Grammar Works®

Equipping Students with Tools to Master the English Language

Jay W. Patterson

Holly Hall Publications

For information write to the following address:

Grammar Works is a Registered Trademark of The Grammar Works People.

The Grammar Works People
Holly Hall Publications, Inc.
P.O. Box 254
Elkton, MD 21922-0254

Cover design by Brian Michael Taylor

Interior design by Jodee Kulp Digital Design

ISBN: 1-888306-43-2

First Printing, August 1995
Second Printing, April 1996
Third Printing, July 1997
First Printing, New Edition, January, 1999

Printed in the United States of America

10	09	08	07	06	05	04	03	02	01	00	99
12	11	10	9	8	7	6	5	4	3	2	1

Acknowledgments

To my dear wife, Jeanne, whose editorial skills and constant, unfailing encouragement made this text a reality.

To our dear friends, Jeff and Kathy Trites, whose computer knowledge, listening ears, and ever present encouragement of the entrepreneurial spirit became an invaluable resource.

To our dear friends, Paul and Mary Stowman, who were there for us when we most needed them with hospitality, proofreading skills, and an incredible willingness to help us see this project succeed.

To my dear children, Jared and Joel, who went without their father and mother for a season to make this text available to them and other children like them.

To Sharon Madsen, my mentor, whose ardent desire to help children and whose teaching skills became a model for me.

To Taner Eiswald, Bob Kawlewski, and Jodee Kulp who came to my rescue with their computer expertise when I most needed them.

To my editors Jan Dennis, Heather Armstrong, and Kathy von Duyke for their objectivity and love of the truth.

To the many students over the years who have been more than instrumental in helping me to develop the teaching methods contained in this text.

"Understanding how letters and their sounds work together to make words is essential if a person is to read well. Knowing the spelling rules is imperative if we are to spell well and comprehend well. Knowing the job that words can do in a sentence is necessary if we are to write well and think well.

"The understanding of syntax is as much a reading skill as is the understanding of phonemes. We must gain a thorough knowledge of sentence patterns, conjugation of verbs, different parts of speech, and the rules of capitalization and punctuation among other elements if we are to write well and comprehend well. The mastery of foundational syntax is an essential component of higher level reading skills and effective writing."

— Jay W. Patterson

Table of Contents

Part 1:
Teacher's Pages

A Philosophy of Approach

Far too many students today are not faring well in the world of print. Too many are not being equipped properly in a world that mandates communication and well-refined language skills. As teachers and as parents we want our students to succeed. All too often, however, the issue expands beyond success. The issue is really about pure survival.

There are two foundational premises that are germane to the direction of this text. These premises become our vision, our goal, and our well-defined purpose. They should drive our instruction, set our agenda, and determine our priorities.

Explicit phonics builds orthographic expectancies at an automatic level.

Precise grammar builds syntactical expectancies at an automatic level.

A student's success with language is a demonstrated automaticity with phonics and grammar. Students need to be trained. They need methods that work. The typist who masters fingering types swiftly. The pianist who masters technique plays adeptly. The Olympic figure skater spends hours on the ice perfecting a routine. These skills have not come without a price. No skill that is truly a skill comes without a price. Those who teach language and understand these two foundational premises desire this same mastery and automaticity for students. Learning grammar and phonics is essentially no different than learning how to type or how to masterfully play the piano. Teachers want language skills built into the minds of their students. They want these skills to become automatic.

To be automatic is to be so well practiced and so well coached that performance becomes virtually instinctive. Performance becomes spontaneous, involuntary, and unpremeditated. We do because we know. The contrast is also true. We do not because we know not. We do not spell well because we have not learned why words are spelled the way they are. We do not write well because we have not learned how words work together properly.

The neurological record in our minds must be precise. We can know how the words of our language best work together. We can know how the phonemes of our language best work together.

What we expect to see at any point in the writing process or the reading process, whether that includes a certain punctuation mark or a certain spelling of a word, is what we know to be true. We conform our written and spoken language to this practiced standard.

As we endeavor to teach syntax (how words work together), we aim to conform our neurological record to accepted norms for language usage. To make spelling sensible requires explicit or precise instruction in

Children Must Be Successful with Language Skills

"Unless children gain academic success, they will continue to have serious problems. In schools in the central city where I work and in most schools where children fail, the major academic failure recognizable to both the children and the teachers is failure to read. Few problem children read well, many not at all. If children cannot gain some beginning success in reading, our psychological approaches will not work."

William Glasser, M.D.,
from his book
Schools Without Failure

The Cost Is Beyond Measure!

"One of the most heart-breaking sights in American schools today is that of children—once so eager to read—discovering that they are not learning how. There comes over those sparkling eyes a glaze of listless despair. We are not talking here about a few children and scattered schools. We are talking about millions of children and every school in the nation. And the toll in young spirits is the least of it. The toll in the learning and thinking potential of our citizenry is beyond measure."

S. Farnham Diggory, Ph.D.,
former director of the
Reading Study Center at the
University of Delaware

sound/symbol relationships and the rules governing these relationships when phonemes combine together to form words. A proper orthographic (spelling) record that serves a student well is built slowly and persistently over time.

Grammar and syntax work the same way. The two premises above allow us to focus on the why of language instruction. If students do not understand why our language works the way it does, they risk failure and defeat. They are not in control of language. In fact, language may control them. It may confuse them, pummel them, ridicule them, turn them into failures, destroy their confidence, keep them vulnerable, limit their opportunities, and handicap them at the most critical of junctures in their lives.

Grammar As an Academic Discipline

There are two general purposes for grammar.

On the one hand, grammar teaches logic. It is no different than many disciplines, like geometry for example, that do the same thing.

Exacting disciplines require an understanding of function.

Students need to determine the jobs words do and why they do them. Without this understanding of function, vulnerability sets in and higher level thinking skills may not be achieved. I would never take my car to a mechanic who did not understand its function. He must know how a fuel injector works and why it is not working in order to fix it. Communication skills are no different. We must understand how these skills work and why they work that way. We must understand the logic and the function of language in order for it to be our friend.

The second purpose of grammar is as a simple writing tool. Knowledge of grammar improves our writing. Both of these purposes have significant value.

The bottom line is this. We want well practiced, automatic, extremely well sharpened minds with language expectancies that dictate excellence in spelling and reading and writing and speaking, and we want these expectancies to operate at an automatic level.

This becomes the focus of this text.

From the Author

The strength of *Grammar Works* is the sequential, incremental, word-for-word instruction contained in the lessons. If you have never taught grammar or have wondered how best to present it in an orderly way, this text will work for you. It provides a multilevel environment, thus several ages and abilities can be taught together. It provides multitasking for students. Students can be brought into the lessons at their point of need. Older, midrange students, or more advanced students, can review and highlight lessons while younger or less advanced students are being introduced to these concepts for the first time. There is built-in review. Besides these benefits, the student will create a beautiful grammar notebook that will become a resource for years to come.

Grammar Works may be used as a multisensory method for teaching foundational syntax. It is designed to complement any reading program and may be used at any grade level K–8 during the first years of language instruction. When combined with the reading program of your choice, *Grammar Works* is designed to provide a solid program for teaching foundational language arts skills.

I have discovered that many teachers are apprehensive about how to effectively teach grammar. They are unsure about what to teach, how to teach it, or when to teach it. *Grammar Works* is designed to alleviate much of that apprehension. It provides word for word instruction. It lays out each lesson in a sequential, incremental manner, helping both student and teacher begin to understand the nature of grammar and how language works. It provides the understanding for why we teach grammar and how best to deliver it. This is a significant benefit to instruction.

The effectiveness of *Grammar Works* is that it empowers teachers to present this necessary discipline precisely and with confidence.

Grammar Works is designed to empower the student, as well, by developing what is called attentional capacity. Attentional capacity is the strength of our mind that helps us pay attention to the smallest of details. Paying attention to the details of language matters. The greater the attentional capacity, the greater the comprehension of the student, and the greater the student's capacity to effectively and efficiently communicate.

Grammar Works is designed to provide an arsenal of tools for the proper use of foundational syntax. This foundational material teaches why and how to put words together properly to form sentences and then paragraphs, letters, book reports, and summaries, among others materials.

Not all grammar principles are covered in *Grammar Works*; some advanced ones are covered in *Advanced Grammar Works*. The

The Imperative for Comprehension: Attentional Capacity

"The mind 'frees up' for comprehension operations only after decoding operations become automatic. If you try to teach comprehension skills before then, you will generate a cycle of confusion: The attentional capacity necessary for mastering decoding will be drained by attempts to 'remember the main idea', and capacity for comprehending will be simultaneously drained by decoding efforts. So neither Stage 2 nor Stage 3 mastery is achieved. This is essentially the current state of 95 percent of our seventeen-year-olds."

S. Farnham Diggory, Ph.D., former director of the Reading Study Center at the University of Delaware

Teaching Language Is the Highest Profession

"The historian-philosopher Will Durant says, '. . .civilization grows upon the study of the written records of man's past thinking achievements in philosophy . . .' Civilization is not inherited, its advance depends upon the ability of each generation to fully communicate and teach its children the great heritage from the recorded wisdom of past ages. Teaching language to children is therefore the highest profession in every age. The best teaching method is of vital importance."

Mrs. Romalda Spalding, author of *Writing Road to Reading*

advanced text is a supplement designed to build and expand upon the foundational principles in *Grammar Works*. Students in *Advanced Grammar Works* will identify infinitives, participles, and gerunds. They will identify and use noun, adjective, and adverb dependent clauses just to name a few. The goals toward which we are striving are basic. We want students who have finished *Grammar Works* to be able to create, understand, and demonstrate with automaticity the concepts and principles contained in their *Grammar and Composition Notebook* that they will write as the teacher takes them through the *Grammar Works* lessons. This goal is accomplished as the students work through five levels of instruction.

Grammar Works is laid out for K–8, but there will be students who can accomplish this material in much less time. The **"Scope and Sequence"** advises that the grade level designations are only rough guidelines. A demonstrated, reasonable mastery by a student is the permission to move on in the **"Scope and Sequence."**

The lower level students will be taught using the lessons and portions of lessons designated for their grade level. All skills will be reviewed and new lessons or portions of lessons will be added each year that a student works through this method.

If you live in a state where there is a lot of snow as we do, people learn the "breaking through a snowdrift" technique. The first attempt we make to drive through the snowdrift results in our getting stuck. We can drive backward, but not forward. Therefore, we back up and make another run for it. This time we get a little farther before we get stuck. We continue to back up, make another run for it, and get a little farther, a little faster, with greater ease each time until we break through to the other side.

This word picture is how *Grammar Works* and the reading method *Writing Road to Reading* or any good method of instruction should be used. The students are expected to gain greater mastery of more and more skills each time they make another run for it until they finally break through to the other side. They have learned and, ideally, mastered all the necessary skills taught.

Please keep in mind that the speed with which your child gains confidence with this material will depend upon developmental readiness. Some of you may choose to teach these lessons well only once in the lower grades and perhaps once in the upper grades after which you would use the grammar notebook they have produced as a resource for reinforcing these mechanics of the English language. Some of you may see the need to follow the **"Scope and Sequence"** for each year for each grade level. This kind of flexibility exists. If you choose to do the "once well" method, be sure to familiarize yourself with the sequence in which these lessons are introduced.

When your child is reading and spelling 50–100 words, turn to **"Lesson 1: Sentences—Writing Words in Sequence."** Introduce the child to the idea that there are rules that sentences must follow that keep them organized so that people who read them can understand them. Do not expect perfection. This is the introductory phase. Refinement comes as the need for reinforcement arises. It is important that children know from the start that there are guidelines for what they are doing so that these lessons are not a surprise or a source of frustration when there is a need for those guidelines to be encouraged.

Grammar Works is divided into five skill levels. They are as follows:

Level K	Kindergarten	**K**
Level 12	Grades 1 and 2	**L12**
Level 34	Grades 3 and 4	**L34**
Level 56	Grades 5 and 6	**L56**
Level 78	Grades 7 and 8	**L78**

Each level has a Scope and Sequence Page that lists the order in which the lessons should be taught. The **Level K** materials are designed to be used for one school year of instruction. The other levels are intended to be used for two years with added lessons the second year.

Where there are different levels of instruction included in one lesson, the level will be designated a **L12, L34, L56,** or **L78** preceding the text to be used with this level. Using colored highlighters can also be a valuable tool during your preparation for that lesson. **Level 12** might be highlighted in yellow, **Level 34** in pink, and so on.

You may notice that some of the teacher dialogue that is designated for **Levels K–2** contains more specific, primary style wording. The author assumes the teacher and students at upper levels will have become accustomed to the routine of the method and will no longer want or need the specificity.

Remember that none of the suggested grade levels are written in marble.

Your student may progress through the levels more quickly or more slowly than suggested. We chose to make the suggested levels quite challenging even for an advanced student. Take the materials at the rate at which they can be mastered. There is no advantage in asking our students to do less than they are able to do. Conversely, we do our students no favor by pushing them beyond what they can handle at their particular developmental stage.

This grammar method will enable a student to create a *Grammar Notebook* similar to the Spelling Notebook of the *Writing Road to Reading* method. It will make use of the words in the Ayres List found in that method. Students will be expected to use a precise handwriting to illustrate the principles of our language and to help build an attention to detail.

Why Can't Johnny Read?

". . . there remains a group of very considerable size in every school who have shown no evidence of any delay or abnormality in either their physical, mental, or emotional development until they have reached school and are confronted with reading, and then they suddenly meet a task which they cannot accomplish."

Samuel T. Orton, M.D., an eminent neurologist in the early part of the twentieth century

Where Has Scholarship Gone?

- *A scholar is one who has curiosity, perseverance, initiative, originality, and integrity; all of which are essential for learning.*

- *A scholar is one who has gained a high degree of mastery in one or more of the academic disciplines by means of long systematic study.*

- *A scholar has acquired the minutiae of knowledge in some special field. A scholar is accurate and possesses skills of investigation and powers of critical analysis in the interpretation of such knowledge.*

- *Scholarship happens when the mind is disciplined to pay attention to the smallest of details.*

We need good teaching methods to improve our students' lives.

Having taught language for over two decades, I am always looking for methods to improve my students' lives. When I was first introduced to Mrs. Romalda Spalding's textbook for teaching reading called *Writing Road to Reading*, I experienced a growing intrigue as I learned the theory and philosophy of this methodology.

Orton's Research Cannot Be Overestimated

"I am deeply indebted to the late Dr. Samuel T. Orton, eminent neurologist and brain specialist, for his years of research and teaching in the field of spoken and written English. It was my privilege while a Bronxville, N.Y., public school teacher to successfully teach an intelligent boy who had a severe writing disability, from kindergarten to the end of second grade, directly under the meticulous supervision of Dr. Orton. This thorough training enabled me then to tutor other similar, though older, children with his guidance, and soon to teach still others by the same techniques without his supervision. He invited me to attend a series of lectures which he gave to the class of pediatricians then graduating from the Columbia College of Medicine. His theory of the functioning of the brain in speaking, writing, and reading and his practical means to prevent or overcome confusions were clear, logical, and highly effective in practice. His book, Reading, Writing, and Speech Problems in Children, *covers this from the medical viewpoint. The value of Dr. Orton's research in this field cannot be overestimated. My contribution has been chiefly to develop Dr. Orton's training into a method for classroom teaching."*

Mrs. Romalda Spalding,
author of *Writing Road to Reading*

When I began to understand the contribution that Dr. Samuel T. Orton made to this text, my intrigue grew into a significant respect for this work. Dr. Orton discovered how best the mind learns how to read through meticulous research conducted earlier in this century. Based upon this research, reading methods emerged to parallel his findings. The more I began to work with this research, the more my respect increased.

In my opinion, there is not a better reading program than the researched-based *Writing Road to Reading* method. It effectively introduces the English language to those who cannot read and greatly helps those who are reading but functioning well below grade level. In fact, I have observed significant benefits when above-average students who appear to already be reading fluently master this method. The results I have experienced are more than encouraging. It fine tunes skills at all levels.

I am persuaded, as I believe anyone will be if they approach this method with an open mind, that once we start on the journey with *Writing Road to Reading* and Dr. Orton, all roads lead to improved reading.

With this in mind, I have tried to parallel my approach to teaching grammar in *Grammar Works* with what Dr. Orton and Mrs. Spalding's method has taught me. I also credit my own mentor, Mrs. Sharon Madsen, for cultivating in me the beginning ideas for a multisensory approach to teaching grammar.

I have called this text *Grammar Works: Equipping Students with Tools to Master the English Language*. It is unashamedly designed to complement the work of both Mrs. Romalda Spalding and Dr. Samuel T. Orton whenever possible.

Focusing on the Why of Instruction: The Bigger Picture

Language mastery and survival are brothers. They go hand in hand. Without mastery of the English language, our culture is at risk.

Our Founding Fathers knew this. Many of them were extremely literate people. Many were well taught. They knew how the English language worked. They were well able to communicate the ideas that created these United States of America. They discovered and demonstrated the power of language.

I believe that those who learn how our language works

- have a growing understanding of the empowering nature of the written and spoken word;

- have a developed accountability to an acceptable standard of English usage and know how to apply it;

- know that ideas conveyed by written and spoken language may have significant consequences;

- are well on their way to becoming independent thinkers able to discern good ideas from bad;

- understand that a Free Republic rests upon the effectual exchange of ideas to the end that truth reigns above all. A populace of able thinkers, writers, and speakers who value a Free Republic will be defenders of what true freedom is all about. To defend it, they must know the language;

- have a confidence that they can contend for the truth in the marketplace of ideas;

- have more marketable job skills.

Nearly Half of All Adults Lack Key Skills

"The article appeared in the Minneapolis Star and Tribune *on Thursday, September 9, 1993. The headline read as follows: 'Literacy Wake-Up Call Study: Nearly Half of Adults Lack Key Skills.' The article is very telling. Fourteen million dollars were spent to find out that '. . . half of all adult Americans read and write English so poorly that it is difficult for them to hold a decent job . . .' Called the 'Adult Literacy in America' study, the study's conclusions underscore the many concerns that experts have had about the millions of high school students earning diplomas but barely able to write and read. The article stated that we have 23 to 27 million Americans who are functionally illiterate. This is not simple illiteracy. These people have been subjected to reading methods that have not worked for them. They have been taught how to read, but the method has not reached them."*

Jay W. Patterson, author of *Grammar Works,* in his article, "Developing Orthographic Expectancies at an Automatic Level: The Pilgrimage"

Students Are Not Prewired for Learning to Read!

"A pervasive error in current reading instructional theory is that children will inductively discover the rules of written language if they are immersed in a written language environment (Goodman & Goodman, 1979; Smith, 1971). Children do, of course, discover the rules of their spoken language through simple immersion—but that is because their brains are prewired for speech. Their brains are not prewired for reading. Left to their own inductive devices, the vast majority of children will not discover how the written language works. What they discover is that they do not understand how it works. And of course they think that is their own fault."

S. Farnham Diggory, Ph.D., former director of the Reading Study Center at the University of Delaware

Let me provide a contrast. **Someone who does not have a mastery in language usage often displays one or more of the following:**

- an inability to read, write, or speak correctly;

- a loss of self esteem and confidence;

- a frustration caused by ineffectual teaching methods;

- an apathetic attitude toward life in general and toward language in particular; I am reminded of Huck Finn's father in Mark Twain's book *The Adventures of Huckleberry Finn* when he found out that Huck could read;

- limited marketable skills for employment if those skills require language mastery.

I have seen it all too often. As the Language Arts Assurance of Mastery teacher in my school district, I am assigned the students who are most academically at risk in language arts. They are coming out of the elementary school far below grade level. They can't write well, spell well, and read well because they haven't been given all the tools they need to master the English language. This is not an isolated situation happening only in my school. It is happening from coast to coast. It is for this reason that I have prepared this text.

I have taught for over 20 years, and my greatest frustration is the student who should know language skills but does not. I believe many of these missing skills should have been in place long ago. There is a pervading philosophy about language acquisition in our schools today that believes students who are missing the boat will eventually catch on. Immerse them in language, let them fall in love with books, and through some magical, mysterious osmosis, these errant expectancies will be virtually self-correcting.

I find inductive discovery, as a chief mode of learning language, to be ineffective and not comprehensive. It is dangerous to leave instruction to chance and assume that students will figure language out for themselves. I believe in using a fine-tuned directed discovery that creatively presents language methodologies in a sequential and incremental manner. That is how we teach other skills. Why should reading, spelling, or grammar be any different?

Inductive discovery may work in a limited way for a certain percentage of the population. There are, however, millions of functionally illiterate people in this country for which it did not work. Some estimates of functional illiteracy go much higher. These people cannot write a simple composition. Why? It is my contention that many of these struggling readers were subjected to reading methods that did not accommodate their learning style.

If I carefully look at those Lake Wobegon students who are above average and appear to read quite fluently, I all too often find that very few of these students can write a paper that is grammatically correct. Even the best students have many gaps in their understanding of how syntax works and should be doing far better.

It is important that students learn grammar and spelling in a systematic way.

Within this text, we will make a practice of asking students to demonstrate a skill only after they have a well-practiced, working knowledge of the components that go into performing that skill.

Teaching grammar in an incremental way is a difficult thing to do. How do we build sequentially so that one lesson adds to the next? So that we do not assume too much? So that we do not take anything for granted?

Certainly children can gain an understanding of sentences before they learn why a noun or a verb performs the way it does. In this text, however, we will not ask students to perform written language until they understand and can explain why they are doing what they are doing.

Why are we doing this? We know that if a student can explain why we do something with language, they understand and will conform to that standard. Students who cannot explain often do not know how to handle language well.

As teachers, we need to keep our expectations high. We do not know and dare not assume how far down the road to language mastery a student can go with encouragement and proper methodology.

As instructors, we need to explain why mastery with language skills is imperative. We need to tell students why what we are doing is important. We need to lead our students to excellence. We must not let mediocre and average become the norm.

We do not know how sharp the students we are teaching really are. Because of this, we need to treat all students as if they were beyond brilliant. They need to believe that they can and must achieve. That is our job as an instructor.

Of course, there will be different levels of mastery. Do not become discouraged if your student does not gain mastery the first time through this material. Mastery takes practice and repetition. That is why this text is designed in the way that it is.

We need to envision a student of character, who has a well disciplined mind, and who can handle the English language like a C. S. Lewis or any great writer who has ever lived. As instructors we need to aspire to this and challenge our students to embrace the same aspirations.

It is with an urgency and a fervor that I jump into the lives of my students. So much is at stake in their lives and in the lives of everyone who is a part of this country. Students need to know the skills *Grammar Works* is trying to teach them, or they may be significantly disadvantaged for the rest of their lives. Too many students don't understand that they are in the midst of a critical preparation time.

Code-Emphasis Methods Produce Better Results

"Most children in the United States are taught to read by what I have termed a meaning-emphasis method. Yet the research from 1912 to 1965 indicates that a code-emphasis method produces better results . . . The results are better, not only in terms of the mechanical aspects of literacy alone, as was once supposed, but also in terms of the ultimate goals of reading instruction-comprehension and possibly even speed reading. The long-existing fear that an initial code emphasis produces readers who do not read for meaning or with enjoyment is unfounded."

Jeanne Chall, Professor Emeritus, Harvard University, from her book, *The Great Debate*

Students Require Systematic Direct Instruction

I see students who initially wanted to survive and succeed. All too often, by the time I get them, many have lost all hope of success because of repeated failure. I see in them too much discouragement and indifference. Inside they are crying. Uncertainties abound. They covet success but don't know how to achieve it. The shadows begin to fall on once bright and eager eyes and their enthusiasm and emerging love for learning wanes. Let us work to turn the lights back on for the sake of each student and for the sake of our country.

Note about Typefaces with an Introduction to the "Three-Step Multisensory Pattern"

In this book we have used a variety of type styles to indicate different elements of communication. The main body of *Grammar Works* is set in Roman type. Names of books, including the student's *Grammar Notebook*, are set in *Italic* type. Names of lessons are set in **"Bold"** type with quotation marks. **Bold** type is also used for emphasis.

An integral part of *Grammar Works* is the **"Three-Step Multisensory Pattern."** This teaching approach lets students use most of their senses—visual, auditory, vocal, kinesthetic, and written—in response to instruction. The **"Three-Step Multisensory Pattern"** uses different type styles, this time to communicate desired teacher directives and student responses. This was done so that we do not need specific instruction accompanying every shift in student–teacher interaction.

Here's how it works. In the first step of the **"Three-Step Multisensory Pattern,"** the teacher gives verbal instructions and writes out the response that the students will write while the students merely watch and listen (visual and auditory response). Step 1 is in "Roman" type with quotation marks. In the second step, the teacher gives verbal instructions and once again writes out the response that the student will write while the students watch and repeat the instructions back to the teacher verbatim (visual, auditory, and vocal response). Step 2 is in *"Italic"* type with quotation marks. In the third step, the teacher gives verbal instructions and watches while the students repeat the instructions and move their pencils to the proper position on the page (auditory, vocal, visual, and kinesthetic response), and then actually write what they are told to write (visual, kinesthetic, and written). The first part of this response (auditory, vocal, visual, and kinesthetic) is in *"Italic"* type with quotation marks; the second part (which adds the actual writing) is in ***"Bold Italic"*** with quotation marks.

It is important to familiarize yourself with this **"Three-Step Multisensory Pattern"** because it is central to the instructional approach of *Grammar Works*. If you have questions, you might want to take some take some time now and turn to pages 90–91 which are sample dialogues modeling the **"Three-Step Multisensory Pattern."** If all this seems complicated now, don't worry. There are numerous places in the text that give you the opportunity to practice this approach.

Scope and Sequence for *Grammar Works*

As we begin the **"Scope and Sequence"** and attempt to develop these syntactical expectancies by working through the lessons, please note that extra practice exercises for many lessons may be found following each lesson. The student worksheets are free to be copied and used to reinforce the content of each lesson. It is through needed practice that we develop skills that eventually become automatic. Use these additional exercises as needed.

Beginning Reading Must Include Systematic, Direct Instruction

"The controversy over how to teach students to read is still raging among educators, public school administrators, and other decision makers. We need to consider programs that are dedicated to the position that beginning reading instruction must include systematic, direct teaching of reading skills and vocabulary knowledge. To do less is a disservice to children and perpetuates the very serious problem of nonreaders."

Norman L. Wilson, Associate Superintendent
Peoria Unified School District, Peoria, Arizona

There Is Much at Stake

"Michael Novak writes, 'Three great lessons have been learned from our century, then, even if the cost of learning them was fearful beyond measure. First, truth matters. Second, for all its manifest faults, even absurdities, democracy is better for the protection of individuals and minorities than dictatorship. Third, for all its deficiencies, even gaping inadequacies, capitalism is better for the poor than either of its two great rivals, socialism and the traditional Third World economy.' He forgot the fourth great lesson of our century. Indeed, the twentieth century has been the bloodiest and most ideological of all time. Ideas have significant consequences. That is self-evident. And Lord Acton was right. Power tends to corrupt and absolute power corrupts absolutely. In fact, power kills. The fourth great lesson is that the act of reading—proficiently, carefully, meticulously, independently, and analytically—really matters, and we in education had better get our act together before the giants of Ignorance and Want squash all of our hopes and dreams and our culture besides."

Jay W. Patterson, author of *Grammar Works*, in his article, "Developing Orthographic Expectancies at an Automatic Level: The Pilgrimage"

Avoid the Great Cataract of Nonsense

"We need intimate knowledge of the past. Not that the past has any magic about it, but because we . . . need something to set against the present . . . A person who has lived in many places is not likely to be deceived by the local errors of his native village: The [person who knows the past] has lived in many times and is therefore in some degree immune from the great cataract of nonsense that pours from the press and the microphone of his own age."

C. S. Lewis from his sermon entitled, "Learning in War-Time"

Instructions for Teaching Level K: Kindergarten

At the kindergarten level in *Grammar Works*, we will be using only the lesson on Handwriting beginning on page 33. Very advanced students may finish **Level K** and begin **Level 12**. The emphasis at **Level K** is the introduction and teaching of precise handwriting. If you are using *Writing Road to Reading*, **Level K** will be extremely helpful as you progress through its "Scope and Sequence." If you are using a different reading method, **Level K** will provide a complete, concise method for teaching beautiful manuscript handwriting.

Kindergarten—What Do I Do First?

1. Read the sections entitled **"The Importance of Manuscript Handwriting"** and **"Foundation Stones Upon Which We Will Build"** immediately following the **"Scope and Sequence"** on page 27.

2. Beginning with **"First Lessons on Manuscript Handwriting"** on page 33, familiarize yourself with the page checkpoints and clock checkpoints and spatial rules talked about therein. You will need to teach these. Also read **"Learning about the Smallest Details of the Written Language: Lines and Curves"** starting on page 38 and **"Introducing Spatial Rules: Understanding the Size of a Space," "Understanding the Concept of Comfortably Close," "Understanding the Concept of Straight,"** and **"Understanding the Concept of Centering"** starting on page 35. There is a multisensory routine that you will need to learn and use with your student. Study the **"Multisensory Pattern"** that is demonstrated in the Sample Dialogue on page 41 for teaching these smallest units of our language.

3. Begin instruction on the **"Learning the Clock and Page Checkpoints"** found in the section entitled **"First Lessons on Manuscript Handwriting"** on page 33. This may require one or more class periods. You will need dotted line penmanship paper. Be sure your student understands the **four page checkpoints** and the **four clock checkpoints** and can locate them without trouble. When they do well, do not hesitate to offer them encouragement. They are experiencing real success with the very first steps of written language development.

4. Introduce and demonstrate the Spatial Rules as found in the section entitled **"Introducing Spatial Rules: Understanding the Size of a Space," "Understanding the Concept of Comfortably Close," "Understanding the Concept of Straight,"** and **"Understanding the Concept of Centering"** starting on

page 35. Complete understanding will come when the student has had ample opportunity to use them. Don't belabor them. Continue to reinforce them as you continue to teach. What does straight mean? How big is a space between words? What is meant by comfortably close? Can we ever touch a top line or a dotted line below?

5. Reread pages 35–41 on **"Learning about the Smallest Details of the English Language: Lines and Curves," "Introducing Spatial Rules: Understanding the Size of a Space," "Understanding the Concept of Comfortably Close," "Understanding the Concept of Straight,"** and **"Understanding the Concept of Centering."** Be sure to hold yourself accountable for the multisensory pattern discussed there.

6. Begin instruction with **"Short Line Segments"** and **"Long Line Segments"** starting on page 43. This exercise will introduce a very important language of instruction. Again, turn to page 41 for the Sample Dialogue of the **"Multisensory Pattern"** if you need to. Students will be involved in learning in the four ways that language is overlaid in the brain: visually, auditorially, vocally, and kinesthetically. They will watch you demonstrate a line or another symbol twice before they put pencil to paper.

7. Work through **"Circle"** and **"Portions of Circle Placements"** on pages 44–46. All of this will take time. These days of instruction are extremely foundational. One important thing they are learning is how to listen carefully.

8. Read **"There Is No Guesswork Here"** following the **"Portion of Circle Placements Definitions"** on pages 46–47.

9. After your student has demonstrated a certain mastery of these first steps, it is time to begin instruction with lower case letters. Teach **"Legal Definitions of Letters a–z"** on page 49. Again use the **"Three-Step Multisensory Pattern."** Of course, we want our students' handwriting at every turn to be beautiful, but beauty needs to be defined within the context of a student's developmental readiness especially as relates to eye-hand coordination. Motor skills will improve with time and the first sincere attempts at penmanship are just as beautiful as the latter, more well practiced, more well refined attempts, and we need to cheer our students on all along the way.

10. Teach **"Capital Letters"** and **"Numerals."** These legal definitions follow after the **"Legal Definitions of Letters a–z."** Use the Multisensory Pattern to teach only a few of these at a time. Practice penmanship daily.

11. At this point *Writing Road to Reading* introduces multiple letter phonograms. Other methods introduce blends and digraphs. Continue reviewing **"Legal Definitions of Letters a–z"** while using your reading method to teach the following: 1) Multiple Letter Phonograms or Blends and Digraphs and 2) Word Analysis Skills which will enable your student to spell and write words and to read what has been written. Be careful to continue holding your student accountable for precise handwriting.

12. When the student has learned enough words to write a simple sentence, begin **Level 12** at Step 2 in **"Lesson 1: Sentences— Writing Words in Sequence"** on page 74. If you are using *Writing Road to Reading*, this will happen after you finish the A–G Section of the Ayres Word List. Remember that this is an introductory phase for writing a sentence. The child is being made aware that guidelines exist to make sentences they have written understandable to those who are reading them. You are creating that awareness, not expecting precise mastery. Refinement is a continuing process.

13. As soon as students are able to complete an *I Can Read* book, *Bob Books*, or some other beginning readers, it is time to begin oral book reports. Look at **"Lesson 41: Writing a Book Report."**

Instructions for Teaching Level 12: Grade 1 and Grade 2

First Year Level 12

By now you know the routine. Review will be fun as both you and your students realize how much easier this is the second time through. You will be able to move much more quickly this year. There may be some legal definitions of letters that may still need to be worked on. Just be sure your students are becoming more proficient and closer to complete mastery through needed practice. Only advanced students will complete all **Level 12** skills by the end of year one. The purpose of year two is for the student to become more automatic in the skills that were covered in year one and also to introduce those **Level 12** skills that were not covered.

Some teachers may want to have a grammar emphasis every year. Some may want to just make sure the principles are eventually understood without grammar every year. Depending upon your teaching style and the learning style of your student, you may want to wait until you are confident your student can cover all the materials in one year and thus eliminate the need to repeat the level. In some cases where students are at different grade levels, waiting a little longer may be desired to teach

As soon as kids can read a simple book, they should begin oral book reports - lesson 41.

There is a significant neurological benefit in requiring precise handwriting.

these lessons to lower and upper level students at the same time. *Grammar Works* allows for that flexibility. As we work through **Level 12,** we will ask the students to record these lessons on loose-leaf penmanship paper. We are still practicing and some day they will be ready to make a beautiful, personal *Grammar Notebook.*

1. **Review all Level K** skills that include handwriting and perhaps simple sentence writing. Don't belabor these. This is a review unless there is an area that requires a concentrated, reteaching effort. Have a couple of days of penmanship practice. Review any legal definitions the student might need to practice. Remember primary emphasis during these vital first years should be on mastering phonics and its sound/symbol relationships and on becoming a beginning reader.

   This next point is very important. **Because most Grade 1 students will not be able to do some of the Sample Page writing with *Grammar Works*, the teacher will demonstrate and the student will only observe the writing and creation of Sample Notebook Pages.** Examples of completed and marked Sample Notebook Pages are included with each lesson. In cases where time resources do not allow for the process of dictation, you may want to allow older, more accomplished students (**L56** and above) to copy the back sections in *Grammar Works*. Keep in mind that copying eliminates the auditory and vocal aspects of multisensory instruction. We strongly encourage the dictation of these pages at all levels in order to maintain a complete multi-sensory impact, but we do understand limited time resources.

   If a Grade 1 student shows an interest in writing these pages as they are able, then you may allow them to do so only as is comfortable without frustration. Depending upon class size, these Sample Pages should be modeled during instruction by the teacher on spiral-bound, classroom-sized flip charts, in a composition notebook, or on penmanship paper.

2. When the student has learned enough words to write a simple sentence, teach **"Lesson 1: Sentences—Writing Words in Sequence"** beginning on page 74. If you are using *Writing Road to Reading* this will happen after you finish the A–G Section of the Ayres Word List. Special note: Sample Dialogue for introducing **"Lesson 1"** using the **"Three-Step Multisensory Pattern"** is found on page 76.

3. After **"Lesson 1"** has been completed, review **declarative, interrogative, imperative,** and **exclamatory sentences, capitalization** of those sentences, and proper **punctuation** of each sen-

tence daily. These have been introduced in **"Lesson 1."** Add new concepts to your daily reviews as they are introduced. You may want to have students write a sentence or two each day on their practice pages if it is not already a part of your reading method or some other subject. Grade 2 students will be able to write sentences that describe places, objects, or characters.

4. As soon as students are able to complete an *I Can Read* book, *Bob Books* or some other beginning readers, it is time to begin oral book reports. Go to **"Lesson 41: Writing a Book Report."**

5. Several concepts that are often taught at this level include the following:

means 'before' Prefixes—*a group of letters coming before a word*
Suffixes—*a group of letters coming after a word*
Contractions (**"Lesson 34"**)—*the shortening of a word by some letters and using an apostro their place*
Synonyms—*2 words of similar or like meanings*
Antonyms—*2 words with opposite meanings*
means 'one' Homonyms—*sounds that are the same but spelled differ*
Syllables—*words or parts of words where a vowel is heard*
Accents—*tells which syllable has the emphasis*
Compound Words—*2 words put together to make 1 new w with a different meaning*

These concepts are taught in *Writing Road to Reading*. Except for contractions, these particular concepts are not specifically covered in *Grammar Works* because most of these are related to reading and word study rather than syntax. If your reading method does not cover them, you will want to supplement.

6. One other concept appropriate for this level is beginning library skills. Please turn to **"Lesson 39: Developing Library Skills"** beginning on page 388. At this level you can teach about book parts, the dictionary, and alphabetizing. Students need to know how to arrange things in alphabetical order. I suggest using rhymes, repetition, or singing the ABC song to teach this skill. (You will need a book with a title page containing the information introduced on page 388, a dictionary, and an encyclopedia.)

7. Teach **"Lesson 4: What Is a Noun?"** on page 92. Refer to Sample Dialogue using the **"Three-Step Multisensory Pattern"** on page 90 that precedes this lesson. After **"Lesson 4"** has been completed, make a **Treasure Hunt Game** by having students discovering and identifying nouns throughout the school day. You may want to begin by adding one noun to a classroom list on a wall chart each day.

Review

8. Teach **"Lesson 36: How Do I Use a Comma?"** on page 357. All that is necessary with this lesson at this level is for the student to understand that commas are used to replace the word "and" when we are listing more than two items. Demonstrate to the student that when there are more than two items being listed, we replace all but the last "and" with commas.

"Johnny and Jim and Joe and I" becomes "Johnny, Jim, Joe, and I". "Pop and milk and tea and water" becomes "Pop, milk, tea, and water". "He and she and it" becomes "he, she, and it".

9. Teach **"Lesson 5: What Are Common and Proper Nouns?"** on page 107 only through Sample Page 9. You may want to add these new types of nouns to the **Treasure Hunt Game**. Challenge students to find a specific type of noun or one of each (common, proper, singular, or plural) on a given day. Keep it an adventure.

10. As you work through the following lessons, the **Treasure Hunt Game** can be expanded. Locate action verbs in a social studies text and list them on an on-going **Action Verb Wall Chart**. Locate adjectives in a science lesson and list them on an ongoing **Adjective Wall Chart**.

11. Teach **"Lesson 6: What Is an Article?"** on page 114.

12. Teach **"Lesson 7: What Is an Action Verb?"** on page 117.

13. Teach **"Lesson 14: What Is an Adjective?"** on page 177.

14. Teach Cursive Writing at the end of Grade 2. The lesson called **"Transforming Manuscript Handwriting into Cursive"** is found on page 65 in the handwriting section following the **"Legal Definitions of Numerals."**

Second Year Level 12

Repeat the same objectives in the same order. Students should be exhibiting confidence and mastery especially in the first skill levels. You should be able to review quite quickly.

Only advanced students will have completed all **Level 12** skills by the end of year one. The purpose of year two is for the student to become more automatic in the skills that were covered in year one and to introduce those **Level 12** skills that were not covered.

If you feel your students are advanced enough, you may begin having them write what is dictated from the lessons on loose-leaf penmanship paper. If this task becomes overwhelming, adjust the amount you have the student write accordingly. Writing just the title or one sentence a day may be all some students can handle comfortably.

Grade 2
Practice writing from dictation

Cursive is often taught at the end of second grade or the beginning of third grade. We have included a lesson on **"Transforming Manuscript Handwriting into Cursive"** that is found in our handwriting section following the **"Legal Definitions of Numerals"** on page 62. Knowing the legal definitions for making lower case manuscript letters will make learning cursive easier. You may want to begin introducing cursive and even using it for writing assignments in other subjects. To keep building and reinforcing attention to detail, please keep using and requiring precise manuscript on *Grammar Works* practice pages.

If a Second Year **Level 12** student is showing good mastery, do not hesitate to start First Year **Level 34.** The primary goal is not to simply finish any particular level of instruction by the end of a given year. The goal should always be to bring your student along at a comfortable pace allowing for both challenge and success. Where you are on the **"Scope and Sequence"** is not as important as how your student is progressing with the material.

Instructions for Teaching Level 34: Grade 3 and Grade 4
First Year Level 34

If you are just starting *Grammar Works* at this level, please go back and teach the handwriting emphasis introduced in **Level K.** The meticulous nature of this emphasis and the rigor necessary to accomplish precise manuscript letters is a discipline that creates attention to detail. Such attentiveness is lacking in too many students, and we use handwriting as a first step in building **attentional capacity.** The same attention to detail is necessary with writing or with any skill. Students need to know how words live together properly and what punctuation is necessary to make their writing clear. Teaching accountability to a handwriting standard is a refining process that requires a strong, disciplined, well-taught, and well-practiced mind. Details need to matter from the very beginning.

Besides the handwriting, this is an ambitious level. Basic reading skills should be well established by this time. This should allow us to begin to move more quickly through *Grammar Works.* Be sure to incorporate a review of **Level 12** Steps 3–5 as needed.

1. **Review handwriting skills** only to the extent it is needed for automaticity and mastery. Revisiting handwriting at this level will highlight the importance of handwriting to this course and will allow for further refinement. Many **K–2** students have been doing developmental work that still needs practice, polishing, and fine-tuning.

2. As you work through **Level 34,** have your students write what is dictated on loose-leaf penmanship paper. These pages should

look like the Sample Pages found in the margin of each lesson and should be saved in a pocket folder. If you are confident that your students have mastered the content of **"Lesson 1: Sentences—Writing Words in Sequence,"** teach Steps 3–6 below on the four different kinds of sentences.

3. Teach **"Lesson 28: What Is a Declarative Sentence?"** on page 285. Begin daily reviews of the definitions students are writing. Ask the questions that are the titles of the lessons they have written and have them answer by reading the definitions aloud.

4. Teach **"Lesson 29: What Is an Interrogative Sentence?"** on page 289.

5. Teach **"Lesson 30: What Is an Imperative Sentence?"** on page 297.

6. Teach **"Lesson 31: What Is an Exclamatory Sentence?"** on page 300.

7. Add a new sentence to one of the student's practice pages for **"Lessons 28–31"** each day until they understand these kinds of sentences. Alternate among declarative, interrogative, imperative, and exclamatory sentences. Encourage students to use the words from their spelling list or their Ayres Word List. Add practice pages as needed.

8. Teach **"Lesson 42: Writing Paragraphs"** on page 422.

9. Teach **"Lesson 39: Developing Library Skills"** on page 388. Introduce other dictionary skills. Introduce encyclopedias and other research tools as needed. (You will need a book with a title page containing the information introduced on page 388, a dictionary, and an encyclopedia.)

10. Teach **"Lesson 41: Writing a Book Report"** on page 416. Have students practice responding to the key questions using complete sentences. You may want to do this orally the first part of the year. Eventually, have students write their complete sentences, using them to compose very simple paragraphs. Introduce the terms for writing fiction like plot, conflict, or setting.

11. Review **"Lesson 4: What Is a Noun?"** on page 92. Refer to Sample Dialogue using the **"Three-Step Multisensory Pattern"** that precedes this lesson.

12. Review **"Lesson 5: What Are Common and Proper Nouns?"** on page 107.

Ladders take time to climb, but the view from the top is terrific.

So Why Should We Read the Classics?

"So why should we read the classics? For one thing they are the acknowledged touchstones of artistic expression. If we are in a quest for the best that is known and thought in the world, then we will value the classics. The classics matter because art and excellence matter. They have value, not because their ideas are always correct, but because they were composed by superior imaginations capable of producing great art . . . [the classics] put us in touch with the past. Contact with the past liberates us from bondage to the contemporary."

Leland Ryken, Ph.D.,
author of *Realms of Gold: The Classics in Christian Perspective*

13. Complete **"Lesson 5: What Are Common and Proper Nouns?"** on page 107.

14. Introduce **"Lesson 40: Developing Letter Writing Skills"** on page 404. First Year **Level 56** will work with friendly letters, invitations, and thank you notes. Second Year **Level 34** will add business letters.

15. Review **"Lesson 6: What Is an Article?"** on page 114.

16. Review **"Lesson 7: What Is an Action Verb?"** on page 117.

17. Teach **"Lesson 8: What Is a Personal Pronoun?"** on page 125.

18. Teach **"Lesson 10: Let's Learn How to Conjugate"** on page 137. Use only the first three tenses introduced. Go as far as is comfortable without overwhelming your students. Continue to review definitions daily, but begin a rotating schedule.

19. Teach **"Lesson 11: What Is a Helping Verb?"** on page 151.

20. Teach **"Lesson 12: What Is a Linking Verb?"** on page 158.

21. Review **"Lesson 14: What Is an Adjective?"** on page 177.

22. Teach **"Lesson 18: The Three Simples: Sentence Pattern 1"** on page 210.

23. Teach **"Lesson 34: What Is an Apostrophe?"** on page 335.

24. Teach **"Lesson 35: When Do I Use a Period?"** on page 352.

25. Teach **"Lesson 36: How Do I Use a Comma?"** on page 357.

26. Teach **"Lesson 37: What Are Quotation Marks?"** on page 365.

27. Practice **punctuation** by having students occasionally use the period, the comma, the apostrophe, and quotation marks in writing short explanations, descriptions, or narrations. Using practice exercises at the end of **"Lessons 34–37,"** have students add only those forms of punctuation to which they have been introduced at this level.

Second Year Level 34

Once again, review will go quickly and students should be praised for and encouraged to recognize how very much they already know. By this stage they may need to be informed that they will be expected to do many of the same things in the same manner as they were required to do last year. We repeat these lessons to improve and polish these skills and to allow for them to become more automatic. We again will use only loose-leaf penmanship paper.

In the Second Year **Level 34** introduces business letters. The linking verb list and verb conjugation should be more automatic. Add more tenses in the lesson on conjugating as the students are able. Book reports and other very short reports requiring some library skills may be assigned occasionally. Remember to always challenge but never over-whelm.

Instructions for Teaching Level 56: Grade 5 and Grade 6
First and Second Year Level 56

At this level, we will be doing much of *Grammar Works* in the order in which it is written. If you have not used *Grammar Works* before and you are starting older students at this level, be sure to teach **"Lesson 39,"** **"Lesson 40,"** and **"Lesson 41"** skills that have already been covered in previous levels of the **"Scope and Sequence."**

First and Second Year **Level 56** students will take dictation directly into their *Grammar and Composition Notebook*. **Level 56** objectives may be repeated during the second year. At this level, have students record lesson names in the **"Table of Contents"** and on the title line of each lesson's page exactly as the lessons dictate. Continue to require precise handwriting referring to legal definitions for letter formation only as needed. Refer to the beginning paragraph in **Level 34.**

1. Begin by working your way through **"Lessons 2–12"** and **"Lesson 14."** These lessons should now be recorded in the students' *Grammar Notebook*. By now much of this will be review. Some lessons will be done in more depth than they have been before. There will still be portions of lessons not intended for introduction until **Level 78.** Teach everything in each lesson except for **Level 78.**

2. Teach **"Lesson 41: Writing a Book Report"** on page 388.

   Always adjust instruction and the amount of writing you require according to the frustration level of the student. You have more than one year to get this notebook right. Review grammar definitions as needed on a rotating basis.

3. Teach **"Lesson 15: What Is an Adverb?"** on page 186.

4. Teach **"Lesson 16: What Is a Preposition?"** on page 194.

5. Teach **"Lesson 17: What Is a Coordinating Conjunction?"** on page 204.

6. Review **"Lesson 18: The Three Simples: Sentence Pattern 1"** on page 210.

What Is the True Purpose of Great Literature?

"In the great tradition of true education, how have wisdom and virtue been cultivated in the young person? Why, chiefly through the study of a body of great litera-ture . . . It was meant to develop character and imagination through examples, precept, and an imagery conceived in noble minds . . . the purpose of humane liter-ature in the core curricu-lum is to help to maintain order in the human soul; to teach young people what it is to be fully human; to impart the cardinal virtues by the art of persuasion, not by extor-tion merely . . . The time has come for us to renew the study of literature as a source of good charac-ter, moral imagination, and right reason."

Russell Kirk from his essay "Traditions of Thought and the Core Curriculum"

What is happening to the human soul in our culture when too many students struggle with reading and grammar and compre-hension of the very litera-ture that could provide them a noble mind to the end that good character is established for the next generation? How do we measure the cost of illiteracy?

What Has Happened to the Complex Sentence?

"Wherever we turn we are confronted with barbarism. I am not referring to the mass culture barbarism of advertising jingles and television comedies, but to the political, intellectual, and moral leadership of this society. No one, it seems, can string together more than a few words without committing a grammatical solecism or indulging in the language of the gutter. The complex sentence has practically disappeared from the political debate and newspaper editorials, and with it has gone complex thought. The nation that once sat at the feet of Webster and Calhoun, Lincoln and Douglas, has learned to endure debates and press conferences in which carefully memorized statistics replace logic, and both parties seek to outdo each other in bad manners. Let me make it clear. I am not

7. Teach **"Lesson 19: What Is a Complete Subject and Predicate?"** on page 219.

8. Teach **"Lesson 20: What Is Sentence Pattern 2?"** on page 225.

9. Teach **"Lesson 21: What Is Sentence Pattern 3?"** on page 229.

10. Teach **"Lesson 42: Writing Paragraphs"** on page 422.

11. Teach **"Lesson 40: Developing Letter Writing Skills"** on page 404.

12. Periodically assign written paragraphs, letters, and book reports. Written assignments in other subject areas should provide opportunities for practice. For instance, if the students' science book suggests assigning a report on a particular topic, use this as a grammar and composition assignment. Some students will be eager to do more writing besides. Other students may find even one such assignment each week to be very challenging.

13. Teach **"Lesson 39: Developing Library Skills"** on page 388. (You will need a book with a title page containing the information introduced on page 388, a dictionary, and an encyclopedia. You may want to have any of the reference books introduced in this lesson.)

14. Teach **"Lesson 43: Creating an Outline"** on page 428.

15. Teach **"Lesson 44: Writing a Summary"** on page 432.

16. Dictate into students' *Grammar Notebooks* **"Lessons 28–31"** on pages 285–307 and **"Lessons 33–37"** on pages 320–378.

If you determine that your students need to work through **Level 56** and **Level 78** two years in a row, they will start a new *Grammar Notebook* each year. By the time they have finished with Second Year **Level 78,** the students' last notebook will look like the Sample Pages in the back of *Grammar Works* with all the markings added. The proper markings are included in the Sample Pages of each lesson located in the margins. The markings tell us that our students understand the concepts of each lesson. Remember that mastery takes practice. Someday your students will thank you for properly equipping them for a world dependent upon communication skills.

Instructions for Teaching Level 78: Grade 7 and Grade 8
First and Second Year Level 78

1. Skills acquired by mastering **"Lessons 39–44"** are used for doing research, making outlines, writing reports and summaries, letter writing, and the like. They have been taught to varying degrees at previous levels. Review or teach the particular skill that the student will need for assignments given in other subject areas. If you have not taught *Grammar Works* before and are starting older students at this level, you may choose to go back and teach those portions of **"Lessons 39–44"** that have been covered in previous levels of the **"Scope and Sequence."** Much of it may be familiar material already.

2. Begin giving dictation at **"Lesson 2"** on page 85 and continue through to **"Lesson 12."** Note the Samples Pages as given in each lesson in the margin. Review definitions daily by asking the questions that are the lesson titles. Do them on a rotating basis when you have introduced more than can be comfortably reviewed each day.

3. Teach **"Lessons 14–18"** starting on page 177.

4. Teach **"Lesson 13: Is It a Linking, Helping, or Action Verb?"** on page 164.

5. Teach **"Lesson 22: What Is Sentence Pattern 4A?"** on page 237.

6. Teach **"Lessons 19–21"** starting on page 219 and **"Lessons 23–44"** starting on page 243.

Remember that each year of **Level 56** and **Level 78** your students will start a new notebook. We want the students' last notebooks to be their very best work. We want their pages beautifully written and looking like the Sample Pages in the back of *Grammar Works* with added markings.

Congratulations! You have persevered. You have completed Level 78!!

talking exclusively or even primarily about style. It is the quality of thought and the substance of their moral vision which ought to appall ordinary citizens. It clearly does not. Cynical and untalented politicians continue to get elected, newspapers are still subscribed to, and the books of Norman Mailer and E. L. Doctorow routinely make the best-seller list. This could not happen in a country where a significant fraction of the populace had received even a mediocre education."

Thomas Fleming in his essay entitled, "The Roots of the American Culture: Reforming the Curriculum"

The Importance of Manuscript Handwriting

Learning anything requires that we start with the smallest details related to our area of study and work toward a greater understanding of each detail. This greater understanding will come only if we understand each component part at the simplest level. Understanding comes when the foundational concepts are mastered.

Handwriting has those small details. In fact, we believe that the mastery of handwriting and its importance to the proper development of reading skills is vital. Handwriting as a means to better encoding, decoding, and comprehension skills is far more important than most people know.

According to Dr. Orton's research, there is significant neurological benefit in requiring a precise neurological record together with the sounds associated with these symbols. While *Grammar Works* is not designed to teach phonics, it will teach a precise handwriting method to make all the letters of our alphabet.

This *Grammar Works* book begins with a unit on how to teach handwriting. Before we actually jump into the grammar lessons and begin to record what the student is learning, we need to master precise manuscript handwriting. Sample Pages of the *Grammar Notebook* are found at the back of this text. Samples Pages with markings are also found in the margin of each lesson. We want our students to develop beautiful manuscript handwriting.

This first emphasis on handwriting may take some time to master. Take whatever time is necessary to help your student make the change from what they have been doing to this way of forming letters. This is especially important if they have struggled with handwriting in the past.

Foundation Stones upon Which We Will Build

There are certain presuppositions upon which this method of instruction is based. Let me list these.

1. As mentioned earlier, the smallest details of any task need to be mastered before moving to a greater proficiency of understanding or skill.

2. Accountability to these smallest details is required if higher level thinking skills and success are to be realized.

3. We are prewired to speak, but we are not prewired to read or write. Skills and the details that result in successful reading and writing must be taught one small step at a time.

Learning anything requires that we start with the smallest details related to our area of study and work toward a greater understanding of each detail.

Note to the Teacher:

*In this unit on handwriting, an effort has been made to present students with precise legal definitions of all letters and numbers. The margins also contain hand-drawn samples of each of these. The Sample Pages, however, use mechanical letter representation, not hand-drawn letters. Consequently, the letters on the Sample Pages will not correspond to the legal definitions. Thus, when checking student manuscript handwriting, always reference the hand-drawn samples in the chapter, "**The Legal Definitions of Letters and Numerals.**"*

4. There are many people who cannot inductively discover the rules of the English language simply by being immersed in a reading environment. For those people, the smallest details of reading and grammar must be taught and well practiced.

While a professor at the University of Delaware, S. Farnham Diggory wrote a paper entitled, "From Theory to Practice in Reading." According to her paper, students need to be able to discriminate at the earliest levels of reading development, the smallest details that make up letters: short lines, long lines, circles, and portions of circles. At higher levels, we have a need to recognize and use grammatical forms and to develop semantic skills like story telling or the comparing and contrasting of points of view in two different novels. There is an interconnectedness to all of this. The beginning details of those earliest levels of reading development are ever present. The details of language instruction will always and forever be essential. It is these smallest of details to which we will turn in this text.

Samples of Student Writing

Shari was a junior high special education student who was in my classroom for two years learning the *Writing Road to Reading* method. Her language skills were at significant risk before she discovered the handwriting methods introduced in *Grammar Works* and which I also use with the *Writing Road to Reading* program.

She lacked confidence before she began relearning the details necessary to establish a precise neurological record of letters and sound/symbol relationships. While she still has a few grammar mistakes, her final paper at the end of two years is a miracle in every respect. She took ownership of her letter formation and found a renewed self-confidence.

It is amazing what students can produce if given the proper tools to accomplish the task. The following examples of handwriting are provided to give you a sense of what students can do. Please take special note of Erika Holder's writing. Hers is a heartwarming story. Before Erika was given the handwriting instruction that appears in this book, she was struggling. Teachers were worried. Parents were worried. Erica's teacher received the information on handwriting found in *Grammar Works* during the summer of 1997. You can see the results for yourself.

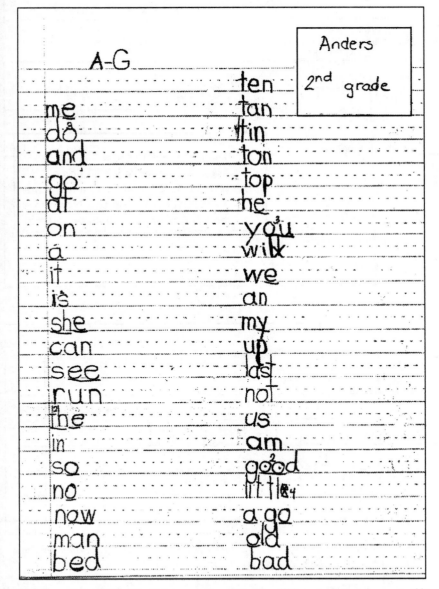

Anders Swendsrud's handwriting as a second grader. This sample is taken out of his Spelling Notebook.

The Erika Holder Story

"Erika was an eight year old second grader in the fall of 1997. She has spina bifida, hydrocephalus, VP shunt, and attention deficit disorder features. (Medical terminology—myelomeningocle S/P closure, hydrocephalus S/P, VP shunt, lower brain stem dysfunction, S/P decompressive lammectomy) She was given the Wechsler Intelligence Scale for Children III by the school psychologist. Scores were in the borderline range. (Performance IQ 65, Verbal IQ 83, Full Scale IQ 72)

"Weaknesses were found in the following areas:

■ Immediate memory/attending skills

■ Visual perceptual functioning

■ Motor speed and visual-motor coordination

■ Non-verbal reasoning and visual organization

"The Occupational Therapist also assessed and found a two-year plus delay with the visual motor coordination and upper limb speed

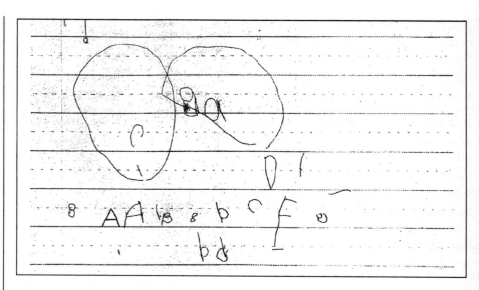

Erika Holder handwriting sample when asked to make letters—2/22/96.

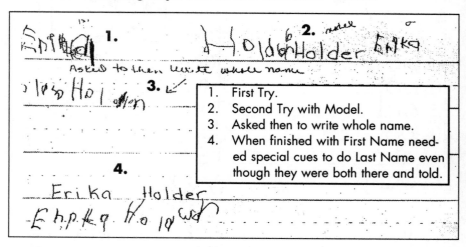

1. First Try.
2. Second Try with Model.
3. Asked then to write whole name.
4. When finished with First Name needed special cues to do Last Name even though they were both there and told.

Erika Holder handwriting sample at occupational therapist—1/9/97.

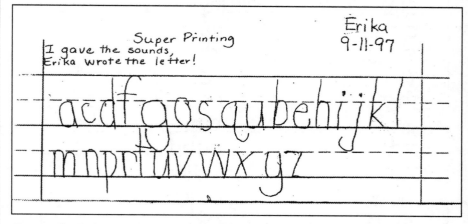

Spacing for Erika is still very difficult, but this was an assessment given after six days of teaching with the Spalding Method, second grade—9/11/97.

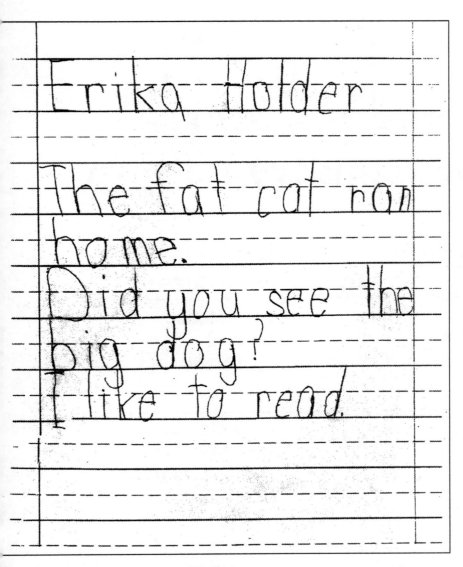

Erika Holder on 10/22/97—a second grader!

and dexterity. The testing also showed she had little or no eye tracking and writing was very difficult for her, as was coloring and drawing. Erika uses an incline board to hold her paper when writing, drawing, or coloring.

"Please note the samples of Erika's work in kindergarten and first grade. At the beginning of second grade, I began the Spalding Program with the handwriting emphasis as taught in Grammar Works. On 9/11/97, I dictated the sounds of the phonograms and Erika correctly wrote each phonogram without assistance (except she forgot to underline the qu). The 10/22/97 paper shows sentence dictation using Erika's spelling words. She wrote the sentences without any cues from me. She still will orally 'walk her way through' forming the phonograms on paper using the legal definitions found in Grammar Works."

Terri Elsey,
Special Education Teacher,
E.N. Nordgaard
Elementary School,
Glenwood, MN

The Three-Step Multisensory Pattern

While the . . .

	TEACHER	STUDENT
Step 1	says and does.	watches and listens.
Step 2	says and does.	watches, listens, and repeats the teacher's words.
Step 3	instructs and watches.	listens, repeats the teacher's words, and writes what the teacher has been demonstrating.

First Lessons on Manuscript Handwriting

Kindergarten

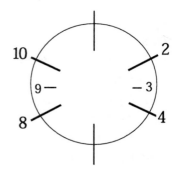

A short section of teacher dialogue follows. Teach those things listed in the manner modeled for you in the teacher dialogue. Please note that for this handwriting section, the dialogue is geared to primary students.

L12P Give each student a piece of loose-leaf penmanship paper with dotted lines. Paper that is 3/8" with margin lines will work well here. If a chalkboard is available, lines and dotted lines can be placed there to demonstrate these first lessons. A musical stave chalk holder works well for making lines. Use chalk in both end holders and the middle holder. Use an eraser to make a dotted line for the middle line. If a chalkboard is not available, working with penmanship paper to demonstrate is just fine.

Learning the Clock Checkpoints

L12 **Step 1** — "We are going to begin to learn how to make letters in a very exact way. We need to do this so there will be a very exact record in our brain of what letters look like. Before we begin making letters, we need to learn about eight special places on our paper that we will call checkpoints. A checkpoint is a place we go to check or make sure that we have followed instructions carefully enough to make our pencil marks in the right place. There are four page checkpoints and four clock checkpoints."

L12 **Step 2** — "Let's learn the clock checkpoints first. If we look at a clock face, we can find numbers to help us tell time. *Can you find 2 on the clock? How about 4 or 8 on the clock? Can you find 10 on the clock? We will also need to learn where 3, 6, 9, and 12 on the clock are. Can you find those?* These locations will be used later to teach the letter 'e' and the numeral '6'. Now let's see if you understand clock checkpoints. I am going to draw a circle without numbers. *Can someone help me locate all the clock checkpoints by putting 'X's' on the circle?*"

L12P Ask students to put an "X" at each of the clock checkpoints as you ask for them.

Learning the Page Checkpoints

L12P Give each student a sheet of penmanship paper. For primary students in a classroom setting, use a prepared chart with penmanship lines or a chalkboard to demonstrate.

L12 **Step 3** — "We need to learn the page checkpoints also. The very first page checkpoint we will learn is called the '**Title**

Special note for the teacher:

*When forming letters that fall between the **Top Line** and the **Dotted Line** like the letter "f" , we call the clock checkpoints high 2, high 4, high 8, or high 10. We start forming a letter "f" at **high 2 on the clock**. We need to picture a clock face above the **Dotted Line**.*

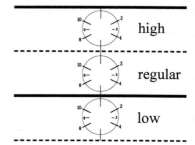

*When forming letters that fall between the **Dotted Line** and the **Baseline** like the letter "o", we call the clock checkpoints regular 2, regular 4, regular 8, and regular 10. We start forming a letter "o" at **regular 2 on the clock**. We need to picture a clock face between the **Dotted Line** and the **Baseline**.*

When forming letters that fall below the Baseline like the letter "g", we call the clock checkpoints low 2, low 4, low 8, or low 10. The tail on the letter "g" rounds from low 4 to low 8. We need to picture a separate clock face below the Baseline. There are three separate places where a clock face will be needed.

We will introduce this information as we go along.

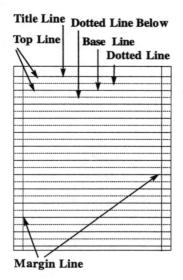

Line'. It is the very top line on our penmanship paper. *Will you point to the Title Line on your paper while I do it on my paper?* Great! You've found the Title Line! How many lines can be the very top line on our page?"

STUDENTS: "There is only one top line that is the very top line. Is that right?"

TEACHER: "That is correct. Therefore, there can be only one Title Line on our page."

L12P Praise them for finding the Title Line. We will ask them to point to it again during this teaching session.

L12 **Step 4 —** "The line just under the Title Line looks like a series of dots so we call it the **'Dotted Line'.** *Can you point to the Dotted Line?* Good job. There are many Dotted Lines on our page. Let's learn the other page checkpoints."

L12 **Step 5 —** "We have learned that the very top line is called a 'Title Line'. It is the only Title Line on our page. Of course there can be other top lines, but there is only one Title Line. The next line below the Title Line is called the 'Dotted Line'. *Say 'Dotted Line' and point to it.*"

STUDENTS: *"Dotted Line."*

TEACHER: *"Say 'Title Line' and point to it."*

STUDENTS: *"Title Line."*

TEACHER: "Well done. The solid line below this first Dotted Line is called a **'Baseline'.** The Baseline is where we write our letters. And every **Dotted Line Below** any particular Baseline is called the 'Dotted Line Below'. *Say 'Baseline' and point to it.*"

STUDENTS: *"Baseline."*

TEACHER: *"Say 'Dotted Line Below' and point to it."*

STUDENTS: *"Dotted Line Below."*

TEACHER: "Very good. On what line do we place our letters?"

STUDENTS: "We place our letters on a Baseline."

TEACHER: "Thank you for being such a good listener. There can be many Baselines on a page. There can be many **Top Lines** on a page. A Baseline for one set of letters that we write will be a Top Line for another set of letters. A Dotted Line for one set of letters can be a Dotted Line Below for a different set of letters. What they are called depends upon where we are writing our letters and words. We always begin writing our words on a Baseline."

L12P Reinforce these during these early days until students can readily identify these checkpoints. Point to one of these checkpoints and ask them to tell you its name.

Introducing Spatial Rules: Understanding the Size of a Space

L12 **Step 6 —** "We also need to learn some very important **spatial rules.** These rules will help us place letters properly on our paper. We need to understand how big a **space** is because all our words are written with one space between them. And every letter is only as wide as one space. Sometimes when we write, we start our writing by moving in five spaces. We call that **indenting.** A group of sentences about one topic is called a paragraph, and we start a new paragraph by indenting five spaces. But how big exactly is a space on a piece of paper? Is it the size of an elephant?"

Spacing indenting paragraphs

STUDENTS: "That is too big."

TEACHER: "Is it the size of a basketball?"

STUDENTS: "That is still too big."

TEACHER: "Let me show you how big a space is."

L12P Understanding the size of a space is a very subjective concept for a primary student. We will teach at first that a space is the same size as **Short Line Segment 3** that will be taught shortly. Later the definition of a space will become the letter "o". In the *Writing Road to Reading* method, students call a space, **the space of an /ah, o, oo/.** They say the sounds that the letter "o" says in English. /Ah/ as in the word "on", /o/ as in the word "go", /oo/ as in the word "do".

L12 **TEACHER:** "There are two ways to learn how big a space is. Let's work with the first one. I am going to put my pencil on a Dotted Line. I am going to pull a straight line on that Dotted Line until that line is exactly as wide as a space. Remember that a space is how wide a letter is. Please help me. Here I go."

a space is just as wide as the letter "o"

L12P You can have some fun here. Keep pulling your pencil for inches on that dotted line and ask if they think this is the size of a space. Make an infinitesimally small line and ask them if they think this is the size of a space. Eventually get around to the approximate size of a space. It is as wide as a letter "o". The second way to show a space is to put a circle on a baseline and tell them that a space is also as wide as this circle. Some students might know that this is the letter "o".

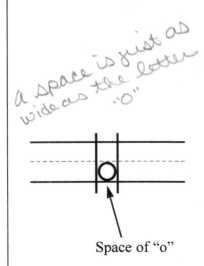

Space of "o"

L12 **TEACHER:** "The second way to show a space is to put a circle on a baseline and have the top of the circle touch the Dotted Line and the bottom of the circle touch the Baseline. This is how we make a letter 'o'. A space is just as wide as a letter 'o'.""

Understanding the Concept of Comfortably Close

L12   **Step 7 —** "We also need to understand that letters in a word that we write on a Baseline sit comfortably close to each other and that they do not touch the Top Line or the Dotted Line Below. If we let them touch the Top Line or the Dotted Line Below, our paper will become crowded and hard to read. Our brain needs white space to 'breathe.' We keep all letters comfortably close to each other and to the Top Line and the Dotted Line Below. The concept of **'comfortably close'** is sometimes hard to understand. It is best taught through demonstration. Do I have a volunteer who could help me?"

JOHN: "I will volunteer."

TEACHER: "Thank you, John. Please watch me."

L12P   Walk as far away from John as you can get without leaving the room. (Coffee is later.)

TEACHER: "John, do you think that I am comfortably close to you where I am standing?"

JOHN: "You are way too far away. You have to come back this way."

L12P   Come back to John and get too close. Crowd John. Push John a little with your shoulder. Hug John. Put your face next to John and ask the following:

TEACHER: "John, am I comfortably close now?"

JOHN: "Now you are too close."

L12P   Now stand comfortably close. We hope they will see that you were too far away at first and then you were too close, but now like the porridge belonging to Goldilocks, you are j-u-s-t right.

TEACHER: "Am I comfortably close now?"

JOHN: "Yes, you are."

TEACHER: "When we learn to write letters, we must remember that each letter in a word must be comfortably close to the next one. They are never too close. They are never too far away. They must be comfortably close."

Understanding the Concept of Straight

L12   **Step 8 —** "We also need to know what the word **'straight'** means. Our letters need to be straight. Look at a piece of penmanship paper. Do you see the red lines running up and down the page. There are only two of them. We call these lines **'Margin Lines'**. *Can you say 'margin lines'?"*

STUDENTS: *"Margin lines."*

TEACHER: "Margin lines become our measure of what straight means. We want our letters to be straight. Straight means that any up and down lines that we put on our paper must look just like our margin lines. All our letters must be straight like the margin lines are straight. They cannot be slanted.

"Margin lines are like football goalposts. We score if we can make our letters straight. The margin lines also are used to get us started when we write a new baseline of letters. When we begin a new baseline of letters, the first letter is comfortably close to the margin line. The letter never touches the margin line."

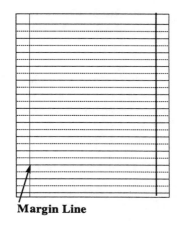

Margin Line

Understanding the Concept of Centering

L12 **Step 9** — "We also need to understand another spatial concept that we call **'centering'**. To learn to center a word or title between two margin lines is like kicking a field goal between two goalposts. It will take some practice. We need to be able to find the middle. Look at you paper again. Can you put your pencil right in the middle of the page on the **Title Line?"**

STUDENTS: "Sure, no problem."

TEACHER: "If you can find the middle, centering a word or a title won't be much of a problem. When we write a title on a Title Line, we'll need to practice centering the title so we have the whole title exactly in the middle. We'll have a chance to practice this more later."

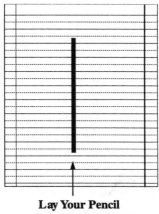

**Lay Your Pencil
on the Center
Between the Margins**

Centering

Checking for Mastery

L12P These checkpoints and spatial concepts are so very important. Once we have taught these, we need to make sure that they are understood. To test their understanding of both the checkpoints and spatial concepts, ask your students to demonstrate their knowledge of the following:

- Where is the Title Line?
- Point to a Dotted Line.
- Point to a Dotted Line Below.
- On the circle on the board, can you find for me 2 on the clock?
- Point to a Baseline. Can this be used as a Top Line?
- How can I tell the difference between a Top Line and a Baseline?
- On the circle on the board, can you find 8 on the clock? 10 on the clock? 4 on the clock?
- What does straight mean?
- How big is a space between words?
- How close should my letters be?
- Can my letters ever touch a Top Line or Dotted Line Below? Why?

ORAL QUIZ HERE ON UNDERSTANDING THESE CONCEPTS

A typical reading of the first legal definition found on the following pages including this directional language in italics would look like this:

"Starting on the first available baseline, (Pause and make sure students are where they should be. Point of their pencil should be on that baseline.) comfortably close to the left red margin line, (Pause and check again. Point of their pencil should be on the same baseline but now comfortably close to the margin line.) starting on the dotted line, (Pause. Check and see that they have moved their pencil to the dotted line and are still comfortably close to the margin line.) pull a straight line down to the baseline. (This line should be as straight as the margin line.) Stop and lift my pencil."

A second example of directional language would begin as follows:

"Starting comfortably close to the last line segment (or the last letter) . . . " then you would give the legal definition of the letter or the short line that your students were practicing.

These checkpoints and spatial concepts will need to be in place as we begin our actual instruction.

Learning about the Smallest Details of the Written Language: Lines and Curves

Short line segments, long line segments, circles, and portions of circles are used in varying combinations to make what we call letters. It is imperative that we teach these details of handwriting. These details need to be recorded properly in the minds of our students because a certain part of the brain perceives short lines. A different part perceives long lines or slanted lines. A still different part picks up on circles and portions of circles. All of these smallest details work in concert to create a letter's particular neurological record. This record allows us sound/symbol relationships that create words; these well-founded relationships create decoding and encoding skills. It is highly likely that those who struggle with reading may have never had these smallest details embedded. They may never have had a precise and comprehensive sound/symbol relationship embedded either.

Dr. S. Farnham Diggory, while a reading professor at the University of Delaware, discussed this issue of embedding these smallest of details in a student's mind. She wrote a paper entitled "From Theory to Practice in Reading" presented at the Annual Conference of the Reading Reform Foundation in San Francisco in July of 1987. In that paper she states, "Actually, there are parts of your brain which are specialized for vertical lines, diagonal lines, horizontal lines and curves among other things. Those parts are activated when you look at print, even though you may not be conscious of that fact." The instruction that follows is designed to embed these details.

You will notice when you get there that the legal definition of each line and curve on the pages following uses the page and clock checkpoints. These definitions will be introducing a very important language of instruction that will later be necessary for learning letter formation.

Finding the Right Place to Start on a Piece of Paper

One more thing that students must understand before the teacher begins dictating is a language of instruction used to get them to the right place on a piece of penmanship paper. The teacher must give directions that are appropriate for each situation. Because these directions change according to each practice situation, they are not included in the legal definitions that are on the following pages. Most of these directions to get students to start at an appropriate place are a matter of common sense. Look at the following examples.

Is it a new day of instruction? Here's what you might say.

L12 **Step 1—** "Students, we are going to learn some new language of instruction. When we start writing on a piece of paper, we have to make sure that we start in the right place. Find the first baseline without any written symbols on it. This first baseline is actually the second solid line from the top. First comes the title line and then the next solid line is called the 'first available baseline'. We call a baseline without written symbols on it 'an available baseline'. We call it that because it is empty and available for us to write on. *Can you put your pencil on the first available baseline?*"

L12P Practice finding the first available baseline, the next available baseline, and so on.

L12 **Step 2 —** "Sometimes if we are told to start writing on the first available baseline, we may have already written four or five lines. What would be the first available baseline then?"

> **STUDENTS:** "The first available baseline would be the next one that has no letters."

> **TEACHER:** "If I ask you to start a letter or a line comfortably close to the margin line on that first available baseline, do I touch the margin line?"

> **STUDENTS:** "No, you would stay a comfortable distance from the margin line."

> **TEACHER:** "If I say to skip a space between letters, do you remember how big a space is?"

> **STUDENTS:** "Yes, a space is how wide a letter is. It is just as wide as a letter 'o'."

L12P As an instructor, you will need to learn how to get your students to the right place on a piece of paper. They need to know where to start. We will give them instructions like the following:

1. "Students, we need to start on the first available baseline, comfortably close to the margin line."

2. "We need to start comfortably close to the last line segment or the last letter."

3. "Students, we need to skip the space of a letter 'o'."

Learning the Instructional Language

In the following chart, you will find a precise, multisensory, word-for-word example of how to teach short line segments, long line segments, circles, and portions of circles. You will need to study this. This example needs to be repeated with each legal definition. By looking closely at this sample dialogue you will see the **"Three-Step Multisensory Pattern."** The first time through the teacher says and does while the student watches and listens. The second time through the teacher says and does while the student watches, listens, and repeats the instructions but waits to do them. The third time through the teacher says and watches while the student says and does on his own penmanship paper.

[handwritten margin note: Learning of instructional language to use with students!]

Sample Dialogue Using the Three-Step Multisensory Pattern with Short Line Segments

SAYS	DOES
TEACHER: "Listen carefully and watch closely: Starting on my first available baseline, comfortably close to the margin line, starting at the dotted line, pull a straight line down to the baseline."	**TEACHER:** Puts the tip of the pencil on the first available baseline comfortably close to the margin and then moves to the point on the dotted line where the line segment should be started and pulls a straight line down to the baseline.
STUDENT: Listens carefully. (Auditory)	**STUDENT:** Watches closely. (Visual)
TEACHER: "Now repeat after me and watch closely. *Starting on my first available baseline, comfortably close to the margin line, starting at the dotted line . . .*"	**TEACHER:** Puts the tip of the pencil on the first available baseline comfortably close to the margin and then moves to the point on the dotted line where the line segment should be started.
STUDENT: "*Starting on my first available baseline, comfortably close to the margin line, starting at the dotted line . . .*" (Auditory and Vocal)	**STUDENT:** Watches closely. (Visual)
TEACHER: "*Pull a straight line down to the baseline.*"	**TEACHER:** Pulls straight line down to the baseline.
STUDENT: "*Pull a straight line down to the baseline.*" (Auditory and Vocal)	**STUDENT:** Watches closely. (Visual)
TEACHER: "*Stop and lift my pencil.*"	**TEACHER:** Stops and lifts pencil.
STUDENT: "*Stop and lift my pencil.*" (Auditory and Vocal)	**STUDENT:** Watches closely. (Visual)
TEACHER: "Now let's say it together and you do it as I watch. *Starting on my first available baseline, comfortably close to the margin line, starting at the dotted line . . .*"	**TEACHER:** Watches student closely.
STUDENT: "*Starting on my first available baseline, comfortably close to the margin line, starting at the dotted line . . .*" (Auditory and Vocal)	**STUDENT:** *Puts the tip of the pencil on the first available baseline comfortably close to the margin and then moves to the point on the dotted line where the line segment should be started.* (Visual and Kinesthetic)
TEACHER: "***Pull a straight line down to the baseline.***"	**TEACHER:** Watches student closely.
STUDENT: "*Pull a straight line down to the baseline.*" (Auditory and Vocal)	**STUDENT:** ***Pulls a straight line down to the baseline.*** (Visual, Kinesthetic, and Written)
TEACHER: "*Stop and lift my pencil.*"	**TEACHER:** Watches student closely.
STUDENT: "*Stop and lift my pencil.*" (Auditory and Vocal)	**STUDENT:** *Stops and lifts pencil.* (Visual and Kinesthetic)

On the previous page is a sample of how to implement the "**Three-Step Multisensory Pattern**" one phrase at a time. The students know precisely what is expected of them. The **"Three-Step Multisensory Pattern"** involves the student auditorially, visually, vocally, and kinesthetically. He hears it, sees it, says it, and does it. This involves all learning styles and what Dr. Orton found to be the four avenues to the brain for overlaying language skills.

The students will eventually be translating the words of instruction that you dictate into precisely made letters. This too will require auditory involvement and kinesthetic action. They will hear what you say and write these letters. There is vocal involvement. You will ask them to repeat the instructions you give phrase by phrase when making the letters. They are hearing the sound of their own voice. You are using directed discovery. There is visual involvement. They will see what you have done on the board and what they have done on their penmanship paper. There will be no guesswork here. Every action is well defined. We will be introducing manuscript writing in this multisensory manner.

L12P Listed on the next pages are the legal definitions for the short line segments, long line segments, circles, and circle placements. You will be taking one legal definition at a time and introducing it in a manner similar to the preceding sample dialogue. **It would be good for you to practice before you start with a student.**

Introduce as many legal definitions as you feel your students can handle each day. Remember to review checkpoints, spatial rules, and the material you introduced the day before.

You know they are mastering the language of instruction when they can do well on a test that you give. Here is an example of how you might test what they should know.

Read the legal definitions you have worked on and see if they are able to write the letter or the symbol you are defining as they listen to your language of instruction. When you know your students are nearing mastery, move on to new material and continue to review as needed.

When you have filled up one baseline with symbols or letters, have students start on the next empty or available baseline.

Balancing Your Expectations with a Student's Development

We would all like to see immediate perfection. Young children, however, may not have the fine motor development to enable them to make exact lines and circles. Always ask students to check whether or not they touched the correct checkpoints. If they can identify the checkpoints, their attempt is successful and they deserve much encouragement and praise even if a line wobbles or a circle is not a perfect circle. Practice over time will make a great difference. Our definition of a beautiful circle or a beautiful line is one that meets all the checkpoints even if they wobble all over the place because of a developmental concern.

TEACHER: "That is a beautiful circle! Wow! You really are concentrating! This is fantastic!

"You really are paying attention to details."

Cartwheels and handstands and pats on the back will be in order.

Starting the Short Line Segments

L12 **Step 1—** "We have already learned about the checkpoints on our penmanship paper. Now we are ready to learn how to make all the symbols that are used in writing letters. I will give you very exact instructions that we call legal definitions.

"Legal definitions are the instructions that tell you exactly where to start your mark on the paper, what shape your mark should be, and where it should stop. When you know the legal definition, you can tell whether or not you have made your mark correctly. You must listen very carefully and do exactly as I say. I want you to listen to my language of instruction.

"When I ask you to repeat what I say, please say the words just as I say them. If the words tell you to go to a certain place, go there. We may have to do more than one of the same definition in order to make it correctly. Here is the first legal definition of a short line segment."

L12P Remember to include the directions for where to begin on the page using the page checkpoints. Remember as well that this directional language may change depending upon where you are on the practice page.

Short Line Segments

1. *"Finding the first available baseline, comfortably close to the margin line, starting on the dotted line, pull a straight line down to the baseline. S&LP"* (S&LP means stop and lift my pencil.)

2. *"Beginning comfortably close to the line just drawn, starting at just below the top line, pull a straight line down to the dotted line. S&LP*

3. *"Finding the next available baseline, starting on the dotted line, pull a straight line on the dotted line in the direction in which we read and write. S&LP"* (When demonstrating this short line segment, move only as far as one space on the dotted line. This will be our first legal definition of a space. Explain that one space is the width of a letter.)

Legal definitions are the instructions that tell you exactly where to start your mark on the paper, what shape your mark should be, and where it should stop. When you know the legal definition, you can tell whether or not you have made your mark correctly.

Legal Definitions

Practice these! with students. on next pg. too!

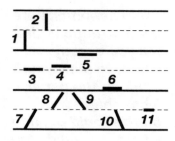

4. *"Beginning comfortably close to the line just drawn, starting at just above the dotted line, pull a straight line just above the dotted line, in the direction in which we read and write, parallel to the dotted line. S&LP*

5. *"Beginning comfortably close to the line just drawn, starting at just below the top line, pull a straight line in the direction in which we read and write, parallel to the top line. S&LP*

6. *"Beginning comfortably close to the line just drawn, starting on the baseline, pull a straight line in the direction in which we read and write. S&LP"* (Again in the demonstration the line should only be as long as a space.)

7. *"Finding the next available baseline, starting one space ahead on the dotted line, make a slanted line down to the left stopping at the baseline. S&LP"* (All slanted lines should occupy one space.)

8. *"Starting one space ahead, at just below the top line, make a slanted line down to the left, stopping at the dotted line. S&LP*

9. *"Beginning comfortably close to the line just drawn, starting at just below the top line, make a slanted line down to the right, stopping at the dotted line. S&LP*

10. *"Starting one space ahead, starting on the dotted line, make a slanted line down to the right, stopping at the baseline. S&LP"*

11. *"Starting one space ahead, starting on the dotted line, make a straight line backwards right on the dotted line for one-half space. S&LP*

Long Line Segments

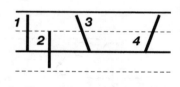

1. *"Finding the next available baseline, starting at just below the top line, pull a straight line down to the baseline. S&LP*

2. *"Beginning comfortably close to the line just drawn, starting on the dotted line, pull a straight line down below the baseline to just above the dotted line below. S&LP"* (None of the letters that extend below the baseline, such as "j" or "p", should touch the dotted line below.)

3. *"Beginning comfortably close to the line just drawn, starting just below the top line, make a slanted line down to the right, stopping at the baseline. S&LP"* (Remember, slanted lines occupy one space.)

4. *"Starting one space ahead, starting at the baseline, make a slanted line up to the right, stopping just below the top line. S&LP"*

Circle Placements

L12P The student needs to have a sense of an imaginary clock face on his penmanship paper. There are also three locations on the penmanship lines that a circle may sit: a high location above the dotted line, a regular location above the baseline, and a low location above the dotted line below. With that understanding let us begin.

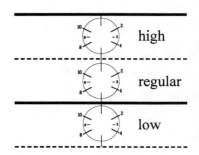

1. *"Finding the next available baseline, starting at regular 2 on the clock, curve up to the dotted line, curve down to regular 10, curve down and around to regular 8, touching the baseline, curve up to regular 4, curve up to regular 2. S&LP"* (Tell your students that we are making a circle like a clock face.)

2. *"Starting comfortably close to my last circle, at just below the top line, at high 2 on the clock, curve up to just below the top line, curve down to high 10, curve down and around to high 8, touching the dotted line, curve up to high 4, curve up to high 2. S&LP"* (Did you notice that this circle placement does not touch the top line?)

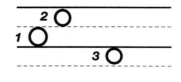

3. *"Starting one space ahead, at just below the baseline, at low 2 on the clock, curve up to the baseline, curve down to low 10, curve down and around to low 8, without touching the dotted line below, curve up to low 4, curve up to low 2. S&LP"*

Portions of Circle Placements

1. *"Beginning comfortably close to the margin, starting at regular 2 on the clock, curve up to the dotted line, curve down to regular 10. S&LP*

2. *"Beginning comfortably close to my last circle portion, starting at regular 4 on the clock, round from regular 4 to regular 8 touching the baseline. S&LP*

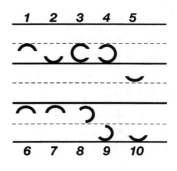

3. *"Beginning comfortably close to my last circle portion, starting at regular 2 on the clock, curve up to the dotted line, curve down to regular 10, curve down and around to regular 8, touching the baseline, curve up to regular 4. S&LP*

4. *"Beginning comfortably close to my last circle portion, starting at regular 10 on the clock, round from regular 10 to regular 2 touching the dotted line. Curve down and around to regular 4. Round from regular 4 to regular 8 touching the baseline. S&LP*

5. *"Beginning comfortably close to my last circle portion, starting below the baseline, at low 4 on the clock, round from low 4 to low 8 just above the dotted line below. S&LP*

6. *"Beginning comfortably close to my last circle portion, starting just below the top line, at high 2 on the clock, curve up to just below the top line, curve down to high 10. S&LP*

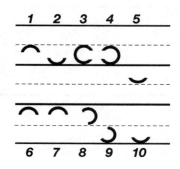

7. *"Beginning comfortably close to my last circle portion, starting just below the top line, at high 10 on the clock, round from 10 to high 2. S&LP*

8. *"Beginning comfortably close to my last circle portion, starting just below the top line, at high 10 on the clock, round from high 10 to high 2 just below the top line, curve down and around to high 4, curve down to the dotted line. S&LP*

9. *"Beginning comfortably close to my last circle portion, starting at regular 12 on the clock, on the dotted line, curve down to regular 2, curve down and around to regular 4. Round from regular 4 to regular 8 touching the baseline. S&LP*

10. *"Beginning comfortably close to my last circle portion, starting at regular 8 on the clock, round from regular 8 to regular 4 touching the baseline. Without lifting my pencil, round from regular 4 to regular 8 over the same curve. S&LP"*

There Is No Guesswork Here

By the time students have worked through these initial legal definitions, they should know their way around a piece of penmanship paper. The language of instruction should be well embedded. They should be able to listen to what you say and translate those words into a kinesthetic response that is very measurable.

It is important to repeat something that was said earlier. There is no guesswork here. This process is teaching at the very first level of reading. Students' brains need to know the features that make up our language. They need to know the smallest details that make up letters. This process should not be ignored.

When teaching reading, we must have precise symbols matched with precise sounds overlaid in the minds of our students. This neurological record must be placed there using all four avenues to the brain. That is why *Writing Road to Reading* and Dr. Samuel T. Orton's research is so powerful. Principle components of the reading process are placed carefully and sequentially into a mind. Students know the symbols and the precise sounds that match those symbols.

We will now move on to the actual letters. When teaching the Spalding Method, these legal definitions of letters are paired with the sounds associated with the letters. Because this is a handwriting emphasis, we shall simply give the alphabet name for the letters we are defining. We do this because some who may use this text have not used Spalding up to this point. If you are familiar with the Spalding phonogram sounds, please use them instead of the letter names at the end of the definitions.

The letter legal definitions to which I was first introduced were developed by Miss Oma Riggs. She was one of Mrs. Romalda Spalding's first-trained *Writing Road to Reading* instructors. I had used her definitions several times daily in my classroom. As a result, I found a need to

Learning the language of instruction is the first key step to success.

Matching the checkpoints provides a legal framework for proper formation of letters.

maintain a more consistent language of instruction. I rewrote these legal definitions to help me present this material in a manner with which I was comfortable and which I have found to be more teacher- and student-friendly.

Wondering how Miss Riggs would feel about my doing that, I contacted her about the change. After reading my revisions, she approved them. These revised definitions as well as the definitions I have developed for capital letters and numerals have worked well in my classroom. They are very teacher- and student-friendly.

Present the legal definitions for the first 26 phonograms of our language in the same multisensory manner as we presented the short line segments, the long line segments, and the circle and portions of circle placements. Remember that there is no guesswork here. These definitions provide a legal framework. Students know if they have made a letter properly or not. Does it match all the checkpoints stated in the definition? If it does not, they are "breaking the law" in a manner of speaking, and there is a need to practice.

Spalding students should know and practice the sounds of these phonograms. Non-Spalding students may use the letter names for now. The emphasis here is not phonics, but handwriting to expedite this grammar text and the *Grammar Notebook* that the students will be making.

Introduce four to six letters each day.

Review all of the previous day's new letters as well as previously taught concepts that students are finding difficult.

Legal Definitions of Letters and Numerals

Legal Definitions of Letters a–z
The Initial 8 Clock Letters

1. ## a

    "Starting at regular 2 on the clock, curve up to the dotted line, curve down to regular 10, curve down and around to regular 8, touching the baseline, curve up to regular 4, curve up to regular 2. Without lifting the pencil, pull a straight line down to the baseline. S&LP and say 'a'." (We will use the alphabet name for these letters if you are using a different reading method than *Writing Road to Reading*.)

2. ## c

    "Starting at regular 2 on the clock, curve up to the dotted line, curve down to regular 10, curve down and around to regular 8, touching the baseline, curve up to regular 4. S&LP and say 'c'."

3. ## d

    "Starting at regular 2 on the clock, curve up to the dotted line, curve down to regular 10, curve down and around to regular 8, touching the baseline, curve up to regular 4. Pull a straight line past regular 2 to just below the top line. Without lifting the pencil, go back down the same line to the baseline. S&LP and say 'd'."

4. ## f

    "Starting just below the top line, at high 2 on the clock, curve up to just below the top line, curve down to high 10. Pull a straight line down through high 8 to the baseline. Stop and lift the pencil. Make a cross just above the dotted line in the direction in which we read and write. S&LP and say 'f'."

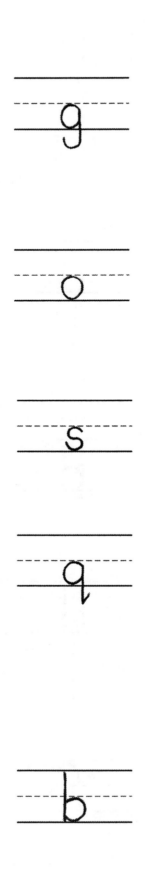

5. **g**

"Starting at regular 2 on the clock, curve up to the dotted line, curve down to regular 10, curve down and around to regular 8, touching the baseline, curve up to regular 4, curve up to regular 2. Without lifting the pencil, pull a straight line down below the baseline and round from low 4 to low 8 without touching the dotted line below. S&LP and say 'g'."

6. **o**

"Starting at regular 2 on the clock, curve up to the dotted line, curve down to regular 10, curve down and around to regular 8, touching the baseline, curve up to regular 4, curve up to regular 2. S&LP and say 'o'." (The letter "o" becomes our new definition of a space. One space is the width of a letter "o".)

7. **s**

"Starting at regular 2 on the clock, curve up to the dotted line, curve down to regular 10, slide across to regular 4 and round from regular 4 to regular 8 making the letter sit on the base line. S&LP and say 's'."

8. **q**

"Starting at regular 2 on the clock, curve up to the dotted line, curve down to regular 10, curve down and around to regular 8, touching the baseline, curve up to regular 4, curve up to regular 2. Without lifting the pencil, pull a straight line down below the baseline to just above the dotted line below. Without lifting the pencil, pull a straight flag at a slant up to the right. S&LP and say 'q'."

The Line Letters

9. **b**

"Starting at just below the top line, pull a straight line down to the baseline. Without lifting the pencil, go back up the same line and round from regular 10 to regular 2 touching the dotted line. Curve down and around to regular 4, curve up to regular 8 touching the baseline. S&LP and say 'b'."

10. **e**

"Starting at regular 9 on the clock, pull a straight line across to regular 3, curve up to regular 2 on the clock, curve up to the dotted line, curve down to regular 10, curve down and around to regular 8, touching the baseline, curve up to regular 4. S&LP and say 'e'."

11. **h**

"Starting at just below the top line, pull a straight line down to the baseline. Without lifting the pencil, go back up the same line and round from regular 10 to regular 2 touching the dotted line. Pull a straight line down to the baseline. S&LP and say 'h'."

12. **i**

"Starting on the dotted line, pull a straight line down to the baseline. Lift the pencil and make a dot just above the dotted line. S&LP and say 'i'."

13. **j**

"Starting one space ahead, on the dotted line, pull a straight line down below the baseline and round from low 4 to low 8 just above the dotted line below. Lift the pencil and make a dot just above the dotted line. S&LP and say 'j'."

14. **k**

"Starting at just below the top line, pull a straight line down to the baseline. Lift the pencil. Starting one space ahead, on the dotted line, make a slanted line down to the left to the first line and then back to the right, matching the first slanted line in length, stopping at the baseline. S&LP and say 'k'."

15. **l**

"Starting at just below the top line, pull a straight line down to the baseline. S&LP and say 'l'."

16. m

"Starting on the dotted line, pull a straight line down to the baseline. Without lifting the pencil, go back up the same line and round from regular 10 to regular 2 touching the dotted line. Pull a straight line down to the baseline. Make two of these. S&LP and say 'm'."

17. n

"Starting on the dotted line, pull a straight line down to the baseline. Without lifting the pencil, go back up the same line and round from regular 10 to regular 2 touching the dotted line. Pull a straight line down to the baseline. S&LP and say 'n'."

18. p

"Starting on the dotted line, pull a straight line down below the baseline to just above the dotted line below. Without lifting the pencil, go back up the same line and round from regular 10 to regular 2 touching the dotted line. Curve down and around to regular 4, curve up to regular 8 touching the baseline. S&LP and say 'p'."

19. r

"Starting on the dotted line, pull a straight line down to the baseline. Without lifting the pencil, go back up the same line and round from regular 10 to regular 2 touching the dotted line. S&LP and say 'r'."

20. t

"Starting just below the top line, pull a straight line down to the baseline. Lift the pencil and make a cross just above the dotted line in the direction in which we read and write. S&LP and say 't'."

21. u

"Starting on the dotted line, pull a straight line down to regular 8 and round from regular 8 to regular 4 touching the baseline, pull a straight line up to the dotted line. Without lifting the pencil, go back down the same line to the baseline. S&LP and say 'u'."

22. **V**

"Starting on the dotted line, make a slanted line down to the right to the baseline. Without lifting the pencil, make another slanted line up to the right, matching in length, stopping at the dotted line. S&LP and say 'v'."

23. **W**

"Starting on the dotted line, make a slanted line down to the right to the baseline. Without lifting the pencil, make another slanted line up to the right, matching in length, stopping at the dotted line. Without lifting the pencil, repeat steps one and two. S&LP and say 'w'."

24. **X**

"Starting on the dotted line, make a slanted line down to the right to the baseline. Lift the pencil and starting directly above on the dotted line, make a slanted line down to the left, matching in length, stopping at the baseline just below where I started. S&LP and say 'x'."

25. **y**

"Starting on the dotted line, pull a straight line down to regular 8, round from regular 8 to regular 4 touching the baseline. Pull a straight line up to the dotted line. Without lifting the pencil, go back down past the baseline and round from low 4 to low 8 just above the dotted line below. S&LP and say 'y'."

26. **Z**

"Starting on the dotted line, pull a straight line for one space in the direction in which we read and write. Without lifting the pencil, make a slanted line down to the left to just below where we started. Without lifting the pencil, pull a straight line on the baseline in the direction in which we read and write, matching the first line in length. S&LP and say 'z'."

Practicing Capital Letters and Numerals

Practice these lower case letters first. Included in this handwriting emphasis on the following pages are legal definitions for capital letters and for numerals. These definitions will also need to be introduced. Older students brushing up on handwriting skills can handle all capital letters in a short time. Younger students need only to practice capitals as they are needed for writing their name or when sentences require a capital letter. If you prefer, you may take a younger student through all of the capitals first, unless the student starts showing frustration.

If students are sincere about these definitions, their handwriting skills should improve quickly. They will be very proud of what they are able to do. I require that the compositions I assign, even for junior high students, be written in this manuscript form on dotted line penmanship paper. Students soon demonstrate mastery by using and practicing beautiful manuscript handwriting.

Research indicates that comprehension is directly related to our effectively and automatically translating sound/symbol relationships into word recognition and then into meaning from a printed page. It is my belief that it is crucial that a precise sound/symbol relationship closely matching the machine printing of textbooks be well established if maximized comprehension is to be achieved at a particular grade level.

To Cursive or Not to Cursive—That Is the Question

Where does cursive writing fit in? Textbooks are not generally written in cursive, and most of a student's time is spent trying to comprehend printed material. Cursive writing has its place. It does have benefits. Signing checks and documents, reading grandmother's letters, hastening the process of note taking, and the pure aesthetics of beautiful handwriting are, perhaps, some of those benefits. But what neurological benefits do students gain from cursive writing? Does comprehension really improve by teaching a student cursive? I have wondered about this and would like to see more research done in this area.

In my daily work with students, it does not appear that their ability to write beautiful cursive improves their comprehension. What I have seen all too often is that students who have poor handwriting also have deficiencies in matching the right sounds with the right symbols in our language. They don't know the sound/symbol relationships. This leads to poor spelling, poor writing, and poor reading skills. In contrast, I have seen reading, writing, and spelling skills improve once precise manuscript handwriting is taught, practiced, and clearly associated with the sounds the letters represent.

There is a place for cursive writing. But based upon my own experience with students, I am beginning to believe that the emphasis on and benefits of teaching cursive writing even before students have mastered neat and legible manuscript may be vastly overrated. We must be careful that classroom instruction leading to cursive writing does not supersede vital steps in reading instruction necessary for literacy. I believe that students should be shown a simple method of changing their manuscript to cursive, but not be required to do volumes of work in this form until manuscript mastery and sound/symbol relationships are well in place.

Regardless of whether or not cursive writing has neurological benefits, it still needs to be taught. A section on how to teach cursive writing entitled **"Transforming Manuscript Handwriting into Cursive"** follows the **"Legal Definitions of Capital Letters and Numerals."**

Legal Definitions of Capital Letters

1. # A

> *"Starting one-half space ahead at just below the top line, make a slanted line down to the left, stopping at the baseline. Stop and lift the pencil.*
>
> *"Starting at the top of the first line, make a matching line, slanted down to the right, stopping at the baseline. Stop and lift the pencil.*
>
> *"Starting at just below the dotted line, connect the two slanted lines by pulling a straight line in the direction we read and write.*
>
> *"S&LP and say 'capital A'."*

2. # B

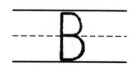

> *"Starting at just below the top line, pull a straight line down to the baseline. Stop and lift the pencil.*
>
> *"Starting at the top of the first line, pull a straight line for one-half space just below the top line in the direction we read and write and curve down to high 2.*
>
> *"Curve down and around to high 4.*
>
> *"Curve down to the dotted line and pull a straight line on the dotted line back to the first line.*
>
> *"Without lifting the pencil, pull a straight line for one-half space on the dotted line in the direction we read and write and curve down to regular 2.*
>
> *"Curve down and around to regular 4. Curve down to regular 6.*
>
> *"Pull a straight line on the baseline back to the first line. S&LP and say 'capital B'."*

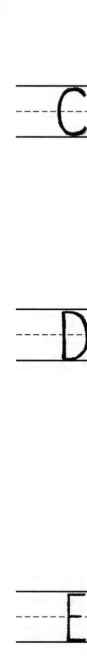

3.

C

"Starting at high 2 on the clock, curve up to just below the top line.

"Curve down to high 10.

"Curve down and around to regular 8.

"Touching the baseline, round from regular 8 to regular 4. S&LP and say 'capital C'."

4.

D

"Starting at just below the top line, pull a straight line down to the baseline. Stop and lift the pencil.

"Starting at the top of the first line, pull a straight line for one-half space just below the top line in the direction we read and write and curve down to high 2.

"Curve down and around to regular 4.

"Curve down to regular 6.

"Pull a straight line on the baseline back to the first line. S&LP and say 'capital D'."

5.

E

"Starting at just below the top line, pull a straight line down to the baseline. Stop and lift the pencil.

"Starting at the top of the first line, pull a straight line for one space, just below the top line in the direction we read and write. Stop and lift the pencil.

"Starting at the dotted line on the first line, pull a straight line for one-half space on the dotted line in the direction we read and write. Stop and lift the pencil.

"Starting at the baseline on the first line, pull a straight line for one space on the baseline in the direction we read and write. S&LP and say 'capital E'."

F

6.

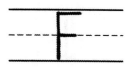

"Starting at just below the top line, pull a straight line down to the baseline. Stop and lift the pencil.

"Starting at the top of the first line, pull a straight line for one space, just below the top line in the direction we read and write. Stop and lift the pencil.

"Starting at the dotted line on the first line, pull a straight line for one-half space on the dotted line in the direction we read and write. S&LP and say 'capital F'."

G

7.

"Starting at high 2 on the clock, curve up to just below the top line.

"Curve down to high 10.

"Curve down and around to regular 8.

"Touching the baseline, round from regular 8 to regular 4.

"Curve up to touch the dotted line.

"Pull a straight line backwards for one-half space on the dotted line. S&LP and say 'capital G'."

H

8.

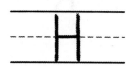

"Starting at just below the top line, pull a straight line down to the baseline. Stop and lift the pencil.

"Moving one space ahead and starting at just below the top line, pull a straight line down to the baseline. Stop and lift the pencil.

"Starting on the dotted line, connect the first and second lines by pulling a straight line in the direction we read and write. S&LP and say 'capital H'."

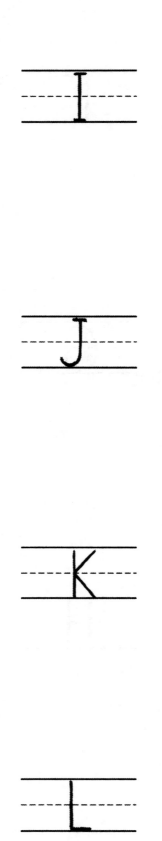

9. I

"Starting one-half space ahead at just below the top line, pull a straight line down to the baseline. Stop and lift the pencil.

"Starting at just before the top of the first line, just below the top line, pull a straight line for one-half space across the top of the first line in the direction we read and write. Stop and lift pencil.

"Starting just before the bottom of the first line, pull a straight line for one-half space on the baseline in the direction we read and write. S&LP and say 'capital I'."

10. J

"Starting one space ahead at just below the top line, pull a straight line down below the dotted line to regular 4.

"Touching the baseline, round from regular 4 to regular 8. Stop and lift the pencil.

"Starting at just before the top of the first line, just below the top line, pull a straight line for one-half space across the top of the first line in the direction we read and write. S&LP and say 'capital J'."

11. K

"Starting at just below the top line, pull a straight line down to the baseline. Stop and lift the pencil.

"Starting one space ahead, just below the top line, make a slanted line down to the left to the intersection of the dotted line and the first line.

"Without lifting the pencil, make a slanted line down to the right stopping at the baseline one space ahead. S&LP and say 'capital K'."

12. L

"Starting at just below the top line, pull a straight line down to the baseline.

"Without lifting the pencil, pull a straight line for one space on the baseline in the direction we read and write. S&LP and say 'capital L'."

13. M

"Starting at just below the top line, pull a straight line down to the baseline. Stop and lift the pencil.

"Starting at the top of the first line, make a slanted line down to the right to the dotted line.

"Without lifting the pencil, make a matching, slanted line up to the right, to just below the top line.

"Without lifting the pencil, pull a straight line down to the baseline. S&LP and say 'capital M'."

14. N

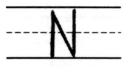

"Starting at just below the top line, pull a straight line down to the baseline. Stop and lift the pencil.

"Starting at the top of the first line, make a slanted line down to the right, stopping at the baseline one space ahead.

"Without lifting the pencil, pull a straight line up to just below the top line. S&LP and say 'capital N'."

15. O

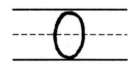

"Starting at high 2 on the clock, curve up to just below the top line.

"Curve down to high 10.

"Curve down and around to regular 8.

"Touching the baseline, round from regular 8 to regular 4.

"Curve up to high 2. S&LP and say 'capital O'."

16. P

"Starting at just below the top line, pull a straight line down to the baseline. Stop and lift the pencil.

"Starting at the top of the first line, pull a straight line for one-half space just below the top line in the direction we read and write and curve down to high 2.

"Curve down and around to high 4.

"Curve down to the dotted line and pull a straight line on the dotted line back to the first line. S&LP and say 'capital P'."

Legal Definitions of Letters and Numerals

17. # Q

"*Starting at high 2 on the clock, curve up to just below the top line. Curve down to high 10.*

"*Curve down and around to regular 8.*

"*Touching the baseline, round from regular 8 to regular 4.*

"*Curve up to high 2. Stop and lift the pencil.*

"*Starting just above and to the left of regular 5, make a slanted line down to the right for one-half space through regular 5 to just below the baseline. S&LP and say 'capital Q'.*"

18. # R

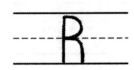

"*Starting at just below the top line, pull a straight line down to the baseline. Stop and lift the pencil.*

"*Starting at the top of the first line, pull a straight line for one-half space just below the top line in the direction we read and write and curve down to high 2.*

"*Curve down and around to high 4.*

"*Curve down to the dotted line and pull a straight line on the dotted line back to the first line.*

"*Without lifting the pencil, pull a straight line for one-half space on the dotted line in the direction we read and write and curve down to regular 2.*

"*Pull a straight line down to the baseline. S&LP and say 'capital R'.*"

19. # S

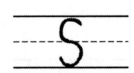

"*Starting at high 2 on the clock, curve up to just below the top line.*

"*Curve down to high 10.*

"*Curve down and around to high 8.*

"*Curve down to the dotted line.*

"*Curve around to regular 2.*

"*Curve down and around to regular 4.*

"*Touching the baseline, round from regular 4 to regular 8. S&LP and say 'capital S'.*"

20\. **T**

"Starting one-half space ahead at just below the top line, pull a straight line down to the baseline. Stop and lift the pencil.

"Starting one-half space before the top of the first line, at just below the top line, pull a straight line for one space across the top of the first line in the direction we read and write. S&LP and say 'capital T'."

21\. **U**

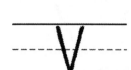

"Starting at just below the top line, pull a straight line down to regular 8.

"Touching the baseline, round from regular 8 to regular 4.

"Pull a straight line up to just below the top line.

"Without lifting the pencil, go back down the same line to the baseline. S&LP and say 'capital U'."

22\. **V**

"Starting at just below the top line, make a slanted line down to the right, stopping at the baseline, one-half space ahead.

"Without lifting the pencil, make a matching, slanted line up to the right, stopping at just below the top line. S&LP and say 'capital V'."

23\. **W**

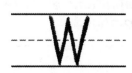

"Starting at just below the top line, make a slanted line down to the right, stopping at the baseline, one-half space ahead.

"Without lifting the pencil, make a matching, slanted line up to the right, stopping at just below the top line.

"Without lifting the pencil, repeat steps one and two. S&LP and say 'capital W'."

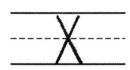

24. X

"Starting at just below the top line, make a slanted line down to the right, stopping at the baseline, one space ahead. Stop and lift the pencil.

"Starting one space ahead at just below the top line, make a matching, slanted line down to the left, intersecting the first line at the dotted line, stopping at the baseline just below where we started. S&LP and say 'capital X'."

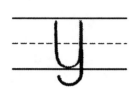

25. Y

"Starting at just below the top line, pull a straight line down to regular 8.

"Touching the baseline, round from regular 8 to regular 4.

"Pull a straight line up to just below the top line. Without lifting the pencil, go back down the same line below the baseline, round from low 4 to low 8 just above the dotted line below. S&LP and say 'capital Y'."

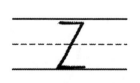

26. Z

"Starting at just below the top line, pull a straight line for one space just below the top line in the direction we read and write.

"Without lifting the pencil, make a slanted line down to the left, stopping at the baseline, just below where I started.

"Without lifting the pencil, pull a straight line on the baseline for one space in the direction we read and write. S&LP and say 'capital Z'."

Legal Definitions of Numerals

Numerals can be made correctly and accurately. We need only follow our legal definitions and then practice.

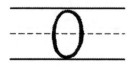

1. 0

"Starting at high 2 on the clock, curve up to just below the top line.

"Curve down to high 10.

"Curve down and around to regular 8.

"Touching the baseline, round from regular 8 to regular 4.

"Curve up to high 2. S&LP and say 'zero'."

2.

1

"Starting at just below the top line, pull a straight line down to the baseline. S&LP and say the number 'one'."

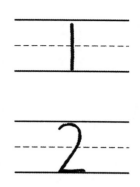

3.

2

"Starting at high 10 on the clock, round from high 10 to high 2 just below the top line.

"Without lifting the pencil, make a slanted line down to the left to the baseline just below the spot where I started.

"Without lifting the pencil, pull a straight line on the baseline for one space in the direction we read and write. S&LP and say the number 'two'."

4.

3

"Starting at high 10 on the clock, round from high 10 to high 2 just below the top line.

"Curve down and around to high 4.

"Curve down to high 6 on the dotted line.

"Without lifting the pencil, curve down to regular 2.

"Curve down and around to regular 4.

"Touching the baseline, round from regular 4 to regular 8. S&LP and say the number 'three'."

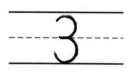

There is no need for guesswork when making numerals.

5.

4

"Starting at just below the top line, pull a straight line down to the dotted line.

"Without lifting the pencil, pull a straight line for one space on the dotted line in the direction we read and write. Lift the pencil.

"Starting at just below the top line, just short of one space ahead of the first line, pull a straight line down to the baseline, intersecting the line at the dotted line. S&LP and say the number 'four'."

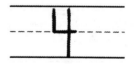

Students need exact definitions to make proper symbols.

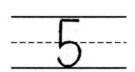

6. **5**

"Starting at just below the top line, pull a straight line down through the dotted line to regular 10 on the clock.

"Curve up to the dotted line.

"Curve down to regular 2.

"Curve down and around to regular 4.

"Touching the baseline, round from regular 4 to regular 8. Stop and lift the pencil.

"Starting at the top of the first line, pull a straight line just below the top line for one space in the direction we read and write. S&LP and say the number 'five'."

7. **6**

"Starting at high 12 on the clock, curve down to high 10.

"Curve down and around to regular 8.

"Touching the baseline, round from regular 8 to regular 4.

"Curve up to regular 2.

"Curve up to the dotted line.

"Curve down to regular 10.

"Curve down to regular 8. S&LP and say the number 'six'."

8. **7**

"Starting at just below the top line, pull a straight line just below the top line for one space in the direction we read and write.

"Without lifting the pencil, make a slanted line down to the left, stopping at the baseline just below the spot where I started. S&LP and say the number 'seven'."

9. # 8

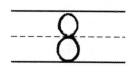

"*Starting at high 2 on the clock, curve up to just below the top line.*

"*Curve down to high 10.*

"*Curve down and around to high 8.*

"*Curve down to the dotted line and around to regular 2.*

"*Curve down and around to regular 4.*

"*Touching the baseline, round from regular 4 to regular 8.*

"*Curve up to regular 10.*

"*Curve up to the dotted line.*

"*Curve up to high 4.*

"*Curve up to high 2. S&LP and say the number 'eight'.*"

10. # 9

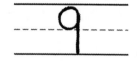

"*Starting at high 2 on the clock, curve up to just below the top line.*

"*Curve down to high 10.*

"*Curve down and around to high 8.*

"*Touching the dotted line, round from high 8 to high 4 .*

"*Curve up to high 2.*

"*Without lifting the pencil, pull a straight line down to the baseline. S&LP and say the number 'nine'.*"

Transforming Manuscript Handwriting into Cursive

The transition from manuscript into cursive is relatively simple. When a student has mastered manuscript, the jump to cursive can happen quickly. I have seen the poorest cursive writers watch their cursive writing go from tragically illegible to very readable and stunningly beautiful. This happens because they now have the foundation, the legal framework if you would, from which to judge the formation of their letters. For this exercise, students will need penmanship paper, lead pencils, and red pencils.

The transition from manuscript into cursive is relatively simple.

When a student has mastered manuscript, the jump to cursive can happen quickly.

abcdefghijklmnopqrstuvwxyz

Example of lower case manuscript a–z sitting on the first available baseline of a practice page

L12 TEACHER: "Now that we have learned the art of manuscript hand-writing and all of you are printing beautiful letters, both capital and lower case, it is time to learn how to write cursive. We need to know how to write cursive so that we can sign our name to a check or so we can read a letter that someone sends to us that is written in cursive.

"Some people think that we can actually write faster in cursive. That would help us if we need to take notes when someone is giving a lecture. I am giving you a new sheet of penmanship paper. On the first available baseline, using manuscript, would you please write the lower case letters in alphabetical order starting with the letter 'a' and going to the letter 'z'. You can see how I have done it on my own paper [or on the board]."

L12P As an instructor you have modeled the printing of the alphabet for the students. Now the students also need to create this model. Encourage them to make this their very best example of manuscript handwriting. Every student will need a red pencil after they are done with this first set.

Step 2:
Placing the Nine Lower Case Cursive Letters Directly Below Their Respective Manuscript Letters

abcdefghijklmnopqrstuvwxyz

Example of these nine lower case cursive letters sitting below their respective manuscript letters on the next available baseline of a practice page

L12 TEACHER: "Wow! That is some of the most beautiful manuscript handwriting I have ever seen. Now watch me closely and listen carefully. There are nine lower case letters whose cursive forms are very different than the manuscript. They are so different that to come up with a legal definition for forming these would be difficult and the definition would be very confusing. We have to use our visual strengths to make these. That isn't the best, but we don't have a choice here.

1. *"On the next available baseline below the manuscript letter 'b', write a cursive 'b' that looks like this. Please use your red pencil and make a beautiful cursive 'b'."* (The teacher will first need to model this cursive "b" for the student. It is placed directly below the manuscript "b". Look at the examples provided in this lesson.)

2. *"Below the manuscript letter 'e', write a cursive 'e' that looks like this.*

3. *"Connected to the cursive letter 'e' and below the manuscript letter 'f', write a cursive 'f' that looks like this.*

4. *"Below the manuscript letter 'k', write a cursive 'k' that looks like this.*

5. *"Below the manuscript letter 'r', write a cursive 'r' that looks like this.*

6. *"Connected to this cursive 'r' and below our manuscript letter 's', write a cursive 's' that looks like this.*

7. *"Below the manuscript letter 'v', write a cursive 'v' that looks like this.*

8. *"Connected to the cursive 'v' and below the manuscript letter 'w', write a cursive 'w' that looks like this.*

9. *"Below the manuscript letter 'z', write a cursive letter 'z' that looks like this.*

"You are doing wonderfully. Remember that even with cursive letters, you still do not touch the top line or the bottom line below."

Step 3:
Writing Another Line of Manuscript Lower Case Letters Leaving Spaces Where the Nine Cursive Letters Are To Go

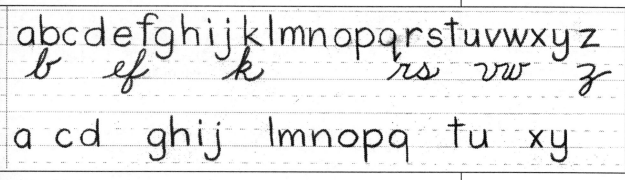

Example of the leaving of a space

Legal Definitions of Letters and Numerals

L12   **TEACHER:** "We will now skip one baseline below these nine new examples. We need some room to think. This next direction is very important.

"Now I want you to begin writing another line of manuscript letters using your regular pencil. This time, however, when you get to the space where one of these nine cursive letters might be located, please skip a space and go to your next manuscript letter. So between the letter 'a' and the letter 'c' please leave a space. Between the letters 'd' and 'g' please leave two spaces because two cursive letters will fit here and so on. When you get to the letter 'q', please leave the flag off. You'll see why in a minute. Watch what I do."

L12P The teacher will need to demonstrate the leaving of a space between the manuscript letters where these nine cursive letters could go. Look at the example provided.

Step 4:
Connecting Our Letters with Curving Red Lines from the Last Checkpoint to the First Checkpoint

Example of connected lettering

Note to the Teacher:

In the above sample and in the sample on page 69 of cursive handwriting, the connecting curves and the nine cursive letters that you and your students will produce in red have been rendered in a grayscale version.

L12   **TEACHER:** "Now here comes the next step. Watch carefully. I need my red pencil [or colored chalk if you are at the board]. I am going to make a series of connecting curves from letter to letter. When we get to the space where one of the nine cursive letters should live, we will make that letter with our red pencil.

"When we write in cursive, we almost always go to the last checkpoint of one manuscript letter and curve to the first checkpoint of the next. It is always last to first except when we encounter one of the nine we have already recorded and in the case of the letter 'x'. Let me demonstrate.

1. "I am placing my red pencil at the last checkpoint for letter 'a' that is on the baseline. I will curve up from this checkpoint and make a cursive 'b' like I have shown you, and then I will curve to the first checkpoint for letter 'c' which is 2 on the clock. *Can you do that?*

2. "I will now pick up my red pencil and move to the last check-point for the letter 'c' that is 4 on the clock. I will now curve to the first checkpoint for the letter 'd' which is 2 on the clock. *Go ahead and try it.*

3. "I think you can handle this. Let's continue. *Curve from the last checkpoint of letter 'd' that is on the baseline and make a cursive 'e' and 'f' and curve to the first checkpoint for letter 'g' which is 2 on the clock.*

4. *"From the last checkpoint of 'g' curve to the first checkpoint of letter 'h' making sure you make a loop on the upper half of the letter 'h' on your way to the checkpoint.*

5. *"From the last point of 'h' to the first point of 'i' which is on the dotted line.*

6. *"From the last point of 'i' to the first point of 'j' which is on the dotted line.*

7. *"From the last point of 'j' which is low 8 we curve up and make a cursive 'k' like I have shown you and we curve to the first point of letter 'l' making a loop on our way.*

8. *"From the last point of letter 'l' curving to the first point of letter 'm'.*

9. *"From the last point of letter 'm' to the first point of letter 'n'.*

10. *"From the last point of letter 'n' to the first point of letter 'o' which is 2 on the clock.*

11. *"From the last point of letter 'o' which is still 2 on the clock to the first point of letter 'p' which is on the dotted line.*

12. *"From the last point of letter 'p' which is 8 on the clock to the first point of letter 'q' which is 2 on the clock.*

13. *"From the last point of letter 'q' before we make the flag which would be just above the dotted line below, curve up and make a loop back to the dotted line to where the baseline and the line we pulled down below the baseline intersect. Continue a curve and make a cursive 'r and 's' to the first point of the letter 't'.*

14. *"From the last point of letter 't' to the first point of letter 'u'.*

15. *"From the last point of letter 'u' make a cursive 'v' and 'w' curving to the first point of letter 'x'.*

16. *"From the bottom of the first slanted line of the letter 'x' curve up to the first point of the letter 'y'.*

17. *"From the last point of the letter 'y' which is low 8, we curve and make a loop into a cursive letter 'z'."*

Step 5:
Now It Is Time to Do Some Serious Practice

L12 **TEACHER:** "If you have watched my example, you can see red connecting lines, and the nine cursive letters that are also written in red, connected to the 17 manuscript letters we wrote with regular pencil. This is really all there is to writing lower case letters in cursive. *Now it is time to practice.*"

Example of connected lettering with two practice lines

L12P Have your students skip one baseline below this demonstration of connected writing and using just regular pencil, have them make another set of cursive lower case letters. Make two or three sets if you would like a good practice session. Tell them they are still responsible to meet all the checkpoints when it is possible to do so. If they are sloppy with meeting the checkpoints when the letter allows, their writing will not be beautiful. Have them practice on a daily basis for a few days. When my students have learned cursive, I give them the option of writing their compositions in cursive. Many still opt for the manuscript in spite of the fact that they now know how to do cursive.

Step 6:
How to Teach Cursive Capitals

To teach cursive capitals, it will be necessary to throw the checkpoints to the wind. You just can't use them. Such is the nature of those nine lower case cursive letters first introduced. Such is the case with most if not all the capital cursive letters. It will be necessary for students to depend on their visual strengths again.

They will need to reproduce the examples as the teacher models these and places them on penmanship paper. Many of these capitals can be directly connected to a lower case letter. Some capitals must stand alone. Please note the suggested form for cursive capitals in this example.

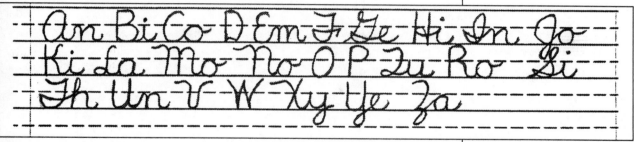

Example of cursive capitals

L12 TEACHER: "We also need to learn how to write cursive capitals. We can't use checkpoints this time. I am going to place these capitals on my paper [or on the board]. You will need to watch carefully so you can do the same on your paper. When I place a lower case letter with one of these capitals, that means that when we use this capital in our writing, we will need to connect it to the second letter in our word. Some capitals don't connect to the second letter. I will write those alone.

"I am going to skip one baseline under my last line of practiced lower case cursive letters. Starting comfortably close to the left red margin line, I will write a cursive capital 'A' with its partner. Every time I write an example of a capital, you may write the same on your paper. It needs to look just like mine. Before we write the next capital, we will skip one space. We will call these capitals by their names. A capital 'A' is called a capital 'A'."

L12P In the same manner, continue to model the rest of these cursive capital letters using the example provided. You will need to use more than one baseline. After they have all been introduced and at least tried once, have your students do some practicing again. Practice is necessary. I hope you have determined already that the writing of cursive letters is really no mystery.

Where we are able to, stay with the checkpoints, it will prove to be an anchor for our cursive writing. We need to have our students practice on a daily basis. We can then begin requiring beautiful cursive in other areas of study. We can still ask our students to pay attention to the details of their writing. Remember that paying attention to details always matters.

Let the Lessons Begin

We will now begin the lessons of the *Grammar Works* text itself. Much foundation has already been laid if the legal definitions for lower case and capitals and numerals have been carefully practiced and reviewed. The lessons that follow have been designed to develop those syntactical expectancies that are necessary if we are going to live well in the world of literacy. Let us begin.

Part 2:
Lessons 1–44

Sentences—Writing Words in Sequence

Rule 1: The first word of a sentence
always begins with a capital letter.

She can see.

Rule 2: We must leave a space between
words when we write.

Rule 3: Every sentence must end with
proper end punctuation.

I can run.
The man can run.
The dog chews a bone.
The boy sits.
The child sings a song.

A sentence is a group of words making
complete sense.

Sample Page A
Lesson 1

Declarative Sentences Practice Page

She can see.
I can run.
The man can run.
The dog chews a bone.
The boy sits.
The child sings a song.
The mother comes home.
We can play.
The girl finds a doll.
The mouse runs.

Sample Page B
Lesson 1

Lesson 1
Sentences—Writing Words in Sequence

LK2P The first purpose of this lesson is to introduce the concept of notebook dictation to students. Students will need to know how notebook pages are created for later lessons. They will eventually be creating a personal *Grammar and Composition Notebook*. To learn how to create a notebook page, students will hear the teacher describing in detail what needs to be written and how it should be recorded on their page.

The first time through **L12** with first graders, the teacher will only model the process of making a notebook page: Sentences—Writing Words in Sequence (Sample Page A in the margin).

First grade students will only watch and listen. We hope second grade students will be ready to watch and listen and actually write this sample of a notebook page. If second graders are not ready, that is still okay. They will just see it modeled again.

It is too much to expect of first graders and even some second graders to write these pages. They still need to see notebook dictation modeled, however. They will hear the teacher describing in detail what will be done. They will see the teacher demonstrate the making of a notebook page on a blackboard, classroom chart, or penmanship paper.

A second vital purpose for **"Lesson 1"** is the introduction of basic sentence writing. First graders will begin the writing of simple sentences on their own paper at Step 8. They will not write sentences before this step. They will have their own Declarative Sentence Practice Page (Sample Page B in the margin). You will also find a sample dialogue for implementing the **"Three-Step Multisensory Pattern"** within the context of this lesson.

As students continue through this first lesson, they will also begin an Interrogative Sentence Practice Page (Sample Page C), an Imperative Sentence Practice Page (Sample Page D), and an Exclamatory Sentence Practice Page (Sample Page E).

Learning to Create a Notebook Page Using the Three-Step Multisensory Pattern

LK2P Have a piece of penmanship paper ready to demonstrate the following steps. Students should be watching and listening. (Sample Page A that this lesson creates is in the left margin.)

LK2 **Step 1** — "Now that we can read and write many words, we are ready to put words together to form what we call **'sentences'**. In a sentence, several words are written in sequence or one after another. It is important to know that not just any group of words that is spoken or written makes a sentence.

"If I say or write the words 'it, me, on, and', I am putting words together, but they don't make a sentence. Do you know why they don't make a sentence? It is because a sentence is a group of words that makes complete sense. They have to mean something as they work together. The words I just put together don't make sense together, so they are not a sentence."

Step 2 — "Please watch me and listen carefully. At the top of my page, on the title line, centered between the two red margin lines, I will write the following: 'Sentences—Writing Words in Sequence'." (The teacher needs to demonstrate this for the student on a flip chart or a piece of penmanship paper.)

Step 3 — "Counting up three baselines from the bottom, I will write the definition of a complete sentence: 'A sentence is a group of words making complete sense'." (Teacher models this step and writes out this definition.)

Step 4 — "Let's take some words we know, and put them together so that they do make sense. Listen to this sentence: She can see. Let's see if it fits our definition of a good sentence: A sentence is a group of words making complete sense. It has to mean something. Is the sentence 'She can see' a group of words? Yes, it is. Does it make complete sense? Does it mean something? Yes, it does. It fits our definition, so it must be a sentence."

Step 5 — "Before we can write this sentence, we must know three very important rules. Listen very closely and watch me carefully as I write the first rule on my page."

Step 6 — "Skipping one baseline below the title line, starting comfortably close to the left margin line, I will write the following: 'Rule 1: The first word of a sentence always begins with a capital letter'." (Teacher again demonstrates this step and then moves on to the next.)

Step 7 — "Listen carefully and watch closely. Skipping one baseline below Rule 1, comfortably close to the left margin line, I will write the word 'She', beginning with a capital letter." (Teacher writes the word 'She' comfortably close beginning with a capital letter.)

LK2P We now need to involve students in this process vocally. This is so very important. All they have been doing so far is watching and listening. We need to repeat the directions in Steps 2, 3, 6, and 7, indicated by bold type, in order to truly embed language skills using all four avenues to the brain. A large percentage of our students really need this. Also, repeating this gives us a chance to model a notebook page twice. That is always a good policy for a teacher. It is a part of directed discovery. Study the following Sample Dialogue before continuing. It will give you a sense of what you need to do especially with Step 2. We have already done the first step.

Sample Dialogue for Three-Step Multisensory Pattern with Lesson 1

Step 1:
Student Is Involved Only Visually and Auditorially

TEACHER: "Listen carefully and watch closely. At the top of my page, on the title line, centered between the two red margin lines, I will write the following: 'Sentences—Writing Words in Sequence'.

"Counting up three baselines from the bottom, I will write the definition of a complete sentence: 'A sentence is a group of words making complete sense'.

"Skipping one baseline below the title line, starting comfortably close to the left margin line, I will write the following: 'Rule 1: The first word of a sentence always begins with a capital letter'.

"Skipping one baseline below Rule 1, comfortably close to the left margin line, I will write the word 'She', beginning with a capital letter."

STUDENTS: Listen carefully and watch closely while teacher models these steps.

Step 2:
Student Is Involved Visually, Auditorially, and Vocally

TEACHER: "Listen carefully and watch closely, but this time repeat after me. *'At the top of my page, on the title line,'*"

STUDENTS: *"At the top of my page, on the title line,"*

TEACHER: *"centered between the two red margin lines,"*

STUDENTS: *"centered between the two red margin lines,"*

TEACHER: *"I will write the following: 'Sentences—Writing Words in Sequence'."*

STUDENTS: *"I will write the following: 'Sentences—Writing Words in Sequence'."*

TEACHER: Turns the paper over to start on a new side. Models another notebook page so the student can be involved vocally this time. Puts the tip of the pencil on the title line, centered between the two red margin lines. Writes the title demonstrating the spatial concept of centering with an explanation of how to center a title if necessary.

STUDENTS: Listen carefully and watch closely and repeat the instruction phrase by phrase as the teacher models the words of instruction for a second time.

TEACHER: *"Counting up three baselines from the bottom,"*

STUDENTS: *"Counting up three baselines from the bottom,"*

TEACHER: *"I will write the definition of a complete sentence:"*

STUDENTS: *"I will write the definition of a complete sentence:"*

TEACHER: *"'A sentence is a group of words making complete sense'."*

STUDENTS: *"'A sentence is a group of words making complete sense'."*

TEACHER: Counts up three baselines from the bottom of the page, starts comfortably close to the left margin line, and writes the definition of a sentence.

STUDENTS: Listen carefully and watch closely and repeat the instruction phrase by phrase as the teacher models the words of instruction for a second time.

TEACHER: *"Skipping one baseline below the title line,"*

STUDENTS: *"Skipping one baseline below the title line,"*

TEACHER: *"starting comfortably close to the left margin line,"*

STUDENTS: *"starting comfortably close to the left margin line,"*

TEACHER: *"I will write the following: 'Rule 1: The first word of a sentence always begins with a capital letter'."*

STUDENTS: *"I will write the following: 'Rule 1: The first word of a sentence always begins with a capital letter'."*

TEACHER: Skips one baseline below the title line and starts comfortably close to the margin line. Writes the rule.

STUDENTS: Listen carefully and watch closely and repeat the instruction phrase by phrase as the teacher models the words of instruction for a second time.

TEACHER: *"Skipping one baseline below Rule 1,"*

STUDENTS: *"Skipping one baseline below Rule 1,"*

Sample Page A

Sentences—Writing Words in Sequence

Rule 1: The first word of a sentence always begins with a capital letter.

She can see.

Rule 2: We must leave a space between words when we write.

Rule 3: Every sentence must end with proper end punctuation.

I can run.
The man can run.
The dog chews a bone.
The boy sits.
The child sings a song.

A sentence is a group of words making complete sense.

Sample Page A
Lesson 1

TEACHER:	*"comfortably close to the left margin line,"*
STUDENTS:	*"comfortably close to the left margin line,"*
TEACHER:	*"I will write the word 'She', beginning with a capital letter."*
STUDENTS:	*"I will write the word 'She', beginning with a capital letter."*
TEACHER:	Skips one baseline below Rule 1. Starts comfortably close to the margin line. Writes the word 'She'.
STUDENTS:	Listen carefully and watch closely and repeat the instruction phrase by phrase as the teacher models the words of instruction for a second time.

LK2P We will return to this lesson at this point and make further application of this Multisensory Pattern. The preceding Sample Dialogue should give you a pretty good idea about how to implement multisensory instruction with a lesson like this. The key is to involve your students' minds using all four avenues to the brain. We would skip the third step of this process because it requires the student to do the writing. We would not expect that at this time.

Making the Multisensory Pattern Work: The Students Start Their Own Declarative Sentence Practice Page

LK2 **Step 8 —** "We are going to do some of these steps again because I want you more involved in what we do. I am going to turn my page over and start again. We are going to practice making another notebook page. Please watch carefully and listen closely, but this time repeat the exact words that I say phrase by phrase. It is so important that you hear the sound of your own voice. After I hear you say these words, I will do what your words are telling me to do."

LK2P The teacher will now repeat these directions using the Sample Dialogue as a model. Again, you are creating a second model of this same page only this time you are involving the student vocally.

"At the top of my page, on the title line, centered between the two red margin lines, I will write the following: 'Sentences— Writing Words in Sequence'.

"Counting up three baselines from the bottom, I will write the definition of a complete sentence: 'A sentence is a group of words making complete sense'.

"Skipping one baseline below the title line, starting comfortably close to the left margin line, I will write the following: 'Rule 1: The first word of a sentence always begins with a capital letter'.

"Skipping one baseline below Rule 1, comfortably close to the left margin line, I will write the word 'She', beginning with a capital letter."

LK2P As an instructor you now have the start of two models of a notebook page. One is on one side of a page or flip chart. One is on the other side. You have involved your students visually, auditorially, and vocally as you have worked through these initial steps. Now they will become involved kinesthetically. Students will now be given the opportunity to write their very first simple sentence, but that is all they will write. Students should be given a piece of penmanship paper at this time. They need to follow your instructions carefully. This is a BIG deal! Remember to tell them to watch and listen. Remember to have them repeat phrase by phrase the following instructions in italics.

LK2 **Step 9 —** "This is a very important day! You are going to write your very first sentence. Listen and follow directions carefully. Repeat after me. *Starting on my first baseline just under the title line, comfortably close to the left margin line, beginning with a capital 'S', write the first word of my sentence, the word 'She'.* Go ahead and write it."

← Start here!

LK2P Remember. Phrase by phrase. Check to make sure each student has capitalized the word and written it in the correct place.

LK2 **Step 10 —** "Before we can write the next word of our sentence, we must review a rule. One of our spatial rules tells us how big a space is. We know how big a space is, don't we? What letter do we use to tell us how big a space is? That's right! The letter 'o'. Do you know what we have to leave between words when we write? You are correct. We have to leave one space."

Step 11 — "Listen very closely and watch carefully as I write the next rule on my page. You won't have to write this rule yet. You just watch me and listen carefully and repeat after me. *Skipping one baseline under my word 'She' on my paper, starting comfortably close to the left margin line, I will write the following: 'Rule 2: We must leave a space between words when we write'.*"

Step 12 — "Now we can continue. Watch and listen. *On the same baseline as the word 'She', leaving one space after my word 'She', I will write the word 'can'.*"

Step 13 — "Now you try on your paper. Repeat after me. *On the same baseline, leaving one space after my word 'She', write the word 'can'.* Go ahead and write it on your paper."

LK2P Don't forget to check each student's work. Remember to offer encouragement for a job well done! Also remember that you are continuing to make a Sample Notebook Page. Your students are starting their own practice page.

LK2 **Step 14** — "Let's do the next step. Watch and listen. *On the same baseline as 'She can', leaving a space after my word 'can' I will write the word* **'see'**.

Step 15 — "Now you try on your paper. Repeat after me. *On the same baseline as 'She can', leaving a space after my word 'can', write the word* **'see'**."

Step 16 — "Now we need to know our third rule. Watch and listen carefully and repeat after me as I put this rule on my paper. *Skipping one baseline under Rule 2, starting comfortably close to the left margin line, I will write the following: 'Rule 3: Every sentence must end with proper end punctuation'*.

"Now we have written our group of words 'She can see'. They make complete sense. We began the first word with a capital letter, and we left a space between words, but we are still not finished. Our sentence is not finished until people who read it can tell where to stop. We need a special mark to tell people when our sentence ends. We call these special marks end punctuation. *Say the words 'end punctuation'*. What does our third rule say? Every sentence must end with proper end punctuation. *Can you say that rule with me?*

"There are different kinds of end punctuation because there are different kinds of sentences. Each kind of sentence has a special job to do and needs a special punctuation tool to help it do its job. Carpenters need hammers and saws. Plumbers need pipe wrenches. Sentences need end punctuation."

Step 17 — "Our sentence 'She can see', is a sentence that gives us information. It states a fact. We call this kind of a sentence a declarative sentence. *Say the words 'declarative sentence'*. We place a dot called a period on the baseline following this kind of a sentence."

*"On the same baseline on my paper, directly after the word 'see' I will write a **period**.* It looks like this."

Step 18 — "Now you try. Repeat after me. *On the same baseline, directly after my word 'see', write a **period**."*

"Now our sentence is complete. We have a group of words that starts with a capital letter, each word has a space between, the sentence ends with the right end punctuation mark, and it makes complete sense. Congratulations! We now understand how to write a sentence.

"We also are seeing how to make a notebook page. We have a title. We might write down some rules. And we always want to have some examples to help us learn. Sometimes in our lessons we will do the examples first and then write down the rules and the title later. However we choose to do it, it is always important that we watch and listen and follow instructions carefully. We are learning how to pay attention to details. That is so important."

Time to Take an Inventory

LK2P As an instructor please take a small inventory of what this lesson has produced.

You have modeled a Sample Notebook Page. It should look like Sample Page A in the margin except for the extra sentences. These extra sentences will be dictated on another day to reinforce sentence writing. The backside of your sample notebook page is not yet finished. That is okay. We didn't need to finish it this time. We repeated this much to establish the vocal aspect of multisensory instruction. If you want to return or feel the need to return and finish it for the students, you may do so later.

You have established a sense of what it takes to do multisensory instruction for the students. They now know you want them to watch, to listen, to speak, and to write. These are so important. So many students struggle with writing simple sentences. We can help them by simplifying the process and using the four avenues to the brain. When they watch and listen, you are modeling what you expect them to perform. When they watch and listen and add their own voice in directed discovery, you are further embedding the information they need to know. When they watch and listen and speak and then write, they become kinesthetically involved.

You have begun a student Declarative Sentence Practice Page for writing simple declarative sentences. (Note Sample Page B in the margin.) They should keep this page. You will have them writing more simple sentences tomorrow and the next day and so on.

LK2 Continue to dictate the first five declarative sentences we have provided in this lesson in the same manner. They will place these five sentences on their practice page. You will continue to place these five sentences on the Model Notebook Page. These sentences were created using the Ayres word lists A–G, H, and I from the *Writing Road to Reading* method. When practicing in days to come, you could also create other sentences with other words that you are sure your students know.

Introducing Interrogative, Imperative, and Exclamatory Sentences

LK2P "**Lesson 1**" continues with the introduction of three other kinds of sentences. Make sure you have taken enough time to establish a reasonable understanding of declarative sentences before beginning here.

Sentences—Writing Words in Sequence

Rule 1: The first word of a sentence always begins with a capital letter.

She can see.

Rule 2: We must leave a space between words when we write.

Rule 3: Every sentence must end with proper end punctuation.

I can run.
The man can run.
The dog chews the bone.
The boy sits.
The child sings a song.

A sentence is a group of words making complete sense.

Sample Page A
Lesson 1

Declarative Sentences Practice Page

She can see.
I can run.
The man can run.
The dog chews a bone.
The boy sits.
The child sings a song.
The mother comes home.
We can play.
The girl finds a doll.
The mouse runs.

Sample Page B
Lesson 1

Notebook Declarative Sentences

1. She can see.

2. I can run.

3. The man can run.

4. The dog chews a bone.

5. The boy sits.

6. The child sings a song.

7. The mother comes home.

8. We can play.

9. The girl finds a doll.

10. The mouse runs.

Sample Page C
Lesson 1

Notebook Interrogative Sentences

1. Can she see?

2. Can I run?

3. Can the man run?

4. Does the dog chew a bone?

5. Does the boy sit?

6. Does the child sing a song?

7. Does the mother come home?

8. Can we play?

9. Does the girl find a doll?

10. Does the mouse run?

The Interrogative Sentence

LK2P Students will need a new piece of loose-leaf practice penmanship paper and a pencil.

LK2 **Step 1 —** "We need to learn about the three other kinds of sentences and the end punctuation we need to use with each kind. Sometimes we need to ask a question to get some information. We have written the sentence 'She can see' before. To turn it into a question, we put the word 'can' in front of the word 'she'. Now it says 'Can she see?'

"We still need to use all three rules for writing a sentence. How does the first word of every sentence start? What do we have to leave between words in a sentence? How must every sentence end? A capital letter, a space between words, and proper end punctuation? That is correct.

"Because every sentence needs an end punctuation mark, we need to put one at the end of the question we have just made. Because this sentence doesn't **give** information, we cannot end it with a period. This sentence **asks** for information instead, so we must end it with a mark we call a 'question mark'. *Say 'question mark'.* Sentences that ask questions are called 'interrogative sentences'. *Can you say 'interrogative sentences'?*"

Step 2 — "Listen very closely and watch carefully as I write this question on my new page. Skipping one baseline under the title line, starting comfortably close to the left margin line, writing the first word with a capital 'C', and leaving one space between words, I will write the question, 'Can she see?' Pay special attention to how I make the end punctuation mark at the end of the sentence."

Step 3 — "Now you try on your new page. Repeat after me. *Skipping one baseline under the title line, starting comfortably close to the left margin line, writing the first word with a capital 'C', and leaving one space between words, write the question,* **'Can she see?'** Remember to use a question mark as your proper end punctuation."

LK2P Take the examples of declarative sentences they have already written and create questions from them. Have your students write these questions on their Interrogative Sentence Practice Page (Sample Page C). Tell them they need to keep track of this page and their Declarative Sentence Practice Page because they will be coming back to them for more practice on another day.

The Imperative Sentence

LK2P Students will need a new piece of loose-leaf practice penmanship paper and a pencil.

LK2 **Step 1** — "The third kind of sentence about which we need to know is a sentence that asks or tells someone to do something. An imperative sentence makes a request or gives a command. You hear this kind of sentence often. When Mom and Dad say, 'Don't fight', 'Pick up your toys', or 'Go to bed', they are using imperative sentences. Imperative sentences end with a period just like declarative sentences do."

Step 2 — "Watch and listen as I write an imperative sentence on another new practice page. Skipping one baseline under the title line, starting comfortably close to the left margin line, writing the first word with a capital 'R', leaving one space between words, and ending the sentence with a period, I will write 'Run to the school'."

Step 3 — "Now you try on your new page. Repeat after me. *Skipping one baseline under the title line, starting comfortably close to the left margin line, writing the first word with a capital 'R', leaving one space between words, and ending the sentence with a period, I will write* **'Run to the school'.**"

LK2P Use the imperative sentences provided to create an Imperative Sentence Practice Page (Sample Page D) for additional reinforcement of their understanding of this kind of a sentence. Continue dictating, checking, correcting, and encouraging. Do only as many as your students can comfortably handle at one sitting. Remember to use multisensory instruction. You demonstrate first and then get them involved vocally and kinesthetically.

The Exclamatory Sentence

LK2P Students will need a new piece of loose-leaf practice penmanship paper and a pencil.

LK2 **Step 1** — "The last sentence we need to learn is called the exclamatory sentence. It is a sentence that shows lots of excitement. We use a different end punctuation mark for this sentence. We use an exclamation point. It looks like a period with a long line over the top of the period.

"Listen to these examples: 'That was wonderful!' 'What a great day!' 'We won the game!' Are these all sentences? They are each a group of words. They each start with a capital letter. There is a space between each word. There is end punctuation. They each make complete sense. Therefore, they are all sentences. They are all exclamatory sentences."

LK2 **Step 2** — "Watch and listen as I write an exclamatory sentence on my new page. Skipping one baseline under the title line, starting comfortably close to the left margin line, writing the first word with a capital 'D', leaving one space between words, and

Sample Page D
Lesson 1

Notebook Imperative Sentences

1. Run to the school.

2. Play the game.

3. Go to sleep.

4. Say a kind word.

5. Take the train home.

6. Bring the Sunday paper.

7. Call your mother.

8. Come to the play.

9. Make up your mind.

10. Tell the truth.

Exclamatory Sentences Practice Page

Dad was right!
That was hard to do!
We found the gold coin!
Everybody was happy!
What a big ice cream cone that is!

Sample Page E
Lesson 1

Notebook Exclamatory Sentences

1. Dad was right!

2. That was hard to do!

3. We found the gold coin!

4. Everybody was happy!

5. What a big ice cream cone that is!

Where Do I Go from Here?

- **LK** goes to **LK** "**Scope and Sequence**" Step 13.

- **L12** goes to **L12** "**Scope and Sequence**" Step 3.

- **L34** goes to **L34** "**Scope and Sequence**" Step 3.

What Materials Will I Need?

- **LK**, **L12**, and **L34** will need penmanship paper and pencils.

writing an exclamation point at the end of my sentence, I will write, 'Dad was right!'"

Step 3 — "Now you try on your new page. Repeat after me. *Skipping one baseline under the title line, starting comfortably close to the left margin line, writing the first word with a capital 'D', leaving one space between words, and writing an exclamation point at the end of my sentence, I will write,* **'Dad was right!'**"

LK2P Continue dictating, checking, correcting, and encouraging, using the sample sentences provided to create an Exclamatory Sentence Practice Page (Sample Page E). Do only as many sentences as your students can comfortably handle at one sitting. In your students' pocket folders or wherever they keep their practice pages, they should have four different practice pages. One will be used to practice declarative sentences. One will be used to practice interrogative sentences. One will be used to practice imperative sentences. The last one will be used to practice exclamatory sentences. You also will need these four practice pages in order to model the sentence writing you want your student to do. Note the Sample Page models provided for you in the margins.

Lesson 2
Making the Title Page in *My Grammar and Composition Notebook*

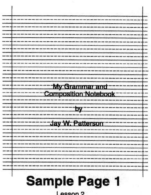

Sample Page 1
Lesson 2

_56P If you have been following the **"Scope and Sequence"**—which can save you much confusion—it is time to create a *Grammar and Composition Notebook*. This is **Level 56**. All of the grammatical principles included in **Level 56** have been well practiced during **Level K1234** of instruction. Now we are going to create the students' very own resource notebook by recording what they already know in a 3/8" dotted line, bound, composition notebook. As you follow the **"Scope and Sequence,"** work to maintain Dr. Orton's multisensory approach where it is appropriate. To learn in a multisensory way, we must hear it, say it, do it, and see it.

Give each student a composition notebook and instruct him or her to turn to the flyleaf page, the first page of penmanship paper opposite the inside cover. Say the following:

_56 **Step 1 —** "This is a special day. We are going to start our *Grammar Notebook*. We are going to begin by writing the title of our new notebook. Remember that every key word in a title is capitalized. *Counting the title line as number one, count down eleven baselines. Starting seven spaces in from the margin line, write the word 'My'.*"

_56P If students struggle with any spelling words, and we hope by **Level 56** they are not struggling too much, they may need to learn a process called orthographic analysis. It is a very important tool that gives reasons for why English words are spelled like they are. While orthographic analysis is not the focus of this book, I personally feel responsible to teach this process to the many students whom I see struggling with spelling. I use the Spalding *Writing Road to Reading* method with them and strongly urge you to consider it as well. Continue to say the following:

_56 **Step 2 —** *"Leaving the space of an 'o' between words, write the word 'Grammar'. Leaving another space, write the word 'and'. Drop down to the next baseline and starting five spaces from the margin line, write the word 'Composition'."*

Note to Teacher:

Key Words are defined as the following: first words, nouns, pronouns, adjectives, verbs, adverbs, subordinating conjunctions (if, because, as, that, etc.). Articles, prepositions (regardless of length), and coordinating conjunctions (and, but, or, for, nor) are lowercased unless they are the first word of the title. "To" in any infinitive usage is also lowercased.

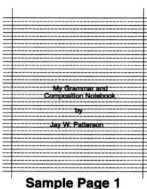

Sample Page 1

Lesson 2

L56 **Step 3 —** *"On the same line as the word 'Composition', leaving a space, write the word **'Notebook'**. The title of our new notebook is . . . Let's read it together,* 'My Grammar and Composition Notebook'."

L56P Always encourage your students and continue to tell them how well they are doing. Continue to say the following:

L56 **Step 4 —** *"Under the title, skip one baseline and on the next baseline, center the word **'by'**. Skip another baseline under the word 'by'. On the next baseline center **your first and last name** between the red margin lines. You may include **your middle initial**. Authors many times include their middle initials."*

L56P To see how the finished product for **"Lesson 2"** should look, refer to the Sample Page diagram in the margin of this lesson. Each of the lessons that follow has a very important and very helpful margin diagram to be used as a benchmark for the instructor. Refer to these often.

Again . . . the Importance of Handwriting!

While mastery of these lessons is our permission to move on, defining mastery needs to include an assessment of the developmental level of a student. Comprehension of the concept may be there while motor skills may be still developing. In this case, we keep moving through the **"Scope and Sequence"** knowing that the motor skills will eventually catch up.

Good handwriting, of course, is the kinesthetic evidence that students are still developing **attentional capacity**. This is the strength of the mind to pay attention to details that matter. It is very important that the student continue to use good handwriting according to the checkpoints and according to proper spatial concepts.

Precise, well-practiced, manuscript handwriting will continue to shape comprehension skills and develop automaticity with reading skills at every level. We are reinforcing an important neurological record necessary for comprehension. It may be slower at first, but development of skills in any area comes slowly. Slow is fast in this case. We can only afford to gain speed if we know we are not sacrificing development.

Expectancies Learned or Reinforced in Lesson 2: Dialogue and Review

1. Why is it important that I follow my teacher's specific instructions? *(I am learning listening skills.)*

2. What do we need to do with key words in every title? *(We capitalize them.)*

3. What does it take to be successful at anything that we do? *(It takes lots of hard work.)*

4. What do authors do? *(They write books.)*

5. Why do I need to use beautiful handwriting? *(I am reinforcing my need to pay very close attention to detail in a disciplined way. I am learning attentional capacity.)*

Where Do I Go from Here?

- **L56** and **L78** go to **"Lesson 3"** on page 88.

What Materials Will I Need?

- **L56** and **L78** will need *Grammar Notebooks* and pencils.

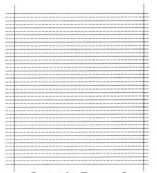

Sample Page 2
Lesson 3 (Blank)

Sample Page 3
Lesson 2–18

Sample Page 4
Lesson 19–32

Lesson 3
Starting the Table of Contents in *My Grammar* and Composition Notebook

L56 **Step 1** — "In your *Grammar Notebook*, starting at the title page which is page 1, *leave a blank page on the back of the title page which is page 2.* We will begin making what is called a 'Table of Contents' on the next page that is page 3.

"A Table of Contents tells our readers what is in our book and on which page they can find it. *On the title line of page 3, center the title 'Table of Contents'.* Do you remember what to do with key words in a title? *Let's write the word 'Table'. Skip a space and write the word 'of'.* Do we capitalize 'of'?"

L56P We do not capitalize the word "of" because it is not a key word in our title. Continue to say the following:

"We do not capitalize words in a title unless they are key words. 'Of' is not a key word. *Skip a space and write the word 'Contents'.*"

Remember to refer to the Sample Pages in the margins of these lessons. They demonstrate what these lessons should be creating. These are a guide for the instructor. As students write numbers, encourage them to conform their numbers to the legal definitions they learned in the handwriting section. Continue to say the following:

L56 **Step 2** — *"Skip one baseline under the title line, and on the next baseline to the left of the margin line, write '7'.* This is our page number for our next lesson on 'Nouns'. *Staying on the left side of the red left margin line, **continue to place numbers vertically until you reach 25.***

*"Turn to page 4 and centered on the title line, write 'Table of Contents (continued)'. Skipping one baseline under the title line, **continue numbering from 26–44.** Again, place the numbers to the left of the margin line. Go on to pages 5 and 6 and center the same title as page 4 'Table of Contents (continued)'. After skipping one baseline on page 5, **continue numbering on the left side of the margin line from 45–63 and on page 6 from 64–76.**"*

Step 3 — *"Counting the title page as page 1, let's count each side of every page. Page 2 is blank. Page 3 would be our Table of Contents. When you get to page 3, **place a beautiful '3' on***

©1998 Grammar Works/Holly Hall Publications, Inc.

the title line, to the right of the red margin line, in the upper right hand corner of the page. The backside of page 3 would be page 4 and so on. **Place the numeral '4' and other even numbers** *in the upper left-hand corner on the title line and to the left of the margin line.* **Continue to number all notebook pages in this manner through page 76.** *Even numbers go in the upper left corner. Odd numbers go in the upper right corner."*

L56P Please note the Sample Notebook Pages provided for you if you have any questions. From this point on we will jump into the content of this course. At the appropriate time in each lesson, students will be asked to return to the Table of Contents and record the title for a particular lesson next to the appropriate page number.

Expectancies Learned or Reinforced in Lesson 3: Dialogue and Review

1. What is a Table of Contents? *(It is a numbered list in the front of a book that tells us what is in a book.)*

2. How do we get organized? *(We take one small step at a time. We take them in the right order.)*

3. Why do I sometimes ask you to repeat my instructions with your own voice? *(We learn best by using multisensory instruction. One of the best tools I have is the sound of my own voice.)*

4. Why do I ask you to carefully write the information to this book? *(We learn best by using multisensory instruction. One of the best tools I have is doing things with my hands. We call this kinesthetics.)*

5. Why do I need to practice? *(Practice makes perfect only if we practice perfectly.)*

Reading comprehension improves when precise sound/symbol relationships are adhered to and reinforced

Sample Page 5
Lesson 32–39

Sample Page 6
Lesson 39–44

Where Do I Go from Here?

- **L56** and **L78** go to "**Lesson 4**" on page 92."

What Materials Will I Need?

- **L56** and **L78** will need *Grammar Notebooks*, pencils, and copies of Worksheets for "**Lesson 4**" starting on page 99.

Sample Dialogue Using the Three-Step Multisensory Pattern with Nouns

SAYS	DOES
First Step — Lesson 4, Step 3:	***First Step — Lesson 4, Step 3:***
TEACHER: "Listen carefully and watch closely. Starting in the first column, counting down 5 baselines from the top, using the title line as number one, comfortably close to the left margin line, write the naming word 'man'."	**TEACHER:** Puts the tip of the pencil on the 5th line where the word should be started. Writes the word "man".
STUDENT: Listens carefully. (Auditory)	**STUDENT:** Watches closely. (Visual)
Second Step	***Second Step***
TEACHER: "Repeat after me and watch closely. *Starting in the first column, counting down 5 baselines from the top, using the title line as number one . . .*"	**TEACHER:** Points with the pencil to the 5th line.
STUDENT: *"Starting in the first column, counting down 5 baselines from the top using the title line as number one . . ."* (Auditory and Vocal)	**STUDENT:** Watches closely. (Visual)
TEACHER: *"comfortably close to the left margin line . . ."*	**TEACHER:** Puts the tip of the pencil at the place on the 5th line where the word should be started.
STUDENT: *"comfortably close to the left margin line . . ."* (Auditory and Vocal)	**STUDENT:** Watches closely. (Visual)
TEACHER: *"write the naming word 'man'."*	**TEACHER:** Writes the word "man".
STUDENT: *"write the naming word 'man'."* (Auditory and Vocal)	**STUDENT:** Watches closely. (Visual)
Third Step	***Third Step***
TEACHER: "Repeat after me and you write while I watch. *Starting in the first column, counting down 5 baselines from the top using the title line as number one . . ."*	**TEACHER:** Watches student point with the pencil to the 5th baseline.
STUDENT: *"Starting in the first column, counting down 5 baselines from the top using the title line as number one . . ."* (Auditory and Vocal)	**STUDENT:** *Points with the pencil to 5th baseline.* (Visual and Kinesthetic)
TEACHER: *"comfortably close to the left margin line . . ."*	**TEACHER:** Watches the student put the tip of the pencil at the place on the 5th line where the word should be started.
STUDENT: *"comfortably close to the left margin line . . ."* (Auditory and Vocal)	**STUDENT:** *Puts the tip of the pencil at the place on the 5th line where the word should be started.* (Voc & K)
TEACHER: *"write the naming word **'man'**."*	**TEACHER:** Watches student write the word "man".
STUDENT: *"write the naming word **'man'**."* (Auditory and Vocal)	**STUDENT:** *Writes the word **"man"**.* (Visual, Kinesthetic, and Written)

Sample Dialogue Using the Three-Step Multisensory Pattern with Nouns

SAYS	DOES
First Step — Lesson 4, Step 6	**First Step — Lesson 4, Step 6**
TEACHER: "Let's write what a noun is. Listen carefully and watch closely. Starting at the bottom of the page, count up 6 baselines and on the 6th baseline, comfortably close to the left margin line, write, 'A noun is a naming word'."	**TEACHER:** Points to the bottom of the page, points to each baseline as they count up 6 baselines, puts the tip of the pencil comfortably close to the left margin line and writes the title in the proper place.
STUDENT: Listens carefully. (Auditory)	**STUDENT:** Watches closely. (Visual)
Second Step	**Second Step**
TEACHER: "Repeat after me and watch closely. *Starting at the bottom of the page . . .*"	**TEACHER:** Points to the bottom of the page.
STUDENT: *"Starting at the bottom of the page . . ."* (Auditory and Vocal)	**STUDENT:** Watches closely. (Visual)
TEACHER: *"count up 6 baselines . . ."*	**TEACHER:** Points to and counts each baseline.
STUDENT: *"count up 6 baselines . . ."* (Aud & Voc)	**STUDENT:** Watches closely. (Visual)
TEACHER: *"and on the 6th baseline, comfortably close to the left margin line . . ."*	**TEACHER:** Puts tip of writing pencil on the 6th baseline at the proper starting place.
STUDENT: *"and on the 6th baseline, comfortably close to the left margin line . . ."* (Aud & Voc)	**STUDENT:** Watches closely. (Visual)
TEACHER: *"write, 'A noun is a naming word'."*	**TEACHER:** Writes the definition.
STUDENT: *"write, 'A noun is a naming word'."* (Auditory and Vocal)	**STUDENT:** Watches closely. (Visual)
Third Step	**Third Step**
TEACHER: *"Now repeat after me and you write as I watch. Starting at the bottom of the page . . ."*	**TEACHER:** Watches student point to the bottom of the page.
STUDENT: *"Starting at the bottom of the page . . ."* (Auditory and Vocal)	**STUDENT:** *Points to the bottom of the page.* (Visual and Kinesthetic)
TEACHER: *"count up 6 baselines . . ."*	**TEACHER:** Watches student point and count.
STUDENT: *"count up 6 baselines . . ."* (Aud & Voc)	**STUDENT:** *Points to and counts baselines.* (Vis & Kin)
TEACHER: *"and on the 6th baseline, comfortably close to the left margin line . . ."*	**TEACHER:** Watches student put the tip of the pencil at the proper starting place.
STUDENT: *"and on the 6th baseline, comfortably close to the left margin line . . ."* (Aud & Voc)	**STUDENT:** *Puts the tip of the pencil at the proper starting place.* (Visual and Kinesthetic)
TEACHER: *"write, **'A noun is a naming word'.**"*	**TEACHER:** Watches student write the definition.
STUDENT: *"write, **'A noun is a naming word'.**"* (Auditory and Vocal)	**STUDENT:** Writes the definition, **'A noun is a naming word'.**" (Visual, Kinesthetic, and Written)

Person	Place	Thing
man	school	bed
boy	street	top
mother	sea	time
child		chance

A noun is a naming word.
A noun names a person, place, or thing.
A singular noun speaks of one.
A plural noun speaks of more than one.

Sample Page 7
Lesson 4

8 What Is a Noun? (continued)	
Ideas	Qualities
democracy	trustworthiness
socialism	loyalty
capitalism	bravery
evolution	courage
creationism	integrity
liberalism	honesty
conservatism	patience
optimism	kindness
pessimism	thriftiness

An idea is a thought or concept
formulated by the mind.
A quality is an inherent feature that makes
a person, place, or thing what they are.

Sample Page 8
Lesson 4

Nouns are naming words.

Nouns name:
- *persons*
- *places*
- *things*
- *ideas*
- *qualities*

Nouns may be singular or plural.

Lesson 4
What Is a Noun?

Let's Think about Naming Words

LK2 "Helen Keller was both blind and deaf. Before she could speak intelligibly, Annie Sullivan, her teacher, needed to introduce the concept of naming. It was not an easy job. Annie had to use signing. The only way to get to Helen's beautiful mind was through kinesthetics. Annie had to use her hands placed in Helen's hands in order to teach her. Helen would feel objects and then Annie would spell those objects into Helen's hands using signing. It was pure perseverance on Annie's part that created the miracle of speech in Helen. Annie would not give up even when Helen was most incorrigible.

"The very first word that Helen said was 'water'. After that Helen discovered, as we all do at some time, that everything in our world has a name. We should never take our understanding of naming for granted. Some of the things we name are very concrete. That means they can be perceived with the five physical senses. Do you remember what those are? Sight, sound, taste, touch, and smell. Other names are concepts or ideas and they are very abstract. Words like 'honesty' and 'freedom' are naming ideas, but we can't smell 'honesty'. We can't taste 'honesty'. The word 'honesty' is abstract and not concrete. It is still a naming word, however. It is time to begin **'Lesson 4.'**"

The Job That Naming Words Do

L12 **Step 1—** "Let's look more closely at naming words. Naming words have a very special job in the English language. They also have a very special name. They are called nouns. *Say the word 'nouns'.* Nouns give us names for people, for places, and for things. Everything and everybody has a name. You have a name. A pencil has a name. Water has a name."

L78 "Nouns also give us names for ideas and for qualities."

L12 "Naming words or nouns may be singular, speaking of only one. Naming words may be plural, speaking of more than one."

L12P Primary students will need more explanation of singular and plural and perhaps a demonstration. Use one pencil and then more than one. Use one student and then more than one.

Give students some examples. What is the plural of the word "man"? What is the plural for the word "boy"? The naming word "boy" is singular. The naming word "boys" is plural. Use as many examples as you need to bring understanding to the concept of singular vs. plural.

Some nouns form the plural by adding an "s" or an "es". Some nouns form the plural by changing the spelling (e.g., "man" changes to "men" in the plural). Still other nouns like the word "deer" do not change at all. Teach the plurals of nouns as students encounter them, telling the students that the dictionary is the standard by which we determine the correct plural form. In **L78** we will discuss in depth the many ways in which plural nouns are formed.

Dictating Nouns

L12P Remember that the students are watching the teacher demonstrate the first year through **L12**. They are doing the writing the second year through if the teacher thinks they are ready. The teacher will need to adapt the language of instruction if he or she is demonstrating. **L12** students who are doing the writing and **L34** need to be given loose-leaf penmanship paper at this time. **L56** and **L78** will go to their notebook.

L12 **Step 2** — "Now we are going to create a list of naming words. I am going to dictate some nouns to you. Dictate means I will say what you should write down and you will write it. But first we need to prepare our page."

L56 *"Let's go to your notebook. Turn to Page 7."*

L12 *"Divide your page into three equal columns. We will create two folded margin lines on our page."*

L12P Dividing paper into three equal columns is no small task. Take some time and demonstrate how to do this. If students are struggling, you may need to demonstrate by actually folding their paper for them the first time.

We are now ready to dictate naming words to our students. You may develop any lists you would like. The list that is included in the margin contains some of the naming words that primary students should have mastered by now. Thus, we hope that spelling will not be an issue.

After you have dictated a word, you may want to ask what the plural form of this word would be. The purpose of this lesson is simply to bring to a conscious level in the minds of our students what the naming process involves and what a naming word can do. Remember that understanding is a priority. Filling up the page with naming words is not.

Ayres List Nouns A–G

man	bed	top
time	chance	boy
book	mace	ice
school	street	hand
ring	mother	land
hat	child	sea

Ayres List H

day	box	door
floor	yard	ball
law	gust	way
home	love	house
year	baby	apple
dog	bread	food

Ayres List I

face	ride	tree
foot	block	spring
plant	river	song
winter	stone	lake
lace	page	end
fall	back	paper
Sunday	show	Monday
moon	letter	thing
form	corn	dance
dinner	doll	egg
zoo	zero	

Ayres List J

sister	cast	band
game	boat	son
sun	race	fire
wire	tire	age
gold	May	line
ship	train	bill
girl	report	side
life	car	word
work	wind	air
name	room	hope
chair	meat	mouse

What Is a Noun?		7
Person	Place	Thing
man	school	bed
boy	street	top
mother	sea	time
child		chance

A noun is a naming word.
A noun names a person, place, or thing.
A singular noun speaks of one.
A plural noun speaks of more than one.

Sample Page 7
Lesson 4

Naming Words

1A.   man

2A.   boy

3A   mother

4A.   child

1B.   school

2B.   street

3B.   sea

1C.   bed

2C.   top

3C.   time

4C.   chance

Column Headings

A.   Person

B.   Place

C.   Thing

L12   **Step 3 —** *"Starting in the first column, counting down five baselines from the top using the title line as number one, comfortably close to the left margin line, write the naming word* **'man'**. *On the next baseline below the word 'man', write the noun* **'boy'.***"*

L12P   Be sure to use these words in a sentence or ask the students to create some good sentences on their own. Continue to dictate the rest of the naming words that you see listed on the Sample Page in the margin. Make sure you are giving specific instructions about where they need to be writing these words. (Which column? Which line?) When this part of the lesson is done, only the naming words listed should be recorded.

Discovering What a Naming Word Does

L12   **Step 4 —** "Let's look at the three lists of nouns that we have written on our paper. Can you see what these nouns in the first column have in common? What do they name?"

STUDENTS: "They name persons."

TEACHER: "What do the words in the second column have in common? What do they name?"

STUDENTS: "They name places."

TEACHER: "What do the naming words in the third column have in common?"

STUDENTS: "They name things."

TEACHER: "Look what we have discovered. A noun names a person, a place, or a thing."

L12   **Step 5 —** "Let's give each of these columns a special title. *In the first column, count down three baselines. Comfortably close to the left red margin line, please write the word* **'Person'**, *capitalized.* Why do we need to capitalize it?"

STUDENTS: "It is a title. We need to capitalize important words in titles."

TEACHER: *"In the second column on the same line as 'Person', comfortably close to the folded margin line, let's write the title* **'Place'**, *capitalized. In the third column, on the same line as 'Person' and 'Place', comfortably close to the folded margin line, let's write the title* **'Thing'**, *capitalized.* We have learned that a noun can be singular or plural. We have learned that a noun can be a person, a place, or a thing."

Defining a Naming Word

L12 **Step 6** — "Everything in our world has to have a name. *Starting at the bottom of the page, count up six baselines and on the sixth baseline, comfortably close to the left margin line, write the following job description of a noun: 'A noun is a naming word'.* Remember to capitalize the first word of your sentence. Remember to add the right end punctuation."

L12P Don't forget to compliment your students. They need encouragement as we all do. Continue to say the following:

L12 **Step 7** — "Let's continue our legal definition of what a noun is. *On the next baseline, directly below your last sentence, starting comfortably close to the left margin line, write the following sentence: 'A noun names a person, place, or thing'.* Nouns also name ideas or qualities, but we won't talk about that until later when it is easier for you to understand.

"On the next baseline, directly below your last sentence, starting comfortably close to the left margin line, add this statement: 'A singular noun speaks of one'. And on the next baseline, directly below the last sentence, write the following: 'A plural noun speaks of more than one'. Can you read with me these very important statements about what a noun is?"

L12P Note that the additional lists provided in this lesson are made up of Ayres List nouns from the A–G list through the J list of the *Writing Road to Reading* method. Ask the students to tell you if the examples you share from this list are nouns that represent people, places, or things. Record as many as you would like. Perhaps start a wall chart if the noun page gets full, or you could make another noun page. Ideas and qualities as nouns will be introduced at a different level.

When dictating these words, make sure you use them in a sentence. Students need to hear how these words can be used as nouns.

When you encounter the words "Sunday" and "Monday" and the month "May" simply say that these words are special and need to be capitalized because we capitalize days of the week and months of the year. The next lesson explains the difference between common and proper nouns. If your student needs a greater challenge, choose nouns from the three categories of people, places, and things from other lists in the Ayres List beyond List J or pull examples from your students' other textbooks.

If you are reading in other books with your students and you come to a special noun that could easily be included in one of the noun columns, take the time to have your student record that noun in the appropriate column. You should always be searching for ways to review and reinforce lessons you have taught.

If you are reading in other books with your students and you come to a special noun that could easily be included in one of the noun columns, take the time to have your student record that noun in the appropriate column. You should always be searching for ways to review and reinforce lessons you have taught.

Ideas	Qualities
democracy	trustworthiness
socialism	loyalty
capitalism	bravery
evolution	courage
creationism	integrity
liberalism	honesty
conservatism	patience
optimism	kindness
pessimism	thriftiness

An idea is a thought or concept formulated by the mind.
A quality is an inherent feature that makes a person, place, or thing what they are.

Sample Page 8
Lesson 4

Nouns

1A.   *democracy*

2A.   *socialism*

3A   *capitalism*

4A.   *evolution*

5A.   *creationism*

6A.   *liberalism*

7A.   *conservatism*

8A.   *optimism*

9A.   *pessimism*

1B.   *trustworthiness*

2B.   *loyalty*

3B   *bravery*

4B.   *courage*

5B.   *integrity*

6B.   *honesty*

7B.   *patience*

8B.   *kindness*

9B.   *thriftiness*

Column Headings

A.   *Ideas*

B.   *Qualities*

Please remember that we are not expecting first graders to write. We are just demonstrating what we want them to be able to do someday.

Let's Get Organized

L56   **Step 8 —** *"Turn to the Table of Contents. On the page 7 line, write the title of this lesson: 'What Is a Noun?' Turn back to page 7.*

L12   *"Centered on the title line, between the two red margin lines, write the title 'What Is a Noun?'* Because this title asks a question, what end punctuation mark do we use after a question?

STUDENTS: "We need a question mark."

TEACHER: "You have done so well. We have created a notebook page. We still have room to add to it when we need to."

L12P **L12** and **L34** are now done with **"Lesson 4."** Turn to the **"Dialogue and Review Questions"** at the end of this lesson. Use the questions that apply to further embed these concepts.

L56P **L56** is now done with **"Lesson 4."** Turn to the **"Dialogue and Review Questions"** at the end of this lesson for further review.

Dictating Words That Are Ideas and Qualities

L78   **Step 1 —** "I am going to dictate some nouns that represent ideas and qualities. *We are going to place these words in their appropriate columns on page 8. You will need to fold a margin line down the middle of page 8."*

L78P   Dictate the words that you see in the Sample Page in the margin for this part of the lesson. Place them in their respective columns. Use each one of them in a sentence. Feel free to use other words you may want your student to think about.

When I was in Boy Scouts, I learned the Law of the Scouts. A scout was to display trustworthiness, loyalty, helpfulness, friendliness, courtesy, kindness, thriftiness, and so on. These are all very abstract nouns. They cannot easily be perceived with the five physical senses. They are neither people, nor places, nor tangible things. Some people might consider them qualities.

Democracy and socialism are ideas. Have your student record these ideas in the first column. They represent a philosophy or way of thinking. Please write words like integrity, honesty, patience, or wisdom in the second column. We can always use more of these qualities in a classroom and in a home. What wonderful topics these would be for compositions. Hint. Hint.

Discovering the Nature of Ideas and Qualities

L78   **Step 2** — *"Look at the list we created in the first column.* What do you know about these words? What do they represent? Can we taste or smell or physically touch what these words mean? They are very abstract, aren't they? These words are used to describe forms of government and the economies of those governments. These words represent the way people think about how life began and about life in general. They represent political frames of reference.

"If we look in a dictionary, we will discover that these words represent a thought, something formulated by the mind, a general concept, a firmly established opinion or belief, or a conviction about how something really should be. We have a name for these kinds of words. We call them **'ideas'**."

L78   **Step 3** — *"Look at the list we created in the second column.* What do you know about these nouns? What do they represent? Can we taste or smell or physically touch what these words mean? Again, they are very abstract, aren't they?

"These words describe the way people live and the character they have in their hearts. They are strong words. If we go to a dictionary, we will discover that these words provide a distinctive feature that makes a person or thing what they are, an inherent characteristic, or a degree of excellence perhaps. We have a name for these kinds of words. We call them **'qualities'**."

L78   **Step 4** — *"Skipping one baseline under the title line, center the subtitle **'Ideas'** in the first column. On the same line in the second column, center the subtitle **'Qualities'**."*

Defining the Concept of Ideas and Qualities

L78   **Step 5** —"We are going to write down a definition for the noun 'Ideas' and the noun 'Qualities'. *Counting up five baselines from the bottom of page 8, starting comfortably close to the left margin line, write the following: **'An idea is a thought or concept formulated by the mind'**. On the next available baseline, write the following: **'A quality is an inherent feature that makes a person, place, or thing what they are'**.*

"Wouldn't these ideas and qualities make great writing projects? I can see it now. A paper entitled, 'What Is the Difference between Democracy and Socialism?' or, 'What Does It Mean to Be Trustworthy?' I am surely glad we are learning about ideas."

8	What Is a Noun? (continued)	
	Ideas	Qualities
	democracy	trustworthiness
	socialism	loyalty
	capitalism	bravery
	evolution	courage
	creationism	integrity
	liberalism	honesty
	conservatism	patience
	optimism	kindness
	pessimism	thriftiness

An idea is a thought or concept formulated by the mind.
A quality is an inherent feature that makes a person, place, or thing what they are.

Sample Page 8
Lesson 4

Column Headings

A.   *Ideas*

B.   *Qualities*

Let's Get Organized

L78 **Step 6 —** *"Turn to the Table of Contents. On the page 8 line, write the title: 'What Is a Noun?' (continued). Turn back to page 8. Centered on the title line, between the two red margin lines, write the same title."*

Expectancies Learned or Reinforced in Lesson 4: Dialogue and Review

1. How does a sentence need to start and end? **L12** *(A sentence needs to begin with a capital letter and end with proper end punctuation?)*

2. What do nouns name? **L12** *(They name persons, places, and things.)* **L78** *(They name ideas and qualities.)*

3. What did Helen Keller discover? **L12** *(That everything has a name.)*

4. Why are nouns so important? **L12** *(Without names for what is in our world we cannot write or speak or communicate with anyone. It would be like we were blind and deaf.)*

5. What does singular mean? **L12** *(This means that there is only one noun.)*

6. What does plural mean? **L12** *(This means we have more than one noun.)*

7. How many different ways are there to form plural nouns? **L12** *(There are many ways. We need to check a dictionary if we are not sure.)*

8. What is an idea? **L78** *(An idea is a thought or a concept formulated by the mind.)*

9. What is a quality? **L78** *(A quality is an inherent feature that makes a person what they are.)*

10. What would be a good exercise for me to do to develop my communication skills? **L78** *(I could write a paper about ideas or qualities with proper syntactical expectancies filled with wonderful thoughts galore!)*

Where Do I Go from Here?

- **L12** goes to **L12** "Scope and Sequence" Step 8.

- **L34**, **L56**, and **L78** go to "Lesson 5" on page 107.

What Materials Will I Need?

- **L12** and **L34** will need penmanship paper and pencils.

- **L56** and **L78** will need *Grammar Notebooks* and pencils.

Practice Exercises for Reinforcement of *Grammar Works* Lessons

Many of the lessons in this text contain Student Worksheets that are designed to reinforce the concepts taught in *Grammar Works*.

These Worksheets provide an opportunity for more practice. The corresponding Teacher's Answer Keys are also included. The Student Worksheets are intended to be copied for student use.

1. The <u>man</u> went to (bed) on [time.]

2. The <u>boy</u> spun the [top] in the (street.)

3. The [book] about [mace] was at (school.)

4. <u>Mother</u> wears a [ring] on her [hand.]

5. The [play] was about a <u>child</u> who wore a [hat.]

6. The (land) and (sea) were covered with [ice.]

7. The [box] behind the [door] was on the (floor.)

8. [Love] in a (home) is like good [food] for all [year.]

9. A lemonade [stand] is in the (yard.)

10. The [dog] eats [bread] in his (house.)

Teacher's Answer Key for Student Worksheet 1:

What Is a Noun?

*Teacher Directions:
To follow is a student worksheet with answers. You may use these exercises however you like. You might go through the worksheet orally with your students on one day and have them identify all of the naming words. The next day you could explain to them the directions for marking persons, places, or things as described below and have them do the worksheet again.*

*Student Directions:
Find all of the naming words in the following sentences.*

<u>Underline</u> those nouns that are speaking of people.

(Circle) those nouns that speak of places.

Put a [box] around those nouns that speak of things.

What Is a Noun?

*Student Directions:
Find all of the naming
words in the following
sentences.*

<u>*Underline those nouns*</u>
*that are speaking of
people.*

*Circle those nouns that
speak of places.*

*Put a box around those
nouns that speak of
things.*

1. The man went to bed on time.

2. The boy spun the top in the street.

3. The book about mace was at school.

4. Mother wears a ring on her hand.

5. The play was about a child who wore a hat.

6. The land and sea were covered with ice.

7. The box behind the door was on the floor.

8. Love in a home is like good food for all year.

9. A lemonade stand is in the yard.

10. The dog eats bread in his house.

1. He sang the |song| on |Sunday.|

2. A |stone| lay near the (river) by a |tree.|

3. The (lake) was pretty during the |fall,| |winter,| or |spring.|

4. The |ball| hit him in the |face.|

5. The <u>baby</u> played with a |doll| trimmed with |lace.|

6. The <u>butcher</u> used the |soap| in the (kitchen.)

7. The |summer| was a |time| for a |lesson| from <u>father.</u>

8. The |clothing| on the |table| was wrapped in |paper.|

9. The <u>people</u> in the (church) prayed for our (country.)

10. He fell when his |foot| slipped off the |track.|

11. We ate |honey,| |cheese,| and an |orange| early in the |morning.|

12. In |August| my <u>uncle</u> will begin |work| for a new |company.|

13. The |weather| affected the |population| of |creatures| in the |mountains.|

Teacher's Answer Key for Student Worksheet 2:

What Is a Noun?

Teacher Directions: You may use these exercises however you like. You might go through the worksheet orally with your students on one day and have them identify all of the naming words. The next day explain to them the directions for marking persons, places, or things as described below and have them do the worksheet again. Nouns in the following sentences are taken from the I through O Ayres List.

Student Directions: Find all of the naming words in the following sentences.

<u>Underline</u> those nouns that are speaking of people.

(Circle) those nouns that speak of places.

Put a |box| around those nouns that speak of things.

What Is a Noun?

Directions: Find all of the naming words in the following sentences.

Underline those nouns that are speaking of people.

Circle those nouns that speak of places.

Put a box around those nouns that speak of things.

1. He sang the song on Sunday.

2. A stone lay near the river by a tree.

3. The lake was pretty during the fall, winter, or spring.

4. The ball hit him in the face.

5. The baby played with a doll trimmed with lace.

6. The butcher used the soap in the kitchen.

7. The summer was a time for a lesson from father.

8. The clothing on the table was wrapped in paper.

9. The people in the church prayed for our country.

10. He fell when his foot slipped off the track.

11. We ate honey, cheese, and an orange early in the morning.

12. In August my uncle will begin work for a new company.

13. The weather affected the population of creatures in the mountains.

1. The police found the sailor in the (palace) on [Saturday.]

2. The [complaint] of the husband caused several [replies.]

3. The thief finally granted the passengers their [liberty.]

4. The (avenue) was prepared for visitors in the [forenoon.]

5. The musician intended to increase his practice [time] for the [director.]

6. The [examination] of the (calculator) by government witnesses was peculiar.

7. The attorney sent a [telegram] on [stationery] because of the political [circumstance.]

8. The [medicine] caused a [sneeze] and a funny [whistle.]

9. The [carriage] was the [object] of the [investigation.]

10. The magnificent [bouquet] was delivered to the (convention.)

Teacher's Answer Key for Student Worksheet 3:

What Is a Noun?

Teacher Directions: You may use these exercises however you like. You might go through the worksheet orally with your students on one day and have them identify all of the naming words. One the next day explain to them the directions for marking persons, places, or things as described below and have them do the worksheet again. Nouns in the following sentences are taken from the P through W Ayres List.

Student Directions: Find all of the naming words in the following sentences.

Underline those nouns that are speaking of people.

(Circle) *those nouns that speak of places.*

Put a [box] around those nouns that speak of things.

What Is a Noun?

Directions: Find all of the naming words in the following sentences.

<u>*Underline those nouns that are speaking of people.*</u>

(Circle) those nouns that speak of places.

Put a |box| around those nouns that speak of things.

1. The police found the sailor in the palace on Saturday.

2. The complaint of the husband caused several replies.

3. The thief finally granted the passengers their liberty.

4. The avenue was prepared for visitors in the forenoon.

5. The musician intended to increase his practice time for the director.

6. The examination of the calculator by government witnesses was peculiar.

7. The attorney sent a telegram on stationery because of the political circumstance.

8. The medicine caused a sneeze and a funny whistle.

9. The carriage was the object of the investigation.

10. The magnificent bouquet was delivered to the convention.

1. In [principle], the [arrangement] for an artillery [campaign] was an extreme [sacrifice].

2. A sensible <u>athlete</u> volunteered to organize <u>employees</u> in a cordial [arrangement].

3. [December] is the [month] when [Christmas] is celebrated.

4. A [Tuesday] in [August] found the [sales] of [The Adventures of Huckleberry Finn] to be off the [charts].

5. <u>Mr. Meyers</u> went to (Europe) on [Thanksgiving].

6. The (Sears Tower) is in (Chicago).

7. The [Civil War] was a tragic [event].

8. A Spanish and German <u>delegation</u> visited the [Washington Monument].

9. Some <u>men</u> received the [Purple Heart] for [valor] shown during the [Vietnam War].

10. Did <u>Charles A. Lindbergh</u> drink [Coca-Cola] while in the [Spirit of St. Louis?]

Teacher's Answer Key for Student Worksheet 4:

What Is a Noun?

Teacher Directions: You may use these exercises however you like. You might go through the worksheet orally with your students on one day and have them identify all of the naming words. On the next day explain to them the directions for marking persons, places, or things as described below and have them do the worksheet again. Many nouns in these sentences are proper nouns or nouns found in the V through Z Ayres List.

Student Directions: Find all of the naming words in the following sentences.

<u>Underline</u> those nouns that are speaking of people.

(Circle) those nouns that speak of places.

Put a [box] around those nouns that speak of things.

What Is a Noun?

Directions: Find all of the naming words in the following sentences.

Underline those nouns that are speaking of people.

(Circle) those nouns that speak of places.

Put a [box] around those nouns that speak of things.

1. In principle, the arrangement for an artillery campaign was an extreme sacrifice.

2. A sensible athlete volunteered to organize employees in a cordial arrangement.

3. December is the month when Christmas is celebrated.

4. A Tuesday in August found the sales of *The Adventures of Huckleberry Finn* to be off the charts.

5. Mr. Meyers went to Europe on Thanksgiving.

6. The Sears Tower is in Chicago.

7. The Civil War was a tragic event.

8. A Spanish and German delegation visited the Washington Monument.

9. Some men received the Purple Heart for valor shown during the Vietnam War.

10. Did Charles A. Lindbergh drink Coca-Cola while in the *Spirit of St. Louis*?

Lesson 5

What Are Common and Proper Nouns?

The Significance of Special Nouns

L12 "In our last lesson, we learned all about nouns. We learned that nouns are naming words and everything has a name. Do you remember what nouns name? Very good. Nouns name persons. Nouns name places. Nouns name things. Sometimes we have to give an extra special name to an extra special noun.

"People have special names. When we were given the personal name that we have, that name was chosen because our parents wanted us to have a special name. Special names are very significant. They can mean much more than just an ordinary common naming word. Some special personal names are taken from the Bible. Some special personal names are given to us because we have a special grandfather or grandmother after whom we are named.

"Whatever special name we have, it means something. When we learn what our name can mean, we can gain a sense of who we are and why we exist and where we are going. Our name can give us a sense of who our parents might want us to become. Sometimes our special name helps us remember our heritage, our personal history, or the history of another personality who may have done something worthy of respect. Personal names are important. In fact they are so important that we begin each one with a capital letter.

"Places also have special names. We don't just say 'city' or 'state'. We say 'Sleepy Eye'. We say 'Minnesota'. These particular naming words all have a history behind them. That is what makes them special. The name 'Sleepy Eye' is the name given to a Sioux Indian Chief who lived in Southern Minnesota. He had an eye that would not open correctly. He had a sleepy eye. His Sioux name was *Ish-tak-ah-bah* which means 'a chief with a sleeping eye' or something like that. They named a city after him. It is an important place to me because that is where I was born. We can look to other cities and states. I wonder how Chicago got its name. I wonder how the state of Texas came to be called Texas. Places have special names and there are reasons for why they are called what they are called. Special places are important, and we show that they are by capitalizing them.

"Things also have special names. We don't just say 'pop' or 'soda' or 'baseball team' or 'candy'. We say 'Coca-Cola' or

What Are Common and Proper Nouns?	9
Common Nouns	**Proper Nouns**
days	Sunday, Monday, and Tuesday
months	January, March, April, June, July, and August
holidays	Christmas, Easter, and Thanksgiving
titles	Miss, Mr., and Mrs. A Tale of Two Cities the President

A common noun is a general naming word that is not capitalized unless it is the first word in a sentence or part of a title. A proper noun is a special, particular naming word that is always capitalized.

Sample Page 9
Lesson 5

10	Common and Proper Nouns (continued)	
continents	Europe, Asia, Africa, Anarctica, Australia, North America, and South America
names of people	John Smith
places	New York City Rocky Mountains
organizations	Boy Scouts of America
products	Coca-Cola
businesses	Sears
historical events	Civil War
nationalities	Norwegian
races	Caucasian
religions	Moslem and Christian
languages	Spanish and German
ships,planes,trains	Titanic
monuments	Lincoln Memorial
awards	Purple Heart
heavenly bodies	Mars and Neptune

Sample Page 10
Lesson 5

Sometimes we have to give an extra special name to an extra special noun.

'Pepsi' or 'Dr. Pepper'. We say 'Cleveland Indians' or 'New York Yankees' or 'Florida Marlins'. We say 'Snickers' or 'Butterfingers' or a 'Baby Ruth' bar. I wonder why they named it a 'Baby Ruth' bar. Why didn't they call it a 'George Washington' bar? Or an 'Abraham Lincoln' bar? Or a 'Davy Crockett' bar? The special names of things have a history, too.

"Companies give special names to the many products that they produce in order to sell those products. Oscar Meyer Wieners, Ivory soap, Wheaties, Microsoft, a Big Mac, and the list goes on. If we don't know what they are, we can't buy them. Special things are important too. How do we show that special things are important? You guessed it. We capitalize them. Our next lesson is about these many special naming words."

L12P Students will need to be given one sheet of loose-leaf penmanship paper. **L56** and **L78** are working in their notebook.

Dictating Special Nouns

L56 **Step 1** — *"Turn to page 9 in your* Grammar and Composition Notebook."

L12P Please remember that first graders are not making these pages. They are watching the teacher model the making of these pages. They first become involved visually and auditorially. Then when you make the second example of a modeled notebook page, they become involved vocally.

As an instructor you must model more than once what you expect of your first grade students. They need to see phrase by phrase what happens when we follow directions carefully. We will now provide specific examples of special, particular nouns that match the general categories of day, month, holiday, and title. You might even want to make some charts that include all of these listings.

L12 **Step 2** — *"Divide your page into two equal columns. In the first column, on the fourth baseline, starting comfortably close to the left margin line, write the word* **'day'**. *Skipping one baseline below the word 'day', write the word* **'month'**. *Skipping two baselines below the word 'month', write the word* **'holiday'**. *Skipping two more baselines, write the word* **'title'**."

Discovering the Name of a Special Noun

L12 **Step 3** — "If everything has a name, what name would we give to a special noun that needs to be capitalized? Let me give you a word picture. If common nouns had to wear a pair of pants, what kind of pants would they wear? I think they would wear blue jeans. Wearing blue jeans is very common when you think about it.

What Are Common and Proper Nouns?   9

Common Nouns	Proper Nouns
days	Sunday, Monday, and Tuesday
months	January, March, April, June, July, and August
holidays	Christmas, Easter, and Thanksgiving
titles	Miss, Mr., and Mrs. A Tale of Two Cities the President

A common noun is a general naming word that is not capitalized unless it is the first word in a sentence or part of a title. A proper noun is a special, particular naming word that is always capitalized.

Sample Page 9
Lesson 5

"You see people wearing blue jeans all over the place. You also see common, ordinary nouns all over the place. Nouns that are like blue jeans are called **'common nouns'**. Because they are common and not special, they are not capitalized.

"What kind of clothes would a special noun wear? I think it is likely that a special noun would dress up in a fancy tuxedo. They get dressed up because they are special. Usually a tuxedo is worn to a special event. Someone who wears a tuxedo feels very special. They are dressed up very properly. That is why we call them **'proper nouns'**. A part of the tuxedo outfit is a capital letter. All proper nouns start with a capital letter.

"We have names for the days of the week. We have names for the months of the year. We have special names for holidays. Some titles are very special. All of the special names and titles are proper nouns. Can we name the days of the week? Can we name the months of the year? Can we name some special holidays? Sure we can. Books have special titles too. People like Abraham Lincoln are given special titles. He is referred to as President Abraham Lincoln. These are proper nouns too.

"I am going to dictate some examples of these special nouns we call proper nouns. *On the same line as the word 'day', in the second column, comfortably close to the folded margin line, write the word 'Sunday', capitalized.* Do you now know why we have to capitalize the word 'Sunday'? That's right. It names a special day of the week."

L12P Please note the list of special nouns included in this lesson. This list is taken from the Ayres List in the *Writing Road to Reading* text. Supplement this list where it is necessary to do so to accommodate the needs of the students.

Continuing Dictation on Your Own

L12P Please continue your dictation of proper nouns in the second column by drawing from the list of proper nouns provided. Word for word instruction is not provided for the completion of this page. You must create your own. Use Step 3 as your model for delivery. Give students instructions about what you want them to write and where you want them to write it. Remember to use these words in a sentence when you dictate.

Note the Sample Page in the margin of this lesson. The student's paper should look something like this when you are done. You may simply follow this page as a model if you would like. Please feel free to add words or delete words if you see the need to do so. Remember that in **L12** the teacher should be simply modeling the making of this page. Some second graders might be able to handle the writing and creating of a notebook page, but asking most first graders would be too much.

Ayres List
Proper Nouns

Sunday	Monday
May	July
Friday	March
June	Tuesday
Mr. or Mrs.	Miss
November	God
April	January
December	October
September	August
Thursday	Saturday
Christmas	Christ
America	American
Wednesday	February
Europe	

What Are Common and Proper Nouns? 9

Common Nouns	Proper Nouns
days	Sunday, Monday, and Tuesday
months	January, March, April, June, July, and August
holidays	Christmas, Easter, and Thanksgiving
titles	Miss, Mr., and Mrs.
	A Tale of Two Cities
	the President

A common noun is a general naming word that is not capitalized unless it is the first word in a sentence or part of a title. A proper noun is a special, particular naming word that is always capitalized.

Sample Page 9
Lesson 5

A common noun is a general naming word that is not capitalized unless it is the first word in a sentence or part of a title.

A proper noun is a special, particular naming word that is always capitalized.

What Are Common and Proper Nouns?	9

Common Nouns	Proper Nouns
days	Sunday, Monday, and Tuesday
months	January, March, April, June, July, and August
holidays	Christmas, Easter, and Thanksgiving
titles	Miss, Mr., and Mrs. A Tale of Two Cities the President

A common noun is a general naming word that is not capitalized unless it is the first word in a sentence or part of a title.
A proper noun is a special, particular naming word that is always capitalized.

Sample Page 9
Lesson 5

L34P Students in **L34** and above should take dictation.

L12P It would be wise to make wall charts with this information available to the students. They need to know all of these of course. For some of the charts like the title chart, you may want to leave room to add titles as you encounter them.

L34P I suggest that for those common nouns where the Ayres List does not offer a complementing special noun, that you provide examples the student will readily identify. For example, Monopoly or Scrabble might be a complementing proper noun for the common noun 'game'.

L12P You may want to use 'Mr.' or 'Mrs.' for examples of titles as well as the title of a book they know. Of course, the key words in every title need to be capitalized.

L56P Also, remind your students that the titles of books and magazines and newspapers and movies are underlined to show that they are titles of major written works. If we are typing a title like these we italicize that title instead of underlining.

L12 **Step 4 —** *"Starting in the first column, skipping one baseline under the title, starting comfortably close to the left margin line, and beginning with a capital letter, write the subtitle '**Common Nouns**'. On the same line in the second column, starting comfortably close to the folded margin line, beginning with a capital letter, write the subtitle '**Proper Nouns**'."*

Defining a Common and a Proper Noun.

L12 **Step 5 —** *"Let's go down to the bottom of our page and write a definition for common and proper nouns. Counting up seven baselines from the bottom, beginning comfortably close to the left margin line, and capitalizing the first word of your sentence, write the following: '**A common noun is a general naming word that is not capitalized unless it is the first word in a sentence or part of a title**'. On the next available baseline write the following: '**A proper noun is a special, particular naming word that is always capitalized**'."*

Let's Get Organized

L56 **Step 6 —** *"Turn to the Table of Contents. On the page 9 line, write the title '**What Are Common and Proper Nouns?**' Turn back to page 9.*

L12 *Centered on the title line, between the two red margin lines, write the title '**What Are Common and Proper Nouns?**' Remember that a question needs to end with a question mark."*

Common Nouns Continued

L34P Look at Sample Page 10 in the margin. Provide students with a sheet of paper.

L56 **Step 1** — *"Turn to page 10 in your* Grammar Notebook.*"*

L34 "There are many general categories other than days of the week or months of the year or holidays or titles that represent proper nouns. Other general categories may include personal names of people and places as well as geographical names; names of organizations, products, business firms, government bodies, historical events and periods, and special events; the names of nationalities, races and religions, and languages; the names of ships, planes, trains, monuments, awards, heavenly bodies, and important documents. Under all of these general categories, we can list words that are wearing a tuxedo. We are going to record some of these general categories and then list some of the proper nouns that go with each."

L34 **Step 2** — *"Skipping one baseline under the title line in the first column, comfortably close to the left margin line, write the word* **'continents'**. *Skipping three baselines, write the words* **'names of'**. *On the next baseline below, write the word* **'people'**. *On the next baseline write the word* **'places'**.*"*

Continuing Dictation on Your Own

L34P You know how to do the rest. Give students directions that will make their pages look like the Sample Page. Remember to use these words, both common and proper, in a sentence when you dictate. How much of this page can be covered in one class period will be determined by your students' progress. Because they are still being careful with their handwriting, it will take time to record these. This time is valuable time. It is worth every painstaking detail. When you jump to the second column, there may be a need to have some spelling lessons.

Let's Get Organized

L56 **Step 3** — *"Turn to the Table of Contents. On the page 10 line, write the title* **'Common and Proper Nouns (continued)'**. *Turn back to page 10."*

L34 *"Centered on the title line, between the two red margin lines, write the title* **'Common and Proper Nouns (continued)'**.*"*

L34 As you dictate, please use Sample Page 9 and Sample Page 10 in the margin as a model.

10	Common and Proper Nouns (continued)
continents	Europe, Asia, Africa, Anarctica, Australia, North America, and South America
names of	
people	John Smith
places	New York City
	Rocky Mountains
organizations	Boy Scouts of America
products	Coca-Cola
businesses	Sears
historical events	Civil War
nationalities	Norweigian
races	Caucasian
religions	Moslem and Christian
languages	Spanish and German
ships,planes,trains	Titanic
monuments	Lincoln Memorial
awards	Purple Heart
heavenly bodies	Mars and Neptune

Sample Page 10
Lesson 5

Expectancies Learned or Reinforced in Lesson 5: Dialogue and Review

1. What are special nouns called that wear tuxedos and begin with a capital letter? **L12** *(Proper Nouns.)*

2. What are the days of the week? **L12** *(Check your wall chart.)*

3. What are the months of the year? **L12** *(Check your wall chart.)*

4. Can you name a special or religious holiday? **L12** *(Check your wall chart.)*

5. What do we need to do with the key words in all titles? **L12** *(We capitalize them.)*

6. What do we do with the names of continents or organizations or special products or the other general categories of special nouns? **L34** *(We capitalize them.)*

7. What do we do with the names of people and specific places? **L12** *(We capitalize them.)*

8. What do we do with the key words in the titles of books, magazines, newspapers, movies, plays, and TV programs? **L34** *(We capitalize them.)*

9. In addition to capitalizing, what else do we do with the titles of special, major written or produced works like books or plays or magazines or newspapers? **L56** *(We underline them if we are writing with a pencil. We italicize them if we are using a typewriter or a word processor.)*

The Pursuit of Excellence Is Found in the Details

Remember to require the use of manuscript for every entry in these *Grammar Notebooks* or on students' practice pages. We are in the very important business of training the human mind to process language better. The mind needs to be trained well. By requiring the use of a precise legal definition for each phonogram, we are requiring the student's mind to be constantly vigilant. The details of life matter. The details of writing matter. Students must be taught to recognize every syntactical and orthographic expectancy and write or speak accordingly.

Syntactical expectancies need to be well taught and well practiced. They are not really expectancies unless the student can explain why a certain word must be capitalized or why a certain punctuation mark must be used in a particular place.

Where Do I Go from Here?

- **L12** goes to **L12** "Scope and Sequence" Step 10.

- **L34** goes to **L34** "Scope and Sequence" Step 14.

- **L56** and **L78** go to **"Lesson 6"** on page 114.

What Materials Will I Need?

- **L56** and **L78** will need *Grammar Notebooks* and pencils.

In my classroom as I work to establish automaticity in my students, I always ask my students to defend their answers. I do not let them say, "Well, it just sounds right."

Grammar is extremely logical and predictable. There are reasons why our language is ordered the way it is. Learning those reasons, understanding those reasons, applying those reasons in our writing and thinking is a discipline that results in an effective mastery of our language. We want our students to be the best, and the best students are very capable of explaining why our language does what it does. They can know how everything fits together and how everything works. When they understand function, they will become good writers.

As instructors we must have high expectations in this regard. Students will rise only to the highest expectation placed before them.

I just left a group of seventh graders. We had only a moment ago finished reading Walt Morey's book called *Kavik, the Wolf Dog*. I shared some biographical information about this well-known author and how he came to love writing. The fact that he didn't like school was very interesting to them. I then suggested that we perhaps consider writing a novel with 12 chapters just like *Kavik, the Wolf Dog*. The kids thought it was an impossible task. But the reality is that the writing of a novel or any major work is only as difficult as the details. This is where we must concentrate our effort. Details will forever matter.

High expectations produce excellence!

The details of life matter.

The details of writing matter.

Students must be taught to recognize every syntactical and orthographic expectancy and write and speak accordingly.

the child
a boy
an apple
the door
a dog
an egg
an hour
an honor

An article is a word that introduces a
noun. There are three articles: "a", "an",
and "the".
The article "an" is used with nouns that
begin with a vowel sound.

Sample Page 11
Lesson 6

Lesson 6
What Is an Article?

Let's Learn about Hunting Dogs

L12 "What do you know about hunting dogs? Some areas of our country use hunting dogs out in the fields or in marshlands to scare up a pheasant or retrieve a duck or goose. One particular kind of hunting dog is called a Pointer. When walking with his master in the field, a well-trained Pointer has a keen awareness of everything around them. The Pointer is sniffing and looking and looking and sniffing.

"If he spots a pheasant, he stops and freezes like a statue. One of his front legs is lifted up. His tail is likely to be straight back. His nose is pointing at that bird telling the master, 'You had better come on over and check this out.'

"Now you hope at this point that the dog knows the difference between a pheasant and a skunk. Hopefully he knows that feathers are not fur and that fur is not feathers. We have three words in our language that know the difference between a noun and other words. They are just like a hunting dog that points.

"These words are looking and sniffing and sniffing and looking. When these three words stop and lift up that front leg and aim that nose, they too are saying 'come on over and check this out.' So let's check out these three words and what they do."

Dictating Hunting Dog Words

L12 Students will need to be given a sheet of loose-leaf penmanship paper.

L56 **Step 1**—"*Turn to page 11 in your* Grammar Notebook.*"*

L12 *"Skipping one baseline below the title line on our page, starting comfortably close to the left margin line, write the following on consecutive baselines.* That means one under the other."

L12P Dictate these examples using each in a sentence. If you wish to develop more examples, use Ayres List Nouns on page 93 for further dictation.

"the child"	*"a boy"*
"an apple"	*"the door"*
"a dog"	*"an egg"*

Discovering Articles and What They Do

L12 **Step 2** — "There are many times in written language that we need to introduce a noun. Look at the examples we have written. What do we know about the word 'child', the word 'boy', the word 'apple', the word 'door', the word 'dog', and the word 'egg'? What kind of words are these? They are nouns aren't they? And how do we know they are nouns? They name a person, a place, or a thing.

"This lesson introduces still another way that we can recognize a noun when we see one. There are three words in the English language whose sole purpose is to point at nouns just like a dog out in the field will point at a pheasant. Let's look more closely at these examples we have written. Can you tell me what you think those three words are? You are right. The words 'a', 'an', and 'the' are our noun pointers. They point to a person, place, thing, idea, or quality. These three words are called articles or noun indicators. They are easy to remember. What are those three words again? The first article is 'a'. The second article is 'an'. The third article is 'the'."

L56 "There is a question that sometimes comes up regarding articles. What part of speech is an article? What job does it really do? Look at these sentences. He bought a watch. He used an egg for the cake. If we use the article 'a' or 'an', are we waving any adjective flags? How many watches are we talking about? How many eggs are there? These two articles imply that there is only one of whatever it is. Both 'a' and 'an' are waving the 'How Many?' flag.

"These two articles therefore fit our legal definition for an adjective. How many eggs are there? How many watches are there? There is only one in each case. Look at the word 'the'. It was the car that we needed. Was it just any car? No. It was 'the' car. What flag is the article 'the' flying? The article 'the' actually flies the flag 'Which One?' It is pointing to a specific car. Because it does, we can say that it is an adjective. The articles 'a', 'an', and 'the' are technically adjectives by definition."

When Do We Use the Article "an"?

L34 **Step 3** — "Why do we need to use the article 'an' instead of the article 'a' with a noun like 'apple'? Why do we need to use 'an' with a noun like 'egg'? Why do we need to use the article 'an' with a word like 'hour'?

"We must know the answer to these questions. All nouns that begin with a **vowel sound** use the article 'an' instead of 'a'. It is simply a rule of our language. Even the word 'hour', that begins its spelling with a consonant letter, must use the article 'an'

The words "a", "an", and "the" are our noun pointers.

They point to a person, place, thing, idea, or quality.

These three words are called articles or noun indicators.

the child
a boy
an apple
the door
a dog
an egg
an hour
an honor

An article is a word that introduces a
noun. There are three articles: "a", "an",
and "the".
The article "an" is used with nouns that
begin with a vowel sound.

Sample Page 11
Lesson 6

Where Do I Go from Here?

- **L12**, **L34**, **L56**, and **L78** go to "Lesson 7" on page 117.

What Materials Will I Need?

- **L12** and **L34** will need penmanship paper, pencils, and copies of Worksheets for "Lesson 7" starting on page 121.

- **L56** and **L78** will need *Grammar Notebooks*, pencils, and copies of Worksheetsfor "Lesson 7" starting on page 121.

because the first sound we hear in the word 'hour' when we pronounce the word is a **vowel sound**. The word 'honor' is another example of the need for the word 'an' based on the initial sound alone. Let's write these examples on our page.

"Directly below 'an egg' on your page, comfortably close to the left margin line, write **'an hour'**. *Directly below 'an hour', comfortably close to the margin line, write* **'an honor'."**

Defining the Noun Pointers That We Call Articles

L12   **Step 4 —** "Now we are going to write the definition of an article at the bottom of our page. *Let's count up five baselines from the bottom. Starting comfortably close to the margin line, remembering to capitalize the first word of each sentence, write these sentences.* **'An article is a word that introduces a noun. There are three articles: "a", "an", and "the".'"**

L34   *"On the next available baseline, starting comfortably close to the margin line, write this sentence.* **'The article "an" is used with nouns that begin with a vowel sound'.** It will take more than one line."

Let's Get Organized

L56   **Step 5 —** *"Turn to the Table of Contents. On the page 11 line, write the title* **'What Is an Article?'** *Turn back to page 11."*

L12   *"Centered on the title line, between the two red margin lines, write the title* **'What Is an Article?'"**

Expectancies Learned or Reinforced in Lesson 6: Dialogue and Review

1. What is the function of the articles "a", "an", and "the" in our language? **L12** *(The function is to simply introduce nouns in the English language.)*

2. What kind of nouns does the article "an" introduce? **L12** *(The article "an" introduces nouns that begin with a vowel sound.)*

Lesson 7
What Is an Action Verb?

The Power Words

L12 "Some words can be really strong and powerful. We need to learn about these kinds of words so we can use them properly."

L34 "As you learn about how powerful words can be, I hope you will begin to learn more and more about using our language. When you do, you will begin to understand why it has been said that the pen is, indeed, mightier than the sword.

"In this lesson, students, we will introduce one of the most powerful kinds of words. These power words are called 'action verbs'. The Nobel Prize-winning author Ernest Hemingway said that nouns and action verbs are the 'bones and sinews of speech.' Bones and sinews are what give our bodies strength and make it possible for us to stand upright and walk and sit up. Without them, our bodies would stand about as well as gingerbread men cut out of finger jello. Language that does not use bones and tendons and muscles and energy will be as weak as those men made of jello. Well-chosen nouns and well-chosen power words make for a strong and healthy and vibrant speaker or writer. The world needs communicators who are able to use language and use it well. Let's look at our lesson."

Dictating the Power Words

L12P **L12** and **L34** students need to be given a sheet of loose-leaf penmanship paper. **L56** and **L78** will work in the *Grammar Notebook.*

L56 *"Turn to page 12 in your* Grammar Notebook."

L12 **Step 1** — "I am going to dictate some action verbs to you. *Let's divide our page into three equal columns by folding properly. Skipping one baseline under the title line, in the first column, comfortably close to the left margin line, write the word* **'do'**."

L12P Dictate the remaining action verbs from Ayres List A–G, H, and I on consecutive baselines. Look at the Sample Page provided. In the first column, dictate the action verbs listed from the Ayres List A–G, using each word in an oral sentence. In the second column, dictate the action verbs from Ayres List H. In the third column, dictate the action verbs found in Ayres List I.

L34P As instructional years go on, feel free to change this list. Include other strong power words you want your students to know. The

---

12	What Is an Action Verb?	
do	eat	miss
go	stand	blow
see	bring	block
run	tell	sing
charge	ask	find
like	sit	take
hand	get	thank
live	call	dance
play	send	
make		
say		
come		

An action verb is a power word that gives strength and energy to a sentence. An action verb expresses action or motion.

Sample Page 12
Lesson 7

Ayres List A–G

do	go
see	run
charge	like
hand	live
play	make
say	come

Ayres List H

eat	stand
bring	tell
ask	sit
get	call
send	

Ayres List I

miss	blow
block	sing
find	take
thank	dance

Sample Page 12

Lesson 7

Ayres List A–G

do	go
see	run
charge	like
hand	live
play	make
say	come

Ayres List H

eat	stand
bring	tell
ask	sit
get	call
send	

Ayres List I

miss	blow
block	sing
find	take
thank	dance

words provided are designed to be only a sampling. Take this list on the Sample Page and find new power words. Teach your students to use a thesaurus to find even more.

Discovering the Nature of a Power Word

L12 **Step 2 —** "These power words or action verbs are very important. They move strong nouns to where they need to go like we move a wheelbarrow full of gravel to where it needs to go. Can you move a wheelbarrow full of gravel? If you can, you are very strong. Words can be like that."

L78 "Power words can also move strong ideas to where they need to go."

L78P Find some examples of writing that convey strong ideas. Use Dr. Martin Luther King's "I Have a Dream" speech. Use the Declaration of Independence. Go to an editorial in your local newspaper. Find a recent speech by someone you respect and admire. Look for power words. Analyze the text. Understand how some of the best communicators in our past and in the present use power words to accomplish their purpose. People who write with such a purpose know that ideas have far-reaching consequences.

L12 "Imagine your body without muscles. Written or spoken language without good power words will produce writing and speaking that is like jello. It will be very shaky and weak. We wouldn't want to build a house out of jello. Would you like to live in a house made out of jello? What would happen if it rained? Do you think that jello words would be strong enough to help you push a wheelbarrow full of gravel?

"Let's look at another word picture. It takes a great deal of energy and power to move a train down the tracks. Trains carry such heavy loads. There are other things that are heavy. Look at the space shuttle. Energy and power are needed to lift a space shuttle into orbit. Let's go to the baseball park. Energy and power are needed to swing at a baseball and slug it into the upper deck. We need to use words that have this kind of energy and power. We want powerful writing. We want energized writing."

L56 "Look at this example: I will *do* my best to *improve* my writing. What do the words 'do' and 'improve' add to this sentence? They add strength. They add a decision to do better. They add energy and power. To do is to act, and to act is to be strong. The word 'do' is a strong word of action."

L12 "Do you like pizza? What kind of a sentence could we write about pizza? Look at this example: I will make pizza. What does the word 'make' add to this sentence? It adds the energy to create a pizza. Our stomach is cheering because something wonderful is happening. This word 'make' is a working word. It is working very hard to produce a pizza. Maybe it is a pepperoni with extra cheese!

"Let's look at this sentence: I will run three miles. What is happening in this sentence when we use the word 'run'? The energy and power of the word 'run' is making something happen. The word 'run' is a muscle word. Running three miles is not easy. Do you think you could do it? We want to use words like 'run'. They are full of action. That is why they are called action verbs. Say action verbs. Action verbs are strong and full of energy. They can push wheelbarrows. They can hit homeruns. They can launch a space shuttle. They can move a train down the tracks."

Defining an Action Verb

12   **Step 3 —** *"Now let's write a definition for an action verb. Counting up five baselines from the bottom of your page, comfortably close to the left margin line, capitalizing the first word of each sentence, please write the following: 'An action verb is a power word that gives strength and energy to a sentence. An action verb expresses action or motion.'"*

Let's Get Organized

L56   **Step 4 —** *"Turn to the Table of Contents. On the page 12 line, write the title 'What Is an Action Verb?' Turn back to page 12."*

L12   *"Centered on the title line, between the two red margin lines, write the title 'What Is an Action Verb?'* Are you still using beautiful manuscript handwriting? We want all our work to be precise."

Continued Encouragement Is a Key

Always remember to encourage your students. If they are doing a good job, say it and say it and say it again. "You are an extremely sharp student. Your handwriting is beautiful. You pay such close attention to detail. You have fantastic listening skills." Be creative.

Do whatever it takes to build confidence in your students. If their handwriting is precise and in accord with the legal definitions, wonderful things are happening in their brains. I'll say it again. Details will forever and always matter.

If their minds are being required to pay attention to the smallest detail in our language, foundation is being built. If they can pay attention to these details, they will be able to pay attention to the details that require higher level thinking. Developing mastery with English is a sequential process that requires a demonstration of mastery at every level.

Ernest Hemingway once said, "Nouns and verbs are the bones and sinews of speech."

Our students must understand that using nouns and action verbs is foundational to good writing.

Other Ideas for Reinforcement of Action Verbs

1. Go to any storybook and identify action verbs as you read. Make sure they are action verbs.

2. Check other written materials found in your textbooks and look for these high-energy words.

Expectancies Learned or Reinforced in Lesson 7: Dialogue and Review

1. What is an action verb? **L12** *(An action verb is a power word that gives strength and energy to a sentence. An action verb expresses action or motion.)*

2. What do action verbs do for my writing and speaking? **L12** *(They give power and energy to what I write and speak.)*

3. How can strong nouns and action verbs be compared to bones and tendons? **L12** *(Bones and tendons hold us together. Nouns and verbs hold writing together. Good nouns make pictures in our minds. Good action verbs put energy in those pictures. Because we use strong nouns and verbs, we will do a better job of communicating our thoughts and ideas. We must write with imagery and energy.)*

Where Do I Go from Here?

- **L12** goes to **"Lesson 14"** on page 177.

- **L34**, **L56**, and **L78** go to **"Lesson 8"** on page 125.

What Materials Will I Need?

- Optional: Teaching will be enhanced for **L12** by using adjective question "flags" as described on page177 in **"Lesson 14."**

- **L12** and **L34** will need penmanship paper and pencils. **L12** need copies of Worksheets for **"Lesson 14"** starting on page 182.

- **L56** and **L78** will need *Grammar Notebooks* and pencils.

1. Please (do) the dishes.

2. He will (go) and (see) the men.

3. The teacher will (run) and (make) the call.

4. A bull (charges) a boy in the pasture.

5. (Hand) your book to me and (say) your lines.

6. He has (written) a song we will (sing.)

7. (Ask) the child if he (ate) the whole thing.

8. The mother (took) her children to the play.

9. The dog (dances) for food.

10. (Watch) the cake in the oven so it will not (burn.)

11. Water (freezes) in the winter.

12. A pilot will (fly) his plane.

Teacher's Answer Key for Student Worksheet 1:

What Is an Action Verb?

Teacher Directions: Explain to your student the directions for marking the action verbs and have them complete the worksheet.

Student Directions: (Circle) *the action verbs in the following sentences.*

What Is an Action Verb?

Directions: (Circle) *the action verbs in the following sentences.*

1. Please do the dishes.

2. He will go and see the men.

3. The teacher will run and make the call.

4. A bull charges a boy in the pasture.

5. Hand your book to me and say your lines.

6. He has written a song we will sing.

7. Ask the child if he ate the whole thing.

8. The mother took her children to the play.

9. The dog dances for food.

10. Watch the cake in the oven so it will not burn.

11. Water freezes in the winter.

12. A pilot will fly his plane.

Abraham Lincoln's "Gettysburg Address"

Four score and seven years ago our fathers (brought forth) upon this continent a new nation, (conceived) in liberty and (dedicated) to the proposition that all men are (created) equal.

Now we are (engaged) in a great civil war, (testing) whether that nation or any nation so (conceived) and so (dedicated) can long (endure.) We are (met) on a great battlefield of that war. We have (come) to (dedicate) a portion of that field as a final resting place for those who here (gave) their lives that that nation might (live.) It is altogether fitting and proper that we should (do) this.

But, in a larger sense, we cannot (dedicate)— we cannot (consecrate)—we cannot (hallow) this ground. The brave men living and dead, who (struggled) here have (consecrated) it far above our poor power to (add) or (detract.) The world will little (note) nor long (remember) what we (say) here, but it can never (forget) what they (did) here. It is for us, the living, rather, to be (dedicated) here to the unfinished work which they who (fought) here have thus far so nobly (advanced.)

It is rather for us to be here (dedicated) to the great task remaining before us—that from these honored dead we (take) increased devotion to that cause for which they (gave) the last full measure of devotion; that we here highly (resolve) that these dead shall not have (died) in vain; that this nation under God, shall (have) a new birth of freedom; and that government of the people, by the people, for the people shall not (perish) from the earth.

Teacher's Answer Key for Student Worksheet 2:

What Is an Action Verb?

Teacher Directions: This is another student worksheet to help students understand action verbs. Explain to your student the directions for marking the action verbs in this selection and have them complete the worksheet.

Student Directions: Find and (circle) all the action verbs in this famous selection—Lincoln's "Gettysburg Address."

What Is an Action Verb?

Directions: Find and (circle) *all the action verbs in this famous selection—Lincoln's "Gettysburg Address."*

Abraham Lincoln's "Gettysburg Address"

Four score and seven years ago our fathers brought forth upon this continent a new nation, conceived in liberty and dedicated to the proposition that all men are created equal.

Now we are engaged in a great civil war, testing whether that nation or any nation so conceived and so dedicated can long endure. We are met on a great battlefield of that war. We have come to dedicate a portion of that field as a final resting place for those who here gave their lives that that nation might live. It is altogether fitting and proper that we should do this.

But, in a larger sense, we cannot dedicate— we cannot consecrate—we cannot hallow this ground. The brave men living and dead, who struggled here have consecrated it far above our poor power to add or detract. The world will little note nor long remember what we say here, but it can never forget what they did here. It is for us, the living, rather, to be dedicated here to the unfinished work which they who fought here have thus far so nobly advanced.

It is rather for us to be here dedicated to the great task remaining before us—that from these honored dead we take increased devotion to that cause for which they gave the last full measure of devotion; that we here highly resolve that these dead shall not have died in vain; that this nation under God, shall have a new birth of freedom; and that government of the people, by the people, for the people shall not perish from the earth.

Lesson 8
What Is a Personal Pronoun?

The Jobs That Words Do

L34 "Many people go to a job every day. Some go to build. Some go to bake. Some go to help people in hospitals. Some go to their place of business. Some go to a factory. Some go to an office. There are many kinds of jobs. Carpenters, nurses, lawyers, plumbers, electricians, clerks, custodians, cooks, farmers, ranchers, secretaries, truckers, teachers, managers, pilots, the list goes on and on.

"If we think about words doing different jobs in the same way we think about people doing different jobs, we will understand our language better. All words have a job to do. Some jobs that we do require certain tools. **What kind of tools does a carpenter need?** We could list a hammer, a saw, a screwdriver, or a tape measure. **What kind of tools does a nurse need?** We could list a thermometer, a stethoscope, a hospital bed, or a simple pen to write on a patient's chart.

"What kind of tools do we need to do a good job with the English language? This is a very important list. In our world today, the ability to use the English language well is often the factor that makes special opportunities for employment possible. That is why there are so many people, even in other countries, who learn English. They know that learning the English language is very important.

"In order to properly use English, we all need to understand that words also go to work every day. Some words go to build ideas. Some words go to name people and places and things. Some words go to provide energy to move words down the tracks of meaning. When we understand this and know what these jobs are, these words can become our tools.

"We need many tools to use English correctly and wisely. We need to become craftsmen, artists, and master designers. Then we can build and craft and mold and shape our language. Nothing that is written or spoken today, no essay or news story or speech or telephone conversation, will happen unless the writer or the speaker understands what words can do.

"Some words help us identify people and things. Look at the sentence, 'I went to Washington, D. C.' The word 'I' is doing some work. It has a job. It tells the listener **who** went to Washington, D. C. Look at this sentence, 'I saw you on the Mall in Washington, D. C.' Now another person is involved. What word

---

| What Is a Personal Pronoun? | 13 |

Singular	Plural
I	we
you	you
he, she, it	they

Jared is going to the parade.
He is going to the parade.
The parade had ten marching bands.
It had ten marching bands.
Sally wanted to see the clowns.
She wanted to see the clowns.
Sam, Mark, and I went to the game.
We went to the game.

A personal pronoun is a part of English speech that takes the place of a noun.
A singular pronoun speaks of one.
A plural pronoun speaks of more than one.

Sample Page 13
Lesson 8

tells me that? It is the word 'you', isn't it? The word 'you' is doing a job. Look at this sentence, 'It needed to be repaired'. To what does the word 'it' refer? It refers to something that is broken. Words like 'I' and 'you' and 'it' are words that do a special job in our language. Let's find out more about that job."

Dictating Singular and Plural Personal Pronouns

L34P L34 students need to be given a sheet of loose-leaf penmanship paper. **L56** and **L78** will work in the *Grammar Notebook*.

L56 **Step 1** — *"Turn to page 13 in your* Grammar Notebook.*"*

L34 *"Fold your page into two equal columns. Find the first column. Skipping one baseline under the title line, centered in the first column, write the word* **'Singular'***, capitalized. Find the second column. On the same baseline as the word 'Singular', centered in the second column, write the word* **'Plural'***, capitalized.*

"We are now ready to write some words that we know. *Find the heading 'Singular'. On the first available baseline under the heading 'Singular', comfortably close to the left margin line, write the word* **'I'***. On next available baseline below 'I' write the word* **'you'***. On the next available baseline below 'you' write the three pronouns* **'he'***,* **'she'***, and* **'it'***. Use commas between 'he' and 'she' and between 'she' and 'it'.*

"*Find the heading 'Plural'. On the next available baseline under the heading 'Plural' in the second column, comfortably close to the folded margin line, write the word* **'we'***. Below 'we' let's write the word* **'you'***. Below the word 'you' let's write the word* **'they'***. The word 'they' is the plural form of 'he, she, or it'."*

Discovering the Nature of These Substitute Words

L34 **Step 2** — "I am now going to read a few sentences to help us see how these words work in our language. Listen to these sample sentences. They will help you see what jobs the words like 'I' and 'you' and 'they' actually do. The sentences we will use contain a special common or proper noun for which a special substitute word may be used. The key word here is substitute. What does the word substitute mean? If a coach has a player who needs a rest, what does the coach do? He sends in a substitute. That is the job of words like 'I' and 'you' and 'we'. They are substitutes. They come off the bench when a noun needs a rest. We call these substitute words pronouns.

"These pronouns help our language avoid needless repetition. These pronouns provide efficiency in written and spoken language. Here are some sample sentences."

What Is a Personal Pronoun?   13

Singular	Plural
I	we
you	you
he, she, it	they

Jared is going to the parade.
He is going to the parade.
The parade had ten marching bands.
It had ten marching bands.
Sally wanted to see the clowns.
She wanted to see the clowns.
Sam, Mark, and I went to the game.
We went to the game.

A personal pronoun is a part of English speech that takes the place of a noun.
A singular pronoun speaks of one.
A plural pronoun speaks of more than one.

Sample Page 13
Lesson 8

L34 **Step 3** — "Listen to this sentence. 'Jared [Use a student's name.] is going to the parade.' Who or what is going to the parade? [Pause for student response.] Right! Jared is going to the parade. The name 'Jared' is a noun. It is a special noun. How do we know? It is a personal name that we need to capitalize."

L34 **Step 4** — "Look at the list of substitute words we have written on this page. Which of these words can we substitute or use instead of the noun 'Jared' in our sentence? Let's try the word 'he'. If we substitute the word 'he' for the noun 'Jared', our sentence will read as follows: 'He is going to the parade'. That works well doesn't it? Let's write some sentences on our page.

"Skipping one line below 'he', 'she', and 'it', write the following sentence starting in the first column comfortably close to the left red margin line: 'Jared is going to the parade'. Directly below this sentence, let's give Jared a rest and send in a substitute. We will send in the substitute word 'he'.

"Write the following sentence: 'He is going to the parade'. Do you see how these substitute words work? Because they most often refer to persons, we call them **'personal pronouns'.**"

Continuing Dictation on Your Own

L34P **Step 5** — Continue dictating the following six sentences on consecutive baselines. Look at the Sample Page in the margin for a guide.

> *"The parade had ten marching bands."*
> *"It had ten marching bands."*
> *"Sally wanted to see the clowns."*
> *"She wanted to see the clowns."*
> *"Sam, Mark, and I went to the game."*
> *"We went to the game."*

Continue by discussing the examples that follow. They do not need to be dictated at this time. Have students tell you which substitute words will work.

> *"John and Mark went to the game."*
> *"They went to the game."*
> *"The bucket of water was missing from the well."*
> *"It was missing from the well."*
> *"John went to the game."*
> *"He went to the game."*

Defining a Personal Pronoun

L34 **Step 6** — *"Starting at the bottom of the page, count up six baselines and starting comfortably close to the left margin line, write the following definition of a substitute word: 'A personal*

What Is a Personal Pronoun?		13
Singular	Plural	
I	we	
you	you	
he, she, it	they	

Jared is going to the parade.
He is going to the parade.
The parade had ten marching bands.
It had ten marching bands.
Sally wanted to see the clowns.
She wanted to see the clowns.
Sam, Mark, and I went to the game.
We went to the game.

A personal pronoun is a part of English speech that takes the place of a noun.
A singular pronoun speaks of one.
A plural pronoun speaks of more than one.

Sample Page 13
Lesson 8

pronoun is a part of English speech that takes the place of a noun'. On the next baseline write the following: 'A singular pronoun speaks of one'. On the next baseline write the following: 'A plural pronoun speaks of more than one'."

Let's Get Organized

L56 **Step 7 —** *"Turn to the Table of Contents. On the page 13 line, write the title 'What Is a Personal Pronoun?' Turn back to page 13."*

L34 *"Centered on the title line, between the two red margin lines, write the title 'What Is a Personal Pronoun?'"*

Keep Asking Review Questions

L34P Remember to periodically ask review questions. What does singular mean? What does plural mean? You will also need to explain that the pronoun 'you' can refer to one person or more than one person at a time. It can be singular or plural. That is why it is included in both columns.

Here is another review question. What is the difference between a common and a proper noun? Remember, our goal is mastery with automaticity. Students need to display a growing understanding and a demonstration of that understanding. Always inspect what you expect. Excellent handwriting and precise following of directions are steps that create a wonderful discipline necessary for learning.

Let's Make Some Application

L34 "Now I am going to give you a sentence with a blank in it. What personal pronouns that we have learned in this lesson would work in these blanks?"

L34P Place these sentences on the board or on a piece of paper.

_____ am working very hard to learn proper language skills. *(We can only use the pronoun 'I'.)*

_____ are working very hard to learn proper language skills. *(We can use 'we', 'you', or 'they'.)*

_____ is working very hard to learn proper language skills. *(We can use 'he', 'she', or 'it'.)*

L34 "All of the personal pronouns introduced so far can be fit into these blanks. We call these pronouns subject pronouns because they do the job of a subject. We will learn more about subjects in a later lesson. For now, a subject pronoun is simply the main word of the sentence or the engine that pulls that sentence down the tracks."

L34P For additional practice, look for the use of these pronouns in other textbooks or reading books used by your students.

Expectancies Learned or Reinforced in Lesson 8: Dialogue and Review

1. What does a personal pronoun do? **L34** *(It substitutes for a noun.)*

2. What are the singular personal pronouns? **L34** *(I, you, he, she, and it.)*

3. What are the plural personal pronouns? **L34** *(We, you, and they.)*

4. Why are personal pronouns such an important part of our language? **L34** *(They give nouns a rest so that sentences are efficient and are not repeating words needlessly.)*

5. What is another job in our sentence that a subject personal pronoun does? **L34** *(It pulls a sentence down the tracks.)*

6. What skills does dictation teach us? **L34** *(We learn acute auditory skills. We are challenged to listen. We are sharpening our minds.)*

Where Do I Go from Here?

- **L34** goes to **L34** "Scope and Sequence" Step 18.

- **L56** and **L78** go to "Lesson 9" on page 130.

What Materials Will I Need?

- **L56** and **L78** will need *Grammar Notebooks*, pencils, and copies of Worksheets for "Lesson 9" starting on page 133.

all	neither
another	nobody
any	none
anybody	no one
anyone	nothing
anything	one
each	other
either	others
everybody	some
everyone	somebody
everything	someone
many	something
most	somewhere
much	several

Indefinite pronouns are not specific
about what or whom they are speaking of.
Personal pronouns are quite specific
about what or whom they are speaking of.

Sample Page 14
Lesson 9

A true multisensory approach in the classroom overlays language four different ways in the mind.

Lesson 9

What Are Indefinite Pronouns?

Somebody Is at the Door

L56 "Sometimes when a friend comes to visit our home, he or she knocks on the door. We know that **someone** is there because we heard the knock, but until we actually open the door or listen to the voice of the **one** behind the door, we won't know exactly who is there. It could be **anybody.** Maybe it is a surprise birthday party and **all** your friends are there. **Each** of them may be bringing a present. **Several** presents would really be **something. Anything** would be better than **nothing. Many** presents would be **everyone's** dream.

You can't wait **another** moment. **No one** is going to stop you from letting **everybody** in. You run to the door. **Each** heartbeat brings you closer. **Much** excitement fills the room. **Somebody** is behind that door. Does **anyone** know who is there? Are there **any** clues besides the knock? **Nobody** would try to trick you, would they? **Some** people would, but not your friends. You hear another knock. **Everything** is just peachy. **Which** present shall I open first? You reach for the doorknob. You turn it. You open the door. You can't believe it.

"'Hello,' says the UPS man. 'Will you please sign for this?'"

Dictating These "Behind the Door" Words

L56P **L56** and **L78** will work in the *Grammar Notebook.*

L56 **Step 1 —** *"Turn to page 14 in your* Grammar Notebook. *Divide your page into two equal columns. Skipping one line below the title, write the following 'Behind the Door' words. We call these words 'indefinite pronouns'. Starting comfortably close to the left red margin line, write the word 'all'. Directly below the word 'all', write the word 'another'."*

L56P Continue dictating the remaining words in the list on consecutive baselines. Remember to use these words in a sentence as you dictate. Look at the Sample Page as a guide.

On the next page is a list of indefinite pronouns commonly used in our language. Feel free to add to this list if you can find other indefinite pronouns that are not listed here.

all	*everyone*	*one*
another	*everything*	*other*
any	*many*	*others*
anybody	*most*	*some*
anyone	*much*	*somebody*
anything	*neither*	*someone*
each	*nobody*	*something*
either	*no one*	*somewhere*
everybody	*nothing*	*several*

Discovering the Nature of Indefinite Pronouns

L56 **Step 2** — "Were you wondering who was behind the door in our little story about the knock on the door? I surely was. Listen to these sentences from that story. I have some questions about these sentences.

> **Many** presents would be **everybody's** dream.

> **Somebody** is behind the door.

> **Everything** is just peachy.

"In the first sentence, how **many** presents are there? It says there are **many**. I want to know exactly how **many**. Can you tell me? Look at the word **everybody**. Could you give me the names and addresses of the people who have a dream about getting many presents?

"Let's look at the second sentence. Who exactly is this **somebody** to which the sentence refers? What does he look like? In the third sentence which things are just peachy? It says **everything** is just peachy. I would like to know specifically which things those are. Do we know?

"If you were listening carefully, you should be able to tell me something about the nature of these 'Behind the Door' words. We can't figure out exactly how **many** presents there are by just using the information we are given. We would not be able to give the names and addresses of the people that the word **'everybody'** is talking about. We don't know who they are.

"And if **everything** is just peachy, we cannot know specifically which things are peachy. These 'Behind the Door' words just don't give us a clue. That is why we call them **'indefinite pronouns'**. They are just not definite about any details. It is like being in a fog sometimes. Let's write a definition for these words."

14	What Is an Indefinite Pronoun?
all	neither
another	nobody
any	none
anybody	no one
anyone	nothing
anything	one
each	other
either	others
everybody	some
everyone	somebody
everything	someone
many	something
most	somewhere
much	several

Indefinite pronouns are not specific about what or whom they are speaking of.
Personal pronouns are quite specific about what or whom they are speaking of.

Sample Page 14
Lesson 9

Where Do I Go from Here?

- **L56** and **L78** go to **"Lesson 10"** on page 137.

What Materials Will I Need?

- **L56** and **L78** will need *Grammar Notebooks* and pencils.

Defining an Indefinite Pronoun

L56 **Step 3 —** *"Counting up five baselines from the bottom of our page, starting comfortably close to the left red margin line, write the following legal definition for an indefinite pronoun: 'Indefinite pronouns are not specific about what or whom they are speaking'. You will need two lines to write this. On the next available baseline, write the following: 'Personal pronouns are quite specific about what or whom they are speaking'.*

"Remember now. With indefinite pronouns, we do not know exactly about whom we are talking, the place to which we refer, the thing mentioned, or the exact idea expressed. Indefinite pronouns are vague. They are foggy. We don't know who is behind the door. Look at this sentence. **Someone handed me the hammer.** Do we know who did this? . . . not exactly. Look at this sentence. **He was going somewhere for the weekend.** Do we know where? . . . not exactly. Look at this sentence. **Something was bothering him.** Do we know exactly what was bothering him? . . . not exactly."

Let's Get Organized

L56 **Step 4 —** *"Turn to the Table of Contents. On the page 14 line, write the title* **'What Is an Indefinite Pronoun?'** *Turn back to page 14. Centered on the title line, between the two red margin lines, write the* **same title.** Remember to capitalize the key words in every title."

Expectancies Learned or Reinforced in Lesson 9: Dialogue and Review

1. What is an indefinite pronoun? **L56** *(Indefinite pronouns are not specific about what or whom they are speaking.)*

2. What is a personal pronoun? **L56** *(Personal pronouns are quite specific about what or whom they are speaking.)*

A Lesson in Application

L56 **Step 5 —** "I am going to give you a copy of the story about the knock on the door. I want you to find all the indefinite pronouns that you can in that story. As we look through other materials that we will read, maybe you will be able to find other indefinite pronouns. If you see one, just let me know. I am going to start a wall chart, and we'll make a list of all the indefinite pronouns that we can find."

L56P The following worksheet may be copied for student use. The answers are found at the beginning of this lesson. Each indefinite pronoun is circled.

The Knock on the Door

Sometimes when a friend comes to visit our home, he or she will knock on the door. We know that (someone) is there because we heard the knock, but until we actually open the door or listen to the voice of the (one) behind the door, we won't know exactly who is there. It could be (anybody.) Maybe it is a surprise birthday party and (all) your friends are there. (Each) of them may be bringing a present. (Several) presents would really be (something.) (Anything) would be better than (nothing.) (Many) presents would be (everyone's) dream.

You can't wait (another) moment! (No one) is going to stop you from letting (everybody) in. You run to the door. (Each) heartbeat brings you closer. (Much) excitement fills the room. (Somebody) is behind that door! Does (anyone) know who is there? Are there (any) clues besides the knock? (Nobody) would try to trick you, would they? (Some) people would but not your friends. You hear another knock. (Everything) is just peachy. (Which) present shall I open first? You reach for the doorknob. You turn it. You open the door. You can't believe it!

"'Hello,' the UPS man says. 'Will you please sign for this?'"

Teacher's Answer Key for Student Worksheet 1:

Finding Indefinite Pronouns

Teacher Directions: Your students will need to find all the indefinite pronouns that they can in the following paragraphs. They will need to (circle) the words that are doing the work of an indefinite pronoun.

Student Directions: Find all the indefinite pronouns that you can in the following paragraphs. (Circle) the words that are doing the work of an indefinite pronoun.

Finding Indefinite Pronouns

*Student Directions: Find
all the indefinite pro-
nouns that you can in the
following paragraphs.
(Circle) the words that are
doing the work of an
indefinite pronoun.*

The Knock on the Door

Sometimes when a friend comes to visit our home, he or she will knock on the door. We know that someone is there because we heard the knock, but until we actually open the door or listen to the voice of the one behind the door, we won't know exactly who is there. It could be anybody. Maybe it is a surprise birthday party and all your friends are there. Each of them may be bringing a present. Several presents would really be something. Anything would be better than nothing. Many presents would be everyone's dream.

You can't wait another moment! No one is going to stop you from letting everybody in. You run to the door. Each heartbeat brings you closer. Much excitement fills the room. Somebody is behind that door! Does anyone know who is there? Are there any clues besides the knock? Nobody would try to trick you, would they? Some people would but not your friends. You hear another knock. Everything is just peachy. Which present shall I open first? You reach for the doorknob. You turn it. You open the door. You can't believe it!

"'Hello,' the UPS man says. 'Will you please sign for this?'"

1. (Everybody) brought (something) to exchange.
2. (Anyone) can do (nothing) without really trying.
3. (Many) were left, but (no one) went without.
4. (Neither) of the two boys found (one.)
5. (Each) of us needs (somebody) who cares.
6. Without planning, (anything) might go wrong for (someone.)
7. (All) attended the banquet; (nobody) was absent.
8. (Many) see the value of good choices.
9. (Most) (everyone) learns from their mistakes.
10. (Everything) went well for (some) people; (others) struggled.
11. (Much) can be said for the need for preventive maintenance.
12. (Nobody) will fail if they never give up.

Teacher's Answer Key for Student Worksheet 2:

Finding Indefinite Pronouns

Teacher Directions: Have your students (circle) all indefinite pronouns that they can find on their Worksheet.

Student Directions: (Circle) the indefinite pronouns that you find in these sentences.

Finding Indefinite Pronouns

Student Directions: (Circle) *the indefinite pronouns that you find in these sentences.*

1. Everybody brought something to exchange.

2. Anyone can do nothing without really trying.

3. Many were left, but no one went without.

4. Neither of the two boys found one.

5. Each of us needs somebody who cares.

6. Without planning, anything might go wrong for someone.

7. All attended the banquet; nobody was absent.

8. Many see the value of good choices.

9. Most everyone learns from their mistakes.

10. Everything went well for some people; others struggled.

11. Much can be said for the need for preventive maintenance.

12. Nobody will fail if they never give up.

Lesson 10
Let's Learn How to Conjugate

Using Action Verbs Properly

L34 "Do you remember action verbs? They are the source of energy for our sentences like burning coal that creates the steam necessary to get a locomotive down the tracks. They are the gasoline that provides the energy to get a car down the road. They are the muscle that makes our writing strong. We want to use action verbs that can bench press 500 pounds. If action verbs are that important and indeed they are, we need to know how to use them and use them well. Let's look at one of the ways they are used.

"Verbs are used to tell time in our writing. In this lesson we are going to learn how to tell time using verbs. We have a special word that we use when we use verbs to tell time. We use the word 'tense'. *Please say 'tense'.* In order to tell time using proper verb tense, we have to find the three most important parts of a verb. Knowing these three important parts allows us to speak correctly. Knowing these three important parts allows us to write correctly. Let's learn more about verb tense."

Dictating Some Vital Sentences to Help Us Learn Verb Tense

L34P **L34** students need to be given a sheet of loose-leaf penmanship paper. **L56** and **L78** will work in the *Grammar Notebook.*

L56 **Step 1** — *"Turn to page 15 in your* Grammar Notebook."

L34 *"Skip one baseline below the title line. On the next baseline starting comfortably close to the left margin line and starting with a capital 'T', write the sentence* **'Today I_____'.** *After the word 'I',* **pull a straight line on the baseline for about five spaces. Then place a period after this straight line.** *Later we will fill in this blank with a word.*

"On the next baseline directly below the sentence 'Today I _____', starting comfortably close to the left margin line, write the sentence **'Yesterday I _____'.** *After the word 'I',* **pull a straight line on the baseline for about five spaces. Again, place a period after this straight line.**

"On the next baseline directly below 'Yesterday I _____', write the sentence **'I have _____'. Create a blank followed by a period after the word 'have'.** These three sentence starters are a very

---

Let's Learn How to Conjugate	15

Today I _____.
Yesterday I _____.
I have _____.

Singular	Plural
Present Tense	
I go.	We go.
You go.	You go.
He, she, it goes.	They go.
Past Tense	
I went.	We went.
You went.	You went.
He, she, it went.	They went.
Present Perfect Tense	
I have gone.	We have gone.
You have gone.	You have gone.
He, she, it has gone.	They have gone.

Sample Page 15
Lesson 10

16	Conjugating (continued)

Singular	Plural
Past Perfect Tense	
I had gone.	We had gone.
You had gone.	You had gone.
He, she, it had gone.	They had gone.
Future Tense	
I will go.	We will go.
You will go.	You will go.
He, she, it will go.	They will go.
Future Perfect Tense	
I will have gone.	We will have gone.
You will have gone.	You will have gone.
He, she, it will have gone.	They will have gone.

Sample Page 16
Lesson 10

---

important tool we will use for making the correct word choices when we need to tell time using verbs."

Today I_____.

Yesterday I_____.

I have_____.

L34 **Step 2 —** *"Fold your page to make two columns. Skip one baseline under the sentence starter 'I have_____'. Centered in the first column, write the subtitle* **'Singular'**, *capitalized. On the same baseline centered in the second column, write the subtitle* **'Plural'**, *capitalized."*

L34P Refer to Sample Page 15 as a guide.

L34 **Step 3 —** *"On the next baseline below the two subtitles Singular and Plural, centered between the two red margin lines, write the subtitle* **'Present Tense'**, *capitalizing both words."*

L56 "There are 6 main tenses in the English language. Here are their names. English tenses are called **'present tense', 'past tense', 'present perfect tense', 'past perfect tense', 'future tense', and 'future perfect tense'**. In order to tell time correctly, we must find the three most important parts of any verb. That is why we introduce and record these three sentences: **'Today I _____'**, **'Yesterday I _____'**, and **'I have _____'**. Let's look at some verbs."

L34 **Step 4 —** "Let's begin with the verb 'go'. We need to ask a very important question before we can start telling time with this word. Here is the question. **What are the three most important parts of the verb 'go'?** We must know this before we go any farther. In order to find out this information, we simply need to fill in the blanks of our sentences. We should say the following: 'Today I go. Yesterday I went. I have gone'."

L34 "The first sentence gives us the first most important part of the verb 'go'. We use 'go' with the present tense. The second sentence gives us the second most important part for the verb 'go' used in the past tense. The third sentence gives us the third most important part of the verb 'go' used with the present perfect tense.

"The present tense means it is happening in the present. It is happening right now. The past tense means that the event has happened in the past. The event is over. It is history. Present perfect means the event has happened in the past, but may also be happening in the present. Look at this example. **He has gone for a walk everyday.** He has walked in the past, but he continues to walk in the present. We'll look at the nature of these tenses at a later time. We have determined the principal parts of the verb 'go'.

"The three most important parts of the verb 'go' are 'go', 'went', and 'gone'."

Let's Learn How to Conjugate 15

Today I
Yesterday I
I have

Singular	Plural
Present Tense	
I go.	We go.
You go.	You go.
He, she, it goes.	They go.
Past Tense	
I went.	We went.
You went.	You went.
He, she, it went.	They went.
Present Perfect Tense	
I have gone.	We have gone.
You have gone.	You have gone.
He, she, it has gone.	They have gone.

Sample Page 15
Lesson 10

Step 5 — *"On the next baseline comfortably close to the left margin line, write the simple sentence,* **'I go'**. *On the next baseline directly below 'I go', write* **'You go'**. *And finally on the next baseline directly below 'You go', write the words* **'He, she, it goes'** *leaving a comma after 'he' and 'she'."*

Step 6 — *"On the same baseline as the sentence 'I go', in the second column, comfortably close to the folded margin line, write the sentence* **'We go'**. *On the next baseline directly below 'We go', write the sentence* **'You go'**. *On the next baseline directly below 'You go', write* **'They go'."**

L34 **Step 7** — *"Skip one baseline and on the next baseline, centered between the two red margin lines, write the subtitle* **'Past Tense',** *capitalizing both words."*

Continuing Dictation on Your Own

L34P Dictate the rest of Sample Page 15. Have your students record the past tense "went" and the present perfect tense form "gone" for the verb "go" as found on the Sample Page. Your students will need to know that the **present perfect form is also called the "past participle". The verb form ending with an "ing" like the verb "going" is called the "present participle".** We'll save a discussion on the nature of a participle for another day.

	Singular	*Plural*
Present Tense	I go. You go. He, she, it goes.	We go. You go. They go.
Past Tense	I went. You went. He, she, it went.	We went. You went. They went.
Present Perfect Tense	I have gone. You have gone. He, she, it has gone.	We have gone. You have gone. They have gone.

L34 **Step 8** — "We have just finished **conjugating**. *Please say the word 'conjugating'.* This is the special word that we use when we take one tense at a time using these important parts and add the pronouns 'I, you, he, she, it, we, you, and they' in the proper order. **Conjugating helps us determine the right way to use a verb.** We need to know how to conjugate."

L34P Conjugating seems to be a lost art among students today. Most will look at a teacher with a questioning glance if they are asked to conjugate a verb in the present tense or the past tense or the present perfect tense. Too many students don't understand how verb tenses work. In this lesson we will introduce the art of conjugating using all six of the main tenses that exist in English.

Let's Get Organized

L56 **Step 9 —** *"Turn to the Table of Contents. On the page 15 line, write the title* **'Let's Learn How to Conjugate'.** *Turn back to page 15."*

L34 *"Centered on the title line, between the two red margin lines, write the title* **'Let's Learn How to Conjugate'."**

Discovering the Principal Parts of Verbs

L34 **Step 10 —** "There are many verbs in our language. We need to know the most important parts of all of these verbs. We need to know how to conjugate these same verbs once we have found their principal parts. Let's do some practicing. What are the three most important parts of the verb 'break'?"

L34P This can be the beginning of a practice time. You will find an extensive list of irregular verbs included in this lesson. Our students need to know all of these verbs and their important parts. Take one verb at a time. Take three, four, or five verbs a day. Ask the question, "What are the three most important parts of this verb?"

Give the first part and then use those three sentences. "Today I break. Yesterday I broke. I have broken." Once the three parts have been determined, we need to conjugate that verb in the present, past, and present perfect tenses using those personal pronouns in the proper order.

Also teach your students that there is a difference between regular and irregular verbs. When regular verbs change tense, they are spelled the same but add the past tense ending "ed". For the regular verb "walk", the three most important parts of this verb are "walk, walked, have walked". In almost all cases when irregular verbs change tense, the spelling of the root word is changed.

How to Practice Conjugating with Your Student

L34P From this point on, there will be periodic conversations between the teacher and some very brilliant students who give all the right answers. These can be used as a guide for conversations between you and your students. The students' responses are what you would like your students to eventually say. You may need to take on the role of the students the first time through and then repeat the series of questions another day or another time in hopes that your students can answer the questions and do the exercises with proficiency. Let's give a listen at how an instructional conversation might sound.

L34   **TEACHER:**   "Students, we are going to practice conjugating. Let's start by using the verb 'begin'. What are the three most important parts of the verb 'begin'?"

   STUDENTS: "Today I begin. Yesterday I began. I have begun."

   TEACHER: "Good job. We need to know these most important parts of a verb in order to conjugate. Let's conjugate the verb 'begin' in the present tense. How do we start?"

   STUDENTS: "The conjugation for 'begin' in the present tense is the following: (Notice the use of a complete sentence as an answer to the teacher's question. It is good to have our students answer our questions in complete sentences. We want them to learn to write and think in complete sentences.)

I begin.	We begin.
You begin.	You begin.
He, she, it begins.	They begin."

   TEACHER   "That was excellent. Just for the fun of it, let's add the words Cha! Cha! Cha! after we are done with every tense. We want to make these verbs dance. Let's look at the past tense of 'begin'? Here we need to use the second most important part of the verb. Yesterday I 'began'."

   STUDENTS: "A conjugation of the past tense of 'begin' is the following:

I began.	We began.
You began.	You began.
He, she, it began.	They began.
Cha! Cha! Cha!"	

   TEACHER   "Well done. You are extremely sharp students. You listen so well. Let's try the present perfect tense. Can anyone tell me what time this tense is telling? It's not today. That is present tense. It is not yesterday. That is past pense. When does the present perfect tense happen?"

   STUDENTS: "The present perfect tense happens sometime in the past. It could be two minutes ago, two days ago, or two weeks ago."

Note to Teacher:

As students conjugate, some may observe that third person singular verb forms are different from first and second person singular and all plural forms in some tenses. In other words, they may bring up the issue of noun/pronoun–verb agreement. At this point it is best not to go into all the complexities of subject–predicate agreement, but just to say that when nouns/pronouns and verbs work together, they sometimes take different forms. Why they do that and under what circumstances will be covered later. For now it is enough to learn how to conjugate.

TEACHER "Good answer. Can you conjugate it? Remember that the present perfect tense, the past perfect tense, and the future perfect tense all use the third most important part of the verb 'begin' which is 'begun'."

STUDENTS: "The conjugation of the present perfect tense for the verb 'begin' is the following:

I have begun.	We have begun.
You have begun.	You have begun.
He, she, it has begun.	They have begun.
Cha! Cha! Cha!"	

"I like that Cha! Cha! Cha! part!"

Adding the Last Three Tenses

L56 **TEACHER:** "I think you have it. Now let's add the other three tenses. The other three main tenses use helping verbs to accomplish their job of telling us what time it is when we write. The past perfect tense uses the helping verb 'had'. The future tense uses the helping verbs 'will' or 'shall'. The future perfect tense uses the helping verbs 'will have' or 'shall have'. Can you conjugate in those remaining tenses?"

STUDENTS: "Let us try. The past perfect tense, future tense, and the future perfect tense are the following:

I had begun.	We had begun.
You had begun.	You had begun.
He, she, it had begun.	They had begun.
Cha! Cha! Cha!	

I will begin.	We will begin.
You will begin.	You will begin.
He, she, it will begin.	They will begin.
Cha! Cha! Cha!	

I will have begun.	We will have begun.
You will have begun.	You will have begun.
He, she, it will have begun	They will have begun.
Cha! Cha! Cha!"	

TEACHER "I think you have it. Especially the 'Cha! Cha! Cha!' part! Verbs need to dance. Let's try to find the three most important parts of some of the other verbs we have in our language."

L34P Do daily practice with the verb list provided, until they become familiar with these verb forms. Have fun conjugating. See if your students can accurately conjugate in the first three tenses in under a minute . . . how about accurately in under thirty seconds? Make it a daily routine to practice conjugating three verbs from the verb list each language arts session until they know them.

Dictating Past Perfect, Future, and Future Perfect Tenses

L56 **Step 1** — *"Turn to page 16 in your* Grammar Notebook. *Make two columns by folding a margin line down the middle of your page. Skip one baseline under your title line and in the first column, centered between the left red margin line and the folded margin line, write the subtitle* **'Singular'**, *capitalized. On the same line in the second column, center the subtitle* **'Plural'**, *capitalized. On the next available baseline below 'Singular' and 'Plural', centered between the two red margin lines, write the subtitle* **'Past Perfect Tense'**, *capitalized. Skipping one baseline below the subtitle 'Past Perfect Tense', comfortably close to the left red margin line, write* **'I had gone'**. *On the next baseline below, write* **'You had gone'**. *Below this write* **'He, she, it had gone'."** (Refer to the Sample Page in your margin as a guide.)

L56 **Step 2** — *"On the same line as 'I had gone', in the second column, starting comfortably close to the folded margin line, write* **'We had gone'**. *On the next baseline below, write* **'You had gone'**. *Below this write* **'They had gone'."**

L56P Continue to dictate the rest of Sample Page 16 in the same manner as above.

Let's Get Organized

L56 **Step 3** — *"Turn to the Table of Contents. On the page 16 line, write the title* **'Conjugating (continued)'**. *Turn back to page 16. Centered on the title line, between the two red margin lines, write the* **same title."**

Understanding the Nature of Each of the Six Tenses

L78P The following information is a broader look at the nature of each of the six tenses. You will need to present this material using the examples and the explanations that follow. If you feel that **L56** students can handle this material, by all means introduce it.

L56 "The names given to each tense, that is, past tense, present perfect tense, future perfect tense and so on, are common, traditional, grammatical terms used when talking about the proper form of a verb.

"Each of these six tenses has its own function."

16	Conjugating (continued)	
Singular		Plural
	Past Perfect Tense	
I had gone.		We had gone.
You had gone.		You had gone.
He, she, it had gone.		They had gone.
	Future Tense	
I will go.		We will go.
You will go.		You will go.
He, she, it will go.		They will go.
	Future Perfect Tense	
I will have gone.		We will have gone.
You will have gone.		You will have gone.
He, she, it will have gone.		They will have gone.

Sample Page 16
Lesson 10

The Present Tense

"One function of the **present tense** is used to show action that is happening in the immediate now. Look at this example:

'John drives a car.'

"John's driving is not going to happen in the future. It certainly is not history. John drives that car right now.

"Present Tense can also be written to imply that a process is continuing to happen. This process is still progressing. Look at this example:

'John is driving a car.'

"John's driving is in progress. He is behind that wheel and he is motoring down the road at this very moment. We call this the **'present progressive tense'.**

"Present tense can also imply that some action is habitual. It keeps on happening periodically. Look at this example:

'He practices his speech every day.'

"We don't want to say that he practiced his speech every day and make it something that is over. We want our sentence to mean that this practice has become a habit and it is continuing.

"We also use present tense to communicate a universal truth:

'The earth revolves around the sun.'

"We don't want to say the earth revolved around the sun. That implies that it is over and the earth revolving around the sun is something that is a part of history. We like it when the sun comes up in the morning.

"The 'ing' form of the verb is also called the **'present participle'.** The present participle form is only used as an adjective."

The Past Tense

"The **past tense** is used to show action that happened in the past, but the action is over. The curtains are closed. The final buzzer is a memory. It's a done deal. There is no sense at all that the action is continuing. The past tense ending 'ed' is often used here. Irregular verbs, of course, change their spelling when we move to past tense. Look at these examples:

'The driver stopped the car.'

'We went to the game at the Fargo Dome.'

"Both of these events are in the history books. We can also use the **past progressive tense.** This is a progressing process that happened in the past but is over:

'The driver was stopping the car.'

'We were going to the game.'

"In both cases an ongoing process took place, but it took place in the past."

The Present Perfect Tense

"The **present perfect tense** is used to show action that happened in the past, but we are not exactly sure when it happened or if it happened every time. There is a sense that we cannot really pin point the exact time. The helping verbs 'have' or 'has' are used. This form of the verb is also called the 'past participle':

'They have watched the sunset when on their camping trips.'

"The present perfect tense is also used to show action that has happened in the past and it is still happening in the present. Look at this example:

'He has walked three miles every day for the past month.'

"This sentence shows action that has happened and it is still happening.

"Of course, this tense would not be complete unless we threw in the **present perfect progressive:**

'He has been practicing piano all week.'

"It is happening in the past and there is a continuing of this process through the week."

The Past Perfect Tense

"The **past perfect tense** is used to show action that has happened in the past, but it has happened before some other action or circumstance. It uses the helping verb 'had':

'The player had played well before spraining his ankle.'

"The playing took place before the sprained ankle. We need past perfect tense to be able to capture that sense.

"There is also the **past perfect progressive**. An event was in process in the past before another event affecting that process took place:

'The player had been playing well before spraining his ankle.'

"All these nuances of verb tense are just a part our language. We need to get to know them."

Present Perfect Tense is used to show action that happened in the past, but we are not exactly sure when it happened or if it happened every time.

Past Perfect Tense is used to show action that has happened in the past, but it has happened before some other action or circumstance.

Future Tense is used to show action that will happen at some time beyond the present.

Future Perfect Tense is used to show action that will be finished before some other future action or circumstance.

Do my students know how to use the following:

Today I _____.

Yesterday I_____.

and

I have _____. ?

The Future Tense

"The **future tense** is used to show action that will happen at some time beyond the present. The helping verbs 'will' or 'shall' are used:

'I will study for my test.'

"The future tense is our time machine. We get in and we head for universes unknown. We head for galaxies not traveled. We head for a tomorrow that hasn't been experienced. What would science fiction be without the future? All the Trekkies would disappear into oblivion at warp speed.

"There is also the **future progressive tense**:

'I will be studying for my test in Biology.'

"This becomes a process that is going to happen in the future."

The Future Perfect Tense

"The **future perfect tense** is used to show action that will be finished before some other future action or circumstance. We use the helping verbs 'will' or 'shall' and 'have' or 'had' in combination:

'I will have used all my money before I get home.'

"The first event finished is the running out of money.

"The next event is the getting home. One is finished before the other happens.

"A discussion on the properties and qualities of verbs can go on into infinity. We won't travel through all of infinity at this time. We will save some of infinity for another day."

The Three Principle Parts of Some Common Regular Verbs

L34P We will only use ten examples of common regular verbs here. We are providing these to point out that the three most important parts of these verbs simply add the ending "ed" in the past and the present perfect tense. The root word or base word does not change spelling as we move from one tense to the other.

Present	Past	Present Perfec
love	loved	have loved
count	counted	have counted
walk	walked	have walked
call	called	have called
use	used	have used
laugh	laughed	have laughed
jump	jumped	have jumped
help	helped	have helped
declare	declared	have declared
slip	slipped	have slipped

The Three Principal Parts of Common Irregular Verbs

Present Tense	Past Tense	Present Perfect
abide	abode, abided	have abode, abided
arise	arose	have arisen
awake	awoke, awaked	have awoke, awaked
bear (to bring forth)	bore	have born
bear (to carry)	bore	have borne
beat	beat	have beaten, beat
become	became	have become
befall	befell	have befallen
beget	begat, begot	have begotten, begot
begin	began	have begun
behold	beheld	have beheld
bend	bent	have bent
bereave	bereft, bereaved	have bereft, bereaved
beseech	besought	have besought
bet	bet	have bet
bid	bid	have bid, bidden
bind	bound	have bound
bite	bit	have bitten, bit
bleed	bled	have bled
bless	blest, blessed	have blest, blessed
blow	blew	have blown
break	broke	have broken
breed	bred	have bred
bring	brought	have brought
build	built	have built
burst	burst	have burst
buy	bought	have bought
cast	cast	have cast
catch	caught	have caught
choose	chose	have chosen
cleave (to adhere to something)	cleaved	have cleaved
cleave (to cut or split something)	cleft, clove	have cleft, cloven, cleaved
cling	clung	have clung
clothe	clad, clothed	have clad, clothed
come	came	have come
cost	cost	have cost
creep	crept	have crept
crow	crowed	have crowed
cut	cut	have cut
deal	dealt	have dealt
dig	dug, digged	have dug, digged
dive	dove, dived	have dived
do	did	have done
draw	drew	have drawn
dream	dreamt, dreamed	have dreamt, dreamed
drink	drank	have drunk
drive	drove	have driven

Present Tense	Past Tense	Present Perfect
dwell	dwelt, dwelled	have dwelt
eat	ate	have eaten
fall	fell	have fallen
feed	fed	have fed
feel	felt	have felt
fight	fought	have fought
find	found	have found
flee	fled	have fled
fling	flung	have flung
fly	flew	have flown
forbear	forbore	have forborne
forget	forgot	have forgotten
forsake	forsook	have forsaken
freeze	froze	have frozen
get	got	have got, gotten
give	gave	have given
go	went	have gone
grind	ground	have ground
grow	grew	have grown
hang (to place something)	hung	have hung
hang (to execute)	hanged	have hanged
have	had	have had
hear	heard	have heard
hew	hewed	have hewn, hewed
hide	hid	have hidden, hid
hit	hit	have hit
hold	held	have held
hurt	hurt	have hurt
keep	kept	have kept
kneel	knelt, kneeled	have knelt
knit	knit, knitted	have knit, knitted
know	knew	have known
lay (to put or place)	laid	have laid
lead	led	have led
leave	left	have left
lend	lent	have lent
let	let	have let
lie (to rest or recline)	lay	have lain
lose	lost	have lost
make	made	have made
mean	meant	have meant
meet	met	have met
pay	paid	have paid
put	put	have put
read	read	have read
rend	rent	have rent
rid	rid	have rid
ride	rode	have ridden, rode
ring	rang	have rung

Present Tense	Past Tense	Present Perfect
rise	rose	have risen
run	ran	have run
saw	sawed	have sawn, sawed
say	said	have said
see	saw	have seen
seek	sought	have sought
send	sent	have sent
set	set	have set
shake	shook	have shaken
shed	shed	have shed
shine	shone, shined	have shone, shined
shoe	shod	have shod
shoot	shot	have shot
show	showed	have shown
shred	shred, shredded	have shred
shrink	shrunk, shrank	have shrunk, shrunken
shut	shut	have shut
sing	sang	have sung
sink	sank, sunk	have sunk
sit	sat	have sat
slay	slew	have slain
sleep	slept	have slept
sling	slung	have slung
slink	slunk	have slunk
slit	slit	have slit
smite	smote	have smitten, smote
sow	sowed	have sown, sowed
speak	spoke	have spoken
speed	sped	have sped, speeded
spend	spent	have spent
spin	spun	have spun
split	split	have split
spread	spread	have spread
spring	sprang, sprung	have sprung
stand	stood	have stood
steal	stole	have stolen
stick	stuck	have stuck
sting	stung	have stung
stride	strode	have stridden
strike	struck	have struck, stricken
string	strung	have strung
strive	strove	have striven, strived
sweep	swept	have swept
swell	swelled	have swollen, swelled
swear	swore	have sworn
swim	swam	have swum
swing	swung	have swung
take	took	have taken
teach	taught	have taught

Present Tense	Past Tense	Present Perfect
tear	tore	have torn
tell	told	have told
think	thought	have thought
throw	threw	have thrown
thrust	thrust	have thrust
tread	trod	have trodden, trod
wake	woke, waked	have woke, waked
wear	wore	have worn
weave	wove, weaved	have woven, weaved
weep	wept	have wept
win	won	have won
wind	wound	have wound
wring	wrung	have wrung
write	wrote	have written

Learning to conjugate teaches proper verb usage.

Where Do I Go from Here?

- **L34**, **L56**, and **L78** go to **"Lesson 11"** on page 151.

What Materials Will I Need?

- **L34** will need penmanship paper, pencils, red pencils, and copies of Worksheets for **"Lesson 11"** starting on page 156.

- **L56** and **L78** will need *Grammar Notebooks*, pencils, red pencils, and copies of Worksheets for **"Lesson 11"** starting on page 156.

Expectancies Learned or Reinforced in Lesson 10: Dialogue and Review

1. What purpose does the use of verb tense serve in our language? **L34** *(We need verb tense to tell time.)*

2. What are the names of the basic tenses for writing in English? **L34** *(present, past, present perfect)* **L56** *(future, future perfect, and past perfect tenses)*

3. What are the three starter sentences that help us find the three most important parts of a verb? **L34** *(Today I _____. Yesterday I _____. I have _____.)*

4. What pronouns do we use to conjugate? **L34** *(I, you, he, she, it in the singular. We, you, and they in the plural.)*

5. What are we learning when we practice conjugating? **L34** *(We are learning how to use verbs properly for the purpose of creating better writers and better speakers.)*

Lesson 11

What Is a Helping Verb?

To Be	To Have
am	have
is	has
are	had
was	
were	Others
be, being, been	can
	could
	may, might
To Do	will, shall
do	would
does	must
did	should

I could have been singing in the choir.

A helping verb is a verb that helps the main verb. The helping verb or verbs and the main verb together make a verb phrase.

Sample Page 17
Lesson 11

Everybody Needs a Helper

L34 "We have learned that action verbs give us the energy we need for our writing just like strong legs provide energy to ride a bicycle. Sometimes, in order to get a job done, we need helpers to get all that energy to the right place in the right way. Electricity needs the wire in order to turn on a light. Strong legs need feet with tennis shoes in order to pedal. Action verbs sometimes need this kind of help too. They get the help they need from words that are called helping verbs."

Dictating Helping Verbs

L34P **L34** students need to be given a sheet of loose-leaf penmanship paper. **L56** and **L78** will work in the *Grammar Notebook.*

L56 **Step 1** — *"Turn to page 17 in your* Grammar Notebook.*"*

L34 "We are going to make a list of common helping verbs. *Fold a margin line down the middle of the page. Skipping one baseline below the title line, starting in the first column comfortably close to the left margin line and starting each word with a capital letter, write the subtitle 'To Be'. On the next baseline directly beneath this subheading, comfortably close to the left margin line write the word 'am'. On the next baseline directly beneath 'am', write 'is'."*

L34P Look at the Sample Page 17 provided in your margin. Dictate the remaining helping verbs listed in column one in the same manner as Step 1. Include the second subtitle **"To Do"** as indicated.

L34 **Step 2** — *"Go to the second column. On the same baseline as the subtitle 'To Be', comfortably close to the folded margin line, write 'To Have'. On the next baseline directly beneath 'To Have', write the word 'have'."*

L34P Dictate the remaining helping verbs in column two of Sample Page 17 in the same manner. Include the second subtitle **"Others"** as indicated.

Discovering the Nature of Helping Verbs

L34P Have the students identify these helping verbs and the main action verbs in the sentences below. For practice, have your students identify helpers as they do their work in other subject areas. Another common name for helping verbs uses the word "auxiliary". Auxiliary verbs are helping verbs.

A helping verb is a verb that helps the main verb. The helping verb(s) and the main verb together make a verb phrase.

What Is a Helping Verb? 17

To Be	To Have
am	have
is	has
are	had
was	
were	Others
be, being, been	can
	could
	may, might
To Do	will, shall
do	would
does	must
did	should

I could have been singing in the choir.

A helping verb is a verb that helps the main verb. The helping verb or verbs and the main verb together make a verb phrase.

Sample Page 17
Lesson 11

L56P There will be room to write only one of the following sentences in the students' *Notebook* on page 17. Choose one, and then dictate it to your students. Have your students mark the sentence using the syntactical analysis described below.

> *"I could have been singing in the choir."*
>
> *"I was walking in the park."*
>
> *"He is being shifted to a later time."*
>
> *"We will have seen the eagle three times."*

L34P For more practice, give your students a copy of the worksheet provided at the end of this lesson. Can they identify the helping verbs? Can they identify the main action verbs?

A Beginning Understanding of Syntactical Analysis

L56P Romalda Spalding in *Writing Road to Reading* developed a marking system for the **orthographic analysis** of individual words. Orthographic analysis helps students discover reasons for why and how phonograms work together properly to make words. There are reasons for why words are spelled the way they are. *Grammar Works* uses a very simple marking system for **syntactical analysis.** This process helps students discover reasons for why and how words work together properly to make sentences. There are reasons for why sentences are written the way they are. When we do syntactical analysis, we will mark and label words. Those marks and labels should be done with red pencil.

When you find a verb that you know is doing the job of an action verb, have your students place the letters **"AV"** over that word in red pencil. If you determine the word to be doing the job of a helping verb, have your students place the letters **"HV"** over that word in red pencil. Note the sample sentence on Sample Page 17. There will be more practice with markings as lessons continue to progress. Having once again found helping verbs and action verbs with your student on the student worksheet provided for this lesson, instead of simply underlining them, label them with an **"HV"** or an **"AV"**.

Defining a Helping Verb

L34 **Step 3** — "We are going to write the definition of the helpers we call '**helping verbs**'. We have already listed many of them. *Count up four baselines from the bottom on your page and starting comfortably close to the left margin line, write the following: 'A helping verb is a verb that helps the main verb. The helping verb or verbs and the main verb together make a verb phrase'.*"

Let's Get Organized

L56 **Step 4** — *"Turn to the Table of Contents. On the page 17 line, write the title 'What Is a Helping Verb?' Turn back to page 17."*

L34 *"Centered on the title line, between the two red margin lines, write the title 'What Is a Helping Verb?'"*

When Is a Helping Verb Really an Action Verb?

L56P When a helping verb is used together with an action verb or a linking verb in a verb phrase, that helping verb is truly a helping verb. When a helping verb is the only verb in the sentence, and thus is not used together with any other verb in a verb phrase, we have to call it an action verb. If the helping verbs listed under "To Be" are used alone, they are linking verbs. Look at these examples.

L56 **Step 4** — "Helping verbs can be very sneaky. Just when you think they are helping verbs, they turn around and surprise you and become action verbs. They are very versatile. We need to look at some sentences to show you how this works."

L56P Write these sentences on the board or on a piece of penmanship paper one at a time. Study the teacher–student dialogue that follows and hold a discussion on why the verbs in these sentences are what they are.

> HV + AV
> I have found a good idea.
>
> AV
> I have a good idea.
>
> HV+AV
> I do sing in the choir.
>
> AV
> I do the job carefully.
>
> HV + AV
> I am running the mile.
>
> LV
> I am a student.

Using Student–Teacher Dialogue to Understand Helping Verbs

L56 **TEACHER:** "Look at this first example: 'I have found a good idea'. Are there any words we can conjugate in this sentence?"

> *Helping verbs can be very sneaky. Just when you think they are helping verbs, they turn around and surprise you and become action verbs. They are very versatile.*

STUDENTS: "We can conjugate the word 'have' and the word 'found'. Both have the three very important parts that we need to conjugate. Today I have. Yesterday I had. have had. Today I find. Yesterday I found. I have found. We know that if we can conjugate a word and it makes sense to do so, it is a verb."

TEACHER: "Can you find the word 'find' in our list of helping verbs? It is not there is it? That tells us the word 'find' is not a helping verb. Can you tell what it is?"

STUDENTS: "It fits our definition of an action verb. To 'find' something provides energy to our sentence. We are in motion. It has to be an action verb."

TEACHER: "Great. What does that make the word 'have' then if it is in partnership with an action verb?"

STUDENTS: "It by definition has to be a helping verb, and it can be because it is in my helping verb list."

TEACHER: "Look at this sentence: 'I have a good idea'. What is the only word we can conjugate in this sentence?"

STUDENTS: "The only word we can conjugate is the word 'have' because we can find the three important parts of that verb."

TEACHER: "Is it paired with another verb?"

STUDENTS: "I do not see any other word that we can conjugate. The word 'have' is acting alone."

TEACHER: "If a helping verb is acting alone, it is not a helping verb any more. It is either an action verb if it fits that definition or it is a linking verb if it is in our linking verb list. Can you remember that?"

STUDENTS: "I shall try. How do we mark these helping verbs that really aren't helping verbs anymore and act alone?"

TEACHER: "If it is a linking verb, we use 'LV'. If it is an action verb, we use 'AV'. When we can determine the jobs that words do, they become well-practiced tools that will make our language skills stronger."

L56P The other pairs of sentences will use the same line of reasoning to determine whether the verbs are helping or action or linking verbs. Continue your discussion of the remaining sentences.

Additional Activities for Reinforcing Helping Verbs and Action Verbs

1. For review with verbs, have your students take the three principal parts of any verb and conjugate that verb in the six main tenses they learned in **"Lesson 10."**

2. Throw in a helping verb in some of these conjugations. Instead of just starting with "I run", say "I might run. You might run. He, she, it might run." Use any of the helping verbs that will work for this.

3. Have your students go to any textbook and locate helping verbs that are used there.

Expectancies Learned or Reinforced in Lesson 11: Dialogue and Review

1. What is the job of a helping verb? **L34** *(A helping verb is a verb or verbs that help the main verb.)*

2. What is a verb phrase? **L34** *(The helping verbs and the main verbs together make a verb phrase.)*

3. How do I tell the difference between a helping verb and an action verb or a helping verb and a linking verb? **L56** *(If a helping verb is acting alone, it is either an action verb or a linking verb. If it is an action verb, it shows action. If it is a linking verb, it is also listed on my linking verb list.)*

4. Why are these helping verbs so important? **L78** *(In our last lesson on action verbs, we learned about the nature of each of the six tenses. In order to tell time accurately with verbs, we need to use these helping verbs.)*

5. What do we use to mark helping verbs and action verbs when we do syntactical analysis? **L56** *(We use "HV" for a helping verb. We use "AV" for an action verb.)*

Where Do I Go from Here?

- **L34**, **L56**, and **L78** go to **"Lesson 12"** on page 158.

What Materials Will I Need?

- **L34** will need penmanship paper, pencils, red pencils, and copies of Worksheets for **"Lesson 12"** starting on page 162.

- **L56** and **L78** will need *Grammar Notebooks*, pencils, red pencils, and copies of Worksheets for **"Lesson 12"** starting on page 162.

What Is a Helping Verb?

Teacher Directions: The following Student Worksheet is designed to offer practice in identifying helping verbs in a sentence.

*Explain to your student the appropriate directions for marking helping verbs depending upon their level of instruction and have them complete the worksheet. **L34** will simply underline these helping verbs. **L56** and above will use the label "HV".*

Student Directions: Find all the helping verbs in the following sentences.

Label them according to your teacher's instructions.

1. I am going to the school. *(HV: am)*
2. You will be running in the race. *(HV: will, be)*
3. They were singing a song. *(HV: were)*
4. I have been doing the work myself. *(HV: have, been)*
5. I did play the piano for the concert. *(HV: did)*
6. He has jumped rope for years. *(HV: has)*
7. We could have watched the game. *(HV: could, have)*
8. It might have been accepted earlier. *(HV: might, have, been)*
9. She will have bought the dress before tomorrow. *(HV: will, have)*
10. You must ride to the store. *(HV: must)*
11. They would have drawn the picture if they had known the need. *(HV: would, have, had)*
12. John might lie down for a few minutes. *(HV: might)*
13. The janitor is being driven to the hospital. *(HV: is, being)*
14. The basketball player does bring certain skills to the game. *(HV: does)*
15. A car tire could be made to last forever. *(HV: could, be)*
16. The principal should have known the proper procedure. *(HV: should, have)*
17. I do eat on occasion. *(HV: do)*
18. He may be giving all he can give. *(HV: may, be, can)*
19. They are keeping an eye on him. *(HV: are)*
20. We shall overcome some day. *(HV: shall)*

1. I am going to the school.

2. You will be running in the race.

3. They were singing a song.

4. I have been doing the work myself.

5. I did play the piano for the concert.

6. He has jumped rope for years.

7. We could have watched the game.

8. It might have been accepted earlier.

9. She will have bought the dress before tomorrow.

10. You must ride to the store.

11. They would have drawn the picture if they had known the need.

12. John might lie down for a few minutes.

13. The janitor is being driven to the hospital.

14. The basketball player does bring certain skills to the game.

15. A car tire could be made to last forever.

16. The principal should have known the proper procedure.

17. I do eat on occasion.

18. He may be giving all he can give.

19. They are keeping an eye on him.

20. We shall overcome some day.

What Is a Helping Verb?

Student Directions: Find all the helping verbs in the following sentences.

Label them according to your teacher's instructions.

18	What Is a Linking Verb?

am	tastes
is	looks
are	grows
was	smell
were	sound
becomes	stay
appears	remain
seems	and any form of the
feels	verb "to be"
	(be, being, been)

The child is a boy.
A boy becomes a man.
The apple tastes sour.

A linking verb is a joining word. A linking
verb joins words that describe the subject
or mean the same thing as the subject.

Sample Page 18
Lesson 12

Lesson 12

What Is a Linking Verb?

Linking One Word to Another

L34 "When we are driving down the road, we often see a truck or a car pulling a trailer. We know that car and trailer are linked together somehow. When a farmer needs to haul his hay from the field to the barn, a hay wagon is linked together with the tractor that is pulling it. Before a space shuttle finds its orbit, that space shuttle must somehow be attached to its rocket booster. Hooking one object to another might require a hitch or a pin or a bolt or two. We have words in our language that do the same kind of work. They hitch words together. They link words together. The words they link together are related to each other like a car and a trailer or a tractor and a hay wagon or a space shuttle and its rocket booster. Let's find out about these words that hook one word to another. We call these words linking verbs."

Dictating the Linking Verb List

L34P L34 students need to be given a sheet of loose-leaf penmanship paper. **L56** and **L78** will work in the *Grammar Notebook*.

L56 **Step 1 —** *"Turn to page 18 in your* Grammar Notebook*."*

L34 *"Fold a margin line down the middle of the page. Skipping one baseline beneath the title line, comfortably close to the left margin line, write the word* **'am'***. On the next baseline directly beneath the word 'am', write the word* **'is'***."*

L34P Look at the Sample Page 18 provided. Dictate the remaining linking verbs found there in the same manner as the Sample Page.

Discovering the Nature of a Linking Verb

L34 **Step 2 —** "Let's create some sentences that show a linking verb joining words. *Skipping one baseline under the word 'feels', beginning comfortably close to the left margin line, write the following sentence:* **'The child is a boy'***."*

L34P Dictate the remaining sentences provided, in the same manner as listed on the Sample Page. Hold a discussion like the one that follows to help students understand the nature of a linking verb.

"A boy becomes a man."
"The apple tastes sour."

Using Student–Teacher Dialogue to Understand Linking Verbs

TEACHER: **Step 3 —** "We know that there are words in our language that link one word to another. They join two words together. In the first sentence, 'The child is a boy', what two words are joined together?"

STUDENTS: "The words 'child' and 'boy'."

TEACHER: "You are right. The words joined together are 'child' and 'boy'. We need to ask how those two words are related. Can you see that as nouns they refer to the same person? The 'boy' is **renaming** the 'child'. In a sense the nouns are **equal to one another** in meaning. They refer to exactly the same person. We can name this person using the noun 'child' or using the noun 'boy'. Because they are **equal,** we are looking at the same person regardless of which word we use. Look at the second sentence. 'A boy becomes a man.' What two words are being joined together?"

STUDENTS: "The words 'boy' and 'man'."

TEACHER: "Again you are right. The words 'boy' and 'man' are joined together by the verb 'becomes'. The word 'boy' is being **renamed** by the word 'man'. They are **equal to each other in meaning**. They are naming the same person. Let's look at the third sentence. 'The apple tastes sour.' What do you see?"

STUDENTS: "The word 'apple' and 'sour' are joined together."

TEACHER: "But what is happening this time?"

STUDENTS: "The words 'apple' and 'sour' are not the same thing. They are not renaming an object or a person. They are not equal. The 'apple' is not a 'sour'. In fact, 'sour' isn't even a naming word, is it? What job is the word 'sour' doing?"

TEACHER: "The word 'sour' is telling us about a quality of the apple. It is describing that apple. What do we know about the apple?"

STUDENTS: "The apple has the quality of being sour."

TEACHER: "The verb 'tastes' is on our list that we placed in this lesson. What have we learned about these verbs?"

STUDENTS: "We have learned that these verbs join words that describe or mean the same thing as another word."

L34P Other examples of sentences using these kinds of verbs are provided in the student worksheet that follows this lesson. Help

*Learning how our
language works is
not an easy task.
We need to stay on
target and lead our
students to mastery
through directed
discovery.*

Press on.

Be diligent.

*Great rewards
come to those who
persevere.*

them to discover these verbs and the words that they join. Challenge your students to come up with some of their own examples when you are reviewing this material on another day. There is room to record these examples on their page.

Marking Linking Verbs When We Analyze a Sentence

L56 "When we discover a linking verb in a sentence, we mark that word by placing an 'LV' over the word. That mark stands for linking verb. We call this process of marking words correctly, syntactical analysis. It is a process that helps us think about what jobs words are doing. Let's do Worksheet 1 and mark our linking verbs with an 'LV'. We will use a red pencil to mark our words."

L56P Provide the Worksheet for this lesson. Instead of underlining the verbs this time, have your students label them correctly with an "LV".

You may want to make a chart with a list of these linking verbs displayed. Your students need to know this list very well. Once they know this list, virtually all other verbs may be categorized as action verbs. Because effective writing primarily concerns itself with using action verbs, it will be important for the student to know the difference.

My students can say this list quickly and almost instinctively. When we further develop syntactical analysis, this tool will be important for analyzing sentences. More on this later. For now review this list daily and see how many can say it in one breath without looking at the chart. You will have fun with this list. Students I had years ago can walk up to me today and recite the linking verb list.

Defining a Linking Verb

L34 **Step 4** — *"On the same page, count up five baselines from the bottom and write the definition of a linking verb: 'A linking verb is a joining word. A linking verb joins words that describe the subject or mean the same thing as the subject'."*

Let's Get Organized

L56 **Step 5** — *"Turn to the Table of Contents. On the page 18 line, write the title 'What Is a Linking Verb?' Turn back to page 18."*

L34 *"Centered on the title line, between the two red margin lines, write the title 'What Is a Linking Verb?'"*

18	What Is a Linking Verb?
am	tastes
is	looks
are	grows
was	smell
were	sound
becomes	stay
appears	remain
seems	and any form of the
feels	verb "to be"
	(be, being, been)

The child is a boy.
A boy becomes a man.
The apple tastes sour.

A linking verb is a joining word. A linking verb joins words that describe the subject or mean the same thing as the subject.

Sample Page 18
Lesson 12

Discipline and Practice Are the Foundation Stones of Accomplished Writers

We want students to learn to write effectively. To be able to write effectively, they need to understand that the act of writing is a craft. It is something that can be learned one small piece at a time even as an artist learns how to paint.

As with all goals worth pursuing, skills achieved do not come cheaply. Painstaking practice is necessary. Without practice that requires paying the price, the language skills of our students will fall in a heap on the streets of communication like so much jello. We don't want jello; we want strong minds that come from a fitness program that requires discipline. As an instructor, be mindful that your students need to display mastery at the simplest and most basic levels. **Fundamentals are at the foundation of great men and women.** This text is a step in providing that fitness program.

Additional Activities for Reinforcing Linking Verbs

L34P Be on the look out for linking verbs your students might encounter in other texts. Make a chart collecting those sentences that are found which really use a linking verb. Make sure your students know the list of linking verbs. They should be able to recite this memorized list quickly and efficiently.

Expectancies Learned or Reinforced in Lesson 12: Dialogue and Review

1. What is one thing that linking verbs do? **L34** *(Linking verbs can join two nouns together that refer to the same person or the same thing. These words are equal to one another.)*

2. What is the other job of a linking verb? **L34** *(Linking verbs join words that describe or give special qualities to the noun or pronoun to which they refer.)*

3. How do we mark a linking verb? **L56** *(We place an "LV" over the word that is doing the job of a linking verb.)*

Where Do I Go from Here?

- **L34**, **L56**, and **L78** go to "Lesson 14" on page 177.

What Materials Will I Need?

- **L34** will need penmanship paper, pencils, red pencils, and copies of Worksheets for **"Lesson 14"** starting on page 182.

- **L56** and **L78** will need *Grammar Notebooks*, pencils, red pencils, and copies of Worksheets for **"Lesson 14"** starting on page 182.

- **Optional:** Teaching would be enhanced at all levels by the use of adjective "flags" as suggested on page 177 in **"Lesson 14."**

What Is a Linking Verb?

Teacher Directions:
Explain to your student the directions for marking the linking verbs and have them complete this worksheet. Remember that sometimes the verb "is" is used in partnership with an action verb. If that is the case, it is a helping verb and not a linking verb. **L34** *students will* <u>underline</u> *the linking verbs they find.* **L56** *students and above will label them with "LV".*

Student Directions:
Follow your teacher's directions for marking the linking verbs in the following sentences.

            LV
1.   I <u>am</u> a sharp student.

              LV
2.   You <u>become</u> what you practice.

              LV
3.   The man <u>is</u> a champion in this event.

         LV
4.   He <u>seems</u> so cheerful.

             LV
5.   A teacher <u>grows</u> weary at the end of a day.

              LV
6.   The children <u>look</u> weary at the end of a day.

            LV
7.   A mother <u>is</u> weary at the end of a day.

       LV
8.   I <u>remain</u> confident about his ability.

            LV
9.   The pizza <u>tastes</u> great.

          LV
10. The idea <u>sounds</u> wonderful.

         LV
11. They <u>appear</u> hopeful after the win.

      LV   LV
12. You <u>were</u> right, and I <u>was</u> wrong.

         LV
13. Humility <u>becomes</u> a character quality of great value.

       LV   LV
14. The day <u>smells</u> rosy for a person who <u>is</u> happy.

         LV
15. My grandpa <u>feels</u> better than ever.

       LV
16. I will <u>be</u> a worker at the meeting.

         LV
17. A good car has <u>been</u> a need for the family.

       LV
18. They <u>were</u> late for the bus.

         HV
19. **L56** He <u>is</u> being careful with those eggs.
     (The "is" here is a helping verb.)

                    HV
20. **L56** He will stay true who <u>is</u> trusted true.
     (The "is" here is a helping verb for the action verb trusted.)

1. I am a sharp student.

2. You become what you practice.

3. The man is a champion in this event.

4. He seems so cheerful.

5. A teacher grows weary at the end of a day.

6. The children look weary at the end of a day.

7. A mother is weary at the end of a day.

8. I remain confident about his ability.

9. The pizza tastes great.

10. The idea sounds wonderful.

11. They appear hopeful after the win.

12. You were right, and I was wrong.

13. Humility becomes a character quality of great value.

14. The day smells rosy for a person who is happy.

15. My grandpa feels better than ever.

16. I will be a worker at the meeting.

17. A good car has been a need for the family.

18. They were late for the bus.

19. He is being careful with those eggs.

20. He will stay true who is trusted true.

Student Worksheet 1:

What Is a Linking Verb?

Student Directions: Follow your teacher's directions for marking the linking verbs in the following sentences.

The cat was chasing the mouse.
The mouse became afraid.
The farmer grows corn for the mice.
The mouse might have been caught.
The mouse ran into the farmhouse.
The mice have corn for breakfast.

If a word can be conjugated, it is a verb.
If a main verb is not on the linking verb
list, it is an action verb.
A main verb may have helping verbs.
Linking verbs may be used as helping
verbs.
Use the Is–Are Rule with verbs from "becomes" to "remain" to determine whether
they are linking verbs or action verbs.
If a helping verb is the only verb and is
not a linking verb, it is an action verb.

Sample Page 19
Lesson 13

Lesson 13

Is It a Linking, Helping, or Action Verb?

Hitting the Home Run

L78 "When we play baseball and step up to the plate, how many swings do we get to hit the ball? We get three don't we? If we swing and miss the first time, we hope we can make contact the second time. What happens if we swing the second time and we miss? We have one more chance. We concentrate at the plate. The pitcher gets the sign from the catcher. The ball comes screaming toward home. We know this is the one we will hit. It has to be. We didn't get it the first two times. We swing and make solid contact. The ball sails off the bat. We nailed it. We hit the ball this time.

"We have three swings when our language throws a verb at us. It can throw a linking verb at us. It can throw a helping verb at us. It can throw an action verb at us. This lesson will teach us how to know the difference so we can mark it correctly and hit it out of the ball park."

Dictating Linking, Helping, and Action Verbs

L78 **Step 1** — *"Turn to page 19 in your* Grammar Notebook. *Counting the title line as your first line, count down three baselines. Starting comfortably close to the left red margin line, write the following sentences on consecutive baselines.* We are going to use these sentences for batting practice.

> *'The cat was chasing the mouse.'*
>
> *'The mouse became afraid.'*
>
> *'The farmer grows corn for the mice.'*
>
> *'The mouse might have been caught.'*
>
> *'The mouse ran into the farmhouse.'*
>
> *'The mice have corn for breakfast.'"*

Discovering the Nature of Linking, Helping, and Action Verbs

L78 **Step 2** — "Sometimes linking verbs are called upon to do more than one job. They can be used strictly as a linking verb or they can be called into service as a helping verb. We have seen this. We know from **'Lesson 11: What Is a Helping Verb?'** that 'am, is, are, was, were, be, being, and been' are potential helping verbs. In the last lesson **'What is a Linking Verb?'** we included 'am, is, are, was, were, be, being, and been' on the linking verb list. So are they 'Linking Verbs' or 'Helping Verbs' in a particular sentence? How do we know?"

Understanding the First Sentence

L78 **Step 3** — "We need to study the verbs in our mouse sentences. In the first sentence, 'The cat was chasing the mouse', is the word 'was' a 'linking verb' (LV) or a 'helping verb' (HV)? We know that if 'was' stands alone, it is a linking verb. If it is in partnership with an action verb, it is a helping verb. We need to look for the last word we can conjugate. What is the last word we can conjugate?"

STUDENTS: "We can successfully conjugate the word 'chase'."

TEACHER: "This means 'chase' is a verb if we can conjugate it. The word 'chase' must also be considered an action verb because it is not in my linking verb list nor my helping verb list. It is an action verb because it provides motion and energy and action to our sentence. Therefore, the word 'was' which can be a linking verb if used alone, is being used here as a helping verb because it is in partnership with the action verb 'chase'. We will label 'was' with an 'HV' and 'chasing' with an 'AV'. Let's use a red pencil to make these marks. Is there a subject in this sentence? Who is doing the chasing?"

STUDENTS: "The cat is the subject. It is doing the chasing."

TEACHER: "What job is the word 'mouse' doing?"

STUDENTS: "It is doing the work of a direct object. It answers the question 'What is the cat chasing?' We label it with a DO."

Understanding the Second Sentence: Introducing the Is–Are Rule

L78 **Step 4** — "In the second sentence 'The mouse became afraid', is the word 'became' a linking verb or a helping verb? Or is it maybe an action verb? Well, 'became' can't be a helping verb, because it is not on our helping verb list. Strike one. We need to learn the **Is–Are Rule** if we are going to hit this pitch.

"The Is–Are Rule focuses on only those words on the linking verb list starting with the word 'becomes' and going to the word 'remain'. *Can you give me those verbs?*"

STUDENTS:	*"Becomes, appears, seems, feels, tastes, looks, grows, smell, sound, stay, and remain."*
TEACHER:	"Now we need to ask a question. Can I substitute the word 'is' or 'are' in place of the word 'became' in my sentence, 'The mouse became afraid'? Only one of the two words needs to work. Substituting the word 'is' for the word 'became', we have the following example: 'The mouse is afraid'. Does the sentence still read well? Does it still mean something?"
STUDENTS:	"It reads very well. It still means something."
TEACHER:	"If it does, the verb is a linking verb because it is doing the job of joining words together. We can know the verb 'became' is a linking verb because the Is–Are Rule works. We would mark the word 'became' with an 'LV'. What became afraid?"
STUDENTS:	"The mouse did. That makes the word 'mouse' a subject doesn't it?"
TEACHER:	"That is right. We label the word 'mouse' with an 'S'. If the verb is a linking verb, what job is the word 'afraid' doing?"
STUDENTS:	"It is doing the work of a **predicate adjective (PA)**. It has to be. It is describing the word 'mouse'."
TEACHER:	"Well done. We would need to mark the word 'afraid' with a 'PA'."

Understanding the Third Sentence

L78 **Step 5** — "Look at the third example. 'The farmer grows corn for the mice'. How would we mark 'for the mice'?"

STUDENTS:	"It is a prepositional phrase. We would bracket it and label the object 'mice' with an 'OP'."
TEACHER:	"What is the last word we can conjugate?"
STUDENTS:	"The last word we can conjugate is the word 'grows'."
TEACHER:	"Is the verb 'grows' a linking verb or an action verb?"
STUDENTS:	"It is on my linking verb list, but I am not sure."
TEACHER:	"If we don't know, what do we need to do?"
STUDENTS:	"We need to use the Is–Are Rule."
TEACHER:	"Let's substitute the word 'is' or 'are' in our sentence. It would read: 'The farmer is corn for the mice' or 'The farmer are corn for the mice'. What do you

---

Is It a Linking, Helping, or Action Verb? | 19

The cat was chasing the mouse.
The mouse became afraid.
The farmer grows corn for the mice.
The mouse might have been caught.
The mouse ran into the farmhouse.
The mice have corn for breakfast.

If a word can be conjugated, it is a verb.
If a main verb is not on the linking verb list, it is an action verb.
A main verb may have helping verbs.
Linking verbs may be used as helping verbs.
Use the Is–Are Rule with verbs from "becomes" to "remain" to determine whether they are linking verbs or action verbs.
If a helping verb is the only verb and is not a linking verb, it is an action verb.

Sample Page 19
Lesson 13

think? Is the verb 'grows' a linking verb in the sentence 'The farmer grows corn for the mice'?"

STUDENTS: "It can't be. The sentence doesn't read well at all with either 'is' or 'are' when we substitute these verbs. The meaning of the sentence is totally gone."

TEACHER: "That's right. The Is–Are Rule helps us determine whether one of these linking verbs is doing the work of an action verb or linking verb. If we substitute the linking verb 'is' or 'are' and the sentence still reads well and still means something with one of the two of these words, we have a linking verb as our main verb.

"Did these sentences read well? Did they make sense? Of course not. That means we have experienced the versatility of the English language. In the sentence 'The farmer grows corn for the mice', the verb 'grows' is used as an action verb. In a different sentence it might be used as a linking verb. To determine which it is, we must use the Is–Are Rule. How would we mark the verb 'grow'?"

STUDENTS: "We would have to use the label 'AV'."

TEACHER: "Who or what grows the corn?"

STUDENTS: "The farmer grows the corn. 'Farmer' is our subject and should be labeled with an 'S'."

TEACHER: "How would we mark the word 'corn'?"

STUDENTS: "It tells us what the farmer grew. The word is waving the 'What or Whom' Flag. It has to be a direct object. We would label it with a 'DO'."

TEACHER: "You are correct."

Understanding the Fourth Sentence

L78 **Step 6 —** "Do you see a prepositional phrase in the fourth sentence?"

STUDENTS: "No."

TEACHER: "What is the last word we can conjugate?"

STUDENTS: "The last word we can conjugate is the word 'caught'."

TEACHER: "Who or what might have been caught?"

STUDENTS: "The mouse might have been caught. That makes the mouse the subject."

TEACHER: "How would we mark the words 'might have been'?"

Is It a Linking, Helping, or Action Verb?   19

The cat was chasing the mouse.
The mouse became afraid.
The farmer grows corn for the mice.
The mouse might have been caught.
The mouse ran into the farmhouse.
The mice have corn for breakfast.

If a word can be conjugated, it is a verb.
If a main verb is not on the linking verb list, it is an action verb.
A main verb may have helping verbs.
Linking verbs may be used as helping verbs.
Use the Is–Are Rule with verbs from "becomes" to "remain" to determine whether they are linking verbs or action verbs.
If a helping verb is the only verb and is not a linking verb, it is an action verb.

Sample Page 19
Lesson 13

STUDENTS: "I think they are helping verbs, aren't they? They are in our helping verb list. We would mark them with an 'HV'."

STUDENTS: "I think they are helping verbs, aren't they? They are in our helping verb list. We would mark them with an 'HV'."

TEACHER: "Are you sure? How do we know this?"

STUDENTS: "Let me look at this sentence. I know the verb 'caught' is an action verb because it is not on my linking verb list. Because the words 'might have been' are all included in my helping verb list, and they are in partnership with an action verb, they have to be used as helping verbs here. It makes sense to me."

TEACHER: "You are right."

Understanding the Fifth Sentence

L78 **Step 7 —** "Let's look at the fifth sentence. What do we look for first if we are going to analyze a sentence?"

STUDENTS: "We look for prepositions and their objects."

TEACHER: "Do you see any?"

STUDENTS: "The sentence has the prepositional phrase 'into the farmhouse'. We would bracket this and label 'farmhouse' with an 'OP'."

TEACHER: "We next need to look for the last word we can conjugate. What do you find?"

STUDENTS: "The only word I can conjugate is 'ran'."

TEACHER: "Is the word 'ran' an action verb or a linking verb?"

STUDENTS: "It has to be an action verb, doesn't it?"

TEACHER: "Why?"

STUDENTS: "Well, first of all it is the only word in this sentence that can be conjugated. That makes it a verb right away. Because 'ran' is not on my linking verb list and it is not included in my helping verb list, it has to be an action verb. I would mark it with an 'AV'."

TEACHER: "Do you see why knowing your linking verb list by memory can make this process go so quickly? You are hitting the ball out of the park! Who or what did the running?"

STUDENTS: "The mouse did the running and is our subject."

Sample Page 19
Lesson 13

Is It a Linking, Helping, or Action Verb? 19

The cat was chasing the mouse.
The mouse became afraid.
The farmer grows corn for the mice.
The mouse might have been caught.
The mouse ran into the farmhouse.
The mice have corn for breakfast.

If a word can be conjugated, it is a verb.
If a main verb is not on the linking verb list, it is an action verb.
A main verb may have helping verbs.
Linking verbs may be used as helping verbs.
Use the Is–Are Rule with verbs from "becomes" to "remain" to determine whether they are linking verbs or action verbs.
If a helping verb is the only verb and is not a linking verb, it is an action verb.

Understanding the Sixth Sentence

L78 **Step 8** — "In the sentence 'The mice have corn for breakfast', how do we mark 'for breakfast'?"

STUDENTS: "It is a prepositional phrase. It needs brackets and an 'OP' over the word 'breakfast'."

TEACHER: "What is the last word we can conjugate?"

STUDENTS: "The last word we can conjugate is 'have', but isn't 'have' a helping verb?"

TEACHER: "It certainly is. Here is a rule of our language. When a helping verb other than a form of the verb 'to be' is used alone in a sentence, it stops being a helping verb and becomes an action verb. We would label the word 'have' with an 'AV'. How do we label the words 'mice' and 'corn'?"

STUDENTS: "The word 'mice' is the subject and needs an 'S'. The word 'corn' is the direct object and needs a 'DO'."

Linking, Helping, and Action Verbs: Defining the Differences

L78 **Step 9** — *"Counting up thirteen baselines from the bottom on your page, add the following sentences on consecutive baselines.*

'If a word can be conjugated, it is a verb.'

'If a main verb is not on the linking verb list, it is an action verb.'

'A main verb may have helping verbs.'

'Linking verbs may be used as helping verbs.'

'Use the Is–Are Rule with verbs from "becomes" to "remain" to determine whether they are linking verbs or action verbs.'

'If a helping verb is the only verb and is not a linking verb, it is an action verb.'"

L78P Teach students to ask the following questions to determine how to mark verbs. Before long these questions will become automatic.

Some Verb Questions Your Students Need to Know

1. What is the last word we can conjugate? *(This shows us the main verb in the sentence.)*

The cat was chasing the mouse.
The mouse became afraid.
The farmer grows corn for the mice.
The mouse might have been caught.
The mouse ran into the farmhouse.
The mice have corn for breakfast.

If a word can be conjugated, it is a verb.
If a main verb is not on the linking verb list, it is an action verb.
A main verb may have helping verbs.
Linking verbs may be used as helping verbs.
Use the Is–Are Rule with verbs from "becomes" to "remain" to determine whether they are linking verbs or action verbs.
If a helping verb is the only verb and is not a linking verb, it is an action verb.

Sample Page 19
Lesson 13

How do we know for sure whether or not we have found a verb?

Here are some clues.

1) Can we conjugate the word and does the conjugation make sense? If it does, we know we have a verb. If it shows action, if it provides motion, if it gives energy to the sentence, it is an action verb.

2) Is the verb in question located on our memorized linking verb list? If it is there and is acting alone in a sentence, it might be a linking verb provided it can pass the scrutiny of the Is–Are Rule. If the word is not in my linking verb list, it is in all likelihood doing the work of an action verb. Remind your students to write the "LV", the "HV", and the "AV" labels with a red pencil.

2. Are there verbs that are assisting this last verb? *(This shows us the helping verbs. We label these with an "HV".)*

3. Is the last word we can conjugate on the linking verb list? *(This tells us whether it is an action verb or a linking verb. If it is not on my linking verb list, it is an action verb. We label action verb with an "AV".)*

4. If it is on my linking verb list, is it found in the list from "becomes" to "remain"? *(If it is, it could be either a linking verb or an action verb. We need to pull out the Is–Are Rule.)*

5. Does the Is–Are Rule apply? *(If it does, then the main verb is linking. We label linking verbs with an "LV". If the Is–Are Rule does not apply, the main verb is an action verb, labeled "AV".)*

6. What job is the verb doing? *(This tells us how to label the word. It also tells us what sentence pattern may be in use. Knowing this helps us determine how to use object and subject pronouns that appear in the sentence.)*

One More Time for the Teacher

L78P If any verb is in partnership with an action verb in a sentence, then we know that these verbs are helping verbs because the action verb calls them into service as helping verbs.

We must imagine these action verbs as being bigger and stronger than linking verbs. They become bullies. They come to the list of linking verbs and say, "Fellas, I need help communicating an idea." What will the linking verbs do? They don't really have a choice. They must serve as a helping verb.

If there are no action verbs in sight, then the linking verb smiles and is very happy to remain a linking verb. He prefers to be a linking verb. A linking verb wants to be the big cheese in the sentence. He doesn't want to just help; he wants to join words together. A linking verb feels that joining words together is the more honorable of the two jobs.

Let's Get Organized

L78 **Step 8 —** *"Turn to the Table of Contents. On the page 19 line, write the title 'Is it a Linking, Helping, or Action Verb?' Turn back to page 19. Centered on the title line, between the two red margin lines, write the **same title**."*

Additional Activities for Reinforcing Verbs

L78P Again, have students go to any textbook or literature book and have them do a verb search. Find the verbs that are in each sentence and determine what job they are accomplishing. You should be able to tell if they are doing the work of a helping verb. You should be able to tell if they are doing the work of a linking verb or an action verb. These are the tools of our language and to know how they work is to know how to use our language properly.

Expectancies Learned or Reinforced in Lesson 13: Dialogue and Review

1. What is a linking verb? **L34** *(A linking verb is a joining word. A linking verb joins words that describe the subject or mean the same thing as the subject.)*

2. Why do I need to know my linking verb list? **L34** *(Main verbs not on my linking verb list are action verbs.)*

3. What happens when a word that is on my linking verb list is in partnership with an action verb? **L78** *(The action verb calls the linking verb into service as a helping verb.)*

4. Which linking verbs can also be used as action verbs? **L78** *(The linking verbs from "becomes" to "remain".)*

5. What rule must we use to determine whether a verb from "becomes" to "remain" is an action verb or a linking verb? **L78** *(We must use the Is–Are Rule.)*

6. What is the Is–Are Rule? **L78** *(If we substitute "is" or "are" for one of these linking verbs, and the sentence still reads well and maintains its meaning, this verb is a linking verb. If it does not maintain its meaning, it is an action verb.)*

7. What does a linking verb do? **L34** *(It joins one word to another either as an equal or as a word that describes.)*

Where Do I Go from Here?

- **L78** goes to **"Lesson 22"** on page 237.

What Materials Will I Need?

- **L78** will need *Grammar Notebooks*, pencils, and red pencils.

Is It a Linking Verb, Helping Verb, or Action Verb?

Teacher Directions: Explain to your students the directions for marking the linking verbs, helping verbs, and action verbs, and have them complete this Worksheet.

Student Directions: This Worksheet is an exercise to give you practice in determining the difference between a linking verb, a helping verb, and an action verb.

Place an "LV" over each linking verb.

Place an "HV" over each helping verb.

Place an "AV" over each action verb.

The Is–Are Rule may be needed.

Please use a red pencil to mark these verbs.

             LV
1. Which way is the grocery store?

           HV LV
2. The policeman is being fair to all concerned.

     HV   HV   AV
3. I have been singing in the rain.

     HV   LV
4. I have been sad since yesterday.

               AV
5. The young boy has a flower for his mother.

      HV   HV HV   AV
6. We might have been sleeping late that

   morning.

     LV
7. It remains a mystery.

         HV   AV
8. The team was rejoicing in their success.

       HV   HV   AV
9. The girls will have run 10 miles before 3 P.M.

       HV LV
10. He is being polite by saying so.

1. Which way is the grocery store?

2. The policeman is being fair to all concerned.

3. I have been singing in the rain.

4. I have been sad since yesterday.

5. The young boy has a flower for his mother.

6. We might have been sleeping late that

   morning.

7. It remains a mystery.

8. The team was rejoicing in their success.

9. The girls will have run 10 miles before 3 P.M.

10. He is being polite by saying so.

Is It a Linking Verb, Helping Verb, or Action Verb?

Student Directions: This Worksheet is an exercise to give you practice in determining the difference between a linking verb, a helping verb, and an action verb.

Place an LV over each linking verb.

Place an HV over each helping verb.

Place an AV over each action verb.

The Is–Are Rule may be needed.

Please use a red pencil to mark these verbs.

Comprehensive Checklist 1 for Lessons 1–13

This is really an inventory listing of skills and concepts learned so far. These will make good review questions in the lessons ahead. Write a few appropriate questions suitable to the level of your students into your lesson plans each day. We are striving for mastery and understanding about how our language works. Remember that my permission to move on in this material is a demonstrated mastery keeping the student's developmental level in mind.

1. What are the benefits of beautiful handwriting? **L12** *(It teaches us how to pay attention to the smallest of details.)*

2. What are the checkpoints for? **L12** *(They help us know how to make letters precisely.)*

3. What legal definitions for our letters do we need to review? **L12** *(Let's take a piece of penmanship paper and find out. Make one beautiful line of manuscript lower case letters from a–z. Make one line of capital letters too.)*

4. What are the four ways to get to our brain for purposes of language instruction? **L12** *(Visual, auditory, kinesthetic, and vocal.)*

5. Why is multisensory instruction so important? *(It reaches the mind and embeds language skills where we are strongest and strengthens where we are weakest. It empowers students in their pursuit of language mastery.)*

6. Why do I need to follow instructions precisely? **L12** *(Learning to listen carefully matters. Paying attention to details matters.)*

7. Why is the *Grammar Notebook* so important? **L56** *(It is a record of achievement. It is a record of a beginning understanding of how our language works. It reinforces attention to detail. It is a resource book for future reference. It is a great addition to any portfolio.)*

8. What do we do with key words in a title? **L12** *(We capitalize them.)*

9. What is a noun? **L12** *(A noun is a person, place, thing, idea, or quality.)*

10. What is the difference between a common and a proper noun? **L12** *(Proper nouns are special, particular nouns that need to be honored with a capital letter. Common nouns do not need to be capitalized.)*

11. What do we do with each day of the week, each month of the year, each continent, and each major holiday? **L12** *(We capitalize them.)*

12. What is the role of an article? **L12** *(An article points us to a noun.)*

13. What does an action verb do? **L12** *(It is an energy word that shows motion or action in our sentence.)*

14. What are the personal pronouns that we use to conjugate? **L34** *(I, you, he, she, it, we, you, and they.)*

15. What is the difference between singular and plural? **L34** *(Singular means one. Plural means more than one.)*

16. How do we conjugate a verb in three tenses **L34** in all six tenses? **L56** *(Carefully. Turn to the lesson on conjugating and practice.)*

17. How do we find the three most important parts of a verb? **L34** *(We use "Today I_____". "Yesterday I _____". "I have _____".)*

18. Why do we need to know the three most important parts of the verbs that are on our irregular verb list? **L34** *(Proper verb usage in our writing and speaking requires this.)*

19. What verbs can be used as helping verbs? **L34** *(Turn to the lesson on helping verbs for review. Create a wall chart.)*

20. What is the linking verb list? **L34** *(Turn to the lesson on linking verbs for review. Create a wall chart. Have them memorize this list.)*

21. What do linking verbs do? **L34** *(They join words together that are either equal in meaning or that describe another joining word.)*

22. How can a verb on our linking verb list be used as a helping verb? **L78** *(If a linking verb is in partnership with a main verb it serves as a helping verb.)*

23. What is the Is–Are Rule? **L78** *(It is a rule that helps us determine whether the linking verbs from "becomes to remain" are being used as action verbs. If I can substitute "is" or "are" and the sentence reads well, the main verb is a linking verb. If it does not read well, it is being used as an action verb.)*

24. Why do I need to understand how our language works? **L12** *(If we do not understand how our language works, it controls us and we do not control it. It makes us a slave. We want it to be our servant. Well-practiced, well-polished communication skills are imperative if we expect doors of opportunity to open and stay open in the future.)*

25. What does this statement mean? Precise grammar builds syntactical expectancies at an automatic level. **L12** *(Learning how our language works builds certain expectations about how sentences should be written and how language should be spoken. If we can use these under-standings and they are automatic, language becomes a friend and a sharpened tool. Few obstacles will stand in our way of effectively communicating.)*

Remember that my permission to move on in this material is a demonstrated mastery keeping the student's developmental level in mind.

If mastery on these first lessons has not been achieved as of yet, do not despair. It takes time to create a work of art. It is my hope that each of the students I teach will become something of a work of art. That their eyes will be opened to the power of the printed and spoken word is always an ever-present goal of mine. It takes practice and patience and perseverance and what I have come to call "The Parrot Principle."

I was driving to work one morning listening to the radio, and Joni Eareckson Tada was sharing a delightful story. It is a story that is worth sharing with your student when the time is right.

The Emperor's Parrot

It seems that an artist whose work was in high regard and demand was paid a visit by the Emperor.

"Would you paint my parrot?" the Emperor asked. "I have heard of the fine work that you do, and I desire to have a painting of yours on my palace walls."

The artist was honored. He consented and kept the Emperor's parrot for a short time and then returned it. Days turned into weeks and the Emperor grew impatient. Where was his painting? Had the artist gone back on his word? The Emperor, unable to contain himself any longer, went to the home of the artist.

"Where is my painting that you consented to do?" asked the Emperor.

The artist was a little nervous but said nothing. Instead, he went for an easel and some brushes, a canvas and some paint. In a matter of moments, the artist, before the incredulous eyes of the Emperor, proceeded to paint an exact replica of the Emperor's beloved parrot. Every color was exact. Every feather was perfect and in place. The dignity and beauty of the bird had been captured. The Emperor was speechless.

"If you could do this beautiful work in such a short time, why have you waited until now?" the Emperor said.

The artist motioned for the Emperor to follow him into his studio. When the Emperor entered the room, he immediately knew why. Filling the walls of this artist's studio were paintings of a parrot, the Emperor's parrot, and some paintings were better than others, but none were better than the painting that would hang in the Emperor's palace.

Standing before Kings

End of story. It is a powerful story. **Artistry has a price.** Developing writing skills has a price. Developing speaking skills has a price, but he who is willing will stand before kings. We know even the best of artists have had a teacher, a mentor, or a guide who has lighted the flame that will propel this student to greatness. And so we too must persevere using the smallest details of our discipline. We must allow our students to be well practiced. The greatest of our day came to be who they are because they were faithful in the small things. They did not ignore the fundamentals of their discipline. They understand function. They required of themselves and of their students a mastery without which they could not succeed. If success matters, we can do no less.

Lesson 14
What Is an Adjective?

Somewhere Over the Rainbow

L12 "Nothing is quite so colorful and so beautiful as a rainbow. All the reds and blues and yellows and greens of a rainbow paint the sky after a rain. Perhaps you have heard the story. Some people would actually have us believe that there is a pot of shining gold at the end of every rainbow. All we need to do is go there and fill our pockets. Should we go?

"We also know for certain that somewhere over that rainbow, bluebirds fly. They have to. Dorothy in the Wizard of Oz tells us they do when she sings the song, 'Somewhere over the Rainbow.' Rainbows and a pot of shining gold and bluebirds flying is what this next lesson is all about. It's about beautiful colors and shining pieces of gold and pretty, little birds. It is about rainbow words that shine like gold on the wings of a bluebird. These rainbow words have a name. We call them 'adjectives'."

Dictating Rainbow Words

L12 "In order to find these adjective rainbow words, we need to learn about some clues that let us know when these words are being used in our sentences. We are going to use some bright, colorful flags when we find these words. Adjectives raise these flags and wave them and say, 'Look at me! I am coloring this beautiful sentence. I am waving this flag to let you know where I am. Can you see the rainbow? Can you find the shining gold? Can you watch the darting bluebirds?'"

L12P L12 students need to be given a sheet of loose-leaf penmanship paper. **L56** and **L78** will work in the *Grammar Notebook.*

L56 **Step 1 —** *"Turn to page 20 in your* Grammar Notebook."

L12 "First we are going to learn about these flags."

L12P You will need to provide a list to introduce these flags.

L12 "These adjective rainbow words are sometimes hard to find. We can recognize these words at work by the flag that is flying over them in a particular sentence. There are six basic flags that can fly over an adjective."

L12 *"Skipping one baseline below the title line, comfortably close to the left margin line, write* **'The "What Kind?" flag'.** *On the next baseline, directly below The 'What Kind?' flag, starting comfortably close to the left margin line, write* **'The "How Much?"**

Sample Page 20
Lesson 14

The "What Kind?" flag

The "How Much?" flag

The "How Many?" flag

The "Which?" "Which One?" or "Whose?" flag

The "What Kind?" flag
The "How Much?" flag
The "How Many?" flag
The "Which?", "Which One?", or
"Whose?" flag

The apple has red skin.

An angry dog has no friends.

The tallest building was Sears Tower.

Forty-two cats lived in our house.

Much study is necessary for a hard test.

An adjective is a word that describes or
influences a noun or pronoun.

Sample Page 20
Lesson 14

*flag'. Directly below this flag, write **'The "How Many?" flag'.** On the next consecutive baseline, write **'The "Which?" "Which One?" or "Whose?" flag'."***

L12   Step 2 — *"Skipping one baseline below 'The "Which?" "Which One?" or "Whose?" flag', write the following sentence:* **'The apple has red skin'.** *Skipping one baseline below this sentence, write this sentence:* **'An angry dog has no friends'.** *Skip another baseline. Here is your third sentence.* **'The tallest building was the Sears Tower'.** *Skipping one baseline below the 'Sears Tower' sentence, write the following:* **'Forty-two cats lived in our house'.** *After skipping yet one more baseline, write the last sentence:* **'Much study is necessary for a hard test'."***

Discovering the Nature of Adjective Rainbow Words

L12   Step 3 — "Look at the sentences we have written. We are going to find words that do the job of an adjective coloring the sentences. These colorful words fly the flags that we have listed. These flags will tell us whether or not a word is an adjective. Look at the first sentence. What flag is flying over the word 'red'?"

STUDENTS: "Quite frankly, I don't see any words flying flags."

TEACHER: "That is what I want to teach you. I want you to see things about our language that you haven't seen before. I want you to see how our language works. We don't mean literal flags, of course. We need symbolic flags.

"What we really mean is that these adjective rainbow words are answering a question about another word in our sentence. Each flag we have recorded is a question. If a word in our sentence answers one of these six questions, it is doing the work of an adjective. Let's look again. Of the six questions we have recorded, can you find a word in our first sentence that answers one of these questions?"

STUDENTS: "The word 'red' is a pretty colorful word. Doesn't it answer the question 'What Kind?'"

TEACHER: "That is correct. Which word is being colored by the word 'red'?"

STUDENTS: "The answer is 'skin' isn't it. The word 'red' is doing the work of an adjective because it answers the question 'What Kind?' It colors the word 'skin'. It is not just 'skin' anymore; it is 'red skin'."

TEACHER: "That's right. Can you imagine the word 'red' grabbing the 'What Kind?' flag and waving it as hard as possible trying to get your attention? 'Here I am. Look at me. I am painting the rainbow. I am coloring words. I am shining like gold.' Everybody takes pride in a job well done. The word 'red' is doing its job well. Place a small flag over the word 'red' and write in the question 'What Kind?' It would look something like this. Now we can look at the second sentence."

L12 **Step 4 —** "Our second sentence has words that are waving flags too. Can you find words that are answering our rainbow questions?"

STUDENTS: "The word 'angry' answers the question 'What Kind?' of dog, doesn't it? The word 'no' answers the question 'How Many?' friends. These words are coloring our sentence."

TEACHER: "You are right. Did you see the flags this time?"

STUDENTS: "I did. They were waving those flags as hard as they could. They wanted me to see the wonderful job they were doing."

TEACHER: "Let's honor these two words with a small flag like we did with the word 'red'. Inside the flag for the word 'angry' we will write the question 'What Kind?' Inside the flag for the word 'no' we will write the question 'How Many?' Now I have another question for you. What kind of words are these adjectives coloring?"

STUDENTS: "In the first sentence the word 'red' colored the word 'skin'. In my second sentence the word 'angry' colored the word 'dog' and the word 'no' colored the word 'friends'. 'Friends' are people. 'Dogs' and 'skin' are things. Adjectives color nouns don't they?"

TEACHER: "You have made a very important discovery."

Discovering the Nature of Adjectives on Your Own

L12P The preceding student–teacher dialogue should be modeled as you analyze the remaining three sentences. Use the Sample Page in the margin as a guide to help you understand which words are flying the flags. Help your student find these words that answer our questions. Place a small flag with the appropriate question written inside that flag over each rainbow word.

Sample Page 20
Lesson 14

Get Out a Sewing Machine

If you really want to have fun, make six flags out of some colorful fabric and put one question on each flag. When the students get to a word and they see what question that word is answering, get that flag out and wave it like crazy. Better yet, let one of your students have the privilege of waving it. Have those flags available. Put them in a piece of styrofoam on your desk or table. Plant them in a small vase or depending upon the size you make, put up six flag poles in your yard.

Of course, real people make flags from things like construction paper, self-adhesive mailing labels, toothpicks, and the like.

L78P Indefinite pronouns like "some" or "many" can sometimes serve as an adjective. Look at this sentence: Some children watched the many stars in the sky. The word "some" is waving the "How Many?" flag. The word "many" is waving the same flag. Both words are adjectives and pronouns at the same time. We call them adjectival pronouns.

Defining Adjective Rainbow Words That Shine Like Gold on the Wings of a Bluebird

L12 **Step 5 —** "We need to write the definition of an adjective. *Counting up three baselines from the bottom of your page, please write the following definition of an adjective. Starting comfortably close to the left margin line, write the following:* **'An adjective is a word that describes or influences a noun or pronoun'.** That definition is the official definition. I suppose we could define an adjective as a rainbow word that colors nouns and waves crazy flags. We'll try to remember both."

Let's Get Organized

L56 **Step 6 —** *"Turn to the Table of Contents. On the page 20 line, write the title* **'What Is an Adjective?'** *Turn back to page 20."*

L12 *"Centered on the title line, between the two red margin lines, write the title* **'What Is an Adjective?'"**

Marking Adjectives When We Analyze a Sentence

L56P When we get to the analysis of various sentences, we will mark adjectives by circling them and placing the label "adj." above the circle. To show the job of an adjective, we will then draw an arrow from the circle to the word that it influences. We will show this in later lessons.

Exercises to Reinforce an Understanding of Adjectives

L12P For review, you may want to take a paragraph from a well-known book and have the kids find adjectives by using this concept of flags. They will find them. They will tell you which words are the rainbow words, they will find the pot of gold, and they will see the bluebirds flying.

Also, have your students do the worksheet at the end of this lesson. See how many adjectives they can find on their own.

Reviewing Is Important

L12P I must remind you not to forget to review those skills you have taught in previous lessons. Go to Checklist 2 and write some of those questions that apply into your lesson plans.

L34P It takes moments to ask for the three most important parts of a verb. It takes moments to ask for the conjugation of that verb in the present, past, and present perfect tenses. It takes moments to ask them to recite that wonderful linking verb list.

L12P Point to charts with the names of the days of the week or the months of the year and review. Leave no stones unturned. Mastery is the target. Put your straight arrows in that bow one at a time, draw back slowly and practice the release until hitting the bull's-eye is automatic. Help your students to hit the target in the same way and then watch their faces. A growing confidence emerges. Students begin to hand you writing assignments that are showing an ever-increasing mastery.

Expectancies Learned or Reinforced in Lesson 14: Dialogue and Review

1. What does an adjective do? **L12** *(It is a word that describes or influences a noun or a pronoun.)*

2. What questions does an adjective answer? **L12** *(what kind? how many? how much? which? which one? or whose?)*

Where Do I Go from Here?

- **L12** goes to **L12** "**Scope and Sequence**" Step 14.

- **L34** goes to "**Lesson 18**" on page 210.

- **L56** goes to "**Lesson 41**" on page 416.

- **L78** goes to "**Lesson 15**" on page 186.

What Materials Will I Need?

- **L34** will need penmanship paper, pencils, red pencils, and copies of Worksheets for "**Lesson 18**" starting on page 217.

- **L56** will need *Grammar Notebooks* and pencils.

- **L78** will need *Grammar Notebooks*, pencils, red pencils, and copies of Worksheets for "**Lesson 15**" starting on page 192.

- **Optional:** Teaching will be enhanced at **L78** by using adverb question "flags" as described on page 187 of "**Lesson 15.**"

What Is an Adjective?

Teacher Directions: Explain to your student the directions for marking the following adjectives.

L12 *students should just use* (circles) *to identify adjectives in the following sentences on the Worksheets.*

L56 *and above should* (circle) *each adjective, draw an arrow to the word it influences, and label each adjective with an "adj."*

Student Directions: Listen carefully to the directions your teacher gives you for doing the following sentences.

1. An old red car drove down the long street.

2. The green apple fell from the tall tree.

3. The little man lived on the large boat.

4. Seven games were played under the blue sky.

5. The gold ring was found in the messy room.

6. The blue horse has short legs.

7. The kind lady planted seeds in the window box.

8. We wear summer clothes on hot days.

9. Morning flowers bring early smiles.

10. Tiny bees make sweet honey.

1. An old red car drove down the long street.

2. The green apple fell from the tall tree.

3. The little man lived on the large boat.

4. Seven games were played under the

   blue sky.

5. The gold ring was found in the messy room.

6. The blue horse has short legs.

7. The kind lady planted seeds in the

   window box.

8. We wear summer clothes on hot days.

9. Morning flowers bring early smiles.

10. Tiny bees make sweet honey.

Student Worksheet 1:

What Is an Adjective?

Student Directions: Listen carefully to the directions your teacher gives you for marking the following sentences.

What Is an Adjective?

*Teacher Directions:
Explain to your students
the directions for
marking the following
adjectives.*

L12 *students should just
use* (circles) *to identify
adjectives in this Work-
sheet.*

L56 *and above should
circle each adjective,
draw an arrow to the
word it influences, and
label each adjective with
an "adj."*

*Student Directions:
Listen carefully to the
directions your teacher
gives you for marking the
following sentences.*

1. adj. adj. adj.
   Ten good boys wearing red hats sat by the
   adj.
   cold sea.

2. adj. adj. adj.
   A cold winter night requires a hot fire.

3. adj. adj. adj.
   The public library has many good books.

4. adj. adj.
   A cranky old prospector was suffering from
   adj.
   stiff joints.

5. adj. adj.
   The icy water from this deep well runs

   quickly.

6. adj. adj. adj.
   The new mayor was a kind and helpful man.

7. adj. adj.
   Twenty-three different reasons were given for
   adj.
   the bad accident.

8. adj. adj.
   Six days remained before the last deadline.

9. **L56** adj. adj.
   Some old pictures appeared in the
   adj.
   town newspaper.

10. **L56** adj. adj.
    Most American students enjoy a
    adj.
    shopping mall.

1. Ten good boys wearing red hats sat by the cold sea.

2. A cold winter night requires a hot fire.

3. The public library has many good books.

4. A cranky old prospector was suffering from stiff joints.

5. The icy water from this deep well runs quickly.

6. The new mayor was a kind and helpful man.

7. Twenty-three different reasons were given for the bad accident.

8. Six days remained before the last deadline.

9. Some old pictures appeared in the town newspaper.

10. Most American students enjoy a shopping mall.

What Is an Adjective?

Student Directions: Listen carefully to the directions your teacher gives you for marking the following sentences.

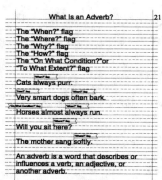

Sample Page 21
Lesson 15

Lesson 15

What Is an Adverb?

More Rainbow Words to Color Our Sky

L56 "In our last lesson, we learned that adjectives are rainbow words that color nouns or pronouns. Can you name one of the adjective flags that tells us when we have an adjective working in our sentence? These words are very important to our writing. They will help the reader see the pictures we want them to see. Instead of an ordinary painting, we could have a beautiful painting of a parrot fit for the palace walls of an emperor. Each color in the painting is just right. Each feather is perfectly placed. Each word in what we write can be just right too. Each word helps to make just the right picture. It creates just the right effect. In this next lesson, we have some more rainbow words, but they don't color nouns and pronouns. That is not their job. These new rainbow words leave the job of coloring nouns and pronouns to an adjective. Let's find out what these new rainbow words are all about."

Dictating Adverb Rainbow Words

L56P If your sewing machine is still working, it's time to get out some different, brightly colored material and make six more flags. You can probably use the same six flagpoles that you put up in the front yard for the last lesson. You won't need to put up six new ones. Concrete is expensive. That would be just too many flagpoles in one yard at any given time. Toothpicks and mailing labels also work very well.

L56 **Step 1** — "In order to find these particular rainbow words, we need to learn some more clues that let us know when these words are being used in our sentences. We are again going to use some bright, colorful flags when we find these words. These new rainbow words raise different flags than adjectives, but they are still waving them and saying, 'Look at me! I am coloring this beautiful sentence. I am waving this flag to let you know where I am.' Can you see the rainbow? Can you find the shining gold? Can you watch the darting bluebirds? These new rainbow words are called adverbs."

L56P **L56** and **L78** will work in the *Grammar Notebook*. If you feel that a lower level student can handle this lesson, by all means do not hesitate to introduce it. The **"Scope and Sequence"** is only a suggested order subject to the needs of the student.

L56 "Turn to page 21 in your *Grammar Notebook*. We are first going to learn about these new flags."

56P You will need to provide a list to introduce these new flags.

L56 "These adverb rainbow words are sometimes hard to find. We can recognize them at work by the imaginary flag that is flying over them in a particular sentence. In addition to the six adjective flags we have already learned, there are six adverb flags that can fly over our sentences. Each flag asks a unique question."

L56 *"Skipping one baseline below the title line, comfortably close to the left margin line, write* **'The "When?" flag'**. *On the next baseline, directly below* 'The "When?" flag', *starting comfortably close to the left margin line, write* **'The "Where?" flag'**. *On the next consecutive baseline, write* **'The "Why?" flag'**. *Directly below this flag, write* **'The "How?" flag'**. *On the next consecutive baselines, write* **'The "On What Condition?" flag'** *or* **'The "To What Extent?" flag'**."

L56 **Step 2**— *"Skipping one baseline below the last recorded flag, write the following sentence:* **'Cats always purr'**. *Skipping one baseline below this sentence, write this one:* **'Very smart dogs often bark'**. *Skip one baseline. Write your third sentence.* **'Horses almost always run'**. *Skipping one baseline below the last sentence, write the following:* **'Will you sit here?'** *After skipping one more baseline, write this sentence:* **'The mother sang softly'**."

The "When?" flag

The "Where?" flag

The "Why?" flag

The "How?" flag

The "On What Condition?" flag

The "To What Extent?" flag

Discovering the Nature of Adverbs: Rainbow Words Coloring Verbs

L56P Understanding how adverbs work and influence other words is a challenge. That is why we have left this until **L56**. Remember that each word has a job to do. Adjectives have the job of answering adjective questions. If we find a word answering one of these questions, we know what it is. We also know that nouns or pronouns are being influenced by this adjective. That is the nature of adjectives. The same is true for adverbs. Adverbs have their questions too. They use their power to influence verbs, adjectives, and other adverbs. They do not and cannot influence a noun or a pronoun. They are restricted in their ability to influence.

If you understand the game of chess, you know that each piece is restricted to a certain movement. The bishops can only move diagonally. The rooks can only move horizontally or vertically. The king can only move one space at a time and so on. Our language does the same thing. Adjectives are restricted in their movement. So are adverbs. The chess master knows what his troops can do. He knows their power. Writers know what words can do. They know their power. A successful writer knows a piece of writing that is a checkmate.

The "When?" flag
The "Where?" flag
The "Why?" flag
The "How?" flag
The "On What Condition?"or
"To What Extent?" flag

Cats always purr.

Very smart dogs often bark.

Horses almost always run.

Will you sit here?

The mother sang softly.

An adverb is a word that describes or
influences a verb, an adjective, or
another adverb.

Sample Page 21
Lesson 15

L56 **Step 3** —"Look at the sentences we have written. We are going to find words that do the job of an adverb. These colorful words fly the flags that we have listed. These flags will tell us whether or not a particular word is a rainbow word. Look at the first sentence. We have used the picture of flying a flag before. Do you see what flag is flying over the word 'always'?"

> **STUDENTS:** "What you really mean is 'What question does the word "always" answer in our sentence?' Is that correct?"

> **TEACHER:** "That is correct. That is what I want to teach you in this lesson. I want you to recognize these new imaginary flags. And you are right. What we really mean when we say 'flying a flag' is that these rainbow words are answering a question about another word in our sentence. Each flag we have recorded is a question. If a word in our sentence answers one of these six questions, it is doing the work of an adverb. Let's look again. Of the six questions we have recorded, can you find a word in our first sentence 'Cats always purr' that answers one of these questions?"

> **STUDENTS:** "The word 'always' answers the question 'When?' doesn't it?"

> **TEACHER:** "That is correct. Do you know which word is being colored by the word 'always'?"

> **STUDENTS:** "The answer is 'purr'. The word 'always' is doing the work of an adverb because it answers the question 'When does the cat purr?' It colors the word 'purr'. The cat is not just 'purring' anymore; it is 'always purring'."

> **TEACHER:** "That's right. The adverb is changing the meaning of the word 'purr' ever so slightly. Imagine the word 'always' grabbing the 'When?' flag and waving it as hard as possible trying to get your attention. 'Here I am. Look at me. I am painting the word "purr". I am making the word "purr" shine like gold.' The word 'always' is doing its job well. *Place a small flag over the word 'always' and write in the question* **'When?'** It would look something like this."

L56 **Step 4** — "Our second sentence 'Very smart dogs often bark' has words that are waving flags too. What question does the word 'often' answer?"

> **STUDENTS:** "The word 'often' answers the question 'When?' just like the word 'always' did.

> **TEACHER:** "You are right. Did you see the flag this time?"

> **STUDENTS:** "I did. 'Often' was waving that flag as hard as it

could. It wanted me to see the important job it was doing. The word certainly answers the question 'When did the dog bark?'"

TEACHER: "Let's honor this word with a small flag like we did with the word 'always'. *Inside the flag for the word 'always' we will write* **'When?'** Now I have another question for you. What kind of words do these adverb rainbow words color?"

STUDENTS: "In the first sentence the word 'purr' was colored by the word 'always'. In my second sentence the word 'bark' was colored by the word 'often'. The words 'purr' and 'bark' are words that I can conjugate. That means these adverbs color verbs, don't they?"

Adverb Rainbow Words Coloring Adjective Rainbow Words

TEACHER: "You have made a very important discovery. Words that answer these new questions can color verbs. They can also color adjectives. Let me show you. What word in our sentence answers the question 'What kind of dogs?'"

STUDENTS: "They are smart dogs aren't they. 'Smart' is an adjective because it answers the question 'What Kind?'"

TEACHER: "Good. You remember adjectives. What other word that remains in our sentence answers the question 'How smart were the dogs?'"

STUDENTS: "The answer has to be the word 'very'. The dogs were 'very smart'. The word 'very' must be an example of an adverb. It is waving the flag 'How?' which is one of our adverb questions."

TEACHER: "So what word does 'very' color? What word is 'very' influencing? What discovery about the nature of these words can you make?"

STUDENTS: "The word 'very' must be coloring the adjective 'smart'. How smart? Very smart. That means that these adverbs can also color an adjective."

Adverb Rainbow Words Coloring Other Adverb Rainbow Words

L56 **Step 5** — "You are catching on. Look at our third sentence: 'Horses almost always run' When do they run?"

STUDENTS: "The word 'always' answers the question 'When do they run?' They 'always run'. The word 'always' is coloring the verb 'run'."

TEACHER: "That is right. Let's look at another word. Can you figure out what question the word 'almost' answers?"

STUDENTS: "It doesn't answer 'When?' or 'Where?' or 'Why?' or 'How?' The word 'almost' seems to be defining a particular situation. This situation is happening almost every time, but not quite every time."

TEACHER: "The word 'almost' is a conditional word. On what condition do the horses always run? They 'almost' always run. 'Almost' colors the word 'always'. It changes the meaning of the word ever so slightly implying that horses don't run all the time, but a large part of the time."

STUDENTS: "We have already determined that the word 'always' is coloring the word 'run'. If 'almost' colors 'always', adverbs can color each other."

TEACHER: "That's right. They are powerful words. Adverbs can influence a verb, an adjective, or another adverb. They are very versatile. Do you understand?"

STUDENTS: "Checkmate."

Discovering the Nature of Adverb Rainbow Words on Your Own

L56P The preceding student-teacher dialogue should be modeled as you analyze the remaining sentences. Use the Sample Page in the margin as a guide to help you understand which words are flying which flags. Record as many sentences as you have room for. Help your students find these words that answer our questions and then have them place a small arrow over that word with the appropriate question written inside that arrow.

Defining Adverbs

L56 **Step 6** — "If a word answers one of these six adverbial questions, it is doing the work of an adverb. *Count up three baselines from the bottom of page 21, and write the following: 'An adverb is a word that describes or influences a verb, an adjective, or another adverb'.*"

Let's Get Organized

L56 **Step 7** — *"Turn to the Table of Contents. On the page 21 line, write the title 'What Is an Adverb?' Turn back to page 21. Centered on the title line, between the two red margin lines, write the same title."*

Sample Page 21
Lesson 15

What Is an Adverb? | 21

The "When?" flag
The "Where?" flag
The "Why?" flag
The "How?" flag
The "On What Condition?" or
"To What Extent?" flag

Cats always purr.

Very smart dogs often bark.

Horses almost always run.

Will you sit here?

The mother sang softly.

An adverb is a word that describes or influences a verb, an adjective, or another adverb.

Marking Adverbs When We Do Syntactical Analysis

L56P When we seriously concentrate on syntactical analysis of sentences, we will mark adverbs much like we mark adjectives. We will circle the adverb that we find, label it with an "adv.", and then draw an arrow from the circle to the word that the adverb influences. Your student will have a chance to do this on the worksheet for this lesson.

Exercises to Reinforce an Understanding of Adverbs

L56P Practice will provide an arena where identification of these parts of speech will come more easily. I encourage you once again to pick up a reading book and go searching for these kinds of words. Your students will begin to notice these flags flying and will be excited to share with you why they are what they are. Every word in English has its job to do.

Expectancies Learned or Reinforced in Lesson 15: Dialogue and Review

1. What do adverbs do? **L56** *(Adverbs describe or influence a verb, an adjective or another adverb.)*

2. What are the adverbial questions? **L56** *(When, where, why, how, and on what condition or to what extent?)*

3. If a word answers one of these questions, what work is it doing? **L56** *(It is doing the work of an adverb.)*

4. What are the adjective questions? **L12** *(What kind, how many, how much, which, which one or whose?)*

5. If a word answers one of these questions, what job is it doing? **L12** *(It is doing the job of an adjective.)*

6. What is the difference between an adjective and an adverb? **L56** *(Adjectives influence nouns and pronouns. Adverbs influence verbs, adjectives, and other adverbs. They each have different questions that they answer.)*

7. How is knowing what words can do similar to playing chess? **L56** *(If we know how our chess pieces move, we can apply strategies that place us in a position of significant advantage. If we know how words work, we can create powerful sentences that also place us in a position of significant advantage.)*

Every word in English has its job to do.

Where Do I Go from Here?

- **L56** and **L78** go to **"Lesson 16"** on page 194.

What Materials Will I Need?

- **L56** and **L78** will need *Grammar Notebooks,* pencils, red pencils, and copies of Worksheets for **"Lesson 16"** starting on page 200.

What Is an Adverb?

Teacher Directions: Explain to your student the directions for marking the adverbs and drawing arrows to the word they influence.

Student Directions: Circle all adverbs, mark them with the label "adv.", and draw an arrow to the word they influence.

1. The doctor *always* arrives *very early*.

2. We worked *hard* and *soon* will reap the rewards.

3. *Very* cold weather *usually* makes cars *hard* to start.

4. Hippopotami *usually* run *rather slowly*.

5. Some sports stars are *extremely well* practiced.

6. The medic *very carefully* opened the car door.

7. He is *rather* slim since he started dieting *recently*.

8. The elevator *suddenly* stopped.

9. The clerk was *perfectly* able to wait *outside*.

10. The book *completely* confused the baker.

11. They *sometimes* watched the sun set.

12. The jogger ran *briskly* through the meadow.

13. The bear growled *loudly yesterday*.

14. The teacher spoke *quite sharply today*.

15. He *successfully* completed the *rather* difficult course.

1. The doctor always arrives very early.

2. We worked hard and soon will reap the rewards.

3. Very cold weather usually makes cars hard to start.

4. Hippopotami usually run rather slowly.

5. Some sports stars are extremely well practiced.

6. The medic very carefully opened the car door.

7. He is rather slim since he started dieting recently.

8. The elevator suddenly stopped.

9. The clerk was perfectly able to wait outside.

10. The book completely confused the baker.

11. They sometimes watched the sun set.

12. The jogger ran briskly through the meadow.

13. The bear growled loudly yesterday.

14. The teacher spoke quite sharply today.

15. He successfully completed the rather difficult course.

What Is an Adverb?

Directions: Circle *all adverbs, mark them with the label "adv.", and draw an arrow to the word they influence.*

Lesson 16

What Is a Preposition?

Where Is Compass Man When You Need Him?

L56 "Have you ever been lost? You look **at a map** and all the roads you thought you needed have suddenly disappeared. You look **at the gas gauge** and it reads empty. You try to start your car and the battery is dead. You forgot your compass **at home.** Where is your hero, Compass Man, when you need him? There isn't a police officer **in sight.** It's getting dark and the batteries **in your flashlight** are dead. You didn't pack a sleeping bag. You didn't pack a toothbrush. A full moon is rising **in the sky.** The wolves are howling **from deep in the woods.** They sound hungry **to you.** You devoured your last Salted Nut Roll hours ago, but you remember something **about surviving on tree bark.**

"'Help!'

"Your cry echoes **through the woods** and **across the valleys** and **down the roads.** You should have brought your cell phone. A moose wanders up **to the car** and licks the headlight. You think it was a moose. Maybe it was Tyrannosaurus Rex! No, it was a moose. You can hear it mooing. Oops! That would make it a cow, wouldn't it?

"'Help!'

"You raise your voice **to the mountaintops** again.

"'Is this what you are looking for?' Compass Man says as he hands you a new Boy Scouts of America compass **with all of the bells and whistles.**

"'Oh, Compass Man. My hero!'

"'Don't mention it,' he says as he walks off **into the moonlit night.** 'You'll be able to find your way now.'

"We have compass words in our language that help keep us from getting lost. These compass words have bells and whistles that tell us the time, give us direction, or provide us with more information. We have a special name that we give to these compass words. We call them 'Prepositions'. Can you say that word? Let's write some of these prepositions."

Dictating and Discovering the Nature of Compass Words

L56 **Step 1** — *"Turn to page 22 in your* Grammar Notebook. *We need to fold our notebook page to make three equal columns.* I am going to give you a list of prepositions that you need to know. *Skipping one baseline below our title line, starting in the first column, starting each word comfortably close to the left margin line, please write the following compass words on consecutive baselines.* I will use each one in a sentence.

'after	below	by
before	beside, besides	except
during	between	for
since	down	like
to	from	of
till, until	in, into	with, within
about	inside, outside	without
above	near	in spite of
across	on, onto	because of
against	over	in addition to
among	through	instead of
around	toward	by means of
at	under	in back of
behind	up, upon	on account of'"

L56P Refer to Sample Page 22 provided in the margin of this lesson as a guide. After the first column looks like the Sample Page, instruct your students to jump to the second column and finally the third column. Be sure to us each word in an oral sentence. While dictating these sentences, point out the prepositions.

Sample Page 22
Lesson 16

Discovering the Object of a Compass Word

L56 **Step 2** — "We have discovered that prepositions can tell us the time, give us direction, or provide more information. We also need to learn something else about these words. They always have a partner that is a noun or a pronoun that follows directly after the preposition. It is possible to have more than one noun or pronoun as a partner. Without these nouns or pronouns, the sentence will make no sense. Look at this example:

He rested after the game.

"The word 'after' is a preposition because it has a partner. What noun is serving as the partner for this preposition?"

STUDENTS: "The word 'game' must be the partner. It is the first noun that I find after the preposition 'after'. I know 'game' is a noun because it is a thing. I also know that 'game' is a noun because the article 'the' has the job of pointing at nouns."

TEACHER: "Good. We call these partners **'objects of the preposition'**. An object and its preposition are called a **'prepositional phrase'**. A preposition and its object always tie themselves to another word in the sentence. In this case the prepositional phrase 'after the game' is being tied to the word 'rested'."

Defining a Preposition

L56 **Step 3 —** *"Counting up six baselines from the bottom of page 22, write the definition of a preposition. Beginning each sentence comfortably close to the left margin line, write the following sentences.*

'A preposition is a word used to relate its object to another word in the sentence.'

'A prepositional phrase begins with a preposition and ends with its object.'

'An object of a preposition (OP) is a noun or a pronoun.'"

Let's Get Organized

L56 **Step 4 —** *"Turn to the Table of Contents. On the page 22 line, write the title **'What Is a Preposition?'** Turn back to page 22. Centered on the title line, between the two red margin lines, write the **same title**."*

An Example of a Compass Word Telling Us the Time

L56 **Step 1 —** *"Turn to page 23 in your* Grammar Notebook. *Let's practice writing some sentences using compass words. Skipping one baseline below our title line, starting comfortably close to the margin line, please write the following sentence: **'He rested after the race'.*** What word is being used as a compass word?"

STUDENTS: "The word is 'after'."

TEACHER: "Can you tell me what job the word 'after' is doing?

STUDENTS: "The word 'after' is telling us when this person rested."

22	What Is a Preposition?	
after	below	by
before	beside, besides	except
during	between	for
since	down	like
to	from	of
till, until	in, into	with, within
about	inside, outside	without
above	near	in spite of
across	on, onto	because of
against	over	in addition to
among	through	instead of
around	toward	by means of
at	under	in back of
behind	up, upon	on account of

A preposition is a word used to relate its object to another word in the sentence.
A prepositional phrase begins with a preposition and ends with its object.
An object of a preposition (OP) is a noun or a pronoun.

Sample Page 22
Lesson 16

What Is a Preposition? (continued) 23

He rested after the race.
He found his wallet between the seats.
The girl walked without her shoes.

With strong workers, a group of Boy Scouts can clear much brush before sundown.

In addition to Boy Scouts, the police asked local citizens for help with the paper drive.

My son has experimented with rockets since 1990 because of an interest in jets.

They leaned against the wind and the rain and walked across the mountains and the prairie.

Sample Page 23
Lesson 16

TEACHER:	"That is correct. Telling time is one of the jobs of a prepositional phrase."

An Example of a Compass Word Giving Us Direction

.56 **Step 2** — *"On the next baseline, please write the second sentence: 'He found his wallet between the seats'.* What is the compass word that is being used in this sentence?"

STUDENTS:	"The word is 'between'."
TEACHER:	"What job is the word 'between' doing?"
STUDENTS:	"The word 'between' is giving me direction so I can see where the wallet was."
TEACHER:	"You are right again. Giving directions is another one of the jobs of a prepositional phrase."

An Example of a Compass Word Giving Us More Information

.56 **Step 3** — *"On the next baseline, please write the next sentence: 'The girl walked without her shoes'.* What is the compass word in this sentence?

STUDENTS:	"The word is 'without'."
TEACHER:	"What job is the word 'without' doing?"
STUDENTS:	"The word 'without' is giving us more information about the girl. She doesn't have shoes on."
TEACHER:	"You are once more correct. Giving more information is another one of the jobs of a prepositional phrase."

Marking Prepositional Phrases Using Syntactical Analysis

.56P Give each student Student Worksheet 1: Finding Prepositional Phrases and Their Objects found in this lesson and continue by saying the following:

.56 **Step 4** — "Let's go looking for prepositions and their objects. To find a compass word or preposition, you must look at the list you have written on page 22 of your *Notebook*. We are going to mark the prepositional phrases that we find. We will place a square bracket in front of any of the words in a sentence that are also found in our preposition list. A square bracket will look like this: **[prepositional phrase].**"

56P You may need to demonstrate how to make square brackets. Put the first sentence without the markings on the board or on paper

22	What Is a Preposition?	
after	below	by
before	beside, besides	except
during	between	for
since	down	like
to	from	of
till, until	in, into	with, within
about	inside, outside	without
above	near	in spite of
across	on, onto	because of
against	over	in addition to
among	through	instead of
around	toward	by means of
at	under	in back of
behind	up, upon	on account of

A preposition is a word used to relate its object to another word in the sentence. A prepositional phrase begins with a preposition and ends with its object. An object of a preposition (OP) is a noun or a pronoun.

Sample Page 22
Lesson 16

A prepositional phrase is a group of words that begins with a preposition and ends with its object.

and make those markings as you work through the Student–Teacher Dialogue that follows. Remember that the objects of prepositions are always the first noun or pronoun you come to after you find a preposition. If there is no noun or pronoun, the word is not doing the job of a preposition because it has no object. It must have an object.

Sometimes there can be two or more nouns or pronouns that serve as objects. When you discuss these sentences with your students, make sure they have the list of prepositions in front of them. They will not need to memorize this list, but as they work with these words, the list needs to become very familiar.

Student–Teacher Dialogue for Finding Prepositional Phrases

L56 **Step 5 —** "Let's look at sentence number one on our worksheet. Does sentence number one, '[With strong workers], a group [of Boy Scouts] can clear much brush [before sundown],' contain any of the words written in your preposition list on page 22?"

STUDENTS: "I see three words. I can find the preposition 'with', the preposition 'of', and the preposition 'before'."

TEACHER: "Right. We need to put a square bracket in front of these words. These brackets tell us where the prepositional phrase starts. Now look for a noun or pronoun following the prepositions you have found. The first noun or pronoun following a preposition is always called the 'object of the preposition'. What do you see?"

STUDENTS: "The first noun that I find after the preposition 'with' is 'workers', after the preposition 'of' is the proper noun 'Boy Scouts', and after the preposition 'before' is the common noun 'sundown'."

TEACHER: "Good job. These words are the objects of these prepositions in this sentence. When you have found these, place a square bracket behind this object. Then to make sure that people can see these objects, label each object by writing the capital letters 'OP' above each one."

L56P Have your students continue their search for prepositional phrases and their objects by working through the rest of the sentences on this worksheet. Have them mark each phrase with square brackets and label each object with "OP". If you find a preposition that has two objects, each must get an "OP". Examples of these sentences with proper markings are provided as a guide on the Sample Page 23 in the back of this book.

L56 **Step 6** — *"Skipping one baseline below the sentence 'The girl walked without her shoes', write the **first four sentences** of our worksheet, skipping one baseline between sentences. Remember to put in **brackets** and **'OP'** labels where they are necessary."*

Let's Get Organized

L56 **Step 7** — *"Turn to the Table of Contents. On the page 23 line, write the title **'What Is a Preposition? (continued)'**. Turn back to page 23. Centered on the title line, between the two red margin lines, write the **same title."***

Additional Activities for Reinforcing Prepositional Phrases

You can take any paragraph from almost any resource and ask students to find prepositional phrases. We are trying to build syntactical expectancies. We want students to recognize these at an automatic level.

Expectancies Learned or Reinforced in Lesson 16: Dialogue and Review

1. What is a prepositional phrase? **L56** *(A prepositional phrase is a group of words that begins with a preposition and ends with its object.)*

2. How do we mark prepositional phrases? **L56** *(We use square end brackets at the beginning and the end of the phrase and we place the label "OP" over the object of that preposition.)*

3. What if there is more than one object? **L56** *(We label each object separately with an "OP".)*

4. How will I know if a word is a preposition? **L56** *(I will need to check my preposition list.)*

5. If I ever get lost on a moonlit night without my compass, what shall I do? **L56** *(Cry "Help!" Compass Man will be on his way.)*

Where Do I Go from Here?

- **L56** and **L78** go to "Lesson 17" on page 204.

What Materials Will I Need?

- **L56** and **L78** will need *Grammar Notebooks*, pencils, red pencils, and copies of Worksheets for **"Lesson 17"** starting on page 208.

Finding Prepositional Phrases

Teacher Directions: Explain to your student the directions for marking the prepositional phrases with brackets and labeling the object of each preposition.

Student Directions: Listen carefully to the directions your teacher gives you for finding each preposition, putting brackets around each [prepositional phrase], and labeling each object of the preposition with an "OP".

1. [With strong workers,] a group [of Boy Scouts] can clear much brush [before sundown.]

2. [In addition to Boy Scouts,] the police asked local citizens [for help] [with the paper drive.]

3. My son has experimented [with rockets] [since 1990] [because of an interest] [in jets.]

4. They leaned [against the wind and the rain] and walked [across the mountains and the prairie.]

5. [Inside the igloo,] the campers stayed warm [without a fire] [until morning.]

6. The cheers [of the crowd] [in back] [of the stadium] came when the flag pole climber reached the top [of the pole.]

7. [Through rose-colored glasses,] the man saw across the expanse [of time] [toward eternity.]

8. Everyone [except John] was running the mile [in six minutes.]

9. We sat [near the gate] so we could walk [over the bridge.]

10. Some scientists think there was a paradise [without sickness and death] [before the fall] [of man.]

1. With strong workers, a group of Boy Scouts can clear much brush before sundown.

2. In addition to Boy Scouts, the police asked local citizens for help with the paper drive.

3. My son has experimented with rockets since 1990 because of an interest in jets.

4. They leaned against the wind and the rain and walked across the mountains and the prairie.

5. Inside the igloo, the campers stayed warm without a fire until morning.

6. The cheers of the crowd in back of the stadium came when the flag pole climber reached the top of the pole.

7. Through rose-colored glasses, the man saw across the expanse of time toward eternity.

8. Everyone except John was running the mile in six minutes.

9. We sat near the gate so we could walk over the bridge.

10. Some scientists think there was a paradise without sickness and death before the fall of man.

Student Directions: Listen carefully to the directions your teacher gives you for finding each preposition, putting brackets around each [prepositional phrase], and labeling each object of the preposition with an "OP".

Finding Prepositional Phrases

Teacher Directions: Explain to your student the directions for marking the prepositional phrases with brackets and labeling the object of each preposition.

Student Directions: Listen carefully to the directions your teacher gives you for finding each preposition, putting brackets around each [prepositional phrase], and labeling each object of the preposition with an "OP".

1. The snowmobile club helped [in the rescue] [of the stranded motorist.]

2. Joey skated [down the street] [near the park.]

3. The old mill [on the Ottertail River] was [on the historic tour.]

4. [Since morning] no further plans were made [for rescheduling] the picnic.

5. A short distance [from the mountaintop] lay the camp [for the climbers.]

6. The girls went swimming [in the lake] [after supper.]

7. [According to the report,] spring weather was coming [from the South.]

8. [During summer] everyone enjoys the fragrance [of blooming flowers.]

9. We waited [inside the bus depot] [for the bus.]

10. Hikers walked [across the bridge] looking [for the trail] [to the lodge.]

11. Sleeping [under the stars] [at night] is an adventure [for most people.]

12. Jumping [into a lake] [without checking] its depth is foolish [for anyone.]

1. The snowmobile club helped in the rescue of the stranded motorist.

2. Joey skated down the street near the park.

3. The old mill on the Ottertail River was on the historic tour.

4. Since morning no further plans were made for rescheduling the picnic.

5. A short distance from the mountaintop lay the camp for the climbers.

6. The girls went swimming in the lake after supper.

7. According to the report, spring weather was coming from the South.

8. During summer everyone enjoys the fragrance of blooming flowers.

9. We waited inside the bus depot for the bus.

10. Hikers walked across the bridge looking for the trail to the lodge.

11. Sleeping under the stars at night is an adventure for most people.

12. Jumping into a lake without checking its depth is foolish for anyone.

Finding Prepositional Phrases

*Student Directions:
Listen carefully to the
directions your teacher
gives you for finding
each preposition, putting
brackets around each
[prepositional phrase],
and labeling each object
of the preposition with
an "OP".*

and
but
or
for
nor
yet
so

The horse and the mule pulled the tractor and the wagon.
The junior choir or the senior choir will be singing.
First we exercise, but then we run.
He cannot avoid the cold, nor can he stop the wind.
Sally had to hurry, for she was late.

A coordinating conjunction is a word that connects other words, phrases, or clauses of equal importance.

Sample Page 24
Lesson 17

Lesson 17
What Is a Coordinating Conjunction?

Proper Use of Connecting Words Is Important

L56 "We live in a day and age when proper connections are vital for communication. The World Wide Web and the Internet can connect us to every corner of the world. The lightning speed of e-mail is connecting the world faster than 'snail mail' ever dreamed possible.

"An e-mail address, of course, has to be entered precisely. Without precision the right connection is impossible. Thousands of homes and businesses are connecting to thousands of web sites. We have seven words in our language that are like the Internet. They make vital connections in our writing between words, phrases, or sentences. Without these connecting words, the wires of communication go down. We have figuratively been disconnected from our server."

Dictating These Connecting Words

L56 **Step 1 —** *"Turn to page 24 in your* Grammar and Composition Notebook. *Skipping one baseline below the title line, starting each word comfortably close to the left margin line, write the following list of connecting words on consecutive baselines:* **'and', 'but', 'or', 'for', 'nor'.** *You may also add* **'yet'** *and the word* **'so'.** *These last two are not so common as the first five, but we will mention them in case you encounter them."*

L56P Sometimes, to make these connecting words come alive, I refer to them as **"and and but"**, and the **"or, for, nor sisters"**. I use a Norwegian accent when saying the sisters' names to spice it up a bit. We all need a little seasoning, and believe me, grammar is no exception.

When I teach grammar, just for fun, I will often "stand on my head" or "swing from the light fixtures" or "hold my breath for ten minutes" just to get a point across. I mean this figuratively of course, but we must do what is necessary to make our teaching come alive.

Cuddling spiders or petting snakes or wrestling alligators might be going a bit far, but you get the point. Personification is one of those sane things that you can do. The three connecting words **"or"**, **"for"**, and **"nor"** are not just dull, dry parts of speech. They are sisters. Perhaps **"and"** and **"but"** could be brothers. That's it! The family unit comes through again.

It's the "or, for, nor sisters" in concert with their two brothers "and and but" and their distant cousins "yet and so". They are playing an old sweet melody known to all: "The Connecting Word Waltz." It doesn't get much better than this. In the next lesson we use the word picture of a steam driven locomotive. Maybe you could let your students "tie you to the railroad tracks." Here is the bottom line. Word pictures together with a little creativity help students. The best teaching provides visual images to embed abstract concepts.

Word pictures together with a little creativity help students. The best teaching provides visual images to embed abstract concepts.

L56 **Step 2** — *"Skipping one baseline below the word 'so', write the following sentences on consecutive baselines.*

> *'The horse and the mule pulled the tractor and the wagon.'*
>
> *'The junior choir or the senior choir will be singing.'*
>
> *'First we exercise, but then we run.'*
>
> *'He cannot avoid the cold, nor can he stop the wind.'*
>
> *'Sally had to hurry, for she was late.'"*

Discovering the Nature of These Connecting Words

TEACHER: "Look at the first sentence: 'The horse and the mule pulled the tractor and the wagon.' The connecting word 'and' is connecting which words?"

STUDENTS: "It is connecting two sets of words. Horse and mule are connected. Tractor and wagon are connected."

TEACHER: "You are right. Look at the second sentence: 'The junior choir or the senior choir will be singing.' The connecting word 'or' is connecting which two phrases?"

STUDENTS: "It is connecting 'the junior choir' and 'the senior choir'."

L56P Point out again to your students that the job of a connecting word is to connect words, phrases, or sentences. Sometimes when trying to help them understand connecting words and the job they do, I provide another word picture. As we are looking at a sentence using a connecting word, I hook my hands together like a hitch and ask, "What is being joined in this sentence . . . what is being hitched together . . . by these connecting words?" This usually helps the students understand. In the last three examples, the connecting words are joining sentences.

> *A coordinating conjunction is a word that connects other words, phrases, or clauses of equal importance.*

TEACHER: "In the third sentence, what is being connected by the word 'but'?"

STUDENTS: "There are two separate sentences. 'First we exercise' is connected to 'Then we run.' I think I understand what these words do."

TEACHER: "Good. Please note that each of these could be a separate sentence if the writer wanted it that way. We have a special name for these kinds of words that connect other words, phrases or other sentences. We call them **'coordinating conjunctions'**."

L56P Continue your discussion of the remaining sentences in the same manner.

Defining Coordinating Conjunctions

L56 **Step 3 —** *"On your page count up three baselines from the bottom and carefully write the following:* **'A coordinating conjunction is a word that connects other words, phrases, or clauses of equal importance.'** Clauses of equal importance are two or more sentences capable of standing alone if the writer would so choose."

Marking Coordinating Conjunctions for Syntactical Analysis

L56 **Step 4 —** "When we are doing **syntactical analysis** to find out what words are doing in a sentence, we mark these coordinating conjunctions by placing a box around them and writing the abbreviation 'conj.' over the top of each box. Let's mark *each conjunction* in this manner in these sentences."

L56P Refer to Sample Page 24 on page 474 as a guide.

Let's Get Organized

L56 **Step 5 —** *"Turn to the Table of Contents. On the page 24 line, write the title* **'What Is a Coordinating Conjunction?'** *Turn back to page 24. Centered on the title line, between the two red margin lines, write the* **same title.**"

Expectancies Learned and Reinforced in Lesson 17: Dialogue and Review

1. What does a coordinating conjunction do? **L56** *(It connects words or phrases or sentences together.)*

2. What are the seven members of the coordinating conjunction family? **L56** *("and", "but", "or", "for", "nor", "yet", and "so")*

3. How do we mark coordinating conjunctions when we analyze a sentence? **L56** *(We place a box around each one and label the box "conj." which stands for conjunction.)*

4. How do we experience success with language? **L12** *(We develop automaticity with language skills one small step at a time. One reason we are likely to experience success in anything we do is because the whole is broken down into smaller, manageable parts. We master the small things. We start to realize that conquering language is possible when it is broken into smaller, manageable pieces. We learn that details really do matter. We start to think, "I can do this." And when we think we can, we do!)*

Where Do I Go from Here?

- **L56** and **L78** go to **"Lesson 18"** on page 210.

What Materials Will I Need?

- **L56** and **L78** will need *Grammar Notebooks*, pencils, red pencils, and copies of Worksheets for **"Lesson 18"** starting on page 217.

What Is a Coordinating Conjunction?

Teacher Directions: Explain to your student the directions for marking the coordinating conjunctions. Have your students do the worksheet.

Student Directions: Locate the coordinating conjunctions and place a box around each one.

Label each coordinating conjunction by placing a small "conj." above each box.

1. Johnny [*conj.* and] Jared went sailing [*conj.* and] canoeing.

2. The teacher [*conj.* or] the principal would attend the meeting.

3. He wanted to go, [*conj.* but] the car would not start.

4. He worked quickly, [*conj.* yet] carefully.

5. The stories were true, [*conj.* but] the newspaper coverage was slanted.

6. He would not attend, [*conj.* nor] would he take time to talk.

7. In Minnesota [*conj.* and] North Dakota, the weather is a friend [*conj.* and] a foe.

8. Call me [*conj.* or] write me as soon as you can.

9. He was insecure, [*conj.* yet] he remained courageous.

10. He ran uptown, [*conj.* so] I followed on a bicycle.

11. Please turn out the lights, [*conj.* so] I can sleep.

1. Johnny and Jared went sailing and canoeing.

2. The teacher or the principal would attend the meeting.

3. He wanted to go, but the car would not start.

4. He worked quickly, yet carefully.

5. The stories were true, but the newspaper coverage was slanted.

6. He would not attend, nor would he take time to talk.

7. In Minnesota and North Dakota, the weather is a friend and a foe.

8. Call me or write me as soon as you can.

9. He was insecure, yet he remained courageous.

10. He ran uptown, so I followed on a bicycle.

11. Please turn out the lights, so I can sleep.

What Is a Coordinating Conjunction?

Student Directions: Locate the coordinating conjunctions and place a box around each one.

Label each coordinating conjunction by placing a small "conj." above each box.

S + AV
S – AV

A cow eats.
A dog barks.
A bird sings.
A boy walks.
A baby cries.

A simple subject is a word about which
something is being said.
A simple predicate is the main verb
plus any helping verbs.
A simple sentence is a group of words
that makes complete sense.

Sample Page 25
Lesson 18

Note to the Teacher:

In a simple sentence pattern, which contains only a subject or subjects and a predicate or predicates, with coordinating conjunctions (where needed), we have chosen to call the predicate(s) and subject(s) "simple" even if there is more than one of them. For example, in the sentence "The dad and his son fished and swam" there are two predicates and two subjects. When there is more than one predicate and subject, some grammar teachers call them compound predicates and compound subjects.

(continued in the margin of the next page)

Lesson 18

The Three Simples: Sentence Pattern 1

L34P When words are put together to form a complete idea or to make a statement, to ask a question or to give a command, there is a special ordered way in which these words must be arranged. We call these methods of organizing a sentence **"a sentence pattern"**. There are generally four different sentence patterns that exist in English. The next lessons will introduce these patterns together with their component parts. We are taking one step of understanding at a time.

Using a Train to Understand Sentence Patterns

L34P In order to provide a word picture for the first sentence pattern, I usually use a steam-driven locomotive. It is a wonderful word picture that easily explains the nature of a simple sentence. We must have an engine and sometimes more than one to pull a train down the tracks. That engine must also have a source of energy to keep it going. Steam-driven locomotives usually have a coal car. Without the coal car, the engine can go nowhere.

This is the dynamic of a sentence. The simple subject is the engine, and the main verb or action verb provides the energy just like a coal car. I draw on the board, as best I can, a model train complete with cowcatcher and a smokestack. There must be smoke coming from the stack of course. In the engine I write a capital "S". In the coal car that is heaped with coal, I write a capital "AV". Please note the Sample Page provided.

My students laugh as I explain the word picture, but they never forget. Can there be more than one coal car? Yes. I tell my students that we can have as many engines and as many coal cars as we need to get this "train of meaning" down the tracks of someone's mind.

Dictating Sentence Pattern 1

L56   **Step 1 —** *"Turn to page 25 in your* Grammar Notebook.*"*

L34P L34 students should be given a piece of loose-leaf penmanship paper.

L34   *"Skipping one baseline below our title line, starting comfortably close to the left margin line, please write the formula for the first sentence pattern. The formula is 'S + AV'. We will use capital* letters. The 'S' stands for 'Subject'. The 'AV' stands for 'Action Verb'. We all understand action verbs. We can conjugate those."

34 **Step 2** — *"One baseline below the sentence pattern 'S + AV', comfortably close to the left margin line, draw **two boxes connected by a line.** Let me put an example on the board. We want these boxes to look like a train. If we would like to, we can add **wheels.** We can add a **smokestack,** but don't forget the **smoke.** Let's make the second box into a coal car. We had better add **coal** to this coal car. We'll need all the energy we can get. Sometimes cows wander onto the tracks so we had better attach a **cow catcher** to the front of the engine."*

34P How elaborate you want to make this train is up to you. Show the kids on the board what a train like this should look like. Make red pencils available to your students for the next step.

34 **Step 3** — *"Using a red pencil, place an 'S' in the engine and an 'AV' in the coal car. When we learn to analyze sentences, we will use a red pencil so we can see it clearly."*

34P By their very nature action verbs are words of energy. That is what makes writing vibrant. We want our student's writing to come alive. We want them to discover what effective writing involves. They need to understand the dynamic of an action verb. They need to overhaul a few engines and get their fingernails dirty. With syntactical analysis we will provide an avenue for that to happen.

Dictating Our Simple Sentences

34 **Step 4** — *"Skipping one baseline below the train, starting comfortably close to the left margin line, write the following sentence: 'A cow eats'. On the next available baseline, directly below 'A cow eats', write the following sentence: 'A dog barks'. Directly below 'A dog barks', write the following: 'A bird sings'. Below 'A bird sings', write the following: 'A boy walks'. One more sentence to go. Below the sentence 'A boy walks', write the sentence 'A baby cries'."*

L34 **Step 5** — "Let's look at these sentences and find the action verbs and the subjects. The action verbs are the words that we can conjugate. The subjects are what the sentence is talking about. We need to put the right labels over these words."

Understanding the Nature of Syntactical Analysis One Step at a Time:

The First Step

L56P The **first step of syntactical analysis** is to find any prepositional phrases in our sentence. We need to turn to our preposition list in

(continued from the margin of the previous page)

In the next lesson we will distinguish between simple subject(s) and predicate(s) and complete subject(s) and predicate(s). Complete subjects and predicates consist of subjects and predicates plus all the words that influence them, such as adjectives, adverbs, and prepositional phrases.

The Three Simples: Sentence Pattern 1 25
S + AV
S – AV

A cow eats.
A dog barks.
A bird sings.
A boy walks.
A baby cries.

A simple subject is a word about which something is being said.
A simple predicate is the main verb plus any helping verbs.
A simple sentence is a group of words that makes complete sense.

Sample Page 25
Lesson 18

1. A cow eats.

2. A dog barks

3. A bird sings

4. A boy walks.

5. A baby cries.

First Step of Syntactical Analysis:

Are there any prepositions?

Second Step of Syntactical Analysis:

Is there a word that can be conjugated?

our notebook. If we find any prepositional phrases, we [bracket] them and label the object of the preposition "OP". Once we have found all the prepositional phrases, we know that any words that remain unmarked contain the sentence pattern.

L56 **Step 6** — "We are going to analyze these sentences. Our first step when we analyze a sentence is to look for all the prepositions and their objects. We need to use brackets and the label 'OP' when we find a prepositional phrase. Check the preposition list in your *Notebook*. Do you see any prepositions in our first sentence, 'A cow eats'?"

> **STUDENTS:** "In the sentence 'A cow eats', we can find no prepositions and therefore no prepositional phrases."

Step Two of Syntactical Analysis

L56 **Step 7** — "If no prepositional phrases can be found, we move immediately to the second step of syntactical analysis. The **second step of analysis** is to find a word that can be conjugated."

L34 "Let's look at our first simple sentence. We need to find a word that we can conjugate. Can we conjugate the word 'cow' in the present, past, and present perfect tenses? If we can, that word is our verb. If we can't conjugate it correctly, then it is not a verb and we need to keep looking."

L34P Go ahead and try conjugating the word "cow" and see what the kids think. Be dramatic. (Note: There is a verb "cow" which means "to make afraid" or "to intimidate". Its usage is not common: "The girls were cowed in a moment". As the word "cow" is used in our sentence, we cannot conjugate it. It is a noun because the article "the" says it is. We cannot conjugate nouns, but it is fun to try.)

L34 **TEACHER:** "In order to conjugate any verb, we need to first find the three most important parts of the verb. What are the three most important parts of the word 'cow'? Today I cow. Yesterday I cowed. I have cowed. With this information we can begin.

> I cow.   We cow.
> You cow.   You cow.
> He, she, it cows. They cow.
> Cha! Cha! Cha!"

> **TEACHER:** "What do you think? Does this conjugation work for you? It surely works for me!"

> **STUDENTS:** "Uh, earth to teacher. Come in please. Something is not quite right with this example. Teacher? Teacher? Oh, boy. My teacher has lost it. Now what have we done? Someone call '911!'"

TEACHER:	"Can one of you get up and 'cow' for me? Maybe this is a new dance step."

_34P Go ahead and dance the cow for your students. Get lost in the pure absurdity of conjugating a noun that cannot be conjugated. Conjugate until the cows come home if you would like. It will get the point across. We can only conjugate verbs.

_34	**STUDENTS:**	"Hello! Is anybody home? Earth to teacher! Come in please."
	TEACHER:	"Yes, my dear students?"
	STUDENTS:	"You can come down from the light fixtures now and bring your cow with you. We get the point."
	TEACHER:	"Oh good. What point did you get?"
	STUDENTS:	"We cannot conjugate the word 'cow' as it is used in this sentence. Therefore, it cannot be an action or a linking verb. It is doing a different job."
	TEACHER:	"Right. Let's try conjugating another word."
	STUDENTS:	"Oh boy."
	TEACHER:	"Can we conjugate the verb 'eats'? Are there three important parts of this verb that can be isolated?"
	STUDENTS:	"Yes, we can. Today I eat. Yesterday I ate. I have eaten.

> I eat.   We eat.
>
> You eat.   You eat.
>
> He, she, it eats.   They eat.
>
> Cha! Cha! Cha!"

_34P If we have taught the lesson on conjugating well, these answers will fly out of their mouths. The students will say, "Yes, teacher, we can conjugate the verb 'eats', and we know the three most important parts of the word 'eats'." What have they found? They have found the energy word. They have found the action verb.

_34	**TEACHER:**	"Good. If we can conjugate a word and it makes sense, we know it is a verb.
_56	**TEACHER:**	"But is the word 'eats' an action or a linking verb?"
_56	**STUDENTS:**	"It has to be an action verb for two reasons. The first is that the word is not on my linking verb list. The second is that I can see action and motion being done by the word 'eats'. It fits the definition we recorded in our notebook for an action verb."

Third Step of Syntactical Analysis:

Who or what is doing the action of the verb?

L56   TEACHER: "You are certainly extremely sharp students. Have we now determined which word is the energy word? Have we determined which word is the coal car?"

L56   STUDENTS: "Yes, we have. The word 'eats' provides the energy for our sentence."

Step Three of Syntactical Analysis

L34   **Step 8** — "Now let's see if we can find the engine or the subject of our sentence."

L56   "This is the third step of syntactical analysis."

L34   "We need to ask the question 'Who or what does the eating?' First, we find the energy source and then we find the word that gets energized just like the 'Energizer Bunny' on TV. Every sentence must be plugged into an energy source. Every sentence must have a coal car. Some sentences have more than one energy source."

L34   STUDENTS: "I know who or what does the eating—it's the cow!"

L34   TEACHER: "Right. Let's mark this sentence. What should we place over the word 'cow' to let everyone know what job the word 'cow' does?"

L34   STUDENTS: "I'd put a capital 'S' over 'cow'. I also know how we should label the word 'eats'. We write 'AV' over the action verb 'eats'."

L34P   Work through the rest of the sentences already dictated in like manner, labeling the subjects and the action verbs.

L56   STUDENTS: "But what do we do with the article 'a'?"

L56   TEACHER: "Do you remember what job the words 'a', 'an', and 'the' do?"

L56   STUDENTS: "They point to nouns. They always point to nouns."

L56   TEACHER: "That's why we aren't even going to mark them. They know what they do, and we know what they do. There are only three of them. Their job is self-evident."

L56   STUDENTS: "Okay, so we won't mark articles."

Defining the Three Simples

TEACHER: "In our first sentence, we picked out one word to describe what our sentence was talking about. What was that word?"

STUDENTS: "It was the word 'cow'. That is what the sentence is all about."

TEACHER:	"We have a name for a word or words that tell us what the sentence is all about. They are called **simple subjects**. What did we find out about the cow?"
STUDENTS:	"We found out that the cow eats."
TEACHER:	"That's right. We have a name for verbs that tell us about the simple subject. These verbs are called **simple predicates**. So what word is the simple predicate?"
STUDENTS:	"It must be 'eats'. It is saying something about the simple subject."
TEACHER:	"Does the sentence 'The cow eats' make complete sense to you?"
STUDENTS:	"Yes, it does. I understand what these words are saying to me."
TEACHER:	"Here is another name. A group of words that makes complete sense is called a simple sentence."

A simple subject is a word about which something is being said.

A simple predicate is the main verb plus any helping verbs.

A simple sentence is a group of words that makes complete sense.

L34 **Step 9 —** *"Let's count up seven baselines from the bottom of the page and write a definition for a simple subject. This is the first of our three simples. Starting comfortably close to the left margin line, write the following: 'A simple subject is a word about which something is being said'.* The simple subject is always in the center ring of our sentence. Everything in a sentence must somehow relate to the subject. It is usually the one key word about which the rest of the sentence speaks."

L34 "Our second simple is the simple predicate. *On the next baseline, under the definition of a simple subject, comfortably close to the left margin line, please write this definition of a simple predicate: 'A simple predicate is the main verb plus any helping verbs'.* So far we have had two simples: the simple subject and the simple predicate."

L34 "Our third simple is a simple sentence. *On the next baseline under the definition of a simple predicate, starting comfortably close to the left margin line, write the following: 'A simple sentence is a group of words that makes complete sense'."*

Sample Page 25
Lesson 18

Let's Get Organized

L56 **Step 10 —** *"Turn to the Table of Contents. On the page 25 line, write the title 'The Three Simples: Sentence Pattern 1'. Turn back to page 25."*

L34 *"Centered on the title line, between the two red margin lines, write the title: 'The Three Simples: Sentence Pattern 1'."*

Where Do I Go from Here?

- **L34** goes to **"Lesson 34"** on page 335.

- **L56** goes to **"Lesson 19"** on page 219.

- **L78** goes to **"Lesson 13"** on page 164.

What Materials Will I Need?

- **L34** will need penmanship paper, pencils, and copies of Worksheets for **"Lesson 34"** starting on page 348.

- **L56** will need *Grammar Notebooks*, pencils, and red pencils.

- **L78** will need *Grammar Notebooks*, pencils, red pencils, and copies of Worksheets for **"Lesson 13"** starting on page 172.

Expectancies Learned or Reinforced in Lesson 18: Dialogue and Review

1. What is the formula for our first sentence pattern? **L34** *(S+AV)*

2. What do the letters "S + AV" stand for? **L34** *(Subject + Action Verb)*

3. How do you conjugate an action verb? **L34** *(Carefully using what they learned in the lesson on conjugating.)*

4. What is a simple subject? **L34** *(It is the main word in a sentence about which something is being said.)*

5. What is a simple sentence? **L34** *(A simple sentence is a group of words that makes complete sense.)*

6. What do we place at the end of a sentence? **L34** *(We must use an end punctuation mark depending on what kind of a sentence it is. If it is a declarative or imperative sentence, we use a period. If it is an interrogative sentence, we use a question mark. If it is an exclamatory sentence, we use an exclamation point.)*

7. How do we mark simple subjects when we do syntactical analysis? **L56** *(We use a capital "S" directly over the word that is doing the job of the subject.)*

8. How do we mark an action verb when we do syntactical analysis? **L56** *(We use a capital "AV" over the word that is doing the job of an action verb.)*

9. What if we cannot conjugate a word in a sentence? **L56** *(If a word cannot be conjugated, it is not a verb.)*

10. How many engines may pull a sentence down the track of meaning? **L56** *(We may use as many engines as we need.)*

11. How many coal cars may be used to provide energy to the subject? **L56** *(We may use as many coal cars as we need.)*

12. How do we mark articles in a sentence when we do syntactical analysis? **L56** *(We do not need to mark articles. There are only three of them and they always so the same job. They point out nouns. We consider them self-evident.)*

         S+   AV
1.   The cat meows in the morning.

         S+ AV+   AV
2.   The bird sings in the trees and flies among

     the clouds.

         S+   S+ AV
3.   The cow and the horse walk across the field.

         S+   AV+   AV
4.   The player jumps and runs on the court.

         S+   AV
5.   The squirrel scampered up the pole.

         S+   S+   AV
6.   The child and his father flew in the plane.

        S+   AV
7.   Proverbs teach about wisdom.

        S+   S+   AV
8.   Fathers and mothers care about their

     children.

        S+   AV
9.   Ice skaters practice hard.

     S+   S+   S+   AV+
10. Jamie, Sally, and Dominic cheered and

       AV
     celebrated after the basketball game.

       S+   AV
11. Ben Franklin awoke early in the morning.

      S+   AV
12. Kathy performed for the President and the

     First Lady.

Sentence Pattern 1

Teacher Directions: Explain to your students the directions for marking Sentence Pattern 1 sentences.

Student Directions: Find the simple predicate(s) in the following sentences by finding the last word in each sentence which can be conjugated. Determine what kind of a verb it is and label it accordingly. Label action verbs with an "AV". If there are two main verbs, label the second verb also and put a plus sign (+) between them. To find the subject, ask "Who?" or "What?" is doing the action in the sentence. Label the simple subject with an "S". If you have more than one answer to the question "What?" or "Who?", you probably have more than one subject. Label each one and put a plus sign (+) between both subjects. Put a plus sign (+) between the last subject (S) and the first action verb (AV) also.

Sentence Pattern 1

Student Directions: Find the simple predicate(s) in the following sentences by finding the last word in each sentence which can be conjugated.

Determine what kind of a verb it is and label it accordingly. Label action verbs with an "AV". If there are two main verbs, label the second verb also and put a plus sign (+) between them.

To find the subject, ask "Who?" or "What?" is doing the action in the sentence. Label the simple subject with an "S". If you have more than one answer to the question "What?" or "Who?", you probably have more than one subject. Label each one and put a plus sign (+) between both subjects. Put a plus sign (+) between the last subject (S) and the first action verb (AV) also.

1. The cat meows in the morning.

2. The bird sings in the trees and flies among the clouds.

3. The cow and the horse walk across the field.

4. The player jumps and runs on the court.

5. The squirrel scampered up the pole.

6. The child and his father flew in the plane.

7. Proverbs teach about wisdom.

8. Fathers and mothers care about their children.

9. Ice skaters practice hard.

10. Jamie, Sally, and Dominic cheered and celebrated after the basketball game.

11. Ben Franklin awoke early in the morning.

12. Kathy performed for the President and the First Lady.

Lesson 19

What Is a Complete Subject and Predicate?

What Does It Take to Build a Tree House?

L56 Let's pretend for a moment and listen in on a conversation between a teacher and her students.

TEACHER: "If you were going to build a tree house, tell me what materials you would need? Would you need nails?"

STUDENTS: "Oh yes. We would need nails and probably some twine and strong rope to make a rope ladder. We would need a secret way to get into the tree house and a secret password too, like the name of the family dog or cat or goldfish or salamander. We would have to make a special place for all of our pet snakes and frogs."

TEACHER: "I see. Would you need boards of all shapes and sizes?"

STUDENTS: "Yes, we would need boards, but we might also need thick cardboard or plywood or carpet scraps or even chicken wire. It's those kind of details that make a tree house a real tree house. We have to make it nice, you know."

TEACHER: "Yes, of course. Would you leave openings for windows?"

STUDENTS: "Of course we would. What's a tree house without a window or a trap door or two? We need to pay attention to the details. You are always telling us that."

TEACHER: "That's right. I should have known. **In anything that we do, we need to remember to pay attention to the details.** We can't forget the windows and we can't forget the chicken wire. We can't forget the carpet and we can't forget the rope."

STUDENTS: "Now you are catching on."

TEACHER: "Everything has to be just right. A real tree house is a tree house that is complete. We have all the details that we need. Am I right?"

STUDENTS: "You are right. You can visit our tree house

26 What Is a Complete Subject and Predicate?

The old, cranky dog was racing across the yard and under the fence.

A wise man walks through life with open eyes.

A shiny car was parked by the curb.

The baseball player dashed to second base.

The three boys quickly jumped over the ditch into the next field.

The complete subject is the simple subject plus all the words that influence it. A complete predicate is the simple predicate plus all the words that influence it.

Sample Page 26
Lesson 19

In anything that we do, we need to remember to pay attention to the details.

26 | What Is a Complete Subject and Predicate?

The old, cranky dog was racing across the yard and under the fence.

A wise man walks through life with open eyes.

A shiny car was parked by the curb.

The baseball player dashed to second base.

The three boys quickly jumped over the ditch into the next field.

The complete subject is the simple subject plus all the words that influence it. A complete predicate is the simple predicate plus all the words that influence it.

Sample Page 26
Lesson 19

anytime. Just remember the password and bring some candy bars and pop when you come. That's how you get to be an honorary member in our club."

TEACHER: "Would I see any salamanders or frogs or snakes if I came?"

STUDENTS: "Now that is a silly question. It's the details that matter, you know."

Dictating the Details of Tree House Building

L56 **Step 1—** "Sentences are like building a tree house. They have to be complete and they have to pay attention to some important details. *Turn to page 26 in your* Grammar Notebook. *I am going to dictate some sentences. Skipping one baseline under the title line, starting each sentence comfortably close to the left margin line, and skipping one baseline after each complete sentence, let's write the following five sentences:*

> *'The old, cranky dog was racing across the yard and under the fence.'*

> *'A wise man walks through life with open eyes.'*

> *'The shiny car was parked by the curb.'*

> *'The baseball player dashed to second base.'*

> *'The three boys quickly jumped over the ditch into the next field.'*"

Discovering the Nature of Sentence Building: Analyzing a Sentence

First Step of Syntactical Analysis:

Are there any prepositions?

L56P Carefully note the following discussion before having students mark these sentences for analysis. Use the Sample Page as your guide. At this level we expect that the teacher will need to supply both the teacher's and students' portions of this discussion. Then again your students may surprise you. Of course, it is highly unlikely that this particular conversation would take place between teacher and student at first. If you follow it through carefully, the steps to understanding how sentences are built and how words work together will begin to emerge.

L56 **Step 2 —** "Look at the first sentence: The old, cranky dog was racing across the yard and under the fence. Let's take it apart and analyze it. What is our first step?"

STUDENTS: "We need to find the prepositions and their objects and mark them."

TEACHER: "Do you see any prepositions?"

STUDENTS: "The word 'across' is in my list of prepositions. The word 'yard' is its object. The word 'under' is in my list and the word 'fence' is its object. I place square brackets around each prepositional phrase and label each object with an 'OP'."

TEACHER: "That is right. Do you see any other prepositions?"

STUDENTS: "No, but I do see a conjunction. It is doing its job very well. It is connecting two prepositional phrases. I remember from one of our last lessons how to mark that. We place a box around it and label it with a 'conj.'"

TEACHER: "Good. What is the next step?"

STUDENTS: "We need to find the last word that we can conjugate. I believe the word 'was' is in both my linking verb and helping verb list. That might be a clue. Hey, look. The verb 'racing' shows action or motion. It has three important parts. 'Today I race. Yesterday I raced. I have raced.' That means it can be conjugated. The word 'racing' is an action verb, for sure. We have learned that. I need to mark it with an 'AV'. That means that 'was' must be a 'helping verb' and needs to be marked with an 'HV'."

TEACHER: "Wow! You have been listening. We have a name for the main verb and all of its helping verbs. Do you remember what it is?"

STUDENTS: "We learned that in our last lesson. It is called a 'simple predicate'."

TEACHER: "Right. Can you tell me what the simple predicate is in 'the old, cranky dog' sentence?"

STUDENTS: "It has to be 'was racing'."

TEACHER: "Correct. When we combine the simple predicate and all the words that influence that predicate, we call it the 'complete predicate'. The complete predicate gives us more information about the subject. What is the complete predicate in 'the old, cranky dog' sentence?"

STUDENTS: "The complete predicate has to be the verb phrase 'was racing' and the two prepositional phrases 'across the yard' and 'under the fence' plus the conjunction 'and'. The complete predicate is the verb phrase plus those other elements."

TEACHER: "Well done. You have found the complete predicate. Let's keep looking. We haven't accounted for all the words yet. Who or what was racing?"

Second Step of Syntactical Analysis:

Is there a word that can be conjugated?

Fifth Step of Syntactical Analysis:

Are there any describing words? If so, what flags do they fly?

Note to the Teacher:

The fourth step of syntactical analysis is missing from this sample dialogue because the information analyzed in the fourth step is covered in later lessons.

STUDENTS: "Of course the dog was racing and that makes the dog the 'simple subject'. If I ask who or what is doing the action in my sentence, I find the simple subject. Am I right?"

TEACHER: "Yes. How do we label a subject?"

STUDENTS: "We place a capital 'S' over the word."

TEACHER: "Are we done with the analysis yet?"

STUDENTS: "No, not yet. We must find the job that every word is doing. We still have to find out what the words 'old' and 'cranky' do. Let me see. They aren't nouns because they don't name persons, places, or things. They aren't pronouns. They aren't in my preposition list. May I use my flags?"

TEACHER: "I think that is a good idea."

STUDENTS: "'When?' 'Where?' 'Why?' 'How?' 'On What Condition?' 'To What Extent?' 'Old' and 'cranky' don't answer any of those questions. That means they can't be adverbs."

TEACHER: "Keep going."

STUDENTS: "Let me go to the adjective questions. 'What kind?' Hey, I found a question that works. What kind of a dog was this dog? It was an 'old' and 'cranky' dog. Both of these words must be doing the work of an adjective."

TEACHER: "How do we mark adjectives?"

STUDENTS: "We circle adjectives, label them with an 'adj.' above the circle, and draw an arrow to the word they influence. In this case it looks like the word 'dog' is being strongly influenced by these two adjectives. It's not just an ordinary dog. It is an old and cranky dog. I am starting to really understand this."

TEACHER: "Well done. Do we mark the article 'the'?"

STUDENTS: "It is self-evident. Its job never changes. An article always points a noun. We don't need to mark it."

TEACHER: "So what is the simple subject?"

STUDENTS: "It is the word 'dog'."

TEACHER: "We have a name for the simple subject combined with all the words that influence it. We call this part of the sentence the 'complete subject'."

STUDENTS: "That makes sense. If the simple predicate and all the words that influence it is called the 'complete predicate', I guess the simple subject and all the words that influence it could easily be called the 'complete subject',"

TEACHER: "You are right. The simple predicate is the main verb and all its helping verbs. Add to this verb phrase all the words that influence it and we have the complete predicate. The simple subject plus all the words that influence it is called the complete subject. I think you are ready to tackle the other sentences."

.56P Analyze and mark the rest of the sentences the students have recorded using the same line of reasoning presented in the preceding dialogue. Use the Sample Page on page 476 as a guide.

Defining a Complete Subject and a Complete Predicate

.56 **Step 3** — *"Counting up four baselines from the bottom on page 26 of your* Notebook, *comfortably close to the left margin line, please write the following:* **'The complete subject is the simple subject plus all the words that influence it'.**

"On the baseline just below the definition of a complete predicate, comfortably close to the left margin line, write the following: **'A complete predicate is the simple predicate plus all the words that influence it'."**

Let's Get Organized

.56 **Step 4** — *"Turn to the Table of Contents. On the page 26 line, write the title* **'What Is a Complete Subject and Predicate?'** *Turn back to page 26. Centered on the title line, between the two red margin lines, write the* **same title."**

Expectancies Learned or Reinforced in Lesson 19: Dialogue and Review

1. What is the simple predicate? **L34** *(It is the main verb and its helping verb or verbs.)*

2. What is the complete predicate? **L56** *(It is the main verb and its helping verb or verbs plus all the words that influence it.)*

3. What is the key word in any sentence about which the predicate speaks? **L34** *(This key word is called the simple subject.)*

4. What is the complete subject? **L56** *(It is the simple subject plus all the words that influence the simple subject.)*

Sample Page 26
Lesson 19

The complete subject is the simple subject plus all the words that influence it.

A complete predicate is the simple predicate plus all the words that influence it.

5. What is the first step of syntactical analysis? **L56** *(The first step requires that we locate and mark all prepositions and their objects.)*

6. What is the second step in syntactical analysis? **L56** *(The second step is to locate and mark correctly the last word in our sentence that can be conjugated and then find helping verbs if there are any.)*

7. What is the third step in syntactical analysis? **L56** *(The third step is to find and mark the simple subject by asking who or what is doing the action if the main verb is an action verb.)*

8. What is the fifth step we learned in syntactical analysis? **L56** *(The fifth step is to fly our adjective or adverb flags over the words not yet accounted for, determine which word they influence, and then mark them accordingly.)*

9. What do we learn when we do syntactical analysis? **L56** *(We learn how and why words work together as they do. To know what words can do will make us a better writer.)*

10. What responsibility does each word in a sentence have? **L56** *(Each word must be responsible to do its job.)*

Further Reinforcement of This Lesson

L56P Before we do additional worksheet exercises, we will cover the material in the next two lessons. At the end of **"Lesson 21,"** you will find two worksheets that will both reinforce this lesson on complete subjects and predicates as well as the material in the two lessons that follow.

Where Do I Go from Here?

- **L56** and **L78** go to **"Lesson 20"** on page 225.

What Materials Will I Need?

- **L56** and **L78** will need *Grammar Notebooks*, pencils, and red pencils.

Lesson 20

What Is Sentence Pattern 2?

L56P The English simple sentence can be quite predictable. That is why we introduce sentence patterns. The first sentence pattern was S + AV. Your students have worked with and analyzed these kinds of sentences. Let's take our students to the next sentence pattern.

Dictating Sentence Pattern 2: The Blueprint

L56 **Step 1** — "When a carpenter builds a house, he follows a pattern called a blueprint. Different blueprints make different houses. It is a step-by-step process. In English, we also have a number of different blueprints called sentence patterns. We use these to build different kinds of sentences.

"Turn to page 27 in your Grammar Notebook. *Skipping one baseline below the title line and starting comfortably close to the left margin line, let's write the formula for our next sentence pattern:* **'S + AV——→DO'.** We have seen the first part of this pattern before. Do you remember what the symbols mean?"

> **STUDENTS:** "The 'S' stands for subject. The 'AV' stands for action verb."

> **TEACHER:** "Great."

L56 **Step 2** — "Let's draw another train. *On the next available baseline below the formula for Sentence Pattern 2, let's create an **engine** followed by a **coal car**, and then we are going to add a **caboose**.* It might look something like this."

L56P Refer to the Sample Page in your margin.

What Is the Difference between a Transitive and Intransitive Verb?

L78 **TEACHER:** "The caboose is very important. The first pattern was missing one. Just for fun, let's say that every train must have a caboose in order to call it a genuine train. Genuine trains need cabooses. If a train is missing a caboose, is Sentence Pattern 1 (S + AV) a genuine train?"

> **STUDENTS:** "No. According to what you have said, if it is missing a caboose, it cannot be a genuine train. You said that genuine trains need cabooses."

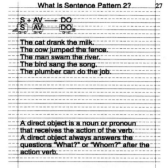

What Is Sentence Pattern 2? 27

S + AV —— DO
S   AV ——→ DO

The cat drank the milk.
The cow jumped the fence.
The man swam the river.
The bird sang the song.
The plumber can do the job.

A direct object is a noun or pronoun that receives the action of the verb. A direct object always answers the questions "What?" or "Whom?" after the action verb.

Sample Page 27
Lesson 20

L78 **TEACHER:** "Just to play with words a little, let's call Sentence Pattern 2 (S + AV———⟩ DO) a 'train' and Sentence Pattern 1 (S + AV) an 'intrain'. What can the prefix 'in' mean?"

STUDENTS: "It can mean 'not'. So you are saying that, by definition, the first sentence pattern is not a genuine train."

TEACHER: "That is right. We have a special name for verbs that pull cabooses. We call an action verb that pulls a caboose a 'train'sitive verb. An action verb that does not pull a caboose is called an 'intrain'sitive verb. Now the real terms are 'transitive' and 'intransitive', but students often have a hard time remembering those terms. Can you remember this play on words?"

STUDENTS: "I think I can. The action verb is transitive if there is a caboose. The action verb is intransitive if there is no caboose."

TEACHER: "That is correct."

Dictating Sentence Pattern 2 Sentences

L56 **Step 3 —** *"Skipping one baseline below our train and starting comfortably close to the margin line, please write the following sentences on consecutive baselines:*

> *'The cat drank the milk.'*
> *'The cow jumped the fence.'*
> *'The man swam the river.'*
> *'The bird sang the song.'*
> *'The plumber can do the job.'"*

L56P We always need to provide enough examples for our students. Create new sentences when needed using Ayres List words or other words that they have already mastered. Slowly but surely the mystery of written language will be unlocked. We want our students to be on their way to mastery.

Discovering the Nature of Sentence Pattern 2

L56 **Step 4 —** "We are going to concentrate on analyzing some Sentence Pattern 2 sentences. If we carefully follow the steps we have learned so far, I think we can figure out what each word's job is and why these sentences work so well. What is the first step in syntactical analysis?"

STUDENTS: "We need to find the prepositions and their objects."

TEACHER: "Do you see any in our first sentence, 'The cat drank the milk'?"

What Is Sentence Pattern 2?   27

S + AV ——⟩ DO
S — AV — DO

The cat drank the milk.
The cow jumped the fence.
The man swam the river.
The bird sang the song.
The plumber can do the job.

A direct object is a noun or pronoun that receives the action of the verb.
A direct object always answers the questions "What?" or "Whom?" after the action verb.

Sample Page 27
Lesson 20

First Step of Syntactical Analysis:

Are there any prepositions?

STUDENTS:	"No, but I do see our second step working."
TEACHER:	"What is that?"
STUDENTS:	"The second step is to find the last word that we can conjugate. The word 'drank' has the three important parts of a verb. Therefore, it can be conjugated. By definition it is an action verb. We would mark 'drank' with an 'AV'."
TEACHER:	"Very good. Let's look at the third step. Who or what is doing the drinking?"
STUDENTS:	"It is the cat. We mark the word 'cat' with an 'S' because it is our simple subject. We don't need to mark the word 'the' because the job of an article is self-evident."
TEACHER:	"We do not know what job the word 'milk' is doing just yet. Let's find out. Is there a word in our sentence that answers the questions 'What?' or 'Whom?'"
STUDENTS:	"The word 'milk' answers the question, 'What did the cat drink?'"
TEACHER:	"Adjectives have their flags. Adverbs have their flags. Direct Objects also have their flags. They are all different. The flags a direct object flies are 'What?' or 'Whom?' If we have a word that answers one of these two questions after an action verb, we know that the word is doing the job of a direct object. We label it with a 'DO'. In this first sentence, the word 'milk' is our direct object. It receives the action of the verb. The cat is drinking the milk. All direct objects are targets for the action of the verb. What do we place over the word 'milk'?"
STUDENTS:	"We place a 'DO' over this word."
L78 TEACHER:	"Is the verb 'drank' a 'train'sitive or 'intrain'sitive verb?"
STUDENTS:	"It has to be a 'train'sitive verb because we have a caboose. We call a caboose a 'direct object' if it flies the flags 'What?' or 'Whom?' If we were missing the caboose, we would have an 'intrain'."
TEACHER:	"Well said. Intransitive verbs have no direct object."
L56 TEACHER:	"Let's analyze some more sentences after you have marked this first sentence."

L56P Continue to work through the remaining sentences to reinforce an understanding of syntactical analysis and the direct object.

Second Step of Syntactical Analysis:

Is there a word that can be conjugated?

Third Step of Syntactical Analysis:

Who or what is doing the action of the verb?

Fourth Step of Syntactical Analysis:

Who or what receives the action of the verb?

Fifth Step of Syntactical Analysis:

Are there any describing words? If so, what flags do they fly?

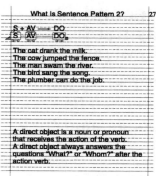

Sample Page 27
Lesson 20

Defining a Direct Object

L56 **Step 5** — *"Turn to the Table of Contents. On the page 27 line, write the title* **'What Is Sentence Pattern 2?'** *Turn back to page 27. Centered on the title line, between the two red margin lines, write the* **same title."**

L56 **Step 6** — *"Count up six baselines from the bottom of page 27. Comfortably close to the left margin line write the definition for a direct object:* **'A direct object is a noun or pronoun that receives the action of a verb. A direct object always answers the questions "What?" or "Whom?" after the action verb'."**

Expectancies Learned or Reinforced in Lesson 20: Dialogue and Review

1. What is Sentence Pattern 2? **L56** *(S + AV—→DO)*

2. Why do we need to use sentence patterns? **L56** *(Sentence patterns give us strong sentences.)*

3. What question does a direct object answer after the action verb? **L56** *("What?" or "Whom?")*

4. What job does the direct object do? **L56** *(It becomes the target for the action of the verb. The subject and the action verb work together to hit this target.)*

5. What kind of an action verb has a direct object? **L78** *(It is a transitive verb. The root "trans" can mean "to carry". A transitive verb is actually carrying its energy and its energized subject and dropping both of them squarely on the direct object.)*

6. What kind of an action verb has no direct object? **L78** *(It is an intransitive verb. It is an action verb, but it is carrying its energy to no particular word. It is missing the caboose.)*

7. Why does every word have a job to do? **L56** *(It is the nature of language. Words are able to do work so we can communicate ideas and thoughts. Our future success depends on effective communication. We must learn to harness these workhorses in order to empower our writing.)*

8. What is syntactical analysis? **L56** *(It is the accounting of every job that each word in a sentence does.)*

9. What are the steps of syntactical analysis that we have learned so far? **L56** *(1. Find the prepositional phrases. 2. Find the last word we can conjugate. 3. Find the simple subject. 4. Find the direct object. 5. Find the adjectives and adverbs.)*

Where Do I Go from Here?

- **L56** and **L78** go to **"Lesson 21"** on page 229.

What Materials Will I Need?

- **L56** and **L78** will need *Grammar Notebooks,* pencils, red pencils, and copies of Worksheets for **"Lesson 21"** starting on page 233.

Lesson 21
What Is Sentence Pattern 3?

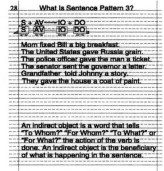

Sample Page 28
Lesson 21

Sentence Patterns: They Are Everywhere We Go

L56 "As you read newspapers and magazines or listen to radio or television, you will see and hear sentence patterns wherever you turn. Without these patterns there can be no English sentences. These patterns are the trains used to transport meaning to our minds. They move down the tracks of language loaded with cargo. Getting that cargo of meaning to its destination is what writing and communicating is all about.

"Well-written sentences never derail. Good writers work hard to transport ideas smoothly and efficiently from their mind to the reader's mind. This lesson teaches us about another one of these Sentence Patterns. **Sentence Pattern 3 sentences have a subject, an action verb, a direct object, and one additional railway car.** Let's find out what the new car is."

Dictating Sentence Pattern 3: The Blueprint

L56P Remember that **L56** and **L78** continue to work in the *Grammar Notebook*. The **"Scope and Sequence"** is only a suggested order. It is subject to the needs of the student. If you feel that a lower level student needs to understand sentence patterns or any other lesson before the **"Scope and Sequence"** gets them there, by all means do not hesitate to introduce it. Continue to use the Sample Pages included in the margin of each lesson as a guide.

L56 **Step 1 —** *"Turn to page 28 in your* Grammar Notebook. *Skipping one baseline under the title line, starting comfortably close to the left margin line, write the following blueprint for this new sentence pattern: 'S + AV→IO + DO'.* We are adding a new car to our train. It is an extra passenger car.

"Do we need an extra passenger car to get down the tracks? Sometimes we do. In order to say what we really need to say, we need to choose just the right words at just the right time. We call this new passenger car an **'indirect object'.** In analysis we label an indirect object with an **'IO'.**"

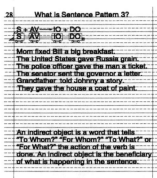

*Precise grammar
builds syntactical
expectancies at an
automatic level.*

*Syntactical Analysis
builds sentence
sense.*

L56 **Step 2 —** *"On the next available baseline below our new pattern, let's draw another **train** together. We need the **engine** for our **subject**. We need the **coal car** for our **verb**. The **next car** will be our **indirect object**. The **caboose** will be our **direct object**.* Place the appropriate labels inside each car or engine. When you are finished, it should look like mine."

Dictating Sentences That Use Sentence Pattern 3

L56 **Step 3 —** *"Skipping one baseline below our train and starting comfortably close to the margin line, please write the following sentences on consecutive baselines:*

> *'Mom fixed Bill a big breakfast.'*
> *'The United States gave Russia grain.'*
> *'The police officer gave the man a ticket.'*
> *'The senator sent the governor a letter.'*
> *'Grandfather told Johnny a story.'*
> *'They gave the house a coat of paint.'"*

Discovering the Nature of an Indirect Object

L56 **Step 4 —** *"Do you know what the word 'beneficiary' means?"*

STUDENTS: "I am afraid I do not."

TEACHER: "What do we do if we do not know what a word means?"

STUDENTS: "We head for our trusty dictionary."

TEACHER: "And what does it say 'beneficiary' means?"

STUDENTS: "The word 'beneficiary' means 'one that benefits from something'. That is what the dictionary says."

TEACHER: "Look at this sentence: *'My mother gave Kari presents'*. Can you see who is benefiting from the gift giving?"

STUDENTS: "It is Kari. She must be the beneficiary."

TEACHER: "That is right. And just like adjectives and adverbs and direct objects have their particular flags, so do indirect objects. There are four different flags that tell you if a word is doing the job of an indirect object. You need to know these questions. An indirect object answers the questions 'To Whom?' 'For Whom?' 'To What?' and 'For What?'"

Let's look at the first sentence we have written. If 'Mom' is the subject of our sentence and 'fixed' is our action verb, and we have used the direct object flags to find that the word 'breakfast' is our caboose, how do we go about finding the 'beneficiary' of the action of our sentence? Who benefits from Mom fixing a big breakfast?"

STUDENTS: "Bill does."

TEACHER: "Right. If we can find the person benefiting from the sentence's message, we have found the indirect object. What are the indirect object questions again?"

STUDENTS: "The questions are 'To Whom?' 'For Whom?' 'To What?' or 'For What?'"

TEACHER: "So let's use one of them and see if we are right. Mom fixed a big breakfast 'For Whom?'"

STUDENTS: "The answer is 'Bill'. 'Bill' is the indirect object. 'Bill' is the one in the sentence that is benefiting from Mom's actions."

TEACHER: "Good job. How do we mark an indirect object?"

STUDENTS: "We place an 'IO' over the word that is doing the work of an indirect object. But it seems that IO's aren't doing much work. They just sit around and get all the benefits."

TEACHER: "I guess we have to think that receiving benefits is a hard job. Somebody or something has to do it. Wouldn't you like chores at home like getting gifts, or receiving money, or having people do things for you?"

STUDENTS: "I think I could handle being an indirect object."

L56P Have students do syntactical analysis and properly mark the rest of the sentences on their notebook page. For review encourage students to create these kinds of sentences on their own. Making an indirect object work in a sentence is sometimes a challenge. See what you can do.

Defining an Indirect Object

L56   **Step 5** — *"From the bottom of page 28, count up six baselines and write the following: 'An indirect object is a word that tells "To Whom?" "For Whom?" "To What?" or "For What?" the action of the verb is done. An indirect object is the beneficiary of what is happening in the sentence'."*

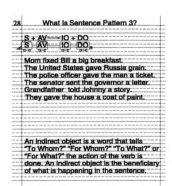

Sample Page 28
Lesson 21

Let's Get Organized

L56 **Step 6-** *"Turn to the Table of Contents. On the page 28 line, write the title **'What Is Sentence Pattern 3?'** Turn back to page 28. Centered on the title line, between the two red margin lines, write the **same title.""***

Expectancies Learned or Reinforced in Lesson 21: Dialogue and Review

1. What is an indirect object? **L56** *(An indirect object is the beneficiary of the action of the sentence.)*

2. What questions does an indirect object answer? **L56** *("To Whom?" or "For Whom?" or "To What?" or "For What?")*

3. What is the blueprint for Sentence Pattern 3? **L56** *(S + AV———→IO + DO)*

4. How do I do syntactical analysis? **L56** *(I must take one step at a time in the proper sequence.)*

Where Do I Go from Here?

- **L56** goes to **"Lesson 42"** on page 422.

- **L78** goes to **"Lesson 23"** on page 243.

What Materials Will I Need?

- **L56** and **L78** will need *Grammar Notebooks*, pencils, and red pencils.

©1998 Grammar Works/Holly Hall Publications, Inc.

                    S+   AV   adv.   OP
1. The path swerved (sharply) to the right.]

        S+   conj.   S+   AV→ DO   adj.
2. Malamutes [and] huskies have wolf [in (their)
    OP
   heritage.]

        S+   HV+   HV+   AV   adj.
3. Chimneys should be cleaned [after (each)
    adj.   OP
   (burning) season.]

        S+   OP   AV→
4. Deposits [from the Mississippi River] build a
   DO   OP
   delta [near New Orleans.]

     S+   AV   adv.   OP
5. Sue walked (slowly) through the store.]

        S+   AV →IO +   DO
6. Grandfather gave Sammy the cake.

           S+   AV→ DO + DO+ conj. DO
7. The zoo had lions, tigers, [and] bears.

   interj.
   Oh my!

     S+   AV ———→ DO+ conj.   DO
8. We own a goldfish [and] a parrot.

     S+   AV ———→ adj. DO+ conj.   adj.
9. We sighted a (bald) eagle [and] a (red-tailed)
     DO   OP
   hawk [on our field trip.]

           S+   AV ——→ adj.   IO+ DO
10. The lawyer fed the (fax) machine letters [for
   adj. OP
   (his) client.]

What Is a Complete Subject and Predicate?

What Is Sentence Pattern 2?

What Is Sentence Pattern 3?

Teacher Directions: Explain to your student the directions and sequence for analyzing sentences on the following worksheet.

These directions are included on the actual student worksheet. They should be getting to know this sequence better and better.

What Is a Complete Subject and Predicate?

What Is Sentence Pattern 2?

What Is Sentence Pattern 3?

*Student Directions:
Analyze the sentences using
these five steps.
1. Find the prepositions and
their objects first. Label
these using [brackets] and
the "OP".
2. Find the last word you
can conjugate together with
its helping verb(s) and
label with "HV" or "AV"
accordingly.
3. Ask the questions
"Who?" or "What?" is
doing the action of the verb.
These are the subject(s).
Label these with an "S".
4. Find all the words that
are flying flags. Circle the
adjectives and adverbs,
label the circled words with
"adj." or "adv." and draw
an arrow to the word they
influence. Label the DO. It
is flying the flag "What?"
or "Whom?" Label the IO.
It is flying the flag "To
Whom?" "For Whom?"
"To What?" or "For
What?"
5. Put boxes around
conjunctions and label
them with a "conj."*

1. The path swerved sharply to the right.

2. Malamutes and huskies have wolf in their heritage.

3. Chimneys should be cleaned after each burning season.

4. Deposits from the Mississippi River build a delta near New Orleans.

5. Sue walked slowly through the store.

6. Grandfather gave Sammy the cake.

7. The zoo had lions, tigers, and bears. Oh my!

8. We own a goldfish and a parrot.

9. We sighted a bald eagle and a red-tailed hawk on our field trip.

10. The lawyer fed the fax machine letters for his client.

1. The cats slept (quietly) [in the sun.]
   S+ AV adv. OP

2. The (four-wheel drive) jeep went [through the ice.]
   adj. S+ AV OP

3. Mother picked (fresh) beans [from the garden.]
   S+ AV→ adj. DO OP

4. Molly threw Sally the ball.
   S+ AV→ IO+ DO

5. Mike made bread, [and] Betsy made chili.
   S+ AV→ DO conj. S+ AV→ DO

6. Maren fed the lambs [with a bottle.]
   S+ AV→ DO OP

7. A (wool) sweater is welcomed [on a (cool) evening.]
   adj. S+ HV+ AV adj. OP

8. The (young) (baseball) player ran (three) miles [at (every) practice.]
   adj. adj. S+ AV→ adj. DO adj. OP

9. The pictures [of (our) (old) depot] were printed [in the magazine.]
   S+ adj. adj. OP HV+ AV OP

10. The (chess) champion won (six) matches [and] lost (only) (two) matches.
    adj. S+ AV→ adj. DO+ conj. AV→ adv. adj. DO

11. The White House sent the Pentagon a (coded) message.
    S+ AV→ IO+ adj. DO

Teacher's Answer Key for Student Worksheet 2:

What Is a Complete Subject and Predicate?

What Is Sentence Pattern 2?

What Is Sentence Pattern 3?

Teacher Directions: Explain to your student the directions and sequence for analyzing sentences on the following worksheet.

These directions are included on the actual student worksheet. They should be getting to know this sequence better and better.

Student Worksheet 2:

What Is a Complete Subject and Predicate?

What Is Sentence Pattern 2?

What Is Sentence Pattern 3?

Student Directions:
Analyze the sentences using these five steps.
1. Find the prepositions and their objects first. Label these using [brackets] and the "OP".
2. Find the last word you can conjugate together with its helping verb(s) and label with "HV" or "AV" accordingly.
3. Ask the questions "Who?" or "What?" is doing the action of the verb. These are the subject(s). Label these with an "S".
4. Find all the words that are flying flags. Ⓒircle the adjectives and adverbs, label the circled words with "adj." or "adv." and draw an arrow to the word they influence. Label the DO. It is flying the flag "What?" or "Whom?" Label the IO. It is flying the flag "To Whom?" "For Whom?" "To What?" or "For What?"
5. Put ⌐boxes¬ around conjunctions and label them with a "conj."

1. The cats slept quietly in the sun.

2. The four-wheel drive jeep went through the ice.

3. Mother picked fresh beans from the garden.

4. Molly threw Sally the ball.

5. Mike made bread, and Betsy made chili.

6. Maren fed the lambs with a bottle.

7. A wool sweater is welcomed on a cool evening.

8. The young baseball player ran three miles at every practice.

9. The pictures of our old depot were printed in the magazine.

10. The chess champion won six matches and lost only two matches.

11. The White House sent the Pentagon a coded message.

Lesson 22
What Is Sentence Pattern 4A?

L78P Most students will have been introduced to the three main sentence patterns that use an action verb before they get to this lesson. Your students should be able to recognize the use of those patterns. They have had practice recognizing those patterns and their component parts.

The final pattern that will be introduced in the next three lessons has three possible forms. Each form uses a linking verb. Your students will soon need to know the linking verb list as recorded in **"Lesson 12: 'What Is a Linking Verb?"**

Dictating Sentence Pattern 4A: The Blueprint

L78　**Step 1** —"We have one more sentence pattern that we need to learn. It comes in three different forms, but in this lesson we will only look at the first form.

"Turn in your Grammar Notebook to page 29. Skipping one baseline under the title line, beginning comfortably close to the left margin line, please write the following formula for Sentence Pattern 4A: 'S + LV'. What do you think the 'LV' stands for?"

STUDENTS: "It must stand for 'linking verb'."

TEACHER: "We have been practicing the linking verb list. Can you say this list for me? You should be able to say it in your sleep."

STUDENTS: "'Am', 'is', 'are', 'was', 'were', 'becomes', 'appears', 'seems', 'feels', 'tastes', 'looks', 'grows', 'smell', 'sound', 'stay', 'remain', and any other form of the verb 'to be' ('be', 'being', or 'been')."

TEACHER: "That was wonderful. We will need to know this list as we work with these next patterns."

L78P Remember to consistently review skills such as conjugating verbs and reciting the linking verb list. Go to the various checklists and make sure their automaticity in these areas is in place. There is no substitute for consistent practice and review over time.

L78　**Step 2** — *"Let's make another train under the formula for Sentence Pattern 4A. This time we will label the coal car 'LV' instead of 'AV'."*

S + LV
S - LV

Present Tense

I am.	We are.
You are.	You are.
He, she, it is.	They are.

Past Tense

I was.	We were.
You were.	You were.
He, she, it was.	They were.

Present Perfect Tense

I have been.	We have been.
You have been.	You have been.
He, she, it has been.	They have been.

Sentence Pattern 4A has at least one subject and one linking verb.

Sample Page 29
Lesson 22

30　Sentence Pattern 4A (continued)

Past Perfect Tense

I had been.	We had been.
You had been.	You had been.
He, she, it had been.	They had been.

Future Tense

I will be.	We will be.
You will be.	You will be.
He, she, it will be.	They will be.

Future Perfect Tense

I will have been.	We will have been.
You will have been.	You will have been.
He, she, it will have been.	They will have been.

I am in the water.
He will be on time.
They were inside the house.
We had been below deck.
She has been in the pool.

Sample Page 30
Lesson 22

Conjugating the Linking Verb "To Be" in All Six Tenses

L78 **Step 3 —** "In order to understand this pattern, we need to learn how to conjugate the verb 'to be' in all of its tenses in both the singular and the plural. It is an irregular verb and can cause some problems. The linking verbs 'am', 'is', 'are', 'was', and 'were' are all used. In the **Present Perfect Tense**, we use the helping verb 'have' and add 'been', which is another form of the verb 'to be'. Listen as I conjugate this verb in the **Present, Past, and Present Perfect Tense**, singular and plural."

	Singular	*Plural*
Present Tense	I am. You are. He, she, it is.	We are. You are. They are.
Past Tense	I was. You were. He, she, it was.	We were. You were. They were.
Present Perfect Tense	I have been. You have been. He, she, it has been.	We have been. You have been. They have been.

L78 **Step 4 —** "We will need to practice this conjugation until we know it well. For now we need to record these various tenses of the verb 'to be' in your notebook. Listen to me as I tell you where these conjugations need to go. *Divide page 29 into two columns. In the first column we will write the 'Singular' forms of the verb 'to be'. In the second column we will write the 'Plural' forms.*"

L78 **Step 5 —** "*On the next available baseline below your train diagram, center the subtitle 'Present Tense' between the red margin lines. Starting one baseline below in the first column, with each sentence of the conjugation comfortably close to the left margin line, write the present tense of the verb 'to be' on consecutive baselines in the singular forms: 'I am.' 'You are.' 'He, she, it is.' In the same manner in the second column, write the present tense of the verb 'to be' in the plural forms: 'We are.' 'You are.' 'They are.'*"

Dictating the Past Tense and the Present Perfect Tense of the Linking Verb "To Be" on Your Own

L78P Using Sample Page 29 in your margin as a guide, dictate the **Past Tense** and the **Present Perfect Tense** of the verb "to be" using the same method used in preceding steps. Skip one baseline if you need to. Center a subtitle if you need to. Begin writing comfortably close to a margin line if you need to. Have your students practice conjugating the verb "to be" on a daily basis until they can conjugate this verb automatically.

Defining Sentence Pattern 4A

L78 **Step 6 —** *"Counting up two baselines from the bottom, beginning comfortably close to the left margin line, write the following definition: 'Sentence Pattern 4A has at least one subject and one linking verb'."*

Let's Get Organized

L78 **Step 7 —** *"Turn to the Table of Contents. On the page 29 line, write the title 'What Is Sentence Pattern 4A?' Turn back to page 29. Centered on the title line, between the two red margin lines, write the **same title**."*

Conjugating the Verb "To Be" in the Past Perfect, Future, and Future Perfect Tenses

TEACHER: **Step 1 —** "We are not done with the verb 'to be'. How do we conjugate the verb 'to be' in the **Past Perfect Tense?** We must use the helping verb 'had'."

STUDENTS: "I had been.   We had been.
You had been.   You had been.
He, she, it had been.   They had been."

TEACHER: "Wonderful. Let's look at the remaining two tenses of the verb 'to be'. The **Future Tense** uses the helping verbs 'will' or 'shall'. Listen as I conjugate this tense.

"I will be.   We will be.
You will be.   You will be.
He, she, it will be.   They will be.

"The **Future Perfect Tense** uses the helping verb 'will' or 'shall' and 'have', and then adds 'been' which is a different form of the verb 'to be'. Listen as I conjugate this tense.

"I will have been. We will have been.
You will have been. You will have been.
He, she, it will have been. They will have been."

Dictating the Past Perfect, Future, and Future Perfect Tenses of the Verb "To Be"

L78 **Step 2** — *"Turn to page 30 in your* Grammar Notebook. *Divide the page into two equal columns. Skipping one baseline below the title line, center the subtitle* **'Past Perfect Tense'** *between the two red margin lines."*

Step 3 — *"Starting one baseline below this subtitle in the first column, with each sentence of the conjugation comfortably close to the left margin line, write the past perfect tense of the verb 'to be' on consecutive baselines in the singular forms:* **'I had been.' 'You had been.' 'He, she, it had been.'** *In the same manner in the second column, write the past perfect tense of the verb 'to be' in the plural forms:* **'We had been.' 'You had been.' 'They had been.'"**

L78P Using Sample Page 30 in your margin as a guide, dictate the **Future Tense** and the **Future Perfect Tense** of the verb "to be" using the same method used in the preceding steps. It is important to have your students practice conjugating the verb "to be" in these various sentences on a daily basis until they can conjugate this verb automatically.

Dictating Sentences Using Sentence Pattern 4A

L78 **Step 4** — *"Skipping one baseline below 'He, she, it will have been', write the following sentences comfortably close to the margin on consecutive baselines:*

> **'I am in the water.'**
> **'He will be on time.'**
> **'They were inside the house.'**
> **'We had been below deck.'**
> **'She has been in the pool.'"**

L78 **Step 5** — *"Analyze these sentences.* **[Bracket]** *each prepositional phrase and mark the object with an* **'OP'**. *Find the linking verbs and label them with an* **'LV'**. *Identify the helping verbs and label them with an* **'HV'**. *Mark each subject with an* **'S'**."

L78P Your student should be able to account for all the words in these sentences. Use the Sample Page on page 480 as a guide.

---

30 | Sentence Pattern 4A (continued)

Past Perfect Tense
I had been. We had been.
You had been. You had been.
He, she, it had been. They had been.

Future Tense
I will be. We will be.
You will be. You will be.
He, she, it will be. They will be.

Future Perfect Tense
I will have been. We will have been.
You will have been. You will have been.
He, she, it will have been. They will have been.

I am in the water.
He will be on time.
They were inside the house.
We had been below deck.
She has been in the pool.

Sample Page 30
Lesson 22

Let's Get Organized

L78 **Step 6 —** *"Turn to the Table of Contents. On the page 30 line, write the title* **'Sentence Pattern 4A (continued)'**. *Turn back to page 30. Centered on the title line, between the two red margin lines, write the* **same title.***"*

Mastery is Important

L78P As teachers we can determine if our students have mastered the skill we have taught. We can ask them to conjugate a verb in the six tenses. We can ask them to give us the linking verb list. We can drill irregular verbs. We can check the handwriting in their notebooks to see if they are exercising that particular attention to detail. We can place sentences before them that require syntactical analysis and watch to see if they follow the step-by-step sequence necessary to find out what job words do.

This method is direct teacher–student instruction. Dictation is hard work. Practicing to bring mastery to students is hard work, but my experience with children who just can't figure out language tells me that syntactical skills and understanding about how language works dare not be left to chance. We must use directed discovery and not inductive discovery. We must be sequential and incremental. We must practice carefully so that language skills become permanent.

Excellence does not come without a price. Personal discipline is necessary. Attention to detail matters. Success in the field of music, in the field of science, on the way to the Olympics, at the Oscars, at the Grammies, or at our chosen vocation comes because skills are important. How much more important is the successful instruction of our children in language skills which are the bedrock foundation for anything they will ever do. Thank you for caring. Please persevere in your pursuit of excellence.

Expectancies Learned or Reinforced in Lesson 22: Dialogue and Review

1. What are the three most important parts of the verb "to be"?
   L78 *(Today I am. Yesterday I was. I have been.)*

2. How do you conjugate the verb 'to be' in all six English tenses?
   L78 *(Students may need to look in Lesson 22 in their Notebooks.)*

3. What is Sentence Pattern 4A? **L78** *(S + LV)*

Dictation is hard work. Practice to bring mastery to students is hard work, but my experience with children who just can't figure out language tells me that syntactical skills and understanding about how language works dare not be left to chance. We must use directed discovery and not inductive discovery. We must be sequential and incremental. We must practice carefully so that language skills become permanent.

4. Why is it important that I know my linking verb list? **L78** *(Knowing this list gives me a quick reference point so that I can tell the difference between an action verb and a linking verb and a helping verb.)*

5. What does successful dictation do for a student? **L78** *(The process creates a mind that is well practiced in the art of listening.)*

6. How do we mark linking verbs? **L78** *(They need to be marked with an LV.)*

7. How do we mark helping verbs? **L78** *(They need to be marked with an HV.)*

8. How do we mark prepositional phrases? **L78** *(They need to be marked with square brackets and the object with the label OP.)*

9. Why do I need to know how to conjugate a verb? **L78** *(To conjugate correctly is to master correct verb usage. We need to know how to use verbs.)*

Further Reinforcement of This Lesson

L78P The practice exercise for this lesson will follow after the next two lessons. We first need to explore two more additional patterns. In the next two lessons we will build on what this lesson on Sentence Pattern 4A has taught us.

Where Do I Go from Here?

- **L78** goes to **"Lesson 19"** on page 219.

What Materials Will I Need?

- **L78** will need *Grammar Notebooks,* pencils, and red pencils.

Lesson 23

What Is a Predicate Adjective? Pattern 4B

Dictating Sentence Pattern 4B

L78 **Step 1** — "The content of **'Lesson 23'** builds on **'Lesson 22.'** The formula for the new sentence pattern introduced in this lesson is S + LV——→PA. We call it 'Sentence Pattern 4B'. The PA in this formula stands for the words **'predicate adjective'.** The predicate adjective is a word that does the job of an adjective and is found in the predicate of our sentence. It always describes the subject. One of the adjective flags flies over every predicate adjective.

"Turn in your Grammar Notebook *to page 31. Counting the title line as number one, count down four baselines. Starting comfortably close to the left margin line, write this new sentence pattern:* **'S + LV——→PA'.**"

L78 **Step 2** — *"We need to create a train for this pattern also. On the next available baseline under the sentence formula, draw three connected boxes. Inside the first box, place a capital* **'S'.** *Inside the second box, place an* **'LV'.** *Inside the third box, place a* **'PA'.** *We need to draw an arrow* ——————→*from the PA to the S and print the word* **'describes'** *above the arrow.* This is what is happening in a sentence that has a PA; the predicate adjective describes the subject. Let's write some examples."

Dictating Sentences That Use Sentence Pattern 4B

L78 **Step 3** — *"Skipping five baselines below your train diagram, starting each sentence comfortably close to the left margin line, write the following sentences on consecutive baselines:*

> *'The man is old.'*
> *'The cow becomes sick.'*
> *'The day seems dreary.'*
> *'The Constitution is long.'*
> *'The player feels happy.'"*

What Do Linking Verbs Actually Do?

L78M Step 4 — "Linking verbs are not words of action. They are words that describe a 'state of being' or a 'state of existing'.

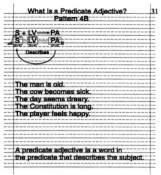

Sample Page 31
Lesson 23

The man is old.

The cow becomes sick.

The day seems dreary.

The Constitution is long.

The player feels happy.

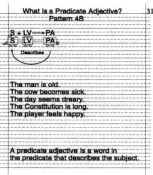

S + LV → PA
S LV PA
Describes

The man is old.
The cow becomes sick.
The day seems dreary.
The Constitution is long.
The player feels happy.

A predicate adjective is a word in
the predicate that describes the subject.

Sample Page 31
Lesson 23

Thus the man in our first sentence 'The man is old' exists in a condition or state of being that is old. Linking verbs do not provide energy or motion to a sentence as an action verb does.

"In our third example, 'The day seems dreary', the day exists in a state of dreariness. When Hamlet begins his famous soliloquy by saying 'To be, or not to be, that is the question . . . ,' he is really saying 'To exist or not to exist . . . To continue my state of being or not to continue . . . '

"This is the nature of a linking verb. It provides a situation within which the subject exists. With an action verb, our subject can walk or talk or jump or do anything we want him to do. With a linking verb the man cannot do anything. He just exists, and we provide him the condition within which he has this state of being."

Discovering the Nature of a Predicate Adjective

L78 **Step 5 —** "Let's look at these few sentences and analyze them using this sentence pattern. The first sentence reads 'The man is old'. Do we have any prepositions in this sentence?"

STUDENTS: "None that I can see."

TEACHER: "Can you find a word that we can conjugate?"

STUDENTS: "We just learned to conjugate the verb 'to be' in **'Lesson 22.'** The verb 'is' is in both my linking verb list and my helping verb list. 'Is' is a linking verb if it acts alone. If there is an action verb that I can conjugate following the linking verb 'is', then it is a helping verb."

TEACHER: "Well, let's look. Can we conjugate the word 'old'?

STUDENTS: "We can't, can we?"

TEACHER: "What does that mean?"

STUDENTS: "It means that the word 'is' is acting independently. We have a linking verb. We have a word that is creating a state of being. But which sentence pattern do we use? Sentence Pattern 4A (S + LV) or 4B (S + LV→PA)? They both have linking verbs."

TEACHER: "Let's take a look. First, let's find the subject. That is our third step in syntactical analysis. We need to ask this question: Who or what 'is'?"

STUDENTS: "The man 'is' and therefore must be our subject. That means we have at least an S + LV pattern."

TEACHER:	"Have we accounted for all the words in our analysis?"
STUDENTS:	"We have not accounted for the word 'old'."
TEACHER:	"What do we know about the man? What flag is flying over the word 'old'?"
STUDENTS:	"I know the man is old. That is a description of the man. It tells me what kind of a man he is. A word that answers the question 'What Kind?' has to be doing the work of an adjective."
TEACHER:	"You are right. Where does this adjective live? Does it live with the subject or does it live with the predicate? Do you remember what those terms mean?"
STUDENTS:	"Yes, I do. A complete subject is what the sentence is about. This sentence is about the man. A complete predicate is the verb or verb phrase plus all the words that influence it, and it says something about the subject. In this case the word 'old' lives in the predicate with the verb 'is'."
TEACHER:	"The word 'old' is doing the job of a **Predicate Adjective,** and we label it by placing a *'PA'* over the word 'old'. Let's practice by doing the other sentences."

Analyzing and Marking the Remaining Sentences

78P Help students analyze and mark the rest of the dictated sentences. Another sample discussion follows to further reinforce an understanding about state of being or state of existing.

TEACHER:	"So what state of being is the word 'Constitution' in our fourth example?"
STUDENTS:	"The Constitution exists as a document that is 'long'. That is all we know based on this sentence."
TEACHER:	"Very good. In what state of being is the player?"
STUDENTS:	"The player is existing in a happy condition."
TEACHER:	"Are the player, the Constitution, or the day doing anything? Are they in motion? Are they in action?"
STUDENTS:	"No, they are not. That once again tells me what the real job of a linking verb is. It creates a condition within which the subject lives."
TEACHER:	"Excellent."

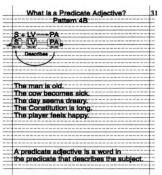

S + LV⟶PA
(S) (LV) [PA]
Describes

The man is old.
The cow becomes sick.
The day seems dreary.
The Constitution is long.
The player feels happy.

A predicate adjective is a word in
the predicate that describes the subject.

Sample Page 31
Lesson 23

*Practice writing
simple sentences
using the sentence
patterns.*

Work for mastery.

*Develop
automaticity.*

*Strengthen
syntactical
expectancies.*

Defining a Predicate Adjective

L78 **Step 6 —** *"Counting up three baselines from the bottom,
starting comfortably close to the left margin line, write the
definiton of a 'predicate adjective': 'A predicate adjective is a
word in the predicate that describes the subject'."*

Let's Get Organized

L78 **Step 7 —** *"Turn to the Table of Contents. On the page 31 line,
write the title 'What Is a Predicate Adjective? Pattern 4B'.
Turn back to page 31. Centered on the title line, between the
two red margin lines, write the title 'What Is a Predicate
Adjective?' On the baseline directly below the title line, center
the title 'Pattern 4B'.*

You Seldom Go Wrong When You Review

We need to circle the wagons and build in opportunities for
review. The Dialogue and Review questions are designed to
help you do that. Place them in your lesson plans. Practice
conjugating verbs. Do noun searches or adjective searches in
other texts. Mark sentences. Wave flags. Find DO's. Wave at
Grandma as she drives by in her new car.

The world is watching what you are doing. Say the linking verb
list until the cows come home. If cows don't work, use sheep.
Conjugate irregular action verbs until there is an Olympic gold
medal hanging around your student's neck. Practice writing
simple sentences using the sentence patterns. Work for mastery.
Develop automaticity. Strengthen syntactical expectancies. And
then rejoice for the day cometh when Little Johnny will not only
read exceptionally well, but he will write and do it superbly.

Expectancies Learned or Reinforced in
Lesson 23: Dialogue and Review

1. What is a predicate adjective? **L78** *(A predicate adjective is a
   word in the predicate that describes the subject.)*

2. What is the formula for Sentence Pattern 4B? **L78**
   (S + LV⟶PA)

3. What does a linking verb create in a sentence? **L78** *(A linking
   verb creates a state of being or a state of existing.)*

4. How do we conjugate the linking verb "to be" in the present
   tense, the past tense, the present perfect tense, the future tense,
   the future perfect tense, and the past perfect tense? **L78**
   (Review "Lesson 22.")

5. What must we do to mark sentences correctly? **L78** *(We must follow the proper sequence for syntactical analysis.)*

6. What happens when we understand what words can do? **L78** *(We gain better control of our language and improve our writing and our speaking.)*

Helping Our Students Understand How Language Works

Throughout these procedures, we are building sentence sense through analytical processes. This will help our students develop syntactical expectancies so they can maximize neurological success and can control language instead of it controlling them. They will then be able to read, write, and comprehend to the best of their ability.

Where Do I Go from Here?

- **L78** goes to "Lesson 24" on page 248.

What Materials Will I Need?

- **L78** will need *Grammar Notebooks,* pencils, red pencils, and copies of Worksheets for **"Lesson 24"** starting on page 254.

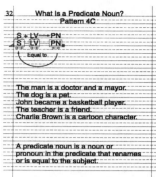

Sample Page 32
Lesson 24

Lesson 24
What Is a Predicate Noun? Pattern 4C

Dictating Sentence Pattern 4C

L78 **Step 1 —** "We have one more major sentence pattern to introduce. We call this pattern **'Sentence Pattern 4C'.** This sentence pattern introduces a new term. We call it the **'predicate noun'.** Some people might use the name 'nominative' instead of 'noun', but using the word 'noun' is just fine.

"Turn to page 32 in your Grammar Notebook. *Counting the title line as number one, count down four baselines from the title line. Starting comfortably close to the left margin line, please write the formula:* '*S + LV*————➔*PN*'. What do all Sentence Pattern 4 sentences have in common?"

STUDENTS: "They all have a linking verb that acts independently."

TEACHER: "That's right."

L78 **Step 2 —** *"Drop down to the next available baseline and let's create our last train. We'll need three boxes again. The first box gets an* **'S'** *for 'subject'. The second box gets an* **'LV'** *for 'linking verb'. The third box this time will have the label* **'PN'**, *which stands for 'predicate noun'. After we have the train drawn and the labels in place, please draw an* **arrow** *from the PN back to the subject. Above this arrow write the words* **'equal to'.** *You will understand why in a moment."*

Dictating Sentences Using Sentence Pattern 4C

L78 **Step 3 —** *"Skipping five lines under the train diagram and starting each sentence comfortably close to the left margin line, write the following sentences on consecutive baselines:*

> *'The man is a doctor and a mayor.'*
> *'The dog is a pet.'*
> *'John became a basketball player.'*
> *'The teacher is a friend.'*
> *'Charlie Brown is a cartoon character.'"*

L78P When a student becomes knowledgeable about how to analyze a sentence, we want the process of analysis to approach automaticity. We hope eventually that a glance will do it. It needs to. In a matter of moments, a sentence is analyzed and accounted for. Proper English usage requires these kinds of informed choices all along the way. Continue to use the Sample Page in your margin as a guide.

Discovering the Nature of Predicate Nouns

L78 **Step 4 —** "We are going to analyze our third sentence and try to account for each word in that sentence. We have learned and continue to practice the premise that every word has a job to do, and when we know what words can do, we can use them better ourselves. Let's analyze 'John became a basketball player'. Our first step is to look for prepositional phrases. Do you see any?"

STUDENTS: "There are none."

TEACHER: "What is the next step in syntactical analysis?"

STUDENTS: "We are to locate the last word in our sentence that can be conjugated. We are trying to find our verb. That will point us toward the right sentence pattern."

TEACHER: "What do you see?"

STUDENTS: "The only word that can be conjugated is 'became'. The three most important parts of that verb are the following: 'Today I become.' 'Yesterday I became.' 'I have become.'"

TEACHER: "Is this a linking verb or an action verb?"

STUDENTS: "I know it is on my linking verb list, but can it pass the Is–Are Rule. That is how we know. When we apply this rule, 'John became a basketball player' changes to 'John **is** a basketball player'. It reads well with this substitute. The verb 'became' is being used as a linking verb."

TEACHER: "If it is a linking verb, we have to use some form of Sentence Pattern 4. Let's reserve judgment on that for the time being. Let's look for the subject. That is our third step. Who or what becomes?"

STUDENTS: "John becomes. Therefore, John is the subject of our sentence."

TEACHER: "The fourth step is locating our third box. If we had determined that our verb was an action verb, we would ask the question, **'What** or **whom** is receiving the action of the verb?' That would give us the direct object.

"Because we have determined that the verb is a linking verb, we ask, **'What** or **who** did John become?' If we get an answer to this question, we have found a

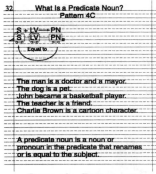

Sample Page 32
Lesson 24

There is only one way to achieve excellence.

We must practice correctly.

A predicate noun is a noun or pronoun in the predicate that renames or is equal to the subject.

word that is either describing or renaming our subject 'John'. If the word that answers that question is a noun, that word is **'equal to'** John. It is the **same** person. If it is a noun, it will not describe John; it will **rename** John. If it is an adjective, it will describe John and be doing the job of a predicate adjective. Is there an answer to that question?"

STUDENTS: "Yes, there is. John becomes a player. The word 'player' is equal to John, represents the same person as John, and renames John."

TEACHER: "We have a name for a word that renames the subject. We call these renaming words **'predicate nouns'.** This means that the word 'player' is our predicate noun. It cannot be a direct object because we do not have an action verb. How do you think we mark a predicate noun?"

STUDENTS: "We label a predicate noun with a 'PN'."

TEACHER: "That is correct. Also, please remember that we may have more than one predicate noun or predicate adjective, just like we may have more than one subject or more than one verb. Is the word 'basketball' being used as a noun?"

STUDENTS: "The word 'basketball' could be a noun, but not this time. Look at the sentence. This time the word 'basketball' answers the question 'What Kind?' What kind of a player was John? He was a basketball player. The word is doing the work of an adjective. We need to circle it, label it with an 'adj.', and draw an arrow to the noun 'player' because that is the word that 'basketball' is influencing."

TEACHER: "Linking verbs create a condition, a state of being, or a state of existing. What condition, state of being, or state of existing is created for John in this sentence?"

STUDENTS: "John's condition or state of being is that of a basketball player."

TEACHER: "You are catching on. Let's do some more practice sentences."

L78P After you have worked through the remaining sample sentences with your students and marked them correctly, create Sentence Pattern 4C sentences on your own. Build some review times into your lesson plans. There is room to record a few more of these sentences on page 32. You can always start a Sentence Pattern 4C wall chart.

Defining a Predicate Noun

L78   **Step 5 —** *"Counting up four baselines from the bottom, starting comfortably close to the left margin line, please write the following: 'A predicate noun is a noun or pronoun in the predicate that renames or is equal to the subject'.* This becomes our working definition for the predicate noun of Sentence Pattern 4C."

Let's Get Organized

L78   **Step 6 —** *"Turn to the Table of Contents. On the page 32 line, write the title 'What Is a Predicate Noun? Pattern 4C'. Turn back to page 32. Centered on the title line, between the two red margin lines, write the title 'What Is a Predicate Noun?' On the next baseline, center the title 'Pattern 4C'."*

Expectancies Learned or Reinforced in Lesson 24: Dialogue and Review

1. What is a predicate noun? **L78** *(A predicate noun is a noun or pronoun in the predicate that renames or is equal to the subject.)*

2. When do we need to use the Is–Are Rule? **L78** *(We need to use the Is–Are Rule to determine if the linking verbs on the linking verb list are doing the job of a linking verb or an action verb.)*

3. How do we find a predicate noun? **L78** *(We find a predicate noun by asking 'What?' or 'Who?' after a linking verb.)*

4. In contrast, how do we find a direct object? **L78** *(We find a direct object by asking 'What?' or 'Whom?' after an action verb. In either case, whether a predicate noun or a direct object, the kind of verb has been determined before we ask these questions. Determining the kind of verb determes the particular sentence pattern in use.)*

5. How can a word like 'basketball' be used in a sentence? **L78** *(Words are very versatile. They can be used as different parts of speech. They can be used in a different part of a sentence pattern. The word 'basketball' can be used as a noun in the subject position, the direct object position, the object of the preposition position, or the predicate noun position. The word 'basketball' can also be used as an adjective.)*

6. How many predicate nouns or predicate adjectives may we have in a sentence? **L78** *(We may have as many as we need.)*

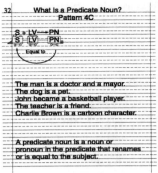

Sample Page 32
Lesson 24

Where Do I Go from Here?

- **L78** goes to **"Lesson 25"** on page 259.

What Materials Will I Need?

- **L78** will need *Grammar Notebooks,* pencils, rulers, copies of Sample Pages 33–35, and copies of Worksheets for **"Lesson 25"** starting on page 262.

Sentence Patterns 4A, 4B, and 4C

Teacher Directions: Explain to your students the directions for analyzing and marking sentences with 4A, 4B, or 4C patterns.

These directions are included on the actual student worksheet. They should be getting to know this sequence better and better.

1. The policeman is (my) friend (and) protector.
   S+   LV→adj.   PN+   conj.   PN

2. He appears cheerful (today).
   S+   LV——→ PA   adv.

3. The soup smells (very) delicious.
   S+   LV   adv.   PA

4. You should have been ready.
   S+   HV+   HV+   LV——→PA

5. He remains strong [for (free) speech.]
   S+ LV——→ PA   adj.   OP

6. I will be a (good) friend.
   S+HV+ LV——→ adj.   PN

7. The farmers (and) workers look tired [during harvest.]
   S+   conj.   S+   LV→PA   OP

8. (Our) cousins were restless [on Easter.]
   adj.   S+   LV——→ PA   OP

9. The (grizzly) bear looked (very) tall (and) angry.
   adj.   S+   LV——→ adv.   PA+   conj.   PA

10. The stranger [in town] was restless.
    S+   OP   LV——→ PA

1. The policeman is my friend and protector.

2. He appears cheerful today.

3. The soup smells very delicious.

4. You should have been ready.

5. He remains strong for free speech.

6. I will be a good friend.

7. The farmers and workers look tired during harvest.

8. Our cousins were restless on Easter.

9. The grizzly bear looked very tall and angry.

10. The stranger in town was restless.

Sentence Patterns 4A, 4B, and 4C

Analyze the following sentences using Sentence Patterns 4A, 4B, and 4C.

1. Find the prepositions and their objects first. Label these using [brackets] and "OP". If you find adjectives influencing OP's, (circle) them, label them with an "adj." and draw an arrow to the OP.

2. Find the last word you can conjugate together with its helping verb(s) and label each one with "LV" or "HV" accordingly.

3. Ask the questions "What?" or "Who?" is being described or renamed. This word is the subject. Label this word with an "S". Remember, you may have more than one subject.

4. Next ask "'What?' or 'Who?' is the subject". If the answer is an adjective in the predicate describing the subject, label this adjective as the "PA". If the answer is a noun in the predicate that renames the subject, label this noun as the "PN". Remember that you may have more than one PA or PN.

5. Find all the other words that are flying flags. (Circle) the adjectives and adverbs, label the circles with "adj." or "adv.", and draw arrows to the word they influence.

6. Put |boxes| around coordinating conjunctions and label them with a "conj."

Sentence Patterns 4A, 4B, and 4C

Teacher Directions: Explain to your students the directions for analyzing and marking sentences with 4A, 4B, or 4C patterns.

These directions are included on the actual student worksheet. They should be getting to know this sequence better and better.

1. The crowd was louder [after the game.]
    S+ LV→ PA   OP

2. Thursday [or] Friday would have been (our) (first) day.
    S+ conj. S+ HV+ HV+ LV adj. adj. PN

3. The students stay interested [in analysis.]
    S+ LV→ PA   OP

4. The witness sounded sad [in court.]
    S+ LV→ PA   OP

5. (Great) treasures remain lost [at sea.]
    adj. S+ LV→ PA   OP

6. John Jones will be president (someday.)
    S+ HV+ LV→ PN   adv.

7. The sport [of golf] has been difficult.
    S+ OP HV+ LV→ PA

8. A (good) parent is a refuge [for a (sad) child.]
    adj. S+ LV→ PN   adj. OP

9. He is being industrious [with the project.]
    S+ HV+ LV→ PA   OP

10. The song sounds unique [and] intriguing.
    S+ LV→ PA+ conj. PA

1. The crowd was louder after the game.

2. Thursday or Friday would have been our first day.

3. The students stay interested in analysis.

4. The witness sounded sad in court.

5. Great treasures remain lost at sea.

6. John Jones will be president someday.

7. The sport of golf has been difficult.

8. A good parent is a refuge for a sad child.

9. He is being industrious with the project.

10. The song sounds unique and intriguing.

Sentence Patterns 4A, 4B, and 4C

Analyze the following sentences using Sentence Patterns 4A, 4B, and 4C.

1. Find the prepositions and their objects first. Label these using [brackets] and "OP". If you find adjectives influencing OP's, (circle) them, label them with an "adj." and draw an arrow to the OP.

2. Find the last word you can conjugate together with its helping verb(s) and label each one with "LV" or "HV" accordingly.

3. Ask the questions "What?" or "Who?" is being described or renamed. This word is the subject. Label this word with an "S". Remember, you may have more than one subject.

4. Next ask "'What?' or 'Who?' is the subject". If the answer is an adjective in the predicate describing the subject, label this adjective as the "PA". If the answer is a noun in the predicate that renames the subject, label this noun as the "PN". Remember that you may have more than one PA or PN.

5. Find all the other words that are flying flags. (Circle) the adjectives and adverbs, label the circles with "adj." or "adv.", and draw arrows to the word they influence.

6. Put [boxes] around coordinating conjunctions and label them with a "conj."

*The Comprehensive
Checklist to the right
gives the teacher ques-
tions to ask students. Use
these questions when you
need them for review.
They will help you deter-
mine whether or not these
principles are well embedded in your students'
minds.*

*On a couple of tests I
gave recently, I pulled out
Abraham Lincoln's
"Gettysburg Address" and
had them do syntactical
analysis on sentences
I knew they understood.
On another test I used the
first page of a short story
by a Nobel Prize-winning
author. We could use an
editorial from* Time *magazine. We could take the
lead story in the* New
York Times. *Print is all
around us. When we do
this, the students will get
the message that some of
the brightest and the best
writers in the present and
in our past are using these
very same grammatical
structures. We want our
students to aspire to excellence. In order to do that
we must provide for them
the very best modeling
that we can.*

Comprehensive Checklist 2 for Lessons 14–24

1. How is mastery achieved? **L34** *(We must practice correctly. We must show perseverance. We must understand why we need to learn our language better.)*

2. What are the adjective questions? **L12** *("What kind?" "How many?" "How much?" "Which?" "Which One?" "Whose?")*

3. What words can an adjective influence? **L12** *(An adjective can influence a noun or a pronoun.)*

4. How do we mark an adjective? **L56** *(We circle adjectives, label them with an "adj.", and draw an arrow to the word they influence.)*

5. What are the adverb questions? **L56** *("When?" "Where?" "Why?" "How?" "On What Condition?" "To What Extent?")*

6. What words can an adverb influence? **L56** *(An adverb can influence a verb, an adjective, or another adverb.)*

7. How do we mark adverbs? **L56** *(We circle them, label them with an "adv.", and draw an arrow to the word they influence.)*

8. How do we recognize a preposition and find its object? **L56** *(We check our preposition list and locate the next noun or pronoun that follows the preposition.)*

9. How do we mark a prepositional phrase? **L56** *(We place [square brackets] at the beginning and end of the phrase and label the object with an "OP".)*

10. What are the coordinating conjunctions and the job that they can do? **L56** *("And", "but", "or", "for", "nor", "yet", and "so". They are used to connect words and phrases and sentences.)*

11. How do you mark coordinating conjunctions? **L56** *(We place a rectangular box around each conjunction, and place the label "conj." over the top of the box.)*

12. Why is practicing grammar correctly so important? **L12** *(If we don't practice correctly, we will never achieve mastery. Language will control us instead of us controlling language. If we are not prepared to use English correctly, our communica- tion skills will be at risk, and doors of opportunity in the future may not open.)*

13. What are simple and complete subjects? **L34** *(A simple subject is the one word about which the rest of the sentence speaks. The complete subject includes the simple subject plus all the words that influence the simple subject.)*

14. What is Sentence Pattern 1? **L34** *(S+AV)*

15. What does a simple sentence do? **L34** *(A simple sentence has at least one subject and one verb and makes complete sense. The simple sentence must have a sentence pattern. A simple sentence must mean something.)*

16. How do we find a verb? **L34** *(If we can find the three most important parts of the word and then conjugate it, we know that it is a verb.)*

17. How do we distinguish between a helping verb, a linking verb, and an action verb? **L78** *(We use our linking verb list, we use our helping verb list, we find the three most important parts of a verb, we conjugate if necessary, and we use the Is–Are Rule if necessary.)*

18. Why is our step-by-step sequence starting with a preposition search necessary to perform syntactical analysis? **L56** *(We must take one step at a time in order to understand how a sentence works.)*

19. What are simple and complete predicates? **L56** *(A simple predicate is the main verb plus all helping verbs. The complete predicate is the main verb plus all the words that influence it.)*

20. What is Sentence Pattern 2? **L56** *(S+AV⟶DO)*

21. How do we find and label a direct object? **L56** *(We find the action verb and ask the questions for "What?" or "Whom?" the action of the verb is done. The word that answers one of these two questions is the direct object. We label a direct object by placing a "DO" over the word.)*

22. How do we know the difference between a transitive ("train"sitive) verb and an intransitive ("intrain"sitive) verb? **L78** *(A transitive verb has a direct object. An intransitive verb has no direct object. A sentence either has a caboose or it doesn't.)*

23. What is Sentence Pattern 3? **L56** *(S+AV⟶IO+DO)*

24. What is a "beneficiary"? **L56** *(A beneficiary is a person or thing that receives benefits.)*

25. Who is the beneficiary in Sentence Pattern 3? **L56** *(The indirect object is always the beneficiary.)*

26. How do we find and label the indirect object? **L56** *(We must ask the questions "To Whom?" "For Whom?" "To What?" and "For What?" the action of the verb is being done. We label an indirect object by placing an "IO" over the word).*

27. What are Sentence Patterns 4A, 4B, and 4C? **L78** *(4A: S+ LV, 4B: S+LV———➔PA, 4C: S+LV———➔PN)*

28. What does a predicate adjective do and how do we mark it? **L78** *(A predicate adjective is in the predicate. It describes the subject and follows the linking verb. We label a predicate adjective by placing a "PA" over the word.)*

29. What does a predicate noun do and how do we mark it? **L78** *(A predicate noun is in the predicate. It renames the subject. We label a predicate noun by placing a "PN" over the word.)*

30. How do we conjugate the verb "to be" in all six English tenses? **L78** *(Turn to **"Lesson 22: What Is Sentence Pattern 4A?"**)*

31. How do we conjugate irregular verbs in all six English tenses? **L34** *(We must learn the three most important parts of each of these verbs. And then . . . there is only one way to achieve excellence. We must practice.)*

Lesson 25

Steps of Syntactical Analysis: Creating Resource Pages

L78P What we have been teaching has intrinsic value beyond the obvious grammar skills. Please read over what follows and share with your students those points that you think would be motivating and encouraging to them.

The Why of Comparative Analysis: The Art of Learning How to Reason to a Satisfactory Conclusion

English syntax offers a wonderful opportunity to learn how to think logically and to do comparative analysis. Geometry does the same thing. The science of argumentation, which is called debate, does the same thing. Learning **syntactical expectancies** offers much more than just information about how to write properly.

Perhaps teachers were trying to teach logic and comparative analysis when they had students diagram sentences years ago. Diagramming had the elements of comparative analysis, but it was too cumbersome, took words out of their context, and most, if not all teachers, really didn't understand that analyzing a sentence and determining why a word is doing what it is doing had benefits beyond the obvious.

The fact that we are learning about how our language works is a bonus. The fact that we are also teaching logic and **comparative analysis** places grammar instruction on the high road.

The resource pages in this lesson are very important pages. They provide the line of reasoning that this text has been trying to teach that allows for **comparative analysis**. Learning how to reason to a satisfactory conclusion is a worthwhile discipline in and of itself. We need to learn how to think logically. We must learn how to think one step at a time.

We do **comparative analysis** every day of our lives in one form or another. We must manage and create causal links all the time. Some, of course, are more obvious than others. If my pipes are leaking now, then my basement will be full of water later. Perhaps I should call a plumber. If I would choose to buy a minivan, then why shouldn't I buy a pickup truck? If this word

Sample Page 33
Lesson 25

Sample Page 34
Lesson 25

Sample Page 35
Lesson 25

can do this job here, then what job will it do somewhere else? If the United States Senate passes this bill, then how will that affect me ten years from now?

We must learn how to think logically and sequentially. It is a necessary life skill. If A equals B and B equals C, then it stands to reason that A equals C. Now such thinking might stand to reason, but too many students today are sitting down when it comes to thinking skills. We all need to learn to stand. If that is the case, then we would be wise to strengthen our minds with exercises that require that kind of thinking.

Dictating the Steps for Syntactical Analysis

L78P Sample Pages 33–35 contain a compilation of those steps of analysis with which your students have been working throughout this text. They have been arranged efficiently in a flowchart that will be easy to follow. Because your students have used the **Steps of Syntactical Analysis** consistently throughout this text, these steps should be familiar and almost automatic by now.

There is no need to work with them further, except to simply record these steps in their *Grammar Notebook* for future reference. It is for this reason that we will depart from the normal dictation process and instruct students to merely copy this information into their notebooks. Make enough copies of Sample Pages 33–35 for each student. Pass these copies out, give the directions that follow, sit back, and watch your students work. Allow more than one class session to accomplish all three pages.

L78 **Step 1 —** *"Turn to page 33 in your* Grammar Notebook. *We are going to make three resource pages and record the various steps that we need to do in order to analyze a sentence. We have already worked with all of these steps at various times in these first lessons. The steps will not be new to you. We just need them recorded for future reference."*

L78 **Step 2 —** *"Skipping one baseline below the title line, comfortably close to the left red margin line, write the first step:* **'1. Are there any prepositional phrases?'** *The rest of the pages are up to you.* **Duplicate what you see.** *If there is a box with the word 'Yes', make a* **box** *in the same place on your Sample Page and place the word* **'Yes'** *in the box. Draw those* **connecting lines** *and follow those lines to the next question or the next box.* **Duplicate what you see.** *See how beautiful you can make each page."*

Let's Get Organized

L78 **Step 3 —** *"Turn to the Table of Contents. On the page 33 line, write the title 'Steps of Syntactical Analysis'. On the page 34 and page 35 lines, write the title 'Steps of Syntactical Analysis (continued)'. Turn back to page 33. Centered on the title line on page 33, between the two red margin lines, write the title 'Steps of Syntactical Analysis'. Centered on the title lines on page 34 and page 35, write the title 'Steps of Syntactical Analysis (continued)'."*

Expectancies Learned or Reinforced in Lesson 25: Dialogue and Review

1. What is comparative analysis? **L78** *(Comparative analysis is the making of correct choices with the available information.)*

2. Why is knowing how to analyze a sentence so important? **L78** *(In addition to becoming better communicators by learning how our language works, we are also learning thinking skills like sequencing, logic, and the drawing of conclusions. Improving our thinking skills is a worthwhile endeavor.)*

3. What are the six steps to analyzing a sentence? **L78** *(1. Find the prepositional phrases. 2. Find the verb(s). 3. Find the subject(s). 4. Find the DO, IO, PN, or PA 5. Find the adjectives and adverbs. 6. Find the conjunctions.)*

Where Do I Go from Here?

- **L78** goes to **"Lesson 26"** on page 266.

What Materials Will I Need?

- **L78** will need *Grammar Notebooks* and pencils.

An Exercise in Syntactical Analysis

Teacher Directions: Explain to your students that they need to analyze the following sentences using the steps of syntactical analysis as recorded in this lesson.

Student Directions: Using the following sentences, let's practice syntactical analysis.

They contain only those grammatical structures to which you have been introduced.

Feel free to use your resource page in your Notebook if you need to.

1. The slippery road became muddy and dangerous.

2. John and Jim raced the car to the school.

3. Horses, cows, and sheep eat hay during the winter.

4. The doctor gave the baby a checkup at the clinic.

5. The dark green cloud floated slowly over the wheat field.

6. The bright morning sun appears on the horizon.

7. I am careful around a hot stove in the wintertime.

8. The student feels sick in the morning before school.

9. The rooster crowed early in the morning.

10. The sleepy, industrious boy rose from bed and did morning chores.

11. Self-control is a good quality.

12. Twenty chickens have been sitting in the tree.

1. The slippery road became muddy and dangerous.

2. John and Jim raced the car to the school.

3. Horses, cows, and sheep eat hay during the winter.

4. The doctor gave the baby a checkup at the clinic.

5. The dark green cloud floated slowly over the wheat field.

6. The bright morning sun appears on the horizon.

7. I am careful around a hot stove in the wintertime.

8. The student feels sick in the morning before school.

9. The rooster crowed early in the morning.

10. The sleepy, industrious boy rose from bed and did morning chores.

11. Self-control is a good quality.

12. Twenty chickens have been sitting in the tree.

An Exercise in Syntactical Analysis

Student Directions: Using the following sentences, let's practice syntactical analysis.

They contain only those grammatical structures to which you have been introduced.

Feel free to use your resource page in your Notebook if you need to.

An Exercise in Syntactical Analysis

Teacher Directions: Explain to your students that they need to analyze the following sentences using the steps of syntactical analysis as recorded in this lesson.

Student Directions: Using the following sentences, let's practice syntactical analysis.

They contain only those grammatical structures to which you have been introduced.

Feel free to use your resource page in your Notebook if you need to.

1. Many people trip and fall on the steep stairway.

2. Yesterday, the hospital released five patients.

3. The little girl yawned quietly and fell into a deep sleep.

4. The choir gave the director an award for excellence.

5. The story remains a mystery to the police.

6. The farmer grows corn.

7. The newspaper will have been running an ad for reporters for two weeks.

8. The New York Times ran an article about the man in the sailboat.

9. Thanksgiving and Christmas are holidays for families.

10. We love fishing, boating, and biking in the summer.

11. The President is a golfer and an outdoorsman.

12. Quietly, the nurse stole into the hospital room and checked the child in the bed.

13. The whole team seemed quiet after the loss.

1. Many people trip and fall on the steep stairway.

2. Yesterday, the hospital released five patients.

3. The little girl yawned quietly and fell into a deep sleep.

4. The choir gave the director an award for excellence.

5. The story remains a mystery to the police.

6. The farmer grows corn.

7. The newspaper will have been running an ad for reporters for two weeks.

8. The New York Times ran an article about the man in the sailboat.

9. Thanksgiving and Christmas are holidays for families.

10. We love fishing, boating, and biking in the summer.

11. The President is a golfer and an outdoorsman.

12. Quietly, the nurse stole into the hospital room and checked the child in the bed.

13. The whole team seemed quiet after the loss.

©1998 Grammar Works/Holly Hall Publications, Inc.

Student Worksheet 2:

An Exercise in Syntactical Analysis

Student Directions: Using the following sentences, let's practice syntactical analysis.

They contain only those grammatical structures to which you have been introduced.

Feel free to use your resource page in your Notebook if you need to.

I run down the beach.
She gave Bill the cake.
They walked carefully.

The student is Jim. Jim is the student.
I am the student. The student is I.

The mother is Jean. Jean is the mother.
She is the mother. The mother is she.

The team members are Wolverines.
The Wolverines are team members.
They are the team members.
The team members are they.

A subject pronoun is any pronoun that
can be used in the subject position.
A subject pronoun may be used as a
subject or as a predicate noun.

Sample Page 36
Lesson 26

Lesson 26
What Is a Subject Pronoun?

Words Can Do So Many Jobs

L78 "We have consistently said that each word in our language has a job to do. Some words are versatile enough to be able to do many jobs. Pronouns have that kind of versatility. In the coming lessons we will learn that pronouns can be used as subjects, objects, adjectives, and predicate nouns."

Dictating Sentences and Discovering the Nature of Pronouns Used As Subjects

L78 **Step 1 —** *"Turn to page 36 in your* Grammar Notebook. *Skipping one baseline under the title line, comfortably close to the margin line, write the following three sentences on consecutive baselines:* **'I run down the beach'. 'She gave Bill the cake'. 'They walked carefully'."**

L78 **Step 2 —** "Let's analyze these three sentences. What words are being used as subjects?"

STUDENTS: "The words 'I', 'she', and 'they' are being used as subjects. They are the words about which the sentences are speaking."

TEACHER: "Right. All the personal pronouns 'I', 'you', 'he', 'she', 'it', 'we', 'you' (plural), and 'they' that we use to conjugate a verb have another name. We can call them **subject pronouns.** They are called this because they can be used in a subject position."

Dictating Sentences Interchanging a Subject Pronoun with a Predicate Noun

L78P When dictating the sentences that follow, please use the Sample Page in the margin as a guide.

L78 **Step 3 —** *"Skipping one baseline below the sentence 'They walked carefully', write the following two sentences on the same baseline:* **'The student is Jim. Jim is the student'.** *On the next available baseline, write the following two sentences on the same baseline:* **'I am the student. The student is I'.**

L78 **Step 4 —** *"Skipping one baseline, write the following two sentences on the same baseline:* **'The mother is Jean. Jean is the mother'.** *On the next available baseline, write the following two sentences on the same baseline:* **'She is the mother. The mother is she'."**

L78   **Step 5 —** *"Skipping one baseline, write the following four sentences on consecutive baselines: 'The team members are Wolverines'. 'The Wolverines are team members'. 'They are team members'. 'The team members are they'."*

Discovering the Nature of the Interchange between a Subject Pronoun and a Predicate Noun

L78   **Step 6 —** "Let's analyze the first set of four sentences. What job is the word 'student' doing in the first sentence?"

STUDENTS: "It is doing the job of a subject."

TEACHER: "What job is the word 'Jim' doing in the first sentence?"

STUDENTS: "It is doing the work of a predicate noun. This is Sentence Pattern 4C, isn't it? The use of the linking verb and a predicate noun tells me this."

TEACHER: "That is right. The sentence pattern is S+LV——→PN. What job is the word 'Jim' doing in the second sentence?"

STUDENTS: "It is doing the job of a subject."

TEACHER: "What job is the word 'student' doing in the second sentence?"

STUDENTS: "It is doing the work of a predicate noun."

TEACHER: "Make an observation here if you can. What do we know about the words 'Jim' and 'student' in these sentences?"

STUDENTS: "One may be substituted for the other."

TEACHER: "Because predicate nouns are equal to their subjects in meaning, they can exchange places in these kinds of sentences. A subject can step up to the plate and be a PN. A PN can step up to the plate and be a subject. You are right. One can be substituted for another. They are interchangeable. They can reverse roles and still have the sentence make sense."

L78   **Step 7 —** "Let's analyze the sentences 'I am the student' and 'The student is I'. What do we learn?"

STUDENTS: "The subject pronoun 'I' and the word 'student' are interchangeable."

TEACHER: "Right. If a pronoun is used in the subject position, it must be a subject pronoun. If a pronoun is used in the PN position, it must also be a subject pronoun.

I run down the beach.
She gave Bill the cake.
They walked carefully.

The student is Jim. Jim is the student.
I am the student. The student is I.

The mother is Jean. Jean is the mother.
She is the mother. The mother is she.

The team members are Wolverines.
The Wolverines are team members.
They are the team members.
The team members are they.

A subject pronoun is any pronoun that
can be used in the subject position.
A subject pronoun may be used as a
subject or as a predicate noun.

Sample Page 36
Lesson 26

A subject and its predicate noun are indeed equal and interchangeable.

Nothing else will work because the two positions are equal. **Proper pronoun usage requires that we know that the subject and predicate noun positions are equal.** Let's see if this holds true with our other examples."

L78P Using the same lines of reasoning, analyze the remaining two sets of four sentences and discover the versatility of a subject pronoun and the nature of the predicate noun position.

As a point of information, some grammar texts use the term 'case' when discussing nouns or pronouns in a subject position. They say that a noun or pronoun is in the **subjective case**. Subjects and predicate nouns are positions in our sentence patterns that require the subjective case. Since the word 'case' is a bit abstract, we will choose to use the term **'subject position'**. Students will be able to relate to the word 'position' because of the use of our sentence patterns.

Defining the Nature of a Subject Pronoun

L78   **Step 8** — *"Counting up five baselines from the bottom of page 36, starting comfortably close to the left margin line, please write the following: 'A subject pronoun is any pronoun that can be used in the subject position'. You may need more than one line to write this definition. On the next available baseline, write the following: 'A subject pronoun may be used as a subject or as a predicate noun'."*

Let's Get Organized

L78   **Step 9** — *"Turn to the Table of Contents. On the page 36 line, write the title 'What Is a Subject Pronoun?' Turn back to page 36. Centered on the title line, between the two red margin lines, write the **same title**."*

One More Example for Discussion

L78   **Step 10** — "Let's analyze these sentences just to see if we understand how subject pronouns can be used as both subjects and predicate nouns. 'John is the plumber.' 'He is the plumber.' 'Sally is the baby sitter.' 'She is the baby sitter.' If the subject and predicate nouns can exchange places, how would these sentences read?

STUDENTS: "They would read like this: 'The plumber is John.' 'The plumber is he.' 'The baby sitter is Sally.' 'The baby sitter is she.' But those sentences with the words 'he' and 'she' interchanged, don't sound right."

TEACHER: "We should never count on how something sounds to determine proper grammar usage. We must be sure that the sentences we write are correct according to the rules of syntax. The subject and the predicate noun must be able to be used interchangeably. Would you say, 'Him is the plumber' or 'Her is the baby sitter'?"

STUDENTS: "No, of course not."

TEACHER: "The proper use of the words 'him' and 'her' is the topic of our next lesson."

Expectancies Learned or Reinforced in Lesson 26: Dialogue and Review

1. What pronouns do we use to conjugate a verb? **L78** *(We use the personal pronouns "I", "you", "he", "she", "it", "we", "you" [plural], "they".)*

2. What is another name for these pronouns? **L78** *(They can be called "subject pronouns" because they are used in the subject position.)*

3. Where may a subject pronoun be used? **L78** *(A subject pronoun may be used in the subject position or the predicate noun position in our sentence.)*

4. Why can a subject pronoun be used as a predicate noun? **L78** *(These two positions in our sentence are equal and interchangeable.)*

5. What does analyzing sentences do? **L78** *(Analyzing sentences teaches us how to think logically. Analyzing teaches us comparative analysis. Analyzing gives us reasons for why words are ordered like they are. Analyzing builds sentence sense so that we know how sentences should be constructed.)*

6. Why shouldn't we determine proper grammar usage by how something sounds? **L78** *(Going by how a word sounds is not reliable. We must go by what is grammatically correct.)*

7. What does conjugating verbs help us to do? **L34** *(It helps us determine the proper usage and the proper verb form for action and linking verbs.)*

8. What is Sentence Pattern 4C? **L78** *(S + LV———→PN.)*

9. What does a predicate noun do? **L78** *(A predicate noun renames the subject and is equal to the subject.)*

Where Do I Go from Here?

- **L78** goes to **"Lesson 27"** on page 270.

What Materials Will I Need?

- **L78** will need *Grammar Notebooks,* pencils, red pencils, and copies of Worksheets for **"Lesson 27"** starting on page 279.

What Is an Object Pronoun? | 37

Subject Pronoun | Object Pronoun
Singular | Singular
I | me
you | you
he | him
she | her
it | it

Plural | Plural
we | us
you | you
they | them

An object pronoun is a form of a personal pronoun used in an object position. An object pronoun may be used as a DO, IO, or OP.

Sample Page 37
Lesson 27

38 | What Is an Object Pronoun? (continued)

Sheri and Joe traveled with John and Betty.

They traveled with them.

The cat and the dog ran over the fence.

They ran over it.

The coach and I tackled the quarterback.

We tackled him.

The mayor gave the police officer a new car yesterday.

He gave her a new car yesterday.

Sample Page 38
Lesson 27

Lesson 27

What Is an Object Pronoun?

Going for the Olympic Gold

L78 "No Olympic champion has become an Olympic champion without paying a significant price in time and energy to develop the skills necessary to compete for the gold. It is no different with language skills. I want each of you to become an Olympic champion, but you must practice. Let's consider these questions. If a baseball player wants to improve his skills, what must he do?"

STUDENTS: "He must practice."

TEACHER: "If piano players want to play classical music and do it like a Mozart or a Beethoven, what must they do?"

STUDENTS: "They must practice."

TEACHER: "If students want to develop into polished writers, what must they do?"

STUDENTS: "They had better polish their writing skills."

TEACHER: "We must be well-practiced in analyzing the jobs that words can do, but practice makes perfect only if we practice perfectly. This lesson introduces a new job for a pronoun. Let's practice."

Dictating the Object Pronouns

L78 **Step 1 —** *"Turn to page 37 in your* Grammar Notebook. *We need to make a folded margin line down the middle of page 37. Skipping one baseline under our title line in the first column, center the subtitle* **'Subject Pronoun',** *capitalizing the first letter of each word."*

L78P Refer to this lesson's Sample Page in the margin as a guide.

L78 **Step 2 —** *"On the next available baseline below this subtitle, center the subtitle* **'Singular',** *capitalized."*

L78 **Step 3 —** "We know that the pronouns 'I', 'you', 'he', 'she', 'it', 'we', 'you' (plural), and 'they' are called 'subject pronouns'. *On the next available baseline just under the subtitle 'Singular', write the singular pronouns* **'I', 'you', 'he', 'she',** *and* **'it'** *comfortably close to the left margin line on consecutive baselines."*

L78 **Step 4 —** *"Skipping one baseline under the last singular pronoun 'it', center in the first column the subtitle* **'Plural',** *capitalized. On the next available baseline, write the plural personal* pronouns *'we'*, *'you'*, and *'they'* on consecutive baselines just under this subtitle *'Plural'*."

L78 **Step 5** — *"Let's go to the second column. On the same line as the subtitle 'Subject Pronoun' that we used in the first column, center in the second column the subtitle **'Object Pronoun'**, capitalized."*

L78 **Step 6** — *"On the next available baseline below the subtitle 'Object Pronoun', center the subtitle **'Singular'**, capitalized.*

Introducing the Object Pronouns

L78 **Step 7** — "I will now introduce you to what our language calls the 'object pronouns'. Object pronouns are only allowed to live in an object position. There are only three object positions that we have learned so far. Do you remember what they are?"

STUDENTS: "Sentence Pattern 3 gives me two of them, is that right?"

TEACHER: "That is correct. The indirect object and the direct object are two of these positions that require the use of an object. What is the third kind?"

STUDENTS: "The third kind must be the object of the preposition. It also requires the use of an object."

TEACHER: "Well done. Let's look at the object pronouns. Some of them change their spelling when we move from the subject pronoun to the object pronoun. For example, the subject pronoun 'I' changes to 'me' when it lives in an object position. *On the same line as the pronoun 'I', starting in the second column, comfortably close to the folded margin line, write the object pronoun **'me'**.*

L78 **Step 8** — *"Below the object pronoun 'me', please write **'you'**.* The subject form of the word 'you' does not change as an object pronoun."

L78 **Step 9** — *"Below the object form of the pronoun 'you' on the same line as the subject pronoun 'he', please write the object pronoun **'him'**.* The subject pronoun 'he' changes to 'him' in the object position."

L78 **Step 10** — *"Below the object pronoun 'him', please write **'her'**.* The subject pronoun 'she' changes to 'her' when used in an object position."

L78 **Step 11** — *"Below the object form of the pronoun 'her', write the object pronoun **'it'**.* The subject pronoun 'it' is like 'you'. It does not change when it is used in an object position."

L78 **Step 12** — "Skipping one baseline below the object pronoun 'it' and on the same line as the subheading '**Plural**' in the first column, center in the second column another subheading '**Plural**'.

L78   **Step 13** — *"Below the subheading 'Plural' in the second column, on the same line as the subject pronoun 'we', write the object pronoun 'us'.* The subject pronoun 'we' changes to 'us' in the object position."

L78   **Step 14** — *"Below the object pronoun 'us', write 'you'.* Again the pronoun 'you' in the plural does not change as we move from subject position to object position."

L78   **Step 15** — *"Below the plural object pronoun 'you', write the object pronoun 'them'.* The subject pronoun 'they' changes to 'them' when it is in an object position."

Discovering the Nature of Object Pronouns

L78   **Step 16** — "You now have recorded the object pronouns that we use in our language. But when do we use them? As we have already mentioned, there are three places in our language and only three places where these object pronouns may be used. These object pronouns may not live any place else. What are those three places again?"

STUDENTS: "Indirect objects, direct objects, and objects of a preposition. DO, IO, and OP."

TEACHER: "You are correct. Two of the places that an object pronoun may live are found in Sentence Patterns 2 and 3. An object pronoun may live in a direct object or indirect object position. The third location where an object pronoun may live is as an object of a preposition."

STUDENTS: "Oh, I get it. So when we find a preposition and its object, we might find an object pronoun as an OP. Let's see if I have this straight. **Subject pronouns may be used only as subjects or predicate nouns. Object pronouns may be used only as a DO, IO, or OP.**"

TEACHER: "Good. Our folded margin line on page 37 becomes a great wall that neither a subject nor an object pronoun can climb. The subject pronouns cannot climb the wall and live where an object pronoun lives. A subject pronoun may only be used as a subject or a predicate noun. The object pronouns may not climb the wall and be used as either a subject or a predicate noun. They must live as a DO, IO, or OP."

Defining Object Pronouns

L78   **Step 17** — *"Counting up five baselines from the bottom of page 37, comfortably close to the left margin line, write the*

What Is an Object Pronoun?	37

Subject Pronoun	Object Pronoun
Singular	**Singular**
I	me
you	you
he	him
she	her
it	it
Plural	**Plural**
we	us
you	you
they	them

An object pronoun is a form of a personal pronoun used in an object position. An object pronoun may be used as a DO, IO, or OP.

Sample Page 37
Lesson 27

following: **'An object pronoun is a form of a personal pronoun used in an object position. An object pronoun may be used as a DO, IO, or OP'.** Let's look at some examples of how these object pronouns are used in our language."

Let's Get Organized

L78 **Step 18** — *"Turn to the Table of Contents. On the page 37 line, please write* **'What Is an Object Pronoun?'** *Turn back to page 37. Centered on the title line, between the two red margin lines, write the* **same title.***"*

Dictating Sentences for Understanding Subject and Object Pronouns

L78P **Step 1** — *"Turn to page 38 in your* Grammar Notebook. *Skipping one baseline under the title line and starting comfortably close to the left margin line, write the sentence* **'Sheri and Joe traveled with John and Betty'.***"*

L78 **Step 2** — *"Skipping three baselines under this sentence and starting on the fourth baseline, comfortably close to the left margin line, write the sentence* **'The cat and the dog ran over the fence'.***"*

L78 **Step 3** — *"Skipping three baselines under this sentence and starting on the fourth baseline, comfortably close to the left margin line, write the sentence* **'The coach and I tackled the quarterback'.***"*

L78 **Step 4** — *"Skipping three more baselines under this sentence and starting on the fourth baseline, comfortably close to the left margin line, write the sentence* **'The mayor gave the police officer a new car yesterday'.** *You may need more than one line for this sentence."*

L78P Place these same sentences on the board and have your students analyze each sentence before continuing the following discussion. Remember to use your Sample Page as a guide.

> "Sheri and Joe traveled with John and Betty."
> "The cat and the dog ran over the fence."
> "The coach and I tackled the quarterback."
> "The mayor gave the police officer a new car yesterday."

Discovering the Nature of Substituting Subject and Object Pronouns

L78 **Step 5** — "In order to understand whether we need to use a subject or object pronoun, we must analyze and mark our

What Is an Object Pronoun?	37

Subject Pronoun Singular	Object Pronoun Singular
I	me
you	you
he	him
she	her
it	it
Plural	**Plural**
we	us
you	you
they	them

An object pronoun is a form of a personal pronoun used in an object position. An object pronoun may be used as a DO, IO, or OP.

Sample Page 37
Lesson 27

38	What Is an Object Pronoun? (continued)

Sheri and Joe traveled with John and Betty.

They traveled with them.

The cat and the dog ran over the fence.

They ran over it.

The coach and I tackled the quarterback.

We tackled him.

The mayor gave the police officer a new car yesterday.

He gave her a new car yesterday.

Sample Page 38
Lesson 27

Subject Pronoun	Object Pronoun
Singular	**Singular**
I	me
you	you
he	him
she	her
it	it
Plural	**Plural**
we	us
you	you
they	them

An object pronoun is a form of a personal pronoun used in an object position. An object pronoun may be used as a DO, IO, or OP.

Sample Page 37

Lesson 27

sentences. Hopefully this process of analyzing and marking will soon become so automatic that we will be able to determine the correct usage without the marking system."

L78P From now on it will be assumed that the instructor is able to help a student determine proper markings for sentences without going into the actual step-by-step discussion that we have done in the past. Turn to the *Grammar Notebook* page for **"Lesson 25: Steps of Syntactical Analysis"** if there is a need for review. For proper pronoun usage, students must be able to quickly analyze a sentence in their minds. We want this analysis to happen automatically.

L78 "Let's use page 37 in our *Notebook* as a resource. We know the subject pronouns are listed in the first column, and the object pronouns are listed in the second column. What pronoun must we use to substitute for our subjects in this first sentence?"

> **STUDENTS:** "I think we need to choose pronouns from the first column because we know they are all subject pronouns."

> **TEACHER:** "That is right. Now let me try to explain how we decide which subject pronouns we need to use. We need to understand the difference between a **First Person Pronoun,** a **Second Person Pronoun,** and a **Third Person Pronoun.** This is a tough concept. Listen closely."

Discovering the Difference between First, Second, and Third Person Pronouns

L78 **Step 6** — "A first person pronoun indicates that the speaker is personally involved in the sentence. The pronouns 'I' and 'we' and 'me' and 'us' are first person pronouns because the speaker is involved personally in the sentence. The second person pronoun indicates that the speaker is directly addressing a listener. The pronoun 'you' is the second person pronoun. As a speaker, you use the pronoun 'you' when you talk to someone. The third person pronoun indicates that the speaker is not involved in the sentence. The third person pronouns are 'he', 'she', 'it', 'him', 'her', 'it', 'they', or 'them'. These pronouns are used when the speaker is observing and stating his observations even though he is not personally involved in the activity."

Since the speaker was not personally involved in this first sentence, the pronoun 'we' cannot be used. Since the speaker was not talking with Sheri and Joe directly, the pronoun 'you' cannot be used. The speaker must use 'they' or 'she' and 'he' because the speaker is merely observing what Sheri and Joe were doing and had no involvement with their activity.

The pronoun 'them' cannot be used because an object pronoun cannot be used in a subject position. This is a hard concept. Do you think you understand?"

.78   **STUDENTS:**   "Let me run this by again. We call 'I', 'we', 'me', and 'us' first person pronouns because the speaker is somehow personally involved in the sentence. The second person pronoun 'you' is used when the speaker is in conversation with someone. The third person pronouns 'he', 'she', 'it', 'him', 'her', 'it', 'they', or 'them' are used when the speaker is not personally involved. The speaker is only observing what is happening, but is not personally involved in the action. How we use these pronouns depends upon their relationship to the speaker. Is this correct?

  TEACHER: "Impressive."

  STUDENTS: "In the sentence 'Sheri and Joe traveled with John and Betty' I believe we should use the plural personal pronoun 'they' because we have two subjects, or we could use the singular pronouns 'she' and 'he'. Regardless of what I choose, I must use third person because I am observing and not personally involved in the sentence. Is that correct?"

  TEACHER: "Thank you for listening so carefully."

roper Use of Pronouns Requires Proper Choices

78P We should not expect mastery of this concept the first time it has been introduced. Students need to know that the choice of a pronoun is determined by who is speaking and whether or not the speaker is personally involved in the action of the sentence. These designations will serve students better when they must choose a point of view from which to write a composition or tell a story. These are higher level concepts that they will eventually need to know. This previous discussion may appear to be cumbersome at first, but proper usage of pronouns requires that these steps of reasoning be in place. Students need to understand why they must make certain choices.

Discovering Object Pronoun Usage in a Prepositional Phrase

L78   **Step 7—** "Are there any other nouns in our sentence where we could substitute pronouns?"

  STUDENTS: "There are two nouns in the prepositional phrase [with John and Betty]."

---

38 What Is an Object Pronoun? (continued)

Sheri and Joe traveled with John and Betty.

They traveled with them.

The cat and the dog ran over the fence.

They ran over it.

The coach and I tackled the quarterback.

We tackled him.

The mayor gave the police officer a new car yesterday.

He gave her a new car yesterday.

Sample Page 38
Lesson 27

Every word in a sentence has a very important job to do.

TEACHER: "What would you say could be used here?"

STUDENTS: "We need to use an object pronoun. By definition the object pronouns may be used in a DO, IO, or OP position and no others. That is what you have told me. So . . . I know I must choose an object pronoun. Let's see. I am the speaker, but I have not been included in this first sentence, so I can't use the object pronoun 'us'. I am not talking to John and Betty personally, so I cannot use the object pronoun 'you'. Since I am only observing what they are doing, and I am not personally involved, I need to use the object pronouns 'them' or 'him' or 'her'."

TEACHER: "Then how could the sentence read?"

STUDENTS: "'They traveled with them', or 'She and he traveled with him and her'."

L78   Step 8 — "That is correct, and you have explained it well. *Skipping one baseline below our original sentence, comfortably close to the margin line, write* **'They traveled with them'**. *And then mark this new sentence with its pronouns accordingly.*"

L78P By way of reminder, a syntactical expectancy is not truly an expectancy unless students can offer a credible explanation for why they are doing what they are doing. When they can explain why, they own the concept and can make application.

L78   Step 9 — "Look at the other sentences. Where could we make proper pronoun substitutions? *Create a new sentence using these pronouns. Write the following new sentences with the proper pronoun substitutions after skipping one line under each original sentence:*

> *'They ran over it.'*
> *'We tackled him.'*
> *'He gave her a new car yesterday.'*"

L78 "In actual language usage, it would be uncommon to find a need to change every noun into an object or subject pronoun. We simply use pronouns to make our language more efficient and less redundant. Technically it would be correct to say our last sentence with all nouns changed to pronouns: 'He gave her it yesterday'. Does this work? Perhaps not. We must use pronoun substitution only when it will help our writing the most."

Let's Get Organized

L78   Step 10 — *"Turn to the Table of Contents. On the page 38 line, write the title* **'What Is an Object Pronoun? (continued)'**. *Turn back to page 38. Centered on the title line, between the two red margin lines, write the* **same title.**"

---

38 | What is an Object Pronoun? (continued)

Sheri and Joe traveled with John and Betty.

They traveled with them.

The cat and the dog ran over the fence.

They ran over it.

The coach and I tackled the quarterback.

We tackled him.

The mayor gave the police officer a new car yesterday.

He gave her a new car yesterday.

Sample Page 38
Lesson 27

A Further Explanation of Proper Pronoun Usage before the Student Worksheet

78 **Step 11** — "I am going to give you another student worksheet to help you make proper pronoun choices. Before I do that, let's look at three examples. These examples will help us understand why we must use the pronouns that we choose.

> (We, us) girls went with (they, them).

"The pronoun 'we' must be used here before the word 'girls' because 'girls' is the subject and pronouns must match the words they describe. These pronouns can be called **adjectival pronouns**. They serve both as a pronoun and as an adjective. We mark such pronouns as if they were adjectives. We use the pronoun 'them' in the second part of the sentence because it is the object of the preposition 'with'.

> (He, him) saw (she, her) at the bakery.

"In this example we must choose 'he' because it is the subject, and we must choose 'her' because 'her' is the direct object.

> (He, him) sold (I, me,) the watch.

"In this example we must choose 'he' again because it is the subject, and we must choose 'me' because it is in an indirect object position."

78P Pass out a copy of the student Worksheet found at the end of this lesson.

Expectancies Learned or Reinforced in Lesson 27: Dialogue and Review

1. Where may subject pronouns be used? **L78** *(Subject pronouns may be used in a subject position or a predicate noun position.)*

2. Where may object pronouns be used? **L78** *(Object pronouns may be used in one of three places: DO, IO, or OP.)*

3. What must we do in order to choose the proper pronoun in a sentence? **L78** *(We must be able to analyze the sentence and determine the function of the pronoun. If it is a subject position or a predicate noun position, we use a subject pronoun. If it is an object position, we must use an object pronoun.)*

4. Why shouldn't we go by how pronouns sound to determine proper usage? **L78** *(How something sounds is not always a reliable guide for pronoun usage. We must know how to analyze and make proper choices accordingly.)*

5. When a pronoun influences a subject, what kind of a pronoun do we use? **L78** *(Pronouns influencing a subject must use a subject pronoun. We must say 'We girls went downtown' not 'Us girls went downtown'.)*

6. How will knowing the four sentence patterns help us? **L78** *(They will be our guide to proper usage of subject and object pronouns.)*

7. Why do we need to analyze a sentence quickly? **L78** *(We need to determine proper pronoun usage.)*

8. What are the singular subject and object pronouns? **L78** *("I", "you", "he", "she", "it", "me", "you", "him", "her", and "it".)*

9. What are the plural subject and object pronouns? **L78** *("We", "you", "they", "us", "you", and "them".)*

10. What are the First Person pronouns and when do we use them? **L78** *(The First Person pronouns are the pronouns "I" and "we" or "me" and "us", and we use them when we are personally involved in a sentence.)*

11. What are the Second Person pronouns and when do we use them? **L78** *(The Second Person pronouns are singular "you" and plural "you", and we use them when talking directly to another person or group. "You" indicates the person who is listening to the message.)*

12. What are the Third Person pronouns and when do we use them? **L78** *(The Third Person pronouns are the pronouns "he", "she", "it", "him", "her", "it", "they", and "them", and they are used when the speaker is observing someone, something, or some group and is not involved in the action of the sentence.)*

Where Do I Go from Here?

- **L78** goes to **"Lesson 28"** on page 285.

What Materials Will I Need?

- **L78** will need *Grammar Notebooks* and pencils.

1. I am searching for them.
   S   OP

2. We looked for her.
   S   OP

3. They watched them.
   S   DO

4. You saw them in the office.
   S   DO

5. He reached him by phone.
   S   DO

6. She and I gave her the message.
   S   S   IO

7. It watched me with glaring eyes.
   S   DO

8. He did it for us and them.
   S   DO   OP   OP

9. She cheered us on.
   S   DO

10. I am she.
    S   PN

Teacher's Answer Key for Student Worksheet 1:

Subject/Object Pronouns

Teacher Directions: Explain to your student the directions for marking the pronouns in these exercises as written on the student Worksheets.

Student Directions: Find the pronouns in these sentences.

Mark them correctly.

If they are object pronouns, what job do they do? Are they a DO, IO, or OP?

If they are subject pronouns, are they an S or a PN?

Subject/Object Pronouns

Student Directions: Find the pronouns in these sentences.

Mark them correctly.

If they are object pronouns, what job do they do? Are they a DO, IO, or OP?

If they are subject pronouns, are they an S or a PN?

1. I am searching for them.

2. We looked for her.

3. They watched them.

4. You saw them in the office.

5. He reached him by phone.

6. She and I gave her the message.

7. It watched me with glaring eyes.

8. He did it for us and them.

9. She cheered us on.

10. I am she.

1. $\overset{S}{((She,)}$ Her) looked for (they, $\overset{OP}{((them))}$.

2. $\overset{S}{((He,)}$ Him) gave (she, $\overset{IO}{(her))}$ the right answers.

3. $\overset{S}{((They,)}$ Them) watched (we, $\overset{DO}{(us))}$swim a mile.

4. $\overset{S}{((We,)}$ Us) girls went to the show with
    (they, $\overset{OP}{(them))}$.

5. $\overset{S}{((They,)}$ Them) went to the show with
    (we, $\overset{adj.}{(us))}\overset{OP}{girls}$.

6. $\overset{S}{((I,)}$ Me) walked over to (he, $\overset{OP}{(him))}$.

7. Sally and $\overset{S}{((I,)}$ me) loved the flowers from
    (he, $\overset{OP}{(him))}$.

8. $\overset{S}{((We,)}$ Us) boys attended the party with
    (they, $\overset{OP}{(them))}$.

9. $\overset{S}{((He,)}$ Him) and $\overset{S}{((she,)}$ her) are $\overset{PN}{((they,)}$ them) of
    whom I speak.

10. $\overset{S}{((She,)}$ Her) threw (we, $\overset{IO}{(us))}$ the rope.

Lesson 27: What Is an Object Pronoun?   **281**

Teacher's Answer Key for Student Worksheet 2:

Subject/Object Pronouns

Teacher Directions: Explain to your student the directions for marking the pronouns in these exercises as written on the student Worksheets.

Student Directions: Circle the correct pronouns in these sentences.

Mark them correctly.

If they are object pronouns, what job do they do? Are they a DO, IO, or OP?

If they are subject pronouns, are they an S or a PN?

Subject/Object Pronouns

Student Directions: (Circle) *the correct pronouns in these sentences.*

Mark them correctly.

If they are object pronouns, what job do they do? Are they a DO, IO, or OP?

If they are subject pronouns, are they an S or a PN?

1.   (She, Her) looked for (they, them).

2.   (He, Him) gave (she, her) the right answers.

3.   (They, Them) watched (we, us) swim a mile.

4.   (We, Us) girls went to the show with (they, them).

5.   (They, Them) went to the show with (we, us) girls.

6.   (I, Me) walked over to (he, him).

7.   Sally and (I, me) loved the flowers from (he, him).

8.   (We, Us) boys attended the party with (they, them).

9.   (He, Him) and (she, her) are (they, them) of whom I speak.

10. (She, Her) threw (we, us) the rope.

1. (They, them) went to the ballpark with
   S

   (we, us).
   OP

2. (He, Him) saw (she, her) at the bakery.
   S   DO

3. Did you see (she, her) or (we, us) down-
                    DO   DO

   town?

4. It must be (he, him) who was after
              PN

   (they, them).
        OP

5. (They, them) glared at (we, us).
   S   OP

6. (We, us) people need (they, them) or
   S   DO

   (she, her) to get done.
        DO

7. (I, me) am (he, him) who must accept
   S   PN

   (she, her) request.
   adj. DO

8. Will you go with (I, me)?
                      OP

9. (He, him) sold (I, me) the watch.
   S   IO

10. (They, them) are in with (we, us) girls
    S   adj. OP

    and John.

Lesson 27: What Is an Object Pronoun? **283**

Subject/Object Pronouns

Teacher Directions: Explain to your student the directions for marking the pronouns in these exercises as written on the student Worksheets.

Student Directions: Circle the correct pronouns in these sentences.

Mark them correctly.

If they are object pronouns, what job do they do? Are they a DO, IO, or OP?

If they are subject pronouns, are they an S or a PN?

Subject/Object Pronouns

Student Directions: Cir-cle the correct pronouns in these sentences.

Mark them correctly.

If they are object pronouns, what job do they do? Are they a DO, IO, or OP?

If they are subject pronouns, are they an S or a PN?

1. (They, them) went to the ballpark with (we, us).

2. (He, Him) saw (she, her) at the bakery.

3. Did you see (she, her) or (we, us) down-town?

4. It must be (he, him) who was after (they, them).

5. (They, them) glared at (we, us).

6. (We, us) people need (they, them) or (she, her) to get done.

7. (I, me) am (he, him) who must accept (she, her) request.

8. Will you go with (I, me)?

9. (He, him) sold (I, me) the watch.

10. (They, them) are in with (we, us) girls and John.

Lesson 28
What Is a Declarative Sentence?

Sample Page 39
Lesson 28

Sentences Have Special Jobs Too

L34 "We should now know that every word has a special job to do. We are learning how to figure out what these jobs are. A noun is a naming word. That is its job. An action verb is a word of energy. That is its job. An adjective is a word that describes a noun or pronoun. That is its job. In the same way, sentences have special jobs to do also. In a sentence, single words work together to make one complete thought in order to accomplish a task. In this lesson we will learn what task a declarative sentence accomplishes."

Dictating Declarative Sentences

L34P Provide loose-leaf penmanship paper for **L34**. **L56** should turn to page 39 of their *Grammar Notebook*. You may have to help students analyze the spelling of some of the words in the sentences below.

L34 *"Skipping one baseline under the title line, starting comfortably close to the left margin line, write this sentence:* **'George Johnson hated the alarm clock'.***"*

Step 2 — *"On the next available baseline, comfortably close, write this sentence:* **'Monarch butterflies emerge from a cocoon'.***"*

Step 3 — *"On the next available baseline, write the next sentence:* **'John, Sally, and Jim sold tickets for the concert'.***"*

Step 4 — *"On the next available baseline, write this sentence:* **'Harriet Tubman was called "Moses"'.***"*

Step 5 — *"On the next available baseline, write the last sentence for this lesson:* **'Spiders are found in the palaces of kings'.***"*

Discovering the Nature of a Declarative Sentence

L56 **Step 6 —** "What do we find out about our first sentence if we analyze it?"

STUDENTS: "There are no prepositional phrases. The word 'hated' can be conjugated and serves as a verb. It has to be an

Hard Work Pays Off

It is important to continually bring the reason we are doing what we are doing to the attention of the students. Occasional references to the character qualities of diligence and dependability and responsibility and the need to "pay the price" will help our students focus on how we accomplish what we are doing.

Hard work pays off. Our students must often be reminded of this. We have a worthy discipline with a worthy goal, and we must urgently and eagerly remind our students exactly how imperative mastery really is. We must convey to our students that, at this moment in their time and space, knowing how language works really matters.

Students must understand the principles. Students must master these lessons. Their ability to attain their full potential is put at significant risk if they do not.

action verb. It is not on my linking verb list. The name George Johnson answers 'Who is doing the hating?' That makes George the subject. What did George hate? He hated the clock so clock is the direct object. The clock receives the action of the verb. The word alarm tells us 'What kind?' of clock it was so it is serving as an adjective influencing the word clock. The sentence is using Sentence Pattern 2: S+AV——→DO. How did we do?"

TEACHER: "You did extremely well."

L34 TEACHER: "We have said that every sentence should make complete sense. What that means is that there is something to learn from each sentence. The only way we can learn is if we are given the facts and all the information that we need in order to think. We cannot think about ideas very well without words. What information do we get from this first sentence? What do we learn?"

STUDENTS: "We learn that George Johnson hates alarm clocks."

TEACHER: "We have a special name for a sentence that gives us factual information. We call these sentences **'declarative sentences'**. Single words work together in a sentence in an ordered way to provide information so that we can learn. They start with a capital letter and end with a period."

L56 TEACHER: "The root word for 'declarative' is the word 'declare'. It is always good to go to the root word and find out what it means. If we look in a dictionary, 'to declare' means 'to make known, to announce, to proclaim, to assert, to reveal, or to prove'."

L34 STUDENTS: "So a declarative sentence tells us something."

L56 STUDENTS: "It introduces whatever it is we need to know. It announces the facts so we can think about them."

L34 TEACHER: "That is correct. Let's do one more declarative sentence."

L56 TEACHER: "What do we find out about our second sentence if we analyze it?"

STUDENTS: "There is one prepositional phrase. The object of the preposition is the word 'cocoon'. The verb 'emerge' is an action verb. I can conjugate it sensibly and it is not in my linking verb list. 'Who or what emerges?' The noun 'butterflies' is serving as the subject of our sentence. The word 'monarch' is serving as an adjective because it answers the question 'What kind of butterfly do we have?' The sentence uses Sentence Pattern 1: S+AV."

L56 TEACHER: "Well done."

L34 TEACHER: "Is our second sentence a declarative sentence?"

  STUDENTS: "The sentence is giving me information about monarch butterflies. I am learning that they emerge from a cocoon. Yes, this is a declarative sentence."

L34P Hold a discussion on the remaining three sentences. Analyze each one, find the job each word is doing, determine the sentence pattern being used, and explain why it is a declarative sentence. Use the Sample Page as a guide.

Defining a Declarative Sentence

L34 **Step 7** — *"Let's count up four baselines from the bottom of our page. Beginning comfortably close to the left margin line, beginning with a capital letter, write the following sentence: 'A declarative sentence states a fact or gives information and always ends with a period'."*

L34P There is room on this page to write declarative sentences that the students have created themselves. Add writing declarative sentences to your lesson plans periodically. Have the students write declarative sentences and then have them read these out loud to you. Record some of these on this page.

Let's Get Organized

L56 **Step 8** — *"Turn to the Table of Contents. On the page 39 line, write the title 'What Is a Declarative Sentence?' Turn back to page 39. Centered on the title line, between the two red margin lines, write the **same title**."*

We All Need Practice Thinking in Complete Sentences

L34P Because I want my students to think and to write in complete sentences, I ask them to practice speaking their thoughts in complete sentences in my classroom. When they are asking or answering questions in my class, I ask them to stand with both feet on the floor and with good posture when they are asking or answering questions. Standing and speaking in complete sentences keeps students alert and gives them practice thinking and speaking in pressure situations.

Continue to pursue excellence.

Be a writer.

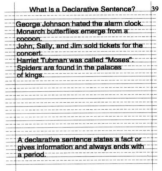

What Is a Declarative Sentence? 39

George Johnson hated the alarm clock.
Monarch butterflies emerge from a cocoon.
John, Sally, and Jim sold tickets for the concert.
Harriet Tubman was called "Moses".
Spiders are found in the palaces of kings.

A declarative sentence states a fact or gives information and always ends with a period.

Sample Page 39
Lesson 28

Expectancies Learned or Reinforced in Lesson 28: Dialogue and Review

1. What is a declarative sentence? **L12** *(A declarative sentence is a sentence that states a fact or gives information.)*

2. What punctuation mark do we use at the end of a declarative sentence? **L12** *(Every declarative sentence needs to end with a period.)*

3. How does standing up on our feet help us when answering a teacher's question? **L34** *(It helps us be very alert.)*

4. What benefits come from answering a teacher's question using a complete sentence? **L34** *(If we can think in complete sentences, we can write in complete sentences.)*

5. Why is a root word so important? **L56** *(A root word is the basic part of a word from which other words may be built. To know what it means is to know what many other words mean.)*

6. How does analyzing sentences help us? **L56** *(Marking sentences helps me to gain an increasing awareness of how sentences are written building in me a "sentence sense" so that I become an excellent writer and speaker.)*

Where Do I Go from Here?

- **L34**, **L56**, and **L78** go to **"Lesson 29"** on page 289.

What Materials Will I Need?

- **L34** will need penmanship paper, pencils, and red pencils.

- **L56** and **L78** will need *Grammar Notebooks,* pencils, and red pencils.

Lesson 29
What Is an Interrogative Sentence?

L34 "This is the second of the four purposes for a sentence. We learned in the last lesson that a declarative sentence states a fact or gives some information. There are lots of these kinds of sentences in English. Sometimes, however, we need to collect information instead of giving it out. We need to ask questions to find the information that we need. We call these kind of sentences 'Interrogative Sentences', and they always end with a question mark."

Dictating Words That Start Interrogative Sentences

L34P L34 students will need a piece of loose-leaf penmanship paper. **L56** and above should turn to page 40 in their *Grammar Notebook*.

L34 **Step 1** — "We are going to make a list of common words that are used to ask many common questions. I want you to start each word in the list with a capital letter. *At the top of your page, skipping a baseline below the title line, comfortably close to the left margin line, write the word 'What?' Place a question mark after this word.*"

L34 **Step 2** — "*On the next baseline, directly under the word 'What?', write the word 'Which?' with a question mark after it.*"

L34 **Step 3** — "*On the next baseline, directly under the word 'Which?', write the word 'Who?' with a question mark after it.*"

L34 **Step 4** — "*On the next baseline, directly under the word 'Who?', write the words 'To Whom?' with a question mark after them.*"

L34 **Step 5** — "*On the next baseline, directly under the words 'To Whom?', write the word 'Whose?' with a question mark after it.* We call these words we have listed so far, **'interrogative pronouns'.** These interrogative pronouns are used to ask many questions. There are other words that we use to ask questions too."

L34 **Step 6** — "*Make three columns by folding margin lines on your page. In the second column on the same line as 'What?', write the following words that may also be used to start questions, placing them on consecutive baselines: 'When?' 'Where?'*"

Sample Page 40
Lesson 29

Sample Page 41
Lesson 29

'Why?' 'How?' In the third column, on consecutive baselines, starting on the same line as 'What?' and 'When?', write five forms of the verb 'to be' all of which can be used to ask a question: 'Am?' 'Is?' 'Are?' 'Was?' 'Were?'. Other helping verbs can also be used to start questions. There are many ways to write a sentence that is a question."

Dictating Interrogative Sentences

L34   **Step 7 —** *"Skipping one baseline below the word 'Whose?', starting comfortably close to the left margin line, write the sentence **'Who was at the ball game with you?'** Don't forget to place a question mark at the end of this sentence."*

L34   **Step 8 —** *"Starting on the next available baseline below our first question, comfortably close to the left margin line, write the sentence **'Which teacher was responsible for the children?'** You may need more than one line."*

L34   **Step 9 —** *"Starting on the next available baseline below our second question, comfortably close to the left margin line, write the sentence **'What is the name of the man?'"***

L34   **Step 10 —** *"Starting on the next available baseline below our third question, comfortably close to the left margin line, write the sentence **'To whom do you refer?'"***

L34   **Step 11 —** *"Starting on the next available baseline below our fourth question, comfortably close to the left margin line, write the sentence **'Whose bicycle needs paint?'"***

L34   **Step 12 —** *"Skipping one baseline below our last example, write the following three sentences on consecutive baselines:*

        'When will we go?'
        'Why was the meeting canceled?'
        'Am I going to the game?'"

Defining an Interrogative Sentence

L34   **Step 13 —** *"Count up three baselines from the bottom of the page and comfortably close to the left margin line, write the following: **'An interrogative sentence asks a question and ends with a question mark'.**"*

Let's Get Organized

L56   **Step 14 —** *"Turn to the Table of Contents. On the page 40 line, write the title **'What Is an Interrogative Sentence?'** Turn back to page 40.*

L34   *Centered on the title line, between the two red margin lines, write the title **'What Is an Interrogative Sentence?'"***

Making the Rounds: Always Inspect What You Expect

34P Walk around the room and offer lots of encouragement where it is merited. Check to see that students are still being diligent in their handwriting efforts. If you are expecting a certain level of performance, then it would be good to see if they are actually meeting that expectation. We are in a training program for the mind. We are teaching listening skills. As we make the rounds, we will see some diligent work in process. Compliment those whose efforts are exemplary. Applaud such efforts lavishly and openly. "Wow! You are doing an incredible job. You are really a detail person. You must be really sharp." As an instructor, keep persevering. Your diligence and caring will be rewarded also.

Discovering the Nature of an Interrogative Sentence

78P The sentences that have been dictated are analyzed in the Sample Page in the margin. Student–Teacher dialogue for the complete analysis of each sentence will need to be developed. Study the following dialogue for an explanation to some of the markings.

78 **Step 1—** "Let's look at some parts of these sentences together and then let's try to analyze these interrogative sentences we have written. What general observation can we make about these sentences?"

> **STUDENTS:** "We can see that these interrogative sentences start with one of the interrogative pronouns we wrote in the first column on page 39. They are seeking information. That is the job of an interrogative sentence. And besides that, they all end with a question mark."

> **TEACHER:** "Well said. If we were to use the personal name John as the answer to the first question, what declarative sentence would give us that information?"

> **STUDENTS:** "Would we substitute the name John for the pronoun 'who'?"

> **TEACHER:** "That's right. The sentence would read, 'John was at the ball game with you'. If we were to analyze this declarative sentence, we would find that the name 'John' is our subject. If we were to analyze the interrogative sentence 'Who was at the ball game with you?' can you figure out which word might be the subject?"

> **STUDENTS:** "Bracketing the prepositional phrases [at the ball game] and [with you] leaves us with the sentence

We are in a training program for the mind.

We are teaching listening skills. As we make the rounds, we will see some diligent work in process.

Compliment those whose efforts are exemplary.

Applaud such efforts lavishly and openly.

'Who was?' Since 'was' is a linking verb here, the interrogative pronoun 'who' must be our subject."

TEACHER: "So we have learned something else. An interrogative pronoun can serve as a subject in a question. Look at the second interrogative question that we recorded. How would you answer the second question? Let's continue to use the name John."

STUDENTS: "John's teacher was responsible for the children."

TEACHER: "This sentence introduces a concept which we will be looking at more closely a few lessons from now. Sometimes we need to show that someone or something 'owns' someone or something else. We call this condition a possessive condition. To possess something is to own it.

L78 "Some people use the word 'case' to refer to this condition. We have mentioned this word 'case' before. Words in the subject position or the object position are said to be in the subjective or objective case. They say that a word that shows ownership is in the possessive case. In our sample declarative sentence, with John substituted for the interrogative pronoun 'Which?' what word is showing a certain ownership or possession of another?"

STUDENTS: "Does John own his teacher?"

TEACHER: "Well, in a manner of speaking, that's right."

STUDENTS: "Wow! Not many students own their own teacher."

TEACHER: "When we write 'John's teacher' we need to punctuate John in a special way. We place an apostrophe before the letter 's'. That shows that John possesses the teacher. How would we mark the word 'John' or the word 'Which?' in this sentence?"

STUDENTS: "We have an answer to the question 'Which teacher?' The pronoun 'Which?' is doing the job of an adjective because it answers one of the adjective questions. We would circle 'Which?', label it with an 'adj.', and draw an arrow to the word 'teacher'."

TEACHER: "That is correct."

When Do We Use Who or Whom?

L78   TEACHER: "Before I have you analyze the rest of these sentences, look at our fourth sentence. Let's learn something new. We learned in our lesson on object pronouns that the object pronoun for the subject pronoun 'I' is 'me'. The object pronoun for 'he' is

	'him'. The object pronoun for 'they' is 'them'. Do you see any pattern in these pronouns when they switch from subject to object?"
STUDENTS:	"Yes, I do. The object pronouns in these three examples all use the letter 'm' in their new spelling."
TEACHER:	"That should tell you something about the pronouns 'who' and 'whom'."
STUDENTS:	"The pronoun 'who' may only be used in a subject position. The pronoun 'whom' may only be used in an object position. Is that correct?"
TEACHER:	"Right. Analyze the sentence 'To whom do you refer?' What do you learn?"
STUDENTS:	"'To whom' is a prepositional phrase. The word 'whom' is the OP."
TEACHER:	"Good thinking. Object pronouns must be used in an object position. 'Whom' is the object form of the subject pronoun 'who'. In this sentence, the interrogative question begins with a prepositional phrase. How versatile our language is."

Using Other Words to Ask Interrogative Questions

56 **Step 2 —** *"Turn to page 41 in your* Grammar Notebook. We need to look at one more aspect of interrogative sentences. It is not always necessary to use interrogative pronouns to ask a question.

"Sometimes all we need to do is put a coal car from a declarative sentence in front of the engine of that sentence to make an interrogative sentence. In other words, we invert or reverse the word order.

"We place a verb in front of a subject instead of the normal word order where the subject is in front of the verb. Usually this coal car that we invert is a helping verb that was there already or that we need to add. Listen to this declarative sentence: 'John was fishing at Lake Reno'."

TEACHER:	"How do we make this into a question?"
STUDENTS:	"We simply change the order of our sentence pattern like you said. We take the HV and put it in front of the subject. It would read 'Was John fishing at Lake Reno?'"
TEACHER:	"Right. Look at this next sentence: John goes uptown regularly. How do we make this a question?"

Interrogative sentences seek information.

A question is created by inverting the word order of a declarative sentence.

Interrogative Sentences (continued) 41

The mailman ate the candy.
Did the mailman eat the candy?

The President and the First Lady attended the Inaugural Ball.
Did the President and the First Lady attend the Inaugural Ball?

Books open doors to the past and make time without wings.
Do books open doors to the past and make time without wings?

Michael Jordan is a super player.
Is Michael Jordan a super player?

Preparation for a career requires study and hard work.
Does preparation for a career require study and hard work?

Sample Page 41
Lesson 29

STUDENTS: "We need to change the verb by adding a helping verb."

TEACHER: "We could use any of the following depending upon our purpose: 'Does John go?' 'Has John gone?' 'Will John go?' 'Could John go?' 'Would John go?' 'Should John go?' When we use the helping verb 'have', 'has', or 'had', we must always use the third most important part of the verb 'go'. This is a rule of our language."

Take Time for Review

L56P When you run into a needed discussion on verbs, take the opportunity to practice a conjugation or two, and throw in a linking verb list review on the side.

L78P Ask what the Adverb Questions are. Ask what the Adjective Questions are. Ask what the Sentence Patterns are and the functions of each part. Drill and review. See how fast your students can conjugate a verb correctly. Time them. How fast can they say the linking verbs and still say this list coherently? Believe me. When they know them, the list will be a blur.

Dictating Declarative Sentences and Creating Interrogative Sentences

L56 **Step 3** — *"Skipping one baseline below the title line on page 41, write the following declarative sentence: **'The mailman ate the candy'**. Skipping two more baselines and starting on the third, use two lines to write the following sentence: **'The President and the First Lady attended the Inaugural Ball'**. Skipping three baselines below this second sentence and starting on the fourth line, write the following declarative sentence using two lines: **'Books open doors to the past and make time without wings'**. Skipping three baselines again and starting on the fourth line, write the following sentence: **'Michael Jordan is a super player'**. Skipping only two baselines and starting on the third line, write our last declarative sentence using two lines: **'Preparation for a career requires study and hard work'**."*

Step 4 — "Before we analyze these declarative sentences, let's look at one more example. Look at this sentence on the board: 'I am going on a trip to New York City'. How would we analyze this sentence?"

STUDENTS: "There are two prepositional phrases with their objects: 'on a trip' and 'to New York City'. The word 'going' is the last word I can conjugate. It is an action verb. I mark it with an 'AV'. The word 'am' is on my linking verb list, but here it is being used as a helping verb. I will mark it with an 'HV'. The subject is the pronoun 'I'."

TEACHER: "Great. Now how do we make this into an interrogative sentence?"

STUDENTS: "We need to change the order of our subject and verb. We will take the verb 'am' and put it in front of the subject 'I'. The interrogative sentence would be the following: 'Am I going on a trip to New York City?'"

L56 **Step 5 —** "Turn your attention to the sentences we have recorded on page 41. *Please **analyze** these at this time.*"

L56P When the students are done, work through a discussion on each sentence to see if these sentences are marked correctly. Use the Sample Page as a guide.

TEACHER: "How might these declarative sentences read if we inverted the word order, added helping verbs where necessary, and changed all these statements into questions?"

STUDENTS: "'Did the mailman eat the candy?'
'Did the President and the First Lady attend the Inaugural Ball?'
'Do books open doors to the past and make time without wings?'
'Is Michael Jordan a super player?'
'Does preparation for a career require study and hard work?'"

TEACHER: *"On the baseline directly below each declarative sentence on page 41, write the **interrogative sentences** you have created from each original declarative sentence."*

Interrogative Sentences (continued)	41

The mailman ate the candy.
Did the mailman eat the candy?

The President and the First Lady attended the Inaugural Ball.
Did the President and the First Lady attend the Inaugural Ball?

Books open doors to the past and make time without wings.
Do books open doors to the past and make time without wings?

Michael Jordan is a super player.
Is Michael Jordan a super player?

Preparation for a career requires study and hard work.
Does preparation for a career require study and hard work?

Sample Page 41
Lesson 29

Let's Get Organized

L56 **Step 6 —** *"Turn to the Table of Contents. On the page 41 line, write the title **'Interrogative Sentences (continued)'**. Turn back to page 41. Centered on the title line, between the two red margin lines, write the title **'Interrogative Sentences (continued)'**."*

Expectancies Learned or Reinforced in Lesson 29: Dialogue and Review

1. What does an interrogative sentence do? **L34** *(It asks a question.)*

2. What punctuation mark do we use at the end of an interrogative sentence? **L34** *(An interrogative sentence always ends with a question mark.)*

3. How do questions begin? **L34** *(Questions may begin with a common interrogative pronoun like "who", "whom", "which", "what", or "whose".)*

4. How else are questions created? **L56** *(Questions may be created by taking a declarative sentence, inverting word order, and adding helping verbs as needed.)*

5. In analysis, an interrogative pronoun might take on what job in the sentence? **L78** *(An interrogative pronoun may serve as a subject, as an adjective, or as an OP.)*

6. What does a word do that shows possession? **L78** *(A possessive word is someone or something that owns someone or something else.)*

7. How do we show possession when we use a personal name like John? **L78** *(We need to add an apostrophe and an "s" to show this ownership.)*

8. What part of the verb must we use when we are using the helping verbs "have", "has", or "had"? **L78** *(We need to use the third most important part of any verb.)*

Where Do I Go from Here?

- **L34**, **L56**, and **L78** go to **"Lesson 30"** on page 297.

What Materials Will I Need?

- **L34** will need penmanship paper and pencils.

- **L56** and **L78** will need *Grammar Notebooks* and pencils.

Lesson 30
What Is an Imperative Sentence?

L34 "A third kind of sentence has a different job than a declarative sentence or an interrogative sentence. Do you remember what job a declarative sentence does?"

    STUDENTS: "A declarative sentence gives us factual information. It makes a statement. 'The sunset is beautiful.' This is a declarative sentence."

    TEACHER: "What is an interrogative sentence?"

    STUDENTS: "An interrogative sentence asks a question. 'Is the sunset beautiful?' is an example of an interrogative sentence."

    TEACHER: "Right. A third job that a sentence can do is also important. Sometimes we need to give orders or a command to someone. On occasion, people need to be given instructions or told what they should do, so we need to have a sentence that helps us do that. We have worked with these kinds of sentences before."

Dictating Imperative Sentences

L34P L34 students should be given a page of loose-leaf penmanship paper. **L56** and above need to turn to page 42 in their *Grammar Notebook.*

L34 **Step 1** — *"Skipping one baseline below the title line on our page, starting six spaces in from the left margin line, write the sentence* **'Clean the house'***. On the next baseline directly below the first sentence, starting six spaces in from the left margin line, write the sentence* **'Go to the backyard'***. On each of the following consecutive baselines, starting six spaces in from the left margin, write the remaining four sentences:* **'Jump in the lake'***.* **'Wash the dishes'***.* **'Run the mile in five minutes'***.* **'Ask the mayor'***. Be sure to place a period at the end of every sentence."*

Discovering the Nature of an Imperative Sentence

L34 **Step 2** — "We need to look carefully at these sentences. Did you notice that something seems to be missing from each sentence? Can you think of what might be missing? To help you, let me ask you a question about our first sentence. Who or what is being told to do the cleaning?"

42	What Is an Imperative Sentence?
(You) Clean the house.	
(You) Go to the backyard.	
(You) Jump in the lake.	
(You) Wash the dishes.	
(You) Run the mile in five minutes.	
(You) Ask the mayor.	

An imperative sentence gives a command or makes a request. An imperative sentence ends with a period.

Sample Page 42
Lesson 30

STUDENTS:	"It sounds like I am suppose to do the cleaning."
TEACHER:	"That is right. What we really want to happen with these kinds of sentences is that the person hearing them understands that they need to do something. What am I needing to do in the second sentence?"
STUDENTS:	"You are needing to go to the backyard."
TEACHER:	"Good. In both of these sentences, a person is being instructed or required to accomplish a task. You should do this. You should do that. The word 'You' is the missing word in every sentence. We just understand that it could be written there, but we never say it and we never write it. So we say that every sentence that gives us an order or makes a request, begins with 'you understood'. Say the term *'you understood'*.
STUDENTS:	*" 'You understood'. "*
TEACHER:	*"Place the word **'You'** in front of every sentence that we have recorded. Capitalize and put **parentheses** around the word 'You' in each sentence.* There is a special name that we give to these kinds of sentences. We call them **'imperative sentences'**. The word imperative means that it has to be done."

Analyzing an Imperative Sentence

L56 **Step 3 —** "We need to analyze these imperative sentences. Can you think of something all of these imperative sentences have in common besides 'you understood'?"

STUDENTS:	"They require some kind of action. If you were talking to me, I would be expected to do something about whatever it was you were saying. It is a command."
TEACHER:	"Look at the sentence 'Clean the house' again. There are no prepositions. What is the last word that we can conjugate?"
STUDENTS:	"It is the action verb 'clean'."
TEACHER:	"Who or what will obey the command? The answer to that question is our subject. 'You' will obey the command, therefore 'you understood' is the subject."
STUDENTS:	"Oh, I get it. When someone is telling me to do something, I am 'you' to him. When I am telling someone else to do something, he is 'you' to me. The pronoun 'you' is always the subject of an imperative sentence."

L78 "Since you are talking to me, you are the speaker. I am receiving your words. We would have to use the second person pronoun 'you'. That's the job of a second person pronoun, to receive the words of the speaker."

L56 STUDENTS: "The sentence could read, 'You clean the house'."

TEACHER: "That is right. Every imperative sentence starts with a verb and leaves off that very important subject 'you understood'. What job does the word 'house' do?"

STUDENTS: "It flies the flag 'What?' after an action verb. It is doing the work of a DO."

TEACHER: "Mark and analyze the rest of these sentences."

42	What Is an Imperative Sentence?

(You) Clean the house.
(You) Go to the backyard.
(You) Jump in the lake.
(You) Wash the dishes.
(You) Run the mile in five minutes.
(You) Ask the mayor.

An imperative sentence gives a command or makes a request. An imperative sentence ends with a period.

Sample Page 42
Lesson 30

Defining an Imperative Sentence

L34 **Step 4** — *"Counting up five baselines from the bottom, comfortably close, please write the following on consecutive baselines: 'An imperative sentence gives a command or makes a request'. 'An imperative sentence ends with a period'."*

Let's Get Organized

L56 **Step 5** — *"Turn to the Table of Contents. On the page 42 line, write the title 'What Is an Imperative Sentence?' Turn back to page 42."*

L34 *"Centered on the title line, between the two red margin lines, write the title 'What Is an Imperative Sentence?'"*

L34P For further review have your students write some imperative sentences of their own.

Expectancies Learned or Reinforced in Lesson 30: Dialogue and Review

1. What does an imperative sentence do? **L34** *(An imperative sentence gives a command or makes a request.)*

2. What does a declarative sentence do? **L34** *(A declarative sentence gives facts and states information.)*

3. What does an interrogative sentence do? **L34** *(An interrogative sentence asks a question.)*

4. What is usually the first written word of an imperative sentence? **L56** *(It is usually an action verb. The sentence expects some kind of action on the part of the receiver of the request.)*

5. What is the subject of every imperative sentence? **L34** *(The subject of every imperative sentence is the pronoun "you".)*

Where Do I Go from Here?

- **L34**, **L56**, and **L78** go to "Lesson 31" on page 300.

What Materials Will I Need?

- **L34** will need penmanship paper, pencils, and copies of Worksheets for "Lesson 31" starting on page 306.

- **L56** and **L78** will need *Grammar Notebooks*, pencils, and copies of Worksheets for "Lesson 31" starting on page 306.

What Is an Exclamatory Sentence? | 43

How special you are!
That was an awesome play at first base!
What a wonderful person he was!
That is hot!
We won the game!
What marvelous eyes you have!
(You): Hit the brakes!
I love Minnesota hotdishes!
Uff Da! Bam! Zap! Pow! Bang! Hurrah!

Exclamatory sentences and interjections
display strong or sudden emotion.
They show excitement!
They always end with an exclamation
point!

Sample Page 43
Lesson 31

Lesson 31

What Is an Exclamatory Sentence?

A Lesson on How Not to Talk Minnesotan

L34 "There is a delightfully amusing book written by Howard Mohr entitled *How to Talk Minnesotan*. In this book we learn that people in Minnesota try not to get too excited about much of anything except for Minnesota hotdishes. If Minnesotans were told that Martians were invading their fair state, they would simply reply, 'Whatever.' They would then yawn and go back to work.

"During a rousing discussion on the weather, Lena might say the following to Ole in her best Scandinavian accent.

"'Ole, I tink there is a blissard outside.'

"Ole would look out the window, blink once or twice, and simply say with all the enthusiasm he could muster, 'You bet, but it could be worse.'

"'But Ole, how will we get to your cousin Sven's house for his good old Minnesota hotdish supper?'

"Ole, not wanting to sound indifferent to the world around him, would respond with a not so resounding 'No problem.' Enthusiasm and emotion are sometimes hard to find among the native peoples of this frozen tundra where it never thaws until July 4.

"'Did you see those fireworks, Ole?'

"'You bet, Lena.

"'Weren't day beautiful den?'

"'Dey're not too bad . . . I've seen worse.' You can see why Ole and Lena get along so well.

"Do Ole and Lena need this next lesson? You bet! It is all about showing enthusiasm and emotion in our writing and our speaking. Before we jump in with both feet, however, let's back pedal like we usually do. Name the three jobs that sentences do that we have learned up to this point."

STUDENTS: "A declarative sentence must either state a fact or give some information. An interrogative sentence may ask for information. An imperative sentence gives a command or makes a request."

TEACHER: "You have listened well. The fourth and last job a sentence can do is the fun one. This sentence also has a cousin that we are going to learn about. They both love to express excitement and emotion."

Dictating Exclamatory Sentences and Interjections

L34P **L34** students should be given a page of loose-leaf penmanship paper. **L56** and above need to turn to page 43 in their *Grammar Notebook*.

L34 **Step 1** — *"Skipping one baseline below the title line, starting comfortably close to the left margin line, write the following sentence: 'How special you are!' On the next baseline under the first sentence, comfortably close to the left margin line, write this sentence: 'That was an awesome play at first base!' Starting on the next available baseline, write the remaining sentences on consecutive baselines: 'What a wonderful person he was!' 'That is hot!' 'We won the game!' 'What marvelous eyes you have!' '(You) Hit the brakes!' 'I love Minnesota hotdishes!' On the next available baseline, write the following: 'Uff Da! Bam! Zap! Pow! Bang! Hurrah!'"*

Discovering the Nature of an Exclamatory Sentence and an Interjection

L34 **Step 2** — "We now know the first three purposes of a sentence. We have practiced them. We can call them by name. We can write them. The fourth and last one is called an exclamatory sentence. The cousin of the **exclamatory sentence** that we will also learn is called the **interjection**. Look at what we have written. How would you say the first sentence if you were talking to someone that was special to you?"

STUDENTS: "With lots of feeling. You would want the person to believe that you really meant what you were saying."

TEACHER: *"Practice saying this sentence."*

STUDENTS: *"'How special you are!'"*

TEACHER: "How do you think Ole might say this to Lena?"

STUDENTS: "He'd probably say, 'I told ya once when we was first married. If anyting changes, I'll let ya know'."

TEACHER: "It sounds like you know Ole quite well. Look at the other sentences. It is important to note here that other kinds of sentences can be made into an exclamatory sentence. The sentence 'We won the game!' is really a

Sample Page 43
Lesson 31

*Interjections are
usually single words
or short phrases.*

*They act alone.
Because they
express strong and
sudden emotion,
they are cousins of
the exclamatory
sentence.*

*What well-known
character is
surrounded by
such interjections
as "Bam!" "Zap!"
"Pow!" "Crash!"
"Bang!" and
"Boom!"*

declarative sentence, but it can show **much** emotion
if we want it to. If we add an exclamation point, it is
both a declarative and an exclamatory sentence.
Everything depends upon what the writer intends.

"Someone learning how to drive a car might hear his
driver education instructor say, 'Hit the brakes!'.
Because we want the reader to know that this could
be a very exciting moment for the student driver, let
alone his teacher, we can end this sentence with an
exclamation point. Not only is this sentence an
imperative sentence, but it becomes an exclamatory
sentence also because of how we are using it.

"Look at the last line. What do you see that is different from the others?"

STUDENTS: "I see individual words and not complete sentences."

TEACHER: "You are right. These are not complete sentences, but
they do express excitement and emotion. These
words are called **interjections**. Interjections are usually single words or short phrases. They act alone.
Because they express strong and sudden emotion,
they are cousins of the exclamatory sentence. What
well-known character is surrounded by such interjections as 'Bam!' 'Zap!' 'Pow!' 'Crash!' 'Bang!' and
'Boom!'?"

STUDENTS: "Sounds like Batman to me."

Analyzing Exclamatory Sentences

L56   Step 3 — "Let's analyze these exclamatory sentences. What
do you discover?"

STUDENTS: "There are sentence patterns, but the subjects appear
later in the sentence. They are not one of the first
words as in a declarative or an imperative sentence."

TEACHER: "Good. Did you find any words that you didn't know
right away?"

STUDENTS: "Help me with the word 'how' as in 'How special
you are!' and the word 'what' as in 'What a wonderful person he was!' or 'What marvelous eyes you
have!'"

Understanding Some Tricky Explanations

TEACHER: "Sometimes tricky words require a trip to a dictionary. Dictionaries tell us the various jobs that words can do. If we do go to the dictionary, we find that the word 'how' is used as an adverb. It can mean 'to what degree, to what amount, or to what extent.' It is also one of our adverb questions. As it is used in the first sentence, it is answering the question 'How special?' although the answer to that question is not obvious.

"Sometimes it helps to invert the word order, create a declarative sentence, and then substitute another word for the tricky word. 'You are very special!' means the same thing as 'How special you are!' The word 'very' answers the question 'How special?'

"'How special are you? To what degree or to what extent are you special? You are very special.'

"The word 'very' must be an adverb because it influences the predicate adjective 'special'. Then we need to draw the conclusion that the word 'how' is like the word 'very'. Both are adverbs. We circle the word 'how', label it an 'adv.', and draw an arrow to the predicate adjective 'special'. Now those are lots of hoops to jump through, and I am thankful we don't always have to work with tricky words."

STUDENTS: "I can understand that. What about the word 'what' in our other examples?

TEACHER: "In the sentences 'What a wonderful person he was!' and 'What marvelous eyes you have!' we have inverted word order again. Both of these examples could be made into declarative sentences: 'He was a wonderful person! You have marvelous eyes!' In doing so, the word 'what' is left out and the sentences still read well.

That is good news. That means that the word 'what' is not grammatically tied to the original sentence pattern. Such is the nature of an interjection. Interjections act independently. We will say that both of these sentences use the word 'what' as an interjection. We will label interjections by simply writing **'interj.'** over the word."

Sample Page 43
Lesson 31

Organizational skills are always an ever-present asset for the student who wants to maximize his learning.

We need to choose order over chaos. Order produces efficiency.

L56P Use the Sample Page in the margin as a guide to further discussions on syntactical analysis.

Defining Exclamatory Sentences and Interjections

L34 **Step 4 —** *"From the bottom of your page, count up six baselines and starting comfortably close to the left margin line, write the following: 'Exclamatory sentences and interjections display strong or sudden emotion'. On the next available baseline below, starting comfortably close to the left margin line, write 'They show excitement!' And on the next baseline below, starting comfortably close to the left margin line, write 'They always end with an exclamation point!'"*

Let's Get Organized

L56 **Step 5 —** *"Turn to the Table of Contents. On the page 43 line, write the title 'What Is an Exclamatory Sentence?' Turn back to page 43.*

L34 *"Centered on the title line, between the two red margin lines, write the title 'What Is an Exclamatory Sentence?'"*

Expectancies Learned or Reinforced in Lesson 31: Dialogue and Review

1. What does an exclamatory sentence do? **L34** *(An exclamatory sentence displays a strong or sudden emotion.)*

2. How do we punctuate an exclamatory sentence? **L34** *(We punctuate an exclamatory sentence with an exclamation point.)*

3. What kinds of sentences may be used as an exclamatory sentence? **L34** *(Declarative and imperative sentences may be used as an exclamatory sentence. If we want them to show emotion, we simply add an exclamation point.)*

4. Why might I need to use a dictionary when analyzing a sentence? **L78** *(The dictionary is a trusted friend in questions regarding grammatical usage. It gives us the various parts of speech a particular word can be and many times provides an example of how it is used.)*

5. What if we encounter some words in a sentence, but we can't figure out how to mark them? **L78** *(Be patient. The English language offers many challenges. Do some research. Invert word order. Use a dictionary. Substitute other words. Find out what*

jobs a difficult word can do. Remember that syntactical analysis needs to be a servant and not a taskmaster. If we cannot account for all of the words, we will happily leave them for another day.)

6. What is an interjection? **L56** *(Interjections usually are a one word part of speech designed to express sudden emotion. They always act alone as with these examples: "Phooey!" "Tarnation!" "Ouch!" They usually precede a further explanation for why the writer is feeling this way. "Uff Da! That was sure a tasty hotdish!")*

7. How are interjections like exclamatory sentences? **L56** *(Interjections are full of emotion just like exclamatory sentences. Interjections, however, act independently. They are not grammatically tied to other words in a sentence.)*

8. Why is learning to be organized so important? **L56** *(Organizational skills are always an ever-present asset for the student who wants to maximize his learning. We need to choose order over chaos. Order produces efficiency.)*

Where Do I Go from Here?

- **L34** goes to **L34** "Scope and Sequence" Step 7.

- **L56** goes to "Lesson 33" on page 320.

- **L78** goes to "Lesson 32" on page 308.

What Materials Will I Need?

- **L56** will need *Grammar Notebooks,* pencils, and copies of Worksheets for **"Lesson 33"** starting on page 326.

- **L78** will need *Grammar Notebooks,* pencils, red pencils, and copies of Worksheets for **"Lesson 32"** starting on page 318.

Declarative, Interrogative, Imperative, and Exclamatory Sentences

Teacher Directions: Use this worksheet for reinforcement after the four lessons on sentences have been completed. Explain to your students the directions for determining the proper responses for these sentences.

Student Directions: Read each of the following sentences.

Label each Declarative Sentence with a "DEC."

Label each Interrogative Sentence with "INT?"

Label each Imperative Sentence with "IMP."

Label each Exclamatory Sentence with an "EX!"

Place the proper end punctuation at the end of every sentence.

IMP. 1. Go call the ambulance!

DEC. 2. The sheep are in the north pasture.

INT? 3. Will you see him in the morning?

EX! 4. What a great day to be alive!

IMP. 5. Stand up and be counted.

INT? 6. Which way is it to the grocery store?

DEC. 7. The snow melts in the spring.

IMP. 8. Melt the ice before you walk on it.

IMP. 9. Sing the song with your whole heart.

INT? 10. Why do you say that?

INT? 11. When is the vacation you planned?

EX! 12. Chocolate chip cookies are great!

INT? 13. Do you like chocolate chip cookies?

DEC. 14. My Grandpa Ahlness told me about Norway.

EX! 15. That was the best show I've ever seen!

IMP. 16. Don't give up the ship!

IMP. 17. Be all that you can be.

DEC. 18. It was a fantastic finish.

INT? 19. Which door did you open?

DEC. 20. Learning grammar makes me a better writer.

_____1. Go call the ambulance

_____2. The sheep are in the north pasture

_____3. Will you see him in the morning

_____4. What a great day to be alive

_____5. Stand up and be counted

_____6. Which way is it to the grocery store

_____7. The snow melts in the spring

_____8. Melt the ice before you walk on it

_____9. Sing the song with your whole heart

_____10. Why do you say that

_____11. When is the vacation you planned

_____12. Chocolate chip cookies are great

_____13. Do you like chocolate chip cookies

_____14. My Grandpa Ahlness told me about Norway

_____15. That was the best show I've ever seen

_____16. Don't give up the ship

_____17. Be all that you can be

_____18. It was a fantastic finish

_____19. Which door did you open

_____20. Learning grammar makes me a better writer

©1998 Grammar Works/Holly Hall Publications, Inc.   Lesson 31: What Is an Exclamatory Sentence?   **307**

Declarative, Interrogative, Imperative, and Exclamatory Sentences

Student Directions: Read each of the following sentences.

Label each Declarative Sentence with a "DEC."

Label each Interrogative Sentence with "INT?"

Label each Imperative Sentence with "IMP."

Label each Exclamatory Sentence with an "EX!"

Place the proper end punctuation at the end of every sentence.

Lesson 32
What Is a Possessive Noun and Pronoun?

It Is Always a Good Time to Review

L78 "Before we jump into this next lesson, we need to be sure that we understand the subject pronouns and the object pronouns and the jobs they do in our language."

Step 1 — "Let's return to the art of conjugating for a moment. We must always pay attention to detail. Who can conjugate the verb 'break' in the present tense, the past tense, and the present perfect tense?"

L78P Take time to conjugate a number of different verbs in all six tenses. Hopefully you have been periodically doing this all along the way. If it is time for lunch, how do you conjugate the verb 'eat'? If it is time for choir practice for the Christmas program, how do you conjugate the verb 'sing'? Seize the moment when you can to reinforce what they need to know.

TEACHER: "What kind of pronoun did we use to conjugate?"

STUDENTS: "We used the subject pronouns."

TEACHER: "Where do we use subject pronouns?"

STUDENTS: "We can only use subject pronouns in a subject position in a sentence."

TEACHER: "What positions are those?"

STUDENTS: "A subject pronoun may be used as a subject or as a predicate noun."

Remembering Our Sentence Patterns

L78P If it is necessary to review the different kinds of sentence patterns, do so at this time.

TEACHER: "Can you name the basic sentence patterns?"

STUDENTS: "We will give it a try.
Pattern 1: S+AV,
Pattern 2: S+AV⟶DO,
Pattern 3: S+AV⟶IO+DO,
Pattern 4A: S+LV,
Pattern 4B: S+LV⟶PA, and
Pattern 4C: S+LV⟶PN. How did we do?"

TEACHER:	"You did wonderfully. Let's see if I can stump you on this one. What are the object pronouns?"
STUDENTS:	"The object pronouns are created from the subject pronouns. The pronoun 'I' becomes 'me'. The pronoun 'you' stays the same in both the singular and plural. The pronoun 'he' becomes 'him'. The pronoun 'she' becomes 'her'. The pronoun 'it' stays the same. On the plural side, the pronoun 'we' becomes 'us'. And finally the pronoun 'they' becomes 'them'."
TEACHER:	"Thank you for letting details matter. Let's play Stump the Student one more time. What is the object pronoun for the word 'who'?
STUDENTS:	"We simply place a letter 'm' in the word to make it an object pronoun."
TEACHER:	"You remembered the letter 'm' didn't you. Name the object positions that we might find in a sentence?"
STUDENTS:	"We might find a direct object. We might find an indirect object. We might find an object of the preposition."
TEACHER:	"Very well done. It is time to introduce another different kind of pronoun. That is what this next lesson is all about."

Dictating Possessive Pronouns

Step 2 — *"Turn to page 44 in your* Grammar Notebook. *Skipping one baseline below the title line, starting each word comfortably close to the left margin line, write each of the subject pronouns, one per line, on consecutive baselines: 'I', 'you', 'he', 'she', 'it', 'we', 'you', and 'they'."*

Step 3 — *"Fold a margin line down the middle of page 44. On the same line as the subject pronoun 'I', starting in the second column, comfortably close to the folded margin line, write the words, 'my, mine'.* We call these kinds of pronouns, **possessive pronouns.** They show us that we own something. 'My' and 'mine' are the possessive forms of the pronoun 'I'."

"On the same line as the subject pronoun 'you', in the second column, starting comfortably close to the folded margin line, write the words 'your, yours'. These are the possessive forms of the pronoun 'you'."

"On the same line as 'he', write 'his' in the second column. On the same line as 'she', write 'her, hers'. On the same line as 'it', write 'its'. On the same line as 'we', write 'our, ours'. On

I	my, mine
you	your, yours
he	his
she	her, hers
it	its
we	our, ours
you	your, yours
they	their, theirs

My car was running in your driveway.
His manner was kind in her presence.
Our plans were changed in spite of their objections.
Your honesty is wonderful!
Our calculator is inaccurate.

A possessive pronoun is a form of the subject pronoun that shows ownership of a noun.

Sample Page 44
Lesson 32

*the same line as the plural 'you', write **'your, yours'**. The singular and plural forms of these possessive pronouns are both the same. On the same line as 'they', write **'their, theirs'**."*

Dictating Sentences Using Possessive Pronouns

L78 **Step 4 —** "Very well done, students. Thank you for listening carefully. Now that we have introduced the possessive pronouns, we are going to write some sentences that demonstrate how they are used. *Skipping a baseline below the pronoun lists, starting each sentence comfortably close to the left margin line, write the following sentences on consecutive baselines:*

'My car was running in your driveway.'

'His manner was kind in her presence.'

'Our plans were changed in spite of their objections.'

'Your honesty is wonderful.'

'Our calculator is inaccurate.'"

Discovering the Nature of a Possessive Pronoun

L78P If your students have trouble knowing how to mark the possessive pronouns, take them through the following discussion.

L78 **Step 5 —** "A possessive pronoun always shows ownership of another noun. If they are 'our plans', whose are they? Who owns them? To whom do they belong? If it is 'your honesty', whose honesty is it?"

STUDENTS: "You own the honesty."

TEACHER: "What question does a possessive pronoun always answer?"

STUDENTS: "It answers the question 'Whose?'"

TEACHER: "That should tell you something. What kinds of words answer the questions 'What kind?' 'How many?' 'How much?' 'Which?' 'Which one?' or 'Whose?'"

STUDENTS: "Adjectives answer those questions. But I thought you said that these were pronouns."

TEACHER: "I did. What does that tell you? Make a discovery."

STUDENTS: "Pronouns can do the work of an adjective. Not only do they show ownership, but they also influence another noun when used in the role of an adjective."

| TEACHER: | "Right. This automatically qualifies a possessive pronoun as doing the work of an adjective. We call such pronouns, **adjectival pronouns,** and we label them as adjectives influencing the noun they are possessing." |

Discussing the Analysis of Possessive Pronoun Sentences

| TEACHER: | "Look at our first sentence. 'My car was running in your driveway.' Do you see any prepositional phrases?" |

| STUDENTS: | "I know 'in your driveway' is a prepositional phrase. The object is driveway. I know the word 'your' shows ownership of the driveway and is therefore a possessive pronoun." |

| TEACHER: | "Is there a flag flying over the word 'your'? What question is being answered by this word?" |

| STUDENTS: | "It answers the question 'Whose?' Therefore as we have discussed before, it is doing the work of an adjective. Am I right?" |

| TEACHER: | "You are right. We have discovered that every possessive pronoun does the work of an adjective. Possessive pronouns tell us 'Whose?' something really is. We call them 'adjectival pronouns' and circle them, label them 'adj.', and draw an arrow to the word they influence. What word does 'your' influence in this case?" |

| STUDENTS: | "It influences the word that it owns, the word 'driveway'." |

| TEACHER: | "Make sure that you label each adjectival pronoun correctly in each of the following sentences." |

L78P Take enough time here to discuss each sentence and its markings. Use the Sample Page on page 494 as your guide. This lesson teaches that possessive pronouns are used as adjectives. They should have no problem understanding the markings of these words in each sentence.

Defining a Possessive Pronoun

L78 **Step 6 —** *"Count up three baselines from the bottom of page 43 and write the following legal definition for a possessive pronoun:* **'A possessive pronoun is a form of the subject pronoun that shows ownership of a noun'.** *You will need more than one line."*

Let's Get Organized

L78   **Step 7 —** *"Turn to the Table of Contents. On the page 44 line, write the title 'What Is a Possessive Pronoun?'. Turn back to page 44. Centered on the title line, between the two red margin lines, write the same title."*

Dictating Sentences Using Possessive Nouns

L78   **Step 1—** *"Turn to page 45 in your* Grammar Notebook. *Skipping one baseline below the title line, starting each sentence comfortably close to the left margin line, write the following sentences on consecutive baselines:*

> *'John's rake was missing.'*

> *'It was Sally's car in the ditch.'*

> *'The governor's race was very tight.'"*

Discovering the Nature of Possessive Nouns

L78   **Step 2 —** "We are learning that in addition to possessive pronouns, the English language also has nouns that act in a possessive manner. These nouns may be either singular or plural, and because they are possessive nouns, we have learned that they use a special punctuation mark. What is the punctuation mark called?"

STUDENTS: "Possessive nouns must have an apostrophe properly placed to denote this ownership. An apostrophe is a comma that always hangs above and between letters at the end of a word."

TEACHER: "Sometimes we have to place the apostrophe directly after the last letter of a word. We will learn more about that in a later lesson. Regardless of where they are used, **possessive nouns need apostrophes. Possessive pronouns do not need apostrophes.** Look at the first sentence. 'Who owns the rake?'"

STUDENTS: "John owns the rake."

TEACHER: "How do we show that John owns the rake?"

STUDENTS: "We place an apostrophe above and between the letters 'n' and 's'."

TEACHER: "If we analyze this first sentence, what do we learn about the word 'John's'?"

STUDENTS:	"This is interesting. The word 'John's' answers the question 'Whose rake?' Therefore, the possessive noun is doing the work of an adjective. Does that make John an adjectival possessive noun?"
TEACHER:	"I think you might be right. Continue your detective work. What jobs do the words 'Sally' and 'governor' do?"
STUDENTS:	"They are waving the flag 'Whose?' They are doing the work of an adjective. We circle them, label them with an 'adj.', and draw an arrow to the word they influence. In this case, the word that is influenced is the word that they own."

L78P Have your students analyze these first three sentences and show how the apostrophe is used in possessive nouns. If you have any questions about the syntactical analysis or markings of these sentences, you may refer to Sample Page 45 on page 495.

Introducing Another Kind of Pronoun

L78 **Step 3 —** "We have already introduced personal pronouns that can be used as subjects or as objects. We now call them 'subject pronouns' or 'object pronouns'. We have also worked with interrogative pronouns that are used to ask a question and indefinite pronouns that aren't as specific. We need to introduce another kind of pronoun. These are called 'demonstrative pronouns'."

"One way that demonstrative pronouns can be used is to point out persons or things. Here are some examples: 'that man', 'these cars', 'this lesson', or 'those pictures'."

Dictating Sentences Using Demonstrative Pronouns

L78 **Step 4 —** *"Skipping one baseline below the sentence 'The governor's race was very tight', write the following sentences on consecutive baselines:*

   'That red book is mine.'

   'These blue coats are hers.'

   'Those black tuxedos are Jim's.'

   'This book is yours.'"

What Is a Possessive Noun?	45

John's rake was missing.
It was Sally's car in the ditch.
The governor's race was very tight.

That red book is mine.
These blue coats are hers.
Those black tuxedos are Jim's.
This book is yours.

Mine is the red book.
Hers is the blue coat.
Jim's is the black tuxedo.

I cannot do that myself.
He walked uptown himself.
They helped with the project themselves.
We did it ourselves.

A possessive noun shows ownership of another noun and needs an apostrophe.

Sample Page 45
Lesson 32

Discovering the Nature of Demonstrative Pronouns

L78 "In analyzing these sentences, what job do the demonstrative pronouns 'this', 'that', 'these', and 'those' do?"

> STUDENTS: "Being the fine analysts that we are, we can tell that these words are pointing out nouns and flying a flag with the question 'Which?' They are doing the work of an adjective."

Discovering the Nature of Possessive Nouns and Pronouns Used as Predicate Adjectives

L78 "Right. Keep analyzing. What job do the words 'mine', 'hers', 'Jim's', and 'yours' do in these sentences?"

> STUDENTS: "We have a linking verb in each sentence. That is a strong clue right away. We see more flags. **Whose** red book? Mine. **Whose** blue coats? Hers. **Whose** black tuxedos? Jim's. **Whose** book? Yours."

> TEACHER: "What does that tell you?"

> STUDENTS: "They are all adjectives. They all follow a linking verb. We must use Sentence Pattern 4B. They are doing the job of a **predicate adjective.** Is that right?"

L78P Put on your professorship glasses and say the following, sounding as intelligent and as academic as you can. Use a British accent if you would like.

L78 "Because they obviously answer the question 'Whose?', that is what we are going to call them. The capacity with which you are able to sequentially deduce the roles that various words contribute to a sentence is both fascinating and intriguing. I dare say that your powers of comparative analysis are increasing one hundred fold. You are becoming academically sound and your ability to garner the specificity of metalinguistics and make direct application is exemplary. In other words, you are sharp! Let's analyze the rest of these sentences."

L78P Have your students finish analyzing the four sentences that illustrate proper use of demonstrative pronouns used as adjectives **and** possessive nouns and pronouns used as predicate adjectives. If you have any questions about the syntactical analysis or markings of these sentences, you may refer to Sample Page 45 on page 495.

Making Grammar Instruction Count

L78P There can be an inherent flaw in most academic instruction whether we look at math or science or social studies or language instruction. It can be dull, dry, and down right uninteresting at times. It doesn't need to be that way. **Standeth thyself on thine head if necessary. Swingeth thyself from the highest tree limb. Get their attention!**

Remember that the instruction of grammar as a discipline has been lost too long. There is a far greater benefit for the student than just language instruction. Kids need to learn to think sequentially, analytically, deductively, comparatively, incrementally, and systematically. Grammar will help them do that.

Discovering That Possessive Nouns and Pronouns Can Also Be Used as Subjects

L78 **Step 5 —** "Skipping one baseline under the sentence 'This book is yours', write the following sentences on consecutive baselines: *'Mine is the red book'. 'Hers is the blue coat'. 'Jim's is the black tuxedo'.*"

L78 **Step 6 —** "Let's analyze these three sentences on our page. What do we learn?"

  STUDENTS: "The possessive pronouns and nouns doing the job of predicate adjectives in our last sentences are now being used as subjects."

L78P Have your students finish analyzing the three sentences that illustrate proper use of possessive nouns and pronouns used as subjects. If you have any questions about the syntactical analysis or markings of these sentences, you may refer to Sample Page 45 on page 495. Help students to discover that possessive nouns and pronouns that were used as predicate adjectives in our last four sentences are now being used as subjects.

The following discussion explains why the words 'mine', 'hers', and 'Jim's' are now being used as subjects.

L78 **Step 7 —** "What these last three sentences are really saying is this: The word 'mine' is a pronoun that means 'my book'. The word 'hers' is a pronoun that means 'her blue coat'. The word 'Jim's' really means 'Jim's tuxedo'. We can see that these possessive nouns and pronouns that are now subjects are equal in meaning with the PN's that are found in the predicate. 'My book' is equal to the 'red book.' 'Her coat' is equal to the 'blue coat'. 'Jim's tuxedo' is equal in meaning to the 'black tuxedo'. This means that the possessive pronouns in these last three sentences are definitely serving as subjects."

What Is a Possessive Noun? | 45

John's rake was missing.
It was Sally's car in the ditch.
The governor's race was very tight.

That red book is mine.
These blue coats are hers.
Those black tuxedos are Jim's.
This book is yours.

Mine is the red book.
Hers is the blue coat.
Jim's is the black tuxedo.

I cannot do that myself.
He walked uptown himself.
They helped with the project themselves.
We did it ourselves.

A possessive noun shows ownership of
another noun and needs an apostrophe.

Sample Page 45
Lesson 32

STUDENTS: "I am beginning to understand."

TEACHER: "Isn't this interesting? Look at what we have learned. Possessive nouns and pronouns can be subjects, and possessive nouns pronouns can also serve in the predicate as a predicate adjective. Now that is versatility!"

Discovering Reflexive Pronouns

L78 **Step 8 —** "There are also **reflexive pronouns** that reflect back to a word already spoken in a sentence. In the sentence 'I can't go myself', the word 'myself' reflects back to the subject pronoun 'I'. Any personal pronouns to which 'self' or 'selves' are added are reflexive pronouns. *Skipping one baseline below the sentence 'Jim's is the black tuxedo', write the following sentences on consecutive baselines:*

'I cannot do that myself.'

'He walked uptown himself.'

'They helped with the project themselves.'

'We did it ourselves.'

"We won't analyze these. We just want some examples of reflexive pronouns recorded in our notebook."

Defining a Possessive Noun

L78 **Step 9 —** *"Counting up two baselines from the bottom of page 45, starting comfortably close to the margin line, write this definition: 'A possessive noun shows ownership of another noun and needs an apostrophe'. You will need more than one line."*

Let's Get Organized

L78 **Step 10 —** *"Turn to the Table of Contents. On the page 45 line, write the title 'What Is a Possessive Noun?' Turn back to page 45. Centered on the title line, between the two red margin lines, write the same title."*

Expectancies Learned or Reinforced in Lesson 32: Dialogue and Review

1. What is the job of a possessive pronoun and noun? **L78** *(The basic job of a possessive noun or pronoun is to show ownership of another noun.)*

2. What do we call possessive pronouns that do the work of an adjective? **L78** *(Possessive pronouns that do the job of an adjective are called adjectival pronouns or predicate adjectives depending upon where they are used.)*

3. Where may subject pronouns be used in a sentence? **L78** *(Subject pronouns may be used in either a subject position or a predicate noun position.)*

4. Where may object pronouns be used in a sentence? **L78** *(Object pronouns may be used in either a DO, IO, or OP position in a sentence.)*

5. How does practicing conjugating help us? **L34** *(Conjugating teaches us to use verbs correctly in our writing.)*

6. What three jobs can a possessive noun or pronoun do in a sentence? **L78** *(A possessive noun or pronoun can do the work of an adjective, a predicate adjective, or a subject.)*

7. What punctuation mark does a possessive noun use to show ownership? **L78** *(Possessive nouns use apostrophes to show ownership.)*

8. What punctuation mark does a possessive pronoun use to show ownership? **L78** *(Possessive pronouns do not use any punctuation. They are possessive by nature.)*

9. What are the demonstrative pronouns and what do they do? **L78** *(The demonstrative pronouns are "this", "that", "these", and "those" and they point at particular nouns.)*

10. What are the reflexive pronouns and what do they do? **L78** *(The reflexive pronouns are any pronouns that end in "self" or "selves", and they reflect back to another word in the sentence.)*

Where Do I Go from Here?

- **L78** goes to **"Lesson 33"** on Page 320.

What Materials Will I Need?

- **L78** will need *Grammar Notebooks*, pencils, and copies of Worksheets for **"Lesson 33"** starting on page 326.

What Is a
Possessive
Pronoun?

*Teacher Directions:
Have your students
produce a syntactical
analysis for each of the
Worksheet sentences.*

*Student Directions:
Analyze these sentences.
Be sure to pay special
attention to the posses-
sive pronouns that you
find. They may be used
as subjects, adjectives, or
predicate adjectives.*

1. My car was near your car.

2. His help was greatly appreciated.

3. His outlook was positive.

4. It may have been yours or mine.

5. The peacock spread its wings.

6. It was their car in his ditch.

7. Theirs was the best performance by far.

8. They had not found their way.

9. The lost wallet was his and not hers.

10. The chauffeur found his billfold in my car.

1. My car was near your car.

2. His help was greatly appreciated.

3. His outlook was positive.

4. It may have been yours or mine.

5. The peacock spread its wings.

6. It was their car in his ditch.

7. Theirs was the best performance by far.

8. They had not found their way.

9. The lost wallet was his and not hers.

10. The chauffeur found his billfold in my car.

What Is a Possessive Pronoun?

Student Directions: Analyze these sentences. Be sure to pay special attention to the possessive pronouns that you find. They may be used as subjects, adjectives, or predicate adjectives.

46 | How Do I Form Plural Nouns?

Rule 1: Regular nouns simply add "s".
dog dogs car cars

Rule 2: Nouns ending in the letters "s","x",
"z","sh", or "ch" add "es".
buzz buzzes dish dishes
church churches bus buses

Rule 3: Letter names, numbers, signs
like $'s, and words talked about as words
are made plural by adding an apostrophe
and an "s".

How many p's did you find in Mississippi?
There were four 10's used in the blueprint.
How many $'s were in the report?
Do count the number of the's on the first
page.

Sample Page 46
Lesson 33

Forming Plural Nouns (continued) | 47

Rule 4: Nouns ending in a consonant followed by a "y" change the "y" to "i" and add "es".
country countries sky skies

Rule 5: Nouns ending in a vowel followed
by a "y" simply add "s".
turkey turkeys monkey monkeys

Rule 6: Most nouns that end in "f" or "fe"
add "s". Some nouns that end in "f" or "fe"
change the "f" or "fe" to "v" and add "es".
chief chiefs knife knives leaf leaves

Rule 7: Irregular nouns change the
spelling of the singular to form the plural.
child children man men mouse mice

Rule 8: Some nouns stay the same in
the singular and plural.
deer deer sheep sheep

Sample Page 47
Lesson 33

48 | Forming Plural Nouns (continued)

Rule 9: Nouns ending in a consonant
followed by the letter "o" simply add "es".
hero heroes tomato tomatoes

Rule 10: Nouns ending in a vowel
followed by the letter "o" simply add "s".
radio radios rodeo rodeos

Rule 11: Musical terms ending in "o"
simply add "s".
piano pianos solo solos

Rule 12: In compound nouns make the
first word plural.
brother-in-law brothers-in-law
sister-in-law sisters-in-law
editor-in-chief editors-in-chief

Sample Page 48
Lesson 33

Lesson 33
How Do I Form Plural Nouns?

L78 "Forming plural nouns can be one of the most challenging grammatical concepts. There are many ways and many rules that we need to look at. We will take them one at a time. We will assume, of course, that we understand that 'singular' refers to one and 'plural' refers to more than one."

Introducing the Rules for Forming Plural Nouns

L56 **Step 1** — *"Turn to page 46 in your* Grammar Notebook. *Skipping one baseline below the title line, starting comfortably close to the left margin line, write the following:* **'Rule 1: Regular nouns simply add "s"'."**

"On the baseline directly below this first rule, starting comfortably close to the left margin line, write the word **'dog'**. On the same line leave one space and write the word **'dogs'**. On the same line leaving one space after 'dogs', write the word **'car'**. On the same line, leaving one space after 'car', write the word **'cars'**. What do we learn from these examples?"

STUDENTS: "It is just as the rule says. Words like dog or car or cat or mule are changed to the plural by simply adding the letter 's'."

L56 **Step 2** — *"Skipping one baseline below the word 'dog', starting comfortably close to the left red margin line, write the following rule:* **'Rule 2: Nouns ending in the letters "s", "x", "z", "sh", or "ch" add "es".** You will need more than one line.

"On the next available baseline, leaving a space between words, write the following: **'buzz'**, **'buzzes'**, **'dish'**, **'dishes'**.

"On the next line leaving one space between each word, write the following: **'church'**, **'churches'**, **'bus'**, **'buses'**. What do we learn from this rule?"

STUDENTS: "We learn that plurals with these endings are formed by adding 'es'.

L56 **Step 3** — *"Skipping one baseline below the word 'church', starting comfortably close to the left red margin line, write the following rule:* **'Rule 3: Letter names, numbers, signs like $'s, and words talked about as words are made plural by adding an apostrophe and an "s".** You will need more than one line.

"Skipping one baseline after the rule, write the following sentences on consecutive baselines: 'How many p's did you find in Mississippi?' 'There were four 10's used in the blueprint.' 'How many $'s were in the report?' 'Do count the number of the's on the first page.' What do we learn from this rule?

> STUDENTS: "We learn that letter names, numbers, signs, and words talked about as words all are made plural by adding an apostrophe and then the letter 's'."

L56P At this point it will be necessary to jump to page 47 in the student's *Notebook*. Watch the Sample Pages in the margin as you progress through this lesson. Don't forget to be a cheerleader. Compliment students on their handwriting, on their ability to follow directions, on their attentiveness, and on their strong, disciplined minds.

L56 **Step 4 —** *"Skipping one baseline below the title line on page 46, starting comfortably close to the left red margin line, write the following rule: 'Rule 4: Nouns ending in a consonant followed by a "y" change the "y" to "i" and add "es".'* You will need more than one line.

"On the next available baseline after the rule, write the following words leaving one space between each word: 'country', 'countries', 'sky', 'skies'. What do we learn from this rule?"

> STUDENTS: "We learn that if a word ending in 'y' has a consonant in front of the letter 'y', we must change the letter 'y' to an 'i' and then add 'es'."

L56 **Step 5 —** *"Skipping one baseline below the word 'country', starting comfortably close to the left red margin line, write the following rule: 'Rule 5: Nouns ending in a vowel followed by a "y" simply add "s".'* You will need more than one line.

"On the next available baseline after the rule, write the following words leaving one space between each word: 'turkey', 'turkeys', 'monkey', 'monkeys'. We call these two rules together *'The "Y" Rules'.* And when you think about it, the letter 'Y' really does rule. It determines everything. What do we learn for this rule?"

> STUDENTS: "Knowing the difference between consonants and vowels is important. If a vowel is in front of the ending letter 'y' of a word, we make the word plural by adding an 's'."

L56 **Step 6 —** *"Skipping one baseline below the word 'turkey', starting comfortably close to the left red margin line, write the following: 'Rule 6: Most nouns that end in "f" or "fe" add "s". Some nouns that end in "f" or "fe" change the "f" or "fe" to "v" and add "es".'* You will need more than one line.

Don't forget to be a cheerleader.

Compliment students on their handwriting, on their ability to follow directions, on their attentiveness, and on their strong, disciplined minds.

> *"On the next available baseline after the rule, write the following words leaving one space between each word:* **'chief'***,* **'chiefs'***,* **'knife'***,* **'knives'***,* **'leaf'***,* **'leaves'***.* What do we learn from this rule?"

STUDENTS: "We learn that most nouns that end in the letters 'f' or 'fe' add a letter 's' and some change the letters 'f' or 'fe' to the letter 'v' before adding 'es'."

L56 **Step 7** — *"Skipping one baseline below the word 'chief', starting comfortably close to the left red margin line, write the following:* **'Rule 7: Irregular nouns change the spelling of the singular to form the plural'***.* You will need more than one line.

> *"On the next available baseline after the rule, write the following words leaving one space between each word:* **'child'***,* **'children'***,* **'man'***,* **'men'***,* **'mouse'***,* **'mice'***.* What do we learn from this rule?"

STUDENTS: "Some words simply change the spelling of the singular to make it plural."

L56 **Step 8** — *"Skipping one baseline below the word 'child', starting comfortably close to the left red margin line, write the following:* **'Rule 8: Some nouns stay the same in the singular and plural'***.* You will need more than one line.

> *"On the next available baseline after the rule, write the following words leaving one space between each word:* **'deer'***,* **'deer'***,* **'sheep'***,* **'sheep'***.* What do we learn from this rule?"

STUDENTS: "Sometimes we do not need to change the spelling when we move from singular to plural."

L78 **Step 9** — *"We need to turn to page 48 in our* Notebook. *Skipping one baseline below the title line, starting comfortably close to the left red margin line, write the following:* **'Rule 9: Nouns ending in a consonant followed by the letter "o" add "es".'** You will need more than one line.

> *"On the next available baseline after the rule, write the following words leaving one space between each word:* **'hero'***,* **'heroes'***,* **'tomato'***,* **'tomatoes'***.* What do we learn from this rule?"

STUDENTS: "Consonant and vowel combinations determine how we make plurals. In this case, the consonant precedes the ending letter 'o' and we need to add the ending 'es'."

L78 **Step 10** — *"Skipping one baseline below the word 'hero', starting comfortably close to the left red margin line, write the following:* **'Rule 10: Nouns ending in a vowel followed by the letter "o" simply add "s".'** You will need more than one line.

---

48   Forming Plural Nouns (continued)

Rule 9: Nouns ending in a consonant followed by the letter "o" simply add "es".
hero heroes tomato tomatoes

Rule 10: Nouns ending in a vowel followed by the letter "o" simply add "s".
radio radios rodeo rodeos

Rule 11: Musical terms ending in "o" simply add "s".
piano pianos solo solos

Rule 12: In compound nouns make the first word plural.
brother-in-law brothers-in-law
sister-in-law sisters-in-law
editor-in-chief editors-in-chief

Sample Page 48
Lesson 33

"On the next available baseline after the rule, write the following words leaving one space between each word: 'radio', 'radios', 'rodeo', 'rodeos'. What do we learn from this rule?"

STUDENTS: "Again I need to sound like a broken record. Knowing our vowel combinations determines how we form plurals. If a word ends with a vowel and the letter 'o', we add the letter 's' to make a word plural."

78 **Step 11 —** *"Skipping one baseline below the word 'hero', starting comfortably close to the left red margin line, write the following: 'Rule 11: Musical terms ending in "o" simply add "s".'* You will need more than one line.

"On the next available baseline after the rule, write the following words leaving one space between each word: 'piano', 'pianos', 'solo', 'solos', 'soprano', 'sopranos', 'allegro', 'allegros'. Rules 9, 10, and 11 are *'The "O" Rules'.* What do we learn from this rule?"

STUDENTS: "Musical terms ending in the letter 'o' just add the letter 's' to make the word plural. And again, the letter 'o' like the letter 'y' helps to determine how we make plurals."

78 **Step 12 —** *"Skipping one baseline below the word 'piano', starting comfortably close to the left red margin line, write the following: 'Rule 12: In compound nouns make the first word plural'.* You will need more than one line.

"On the next available baseline after the rule, write the following words leaving one space between each compound word: 'brother-in-law', 'brothers-in-law'. Go to the next line. Write the following words: 'sister-in-law', 'sisters-in-law'. On the next available baseline below 'sister-in-law', write the following: 'editor-in chief', 'editors-in-chief'. (Some compound nouns like 'two-year-old', 'two-year-olds' break this rule.) What do we learn from this rule?"

STUDENTS: "Would 'sons-in-law' be the plural of 'son-in-law'?"

TEACHER: "Yes."

STUDENTS: "Then I understand. When we have a compound word, we make the first word plural."

L78 **Step 13 —** "One plural rule that we haven't mentioned yet deals with foreign words. We will not include it in the notebook at this time because it is not too frequently encountered. We still need to know about this rule, however. It reads like this: 'Rule 13: Foreign words sometime keep the plural of the original language'. Some examples of this include the following words: 'alumnus' becomes 'alumni' in the plural, or 'hypothesis' becomes 'hypotheses' in the plural."

cat—cats (1)

alto—altos (11)

wife—wives (6)

valley—valleys (5)

ditch—ditches (2)

and—and's (3)

enemy—enemies (4)

goose—geese (7)

mother-in-law— mothers-in-law (12)

8 (the number)— 8's (3)

deer—deer (8)

parenthesis— parentheses (13)

radio—radios (10)

fox—foxes (2)

potato—potatoes (9)

rodeo—rodeos (10)

cello—cellos (11)

duty—duties (4)

moose—moose (8)

knife—knives (6)

horse—horses (1)

R—R's (3)

key—keys (5)

mouse—mice (7)

bill of sale— bills of sale (12)

hypothesis— hypotheses (13)

An Exercise on Forming Noun Plurals

L78P Give each student a piece of practice penmanship paper. Have your students write the singular form of the 26 words (found in the sidebar) as you dictate them. Count it as a spelling test if you would like. After making sure all words are spelled correctly, have your students use pages 46–48 in their *Notebooks* to find the rule for making each of the words plural. Have them write the plural form of the word and then the rule number that applies in parentheses after the singular words you dictated.

L78 **Step 14 —** "We need to do some practicing. I am going to dictate to you ***26 words*** that you need to spell carefully. When we are done, we need to turn to pages 46–48 in our *Notebook* and use the rules to help us decide how to make each of these words plural. Write the ***plural form of the word*** next to the sinfular form and then be sure to write down the ***number of the rule*** that applies."

Plurals Aren't Easy

Is there any wonder why some students struggle with our language? There are so many things to think about. They do need to know these plural rules. They will be using these for the rest of their lives.

Let's Get Organized

L78 **Step 15 —** *"Turn to the Table of Contents. On the page 46 line, write the title* **'How Do I Form Plural Nouns?'** *On the page 47 line, write the title:* **'Forming Plural Nouns (continued)'***. On the page 48 line, write the following title once again:* **'Forming Plural Nouns (continued)'***. Turn back to page 46.*

"Centered on the title line on page 46, between the two red margin lines, write the title **'How Do I Form Plural Nouns?'** *Centered on the title line on page 47, between the two red margin lines, write the title* **'Forming Plural Nouns (continued)'***. Centered again on the title line on page 48, between the two red margin lines, write the title* **'Forming Plural Nouns (continued)'** *one more time. We have used three pages to record the plural rules for nouns."*

Expectancies Learned or Reinforced in Lesson 33: Dialogue and Review

1. What do we add to most regular nouns to make them plural? **L56** *(We add a letter "s" to make most regular nouns a plural.)*

2. How do we make words plural that end in the letters "s", "x", "z", "sh", and "ch"? **L56** *(We simply add "es".)*

3. How do we make nouns plural that end in "y" preceded by a consonant? **L56** *(We change the "y" to "i" and add "es".)*

4. How do we make nouns plural that end in "y" preceded by a vowel? **L56** *(We simply add an "s".)*

5. How are most nouns made plural that end in "f" or "fe"? **L56** *(Most of these kinds of nouns form plurals by adding "s".)*

6. How are a few of these nouns made plural that end in "f" or "fe"? **L56** *(Some form plurals by changing the "f" or "fe" to "v" and adding "es". "Calf" becomes "calves".)*

7. Some plural forms of words are irregular. What do they do to make a word plural? **L56** *(They change the spelling of the root word when moving from singular to plural. "Man" becomes "men". "Mouse" becomes "mice".)*

8. How do some nouns form plurals that end in "o" preceded by a vowel? **L78** *(They simply add an "s" for plural. "Radio" becomes "radios".)*

9. How do some nouns form plurals that end in "o" preceded by a consonant? **L78** *(They add "es" for plural. "Hero" becomes "heroes".)*

10. How do musical terms that end in "o" form plural? **L78** *(They simply add "s" for plural. "Piano" becomes "pianos".)*

11. How do we make a compound nouns plural like in the word "brother-in-law"? **L78** *(We make the main noun of the compound word plural according to the rule that applies for that word. "Brother-in-law" becomes "brothers-in-law".)*

12. What happens to some words that do not change any spelling in the plural? **L56** *(Some nouns stay exactly the same in the singular and plural. "Deer" remains "deer" in the plural.)*

13. How do we make plural the forms of numbers, symbols, words talked about as words, and letters? **L56** *(We make them plural by adding an apostrophe "s". The letter "p" made plural is "p's".)*

14. What do many foreign words make a word plural? **L78** *(They sometimes keep the plural of the original language.)*

15. What do we do if we are not sure how to form the plural of some noun? **L56** *(If there is doubt about the plural form of a noun, we need to check a good dictionary.)*

Any questions on how to form the plural of nouns?

Consult our standard for spelling and for meaning — our trusty dictionary.

Where Do I Go from Here?

- **L56** and **L78** goes to **"Lesson 34"** on page 335.

What Materials Will I Need?

- **L56** and **L78** will need *Grammar Notebooks*, pencils, and copies of Worksheets for **"Lesson 34"** starting on page 348.

How Do I Form Plural Nouns?

Teacher Directions: Have your student write the plural forms of these nouns. Watch number 16; it's tricky.

Student Directions: Write the plural form for each of these nouns.

1.	kiss	1. kisses
2.	shampoo	2. shampoos
3.	convoy	3. convoys
4.	ferry	4. ferries
5.	safe	5. safes
6.	shelf	6. shelves
7.	soprano	7. sopranos
8.	hero	8. heroes
9.	ox	9. oxen
10.	cattle	10. cattle
11.	buzz	11. buzzes
12.	guy	12. guys
13.	army	13. armies
14.	roof	14. roofs
15.	loaf	15. loaves
16.	Jim Smith, Jim Brown	16. the two Jims
17.	mouse	17. mice
18.	daughter-in-law	18. daughters-in-law
19.	comedy	19. comedies
20.	attorney-general	20. attorneys-genera
21.	a	21. a's
22.	10	22. 10's

1. kiss   1._____

2. shampoo   2._____

3. convoy   3._____

4. ferry   4._____

5. safe   5._____

6. shelf   6._____

7. soprano   7._____

8. hero   8._____

9. ox   9._____

10. cattle   10._____

11. buzz   11._____

12. guy   12._____

13. army   13._____

14. roof   14._____

15. loaf   15._____

16. Jim Smith, 16._____
    Jim Brown

17. mouse   17._____

18. daughter-in-law 18._____

19. comedy   19._____

20. attorney general 20._____

21. a   21._____

22. 10   22._____

**Student
Worksheet 1:**

How Do I Form Plural Nouns?

*Student Directions: Write
the plural form for each
of these nouns.*

Comprehensive Checklist 3 for Lessons 25-33

1. What is comparative analysis? **L78** *(Comparative analysis is making correct choices with the available information.)*

2. Why is knowing how to analyze a sentence so important? **L78** *(Not only do we learn how our language works making us a better communicator, but we also are learning thinking skills like sequencing, logic, the drawing of conclusions, and comparative analysis. Improving our thinking skills is a worthwhile endeavor.)*

3. What are the six steps to analyzing a sentence? **L78** *(1. Find the prepositional phrases. 2. Find the verb(s). 3. Find the subject(s). 4. Find the DO, IO, PN, or PA 5. Find the adjectives and adverbs. 6. Find the conjunctions.)*

4. What pronouns do we use to conjugate a verb? **L34** *(We use the personal pronouns "I", "you", "he", "she", "it", "we", "you", "they".)*

5. What is another name for these pronouns? **L78** *(They can be called "subject pronouns" because they are used in the subject position.)*

6. Where may a subject pronoun be used? **L78** *(A subject pronoun may be used in the subject position or the predicate noun position in our sentence.)*

7. Why can a subject pronoun be used as a predicate noun? **L78** *(These two positions in our sentence are equal and interchangeable.)*

8. What does analyzing sentences do? **L78** *(Analyzing sentences teaches us how to think logically. Analyzing sentences teaches us comparative analysis. Analyzing gives us reasons for why words are ordered like they are. Analyzing builds sentence sense so that we know how sentences should be constructed.)*

9. Why shouldn't we determine proper grammar usage by how something sounds in a sentence? **L78** *(Going by how a word sounds is not reliable. We must go by what is grammatically correct.)*

10. What does conjugating verbs help us to do? **L34** *(It helps us determine the proper usage and the proper verb form for action and linking verbs.)*

11. What is Sentence Pattern 4C? **L78** *(Sentence Pattern 4C is S + LV——>PN.)*

12. What does a predicate noun do? **L78** *(A predicate noun renames the subject and is equal to the subject.)*

13. Where may subject pronouns be used? **L78** *(Subject pronouns may be used in a subject position or a predicate noun position.)*

14. Where may object pronouns be used? **L78** *(Object pronouns may be used in one of three places: DO, IO, or OP.)*

15. What must we do in order to choose the proper pronoun in a sentence? **L78** *(We must be able to analyze the sentence and determine the function of the pronoun. If it is a subject position or a predicate noun position, we use a subject pronoun. If it is an object position, we must use an object pronoun.)*

16. Why shouldn't we go by how pronouns sound to determine proper usage? **L78** *(How something sounds is not always a reliable guide for pronoun usage. We must know how to analyze a sentence quickly and make proper choices accordingly.)*

17. When a pronoun influences a subject, what kind of a pronoun do we use? **L78** *(Pronouns influencing a subject must use a subject pronoun. We must say, "We girls went downtown" not "Us girls went downtown".)*

18. How will knowing the four sentence patterns help us? **L78** *(They will be our guide to proper usage of subject and object pronouns.)*

19. What are the singular subject and object pronouns? **L78** *("I", "you", "he", "she", "it", "me", "you", "him", "her", "it".)*

20. What are the plural subject and object pronouns? **L78** *("We", "you", "they", "us", "you", "them".)*

21. What are the first person pronouns and when do we use them? **L78** *(The first person pronouns are the pronouns "I" and "we" or "me" and "us", and we use them when we are personally involved in a sentence.)*

22. What are the second person pronouns and when do we use them? **L78** *(The second person pronouns are singular "you" and plural "you", and we use them when talking directly to another person or group. It is the person who is listening to the message.)*

23. What are the third person pronouns and when do we use them? **L78** *(The third person pronouns are the pronouns "he", "she",*

"it", "him", "her", "it", "they", or "them", and they are used when the speaker is observing and stating his observations even though he is not personally involved in the activity described in the sentence.)

24. What is a declarative sentence? **L12** *(A declarative sentence is a sentence that states a fact or gives information.)*

25. What punctuation mark do we use at the end of a declarative sentence? **L12** *(Every declarative sentence needs to end with a period.)*

26. How does standing up on our feet help us when answering a teacher's question? **L34** *(It helps us to be very alert.)*

27. What benefits come from answering a teacher's question using a complete sentence? **L34** *(If we can think in complete sentences, we can write in complete sentences.)*

28. Why is a root word so important? **L56** *(A root word is the basic part of a word from which other words may be built. To know what it means is to know what many other words mean.)*

29. How does analyzing sentences help us? **L56** *(Marking sentences helps me to gain an increasing awareness of how sentences are written building in me a "sentence sense" so that I become an excellent writer and speaker.)*

30. What does an interrogative sentence do? **L12** *(It asks a question.)*

31. What punctuation mark do we use at the end of an interrogative sentence? **L12** *(An interrogative sentence always ends with a question mark.)*

32. How do questions begin? **L12** *(Questions may begin with a common interrogative pronoun like "who", "whom", "which", "what", or "whose".)*

33. How else are questions created? **L56** *(Questions may be created by taking a declarative sentence, inverting word order, and adding helping verbs as needed.)*

34. In analysis, an interrogative pronoun might take on what job in the sentence? **L78** *(An interrogative pronoun may serve as a subject, as an adjective, or as an OP.)*

35. What does a word do that shows possession? **L78** *(A possessive word is someone or something that owns someone or something else.)*

36. How do we show possession when we use a personal name like John? **L78** *(We need to add an apostrophe and an "s" to show this ownership.)*

37. What part of the verb must we use when we are using the helping verbs "have", "has", or "had"? **L78** *(We need to use the third most important part of any verb. Another name for this is the past participle.)*

38. What does an imperative sentence do? **L12** *(An imperative sentence gives a command or makes a request.)*

39. What is usually the first written word of an imperative sentence? **L56** *(The first written word is usually an action verb. The sentence expects some kind of action on the part of the receiver of the request.)*

40. What is the subject of every imperative sentence? **L34** *(The subject of every imperative sentence is the pronoun "you" understood.)*

41. What does an exclamatory sentence do? **L12** *(An exclamatory sentence displays a strong or sudden emotion.)*

42. How do we punctuate an exclamatory sentence? **L12** *(We punctuate an exclamatory sentence with an exclamation point.)*

43. What kinds of sentences may be used as an exclamatory sentence? **L34** *(Declarative and imperative sentences may be used as exclamatory sentences. If we want them to show emotion, we simply add an exclamation point.)*

44. Why might I need to use a dictionary when analyzing a sentence? **L78** *(The dictionary is a trusted friend in questions regarding grammatical usage. It gives us the various parts of speech a particular word can be and many times provides an example of how it is used.)*

45. What if we encounter some words in a sentence, but we can't figure out how to mark them? **L78** *(We must be patient. The English language offers many challenges. We can do some research. Invert word order. Use a dictionary. Substitute other words. Find out what jobs a difficult word can do. We need to remember that syntactical analysis should be a servant and not a taskmaster. If we cannot account for all of the words, we will happily leave them for another day.)*

46. What is an interjection? **L56** *(Interjections usually are a one word part of speech designed to express sudden emotion. They*

always act alone like with these examples: "Phooey!" "Tarna-tion!" "Ouch!" They usually precede a further explanation for why the writer is feeling this way. "Uff Da! Dat was sure a tasty hotdish!")

47. How are interjections like exclamatory sentences? **L56**
(Interjections are full of emotion just like exclamatory sentences. Interjections, however, act independently. They are not grammatically tied to other words in a sentence.)

48. Why is learning to be organized so important? **L56**
(Organizational skills are always an ever-present asset for the student who wants to maximize his learning. We need to choose order over chaos. Order produces efficiency.)

49. What is the job of a possessive pronoun and noun? **L78** *(The basic job of a possessive noun or pronoun is to show ownership of another noun.)*

50. What do we call possessive pronouns that do the work of an adjective? **L78** *(Possessive pronouns that do the job of an adjective are called "adjectival pronouns" or "predicate adjectives" depending upon where they are used.)*

51. How does practicing conjugating help us? **L34** *(Conjugating teaches us to use verbs correctly in our writing.)*

52. What three jobs can a possessive noun or pronoun do in a sentence? **L78** *(A possessive noun or pronoun can do the work of an adjective, a predicate adjective, or a subject.)*

53. What punctuation mark does a possessive noun use to show ownership? **L78** *(Possessive nouns use apostrophes to show ownership.)*

54. What punctuation mark does a possessive pronoun use to show ownership? **L78** *(Possessive pronouns do not use any punctuation. They are possessive by nature.)*

55. What are the demonstrative pronouns and what do they do? **L78** *(The demonstrative pronouns are "this", "that", "these", and "those" and they point at particular nouns.)*

56. What are the reflexive pronouns and what do they do? **L78** *(The reflexive pronouns are any pronouns that end in "self" or "selves", and they reflect back to another word in the sentence.)*

57. What do we add to most regular nouns to make them plural? **L56** *(We add a letter "s" to make most regular nouns a plural.)*

58. How do we make words plural that end in the letters "s", "x", "z", "sh", and "ch"? **L56** *(We simply add "es".)*

59. How do we make nouns plural that end in "y" preceded by a consonant? **L56** *(We change the "y" to "i" and add "es".)*

60. How do we make nouns plural that end in "y" preceded by a vowel? **L56** *(We simply add an "s".)*

61. How are most nouns made plural that end in "f" or "fe"? **L56** *(Most of these kinds of nouns form plurals by adding "s".)*

62. How are a few of these nouns made plural that end in "f" or "fe"? **L56** *(Some form plurals by changing the "f" or "fe" to "v" and adding "es". "Calf" becomes "calves".)*

63. Some plural forms of words are irregular. What do they do to make a word plural? **L56** *(They change the spelling of the root word when moving from singular to plural. "Man" becomes "men". "Mouse" becomes "mice".)*

64. How do some nouns form plurals that end in "o" preceded by a vowel? **L78** *(They simply add an "s" for plural. "Radio" becomes "radios".)*

65. How do some nouns form plurals that end in "o" preceded by a consonant? **L78** *(They add "es" for plural. "Hero" becomes "heroes".)*

66. How do musical terms that end in "o" form plural? **L78** *(They simply add "s" for plural. "Piano" becomes "pianos".)*

67. How do we make a compound nouns plural like in the word "brother-in-law"? **L78** *(We make the main noun of the compound word plural according to the rule that applies for that word. "Brother-in-law" becomes "brothers-in-law".)*

68. What happens to some words that do not change any spelling in the plural? **L56** *(Some nouns stay exactly the same in the singular and plural. "Deer" remains "deer" in the plural.)*

69. How do we make plural the forms of numbers, symbols, words talked about as words, and letters? **L56** *(We make them plural by adding an apostrophe "s". The letter "p" made plural is "p's".)*

70. What do many foreign words make a word plural? **L78** *(They sometimes keep the plural of the original language.)*

71. Why do I need to understand how our language works? **L78** *(If we do not understand how our language works, it controls us*

and we do not control it. It makes us a slave. We want it to be our servant. Well-practiced, well-polished communication skills are imperative if we expect doors of opportunity to open and stay open in the future.)

72. What does this statement mean? Precise grammar builds syntactical expectancies at an automatic level. **L78** *(Learning how our language works builds certain expectations about how sentences should be written and how language should be spoken. If we can use these understandings and they are automatic, language becomes a friend and a sharpened tool. Few obstacles will stand in our way of effective communication.)*

Lesson 34

What Is an Apostrophe?

Discovering the Apostrophe

L34P Before the class time, write down the following information from this lesson on a piece of penmanship paper: "This is Tommy's bike." "The cat's food was in the pail." "Jim's car ran out of gas." "My teacher's smile was special." "The monkey's banana was in the tree." Of course, they need to be written beautifully. After these examples have been written there, make a beautiful paper airplane out of this piece of penmanship paper and put it out of sight of the students.

34 **Step 1 —** "There is a special trick that some commas can do that no other punctuation marks can do. Do any of you know what that trick is?"

34P Pause.

34 "The commas that do this trick have a special name. They are called **'apostrophes'.** Do you know what trick they can do?"

L34P After a pause, fly the plane!

34 "Look at my paper airplane. The apostrophe is like a paper airplane. It is as if this punctuation mark has wings. Apostrophes are commas that can fly! I have written some sentences on my paper airplane that use apostrophes. These are very special kinds of sentences."

L34P Open the paper airplane and show each student the sentences that you have written. If necessary, put these sentences on the board or on a flip chart so all can see.

"Look at these sentences. Can you see the commas that are flying? These apostrophes don't move once they are in place. Can you figure out one of the jobs they do? Look at the sentences carefully. What do they all have in common? They all talk about someone or something that owns something, don't they? One of the jobs of an apostrophe is to show ownership. If we own something, it belongs to us. If the bike belongs to Tommy, we say it is **Tommy's bike.** If the food belongs to the cat and it is in the pail, we say it is the **cat's food** in the pail."

Discovering the Nature of a Noun That Shows Ownership

L34 **Step 2 —** "There is a very important principle about how to use an apostrophe that we need to discover. Let's look at these

This is Tommy's bike.
The cat's food was in the pail.
Jim's car ran out of gas.
My teacher's smile was special.
The monkey's banana was in the tree.

Singular	Plural	Singular Possessive	Plural Possessive
child	children	child's	children's
turkey	turkeys	turkey's	turkeys'
calf	calves	calf's	calves'
dog	dogs	dog's	dogs'
secretary	secretaries	secretary's	secretaries'
man	men	man's	men's
bear	bears	bear's	bears'
cat	cats	cat's	cats'
mouse	mice	mouse's	mice's

Sample Page 49
Lesson 34

50 What Is an Apostrophe? (continued)

Rule 1: We make singular words show ownership by adding an apostrophe "s" to the end of the word.
My teacher's smile was special.

Rule 2: We make plural words not ending in "s" show ownership by adding an apostrophe "s" to the end of the word.
The children's toys were broken.

Rule 3: We make plural words that end in "s" show ownership by adding an apostrophe after the "s".
The boys' hats were found.

Rule 4: An apostrophe is used to show letters or numbers that are missing in a contraction.
did not didn't will not won't I am I'm
In the fall of '95, we traveled to Alaska.

Sample Page 50
Lesson 34

Who we are and how we model what we would like our students to be is what they will become.

sentences: 'This is Tommy's bike.' 'The cat's food was in the pail.' 'Jim's car ran out of gas.' 'My teacher's smile was special.' 'The monkey's banana was in the tree.' Look at each of the words that own something. What does Tommy own?"

STUDENTS:	"Tommy owns the bike."
TEACHER:	"What does the cat own?"
STUDENTS:	"The cat owns the food."
TEACHER:	"What does Jim own?"
STUDENTS:	"Jim owns the car."
TEACHER:	"What does your teacher own?"
STUDENTS:	"My teacher owns a smile."
TEACHER:	"What does the monkey own?"
STUDENTS:	"The monkey owns the banana."
TEACHER:	"What can we learn from these words?"
STUDENTS:	"Every noun that owns something has a flying comma."
TEACHER:	"Where was the apostrophe placed in every one of these words?"
STUDENTS:	"The apostrophe was placed directly after the word and directly before the letter 's'."
TEACHER:	"This is a rule of our language. A singular noun that owns something needs to have an apostrophe and then the letter 's' added to the end of the word. We need to write these sentences."

Dictating Sentences That Use Nouns That Show Ownership

L34P L34 students will need a piece of loose-leaf practice penmanship paper. **L56** and beyond will need to turn to page 49 in their *Grammar Notebook*.

L34 **Step 3 —** *"Skipping one baseline below the title line, write the following sentences on consecutive baselines: 'This is Tommy's bike'. 'The cat's food was in the pail'. 'Jim's car ran out of gas'. 'My teacher's smile was special'. 'The monkey's banana was in the tree'.*

"We show these nouns own something by flying the comma in the right place. What did we call these flying commas?"

STUDENTS: "They are called 'apostrophes'."

L78 TEACHER: "We have also learned that when pronouns like '*my*' and '*mine*' or '*his*' and '*hers*' own something, they

---

What Is an Apostrophe?   49

This is Tommy's bike.
The cat's food was in the pail.
Jim's car ran out of gas.
My teacher's smile was special.
The monkey's banana was in the tree.

Singular	Plural	Singular	Plural
			Possessive
child	children	child's	children's
turkey	turkeys	turkey's	turkeys'
calf	calves	calf's	calves'
dog	dogs	dog's	dogs'
secretary	secretaries	secretary's	secretaries'
man	men	man's	men's
bear	bears	bear's	bears'
cat	cats	cat's	cats'
mouse	mice	mouse's	mice's

Sample Page 49
Lesson 34

---

are called **'possessive pronouns'**. Nouns like Tommy and cat that also own something are called **'possessive nouns'**."

Dictating Singular and Plural Forms of Nouns

L34   **Step 4** — "We need to write some more examples of nouns that own something. *Fold your page into four equal columns. Skipping one baseline below the last sentence, 'The monkey's banana was in the tree', centered in the first column, write the subtitle **'Singular'**. On the same baseline in the second column, center the subtitle **'Plural'**. On the same baseline in the third column, center another subtitle **'Singular'**. Centered in the fourth column, on the same baseline, write the subtitle **'Plural'**.*"

L78   *"Go to the next available baseline. Centered across both the third and fourth columns, directly below the second set of 'Singular' and 'Plural', write the subtitle **'Possessive'**."*

L34   **Step 5** — *"Skipping one baseline below 'singular' in the first column, comfortably close to the left red margin line, write the following nouns on consecutive baselines:* **'child', 'turkey', 'calf', 'dog', 'secretary', 'man', 'bear', 'cat', 'mouse'.**"

L34   **Step 6** — "We need to record the plural forms of each of these words. *Comfortably close to the first folded margin line in the second column, on the same baseline as its singular form, write the following plural forms on consecutive baselines:* **'children', 'turkeys', 'calves', 'dogs', 'secretaries', 'men', 'bears', 'cats', 'mice'.**"

Discovering the Nature of a Singular Noun That Shows Ownership

L34   **Step 7** — "I am going to write a few more sentences on the board for you to examine. We need to be sure that we know how to use an apostrophe in some other places. Here are the sentences. 'The child's toy was broken.' 'The turkey's scratching attracted the hunter.' 'The calf's milk was in the bottle.' 'The dog's dish is full of good food.' 'The secretary's desk was very well organized.' 'Look at each of the ownership words.' Are they singular or plural?"

STUDENTS: "Each ownership word is singular."

TEACHER: "What have we learned about placing apostrophes in singular nouns like these?"

STUDENTS: "The apostrophes need to be placed directly after the singular form of the word and directly before the added letter 's'."

What Is an Apostrophe?			49

This is Tommy's bike.
The cat's food was in the pail.
Jim's car ran out of gas.
My teacher's smile was special.
The monkey's banana was in the tree.

Singular	Plural	Singular	Plural
		Possessive	
child	children	child's	children's
turkey	turkeys	turkey's	turkeys'
calf	calves	calf's	calves'
dog	dogs	dog's	dogs'
secretary	secretaries	secretary's	secretaries'
man	men	man's	men's
bear	bears	bear's	bears'
cat	cats	cat's	cats'
mouse	mice	mouse's	mice's

Sample Page 49
Lesson 34

This is Tommy's bike.
The cat's food was in the pail.
Jim's car ran out of gas.
My teacher's smile was special.
The monkey's banana was in the tree.

Singular	Plural	Singular Possessive	Plural
child	children	child's	children's
turkey	turkeys	turkey's	turkeys'
calf	calves	calf's	calves'
dog	dogs	dog's	dogs'
secretary	secretaries	secretary's	secretaries'
man	men	man's	men's
bear	bears	bear's	bears'
cat	cats	cat's	cats'
mouse	mice	mouse's	mice's

Sample Page 49
Lesson 34

TEACHER: "We need to record each of these words. *Comfortably close to the folded margin line in the third column, on the same baseline as its singular and plural form, write the following singular forms of these ownership words on consecutive baselines: 'child's', 'turkey's', 'calf's', 'dog's', 'secretary's', 'man's', 'bear's', 'cat's', 'mouse's'.* One more time, what do we do every time we write a singular noun that shows ownership?"

STUDENTS: "We simply add an apostrophe and then the letter 's'."

Discovering the Nature of a Plural Noun That Shows Ownership

L34   Step 8 — "I need to write some more sentences for you to investigate. Look at these sentences. 'The children's toys are broken.' 'The turkeys' range was wet from the rain.' 'The calves' milk was in the bottles.' 'The dogs' dishes need to be cleaned.' 'The secretaries' organization met on Tuesday.' Look at each ownership word. Are they singular or plural?"

STUDENTS: "They all appear to be plural. 'Children' means there is more than one child."

TEACHER: "Where is the apostrophe is these words?"

STUDENTS: "The apostrophe is before the letter 's' in the word 'children' and after the letter 's' in all the other words."

TEACHER: "Good. Keep that in mind."

STUDENTS: "But why is the apostrophe in a different place in 'children' than in the words 'calves' and 'secretaries' and 'turkeys' and 'dogs'?"

TEACHER: "You will soon find out. Look at the words 'turkeys' and 'dogs'? Where is the apostrophe in these words again?"

STUDENTS: "It comes after the letter 's'."

TEACHER: "When we wrote the word 'dog' and 'turkey' and there was only one dog and one turkey and each one owned something, where did the apostrophe go?"

STUDENTS: "When there was only one 'dog' and one 'turkey', it was before the letter 's'."

TEACHER: "What does that tell you?"

STUDENTS: "Oh, I get it. The location of the apostrophe in most words that show ownership tells us whether the word is singular or plural."

TEACHER: "That is right. How do we determine this location?"

STUDENTS: "We have to know the plural form of the noun."

TEACHER: "What is different between the plural form 'children' and all the other plural forms of the words we have listed?"

STUDENTS: "All the other plural forms end in the letter 's'. The word 'children' does not."

TEACHER: "Here is another rule of our language. If the last letter of the plural form ends in the letter 's' like in the word 'dogs', guess where we put the apostrophe?"

STUDENTS: "We place it after the letter 's'."

TEACHER: "If the original plural form of the noun does not need a letter 's' to make it plural, where do we put the apostrophe?"

STUDENTS: "We place it before the letter 's'."

TEACHER: "The placement of the apostrophe is so very important. Irregular nouns like 'child' or 'man' are spelled differently in the plural. They do not need to simply add a letter 's' like many words do to make the plural form."

.34 "Regular nouns like 'dog' or 'turkey' only need to add a letter 's' to make them plural. They do not change spelling. If the apostrophe is used **before** the letter 's' with regular nouns, these ownership nouns are singular. If the apostrophe is **after** the final letter 's', these ownership nouns are plural. And even if a singular noun like 'calf' changes spelling in the plural, making the word 'calves', because the plural form ends in the letter 's', we still place the apostrophe after that letter 's'. **The spelling of the plural form of the noun determines where we place the apostrophe.**"

Dictating Plural Nouns That Show Ownership

.34 **Step 9** — "We need to record the plural forms of each of these ownership words. *Comfortably close to the folded margin line in the fourth column, on the same baseline as its singular form, write the following plural forms of these ownership words on consecutive baselines: 'children's,' 'turkeys',' 'calves',' 'dogs',' 'secretaries',' 'men's,' 'bears',' 'cats',' 'mice's.'* We need to be sure the apostrophe is in the right place."

What Is an Apostrophe?			49

This is Tommy's bike.
The cat's food was in the pail.
Jim's car ran out of gas.
My teacher's smile was special.
The monkey's banana was in the tree.

Singular	Plural	Singular Possessive	Plural Possessive
child	children	child's	children's
turkey	turkeys	turkey's	turkeys'
calf	calves	calf's	calves'
dog	dogs	dog's	dogs'
secretary	secretaries	secretary's	secretaries'
man	men	man's	men's
bear	bears	bear's	bears'
cat	cats	cat's	cats'
mouse	mice	mouse's	mice's

Sample Page 49
Lesson 34

What Is an Apostrophe? 49

This is Tommy's bike.
The cat's food was in the pail.
Jim's car ran out of gas.
My teacher's smile was special.
The monkey's banana was in the tree.

Singular	Plural	Singular Possessive	Plural Possessive
child	children	child's	children's
turkey	turkeys	turkey's	turkeys'
calf	calves	calf's	calves'
dog	dogs	dog's	dogs'
secretary	secretaries	secretary's	secretaries'
man	men	man's	men's
bear	bears	bear's	bears'
cat	cats	cat's	cats'
mouse	mice	mouse's	mice's

Sample Page 49
Lesson 34

50   What Is an Apostrophe? (continued)

Rule 1: We make singular words show
ownership by adding an apostrophe "s"
to the end of the word.
My teacher's smile was special.

Rule 2: We make plural words not
ending in "s" show ownership by adding
an apostrophe "s" to the end of the word.
The children's toys were broken.

Rule 3: We make plural words that end
in "s" show ownership by adding an
apostrophe after the "s".
The boys' hats were found.

Rule 4: An apostrophe is used to show
letters or numbers that are missing in a
contraction.
did not didn't will not won't I am I'm
In the fall of '95, we traveled to Alaska.

Sample Page 50
Lesson 34

Let's Get Organized

L56   **Step 10 —** *"Turn to the Table of Contents. On the page 49 line, write the title* **'What Is an Apostrophe?'** *Turn back to page 49."*

L34   *"Centered on the title line, between the two red margin lines, write the title* **'What Is an Apostrophe?'"**

L34P L34 students need to turn their paper over to the backside to continue the following steps. On the front they should have the five sample sentences with singular ownership nouns and the list of singular and plural words and their ownership forms using the apostrophe. **L56** students and above need to turn to page 50 before continuing the following steps.

Defining Singular and Plural Ownership Nouns

L34   **Step 1 —** *"Skipping one baseline below the title line, comfortably close to the left margin line, write the following:* **'Rule 1: We make singular words show ownership by adding an apostrophe "s" to the end of the word'.** You will need more than one line. *On the next available baseline, write the following sample sentence:* **'My teacher's smile was special'."**

L34   **Step 2 —** *"Skipping one baseline below our sample sentence, comfortably close to the left margin line, write the following:* **'Rule 2: We make plural words not ending in "s" show ownership by adding an apostrophe "s" to the end of the word'.** You will need more than one line. *On the next available baseline, please write the following sample sentence:* **'The children's toys were broken'."**

L34   **Step 3 —** *"Skipping one baseline below our sample sentence, comfortably close to the left margin line, write the following:* **'Rule 3: We make plural words that end in "s" show ownership by adding an apostrophe after the "s"'.** You will need more than one line. *On the next available baseline, please write the following sample sentence:* **'The boys' hats were found'."**

Learning to Use Apostrophes with Contractions

L34   **Step 4 —** "Another job that an apostrophe does is to help make sense out of words we call contractions. Sometimes we do not want to take the time to say two whole words, so we shorten them into one word.

"For instance, instead of saying the words 'do' and 'not' as in the sentence 'I do not know the answer', we often say 'don't'.

Instead of 'can' and 'not' as in the sentence 'I cannot come to the door', we say 'can't'. Instead of 'it' and 'is' as in the sentence 'It is beginning to look a lot like Christmas', we say 'it's'.

"When we write a contraction, we leave out some of the letters from the two words. We want people who are reading to know that we are missing letters. Most of the time we place an apostrophe above and between where our letter or letters are missing. In some words we take out more than one letter. Look at these examples."

34P Write the following two-word combinations on the board one at a time. Discuss each example by asking the question, "How would we make these two words into a contraction?" Write the contraction next to the words from which it was made. Remind your students that in some words we need to take out more than one letter.

Practicing with Contractions

did not ——————→ didn't   I am ——————→ I'm

does not ——————→ doesn't   let us ——————→ let's

has not ——————→ hasn't   he is or he has ——————→ he's

were not ——————→ weren't   it is or it has ——————→ it's

who has or who is ——————→ who's   is not ——————→ isn't

they had or they would →they'd   you have ——————→ you've

we are or we were ——————→ we're   they are ——————→ they're

she had or she would ——→ she'd   you are ——————→ you're

she will ——————→ she'll   will not ——————→ won't

could not ——————→ couldn't   should not ——→ shouldn't

they have ——————→ they've   would not ——————→ wouldn't

have not ——————→ haven't   I will ——————→ I'll

34 **Step 5 —** *"Skipping one line under the example for Rule 3, comfortably close to the margin line, write the following: 'Rule 4: An apostrophe is used to show letters or numbers that are missing in a contraction'. You will need more than one line. On the next available baseline, write these examples leaving one space between each two-word combination and each contraction: 'Did not', 'didn't', 'will not', 'won't', 'I am', 'I'm'."*

"On the next available baseline below the two-word combination 'did not', write the following sentence: 'In the fall of '95, we traveled to Alaska'.

50   What Is an Apostrophe? (continued)

Rule 1: We make singular words show ownership by adding an apostrophe "s" to the end of the word.
My teacher's smile was special.

Rule 2: We make plural words not ending in "s" show ownership by adding an apostrophe "s" to the end of the word.
The children's toys were broken.

Rule 3: We make plural words that end in "s" show ownership by adding an apostrophe after the "s".
The boys' hats were found.

Rule 4: An apostrophe is used to show letters or numbers that are missing in a contraction.
did not didn't will not won't I am I'm
In the fall of '95, we traveled to Alaska.

Sample Page 50
Lesson 34

Rule 1: We make singular words show
ownership by adding an apostrophe "s"
to the end of the word.
My teacher's smile was special.

Rule 2: We make plural words not
ending in "s" show ownership by adding
an apostrophe "s" to the end of the word.
The children's toys were broken.

Rule 3: We make plural words that end
in "s" show ownership by adding an
apostrophe after the "s".
The boys' hats were found.

Rule 4: An apostrophe is used to show
letters or numbers that are missing in a
contraction.
did not didn't will not won't I am I'm
In the fall of '95, we traveled to Alaska.

Sample Page 50
Lesson 34

TEACHER: "In what year did we manage a trip to Alaska?"

STUDENTS: "It was in the year 1995."

TEACHER: "What job did the apostrophe do in our sample sentence?"

STUDENTS: "Instead of taking the place of letters as it usually does, this time it took the place of two numbers."

TEACHER: "That is why we have included the word 'numbers' in Rule 4 because an apostrophe may replace the first two digits in the writing of a year. The sentence really says the summer of 1995. The apostrophe replaces the numerals '1' and '9'."

Let's Get Organized

L56 **Step 6 —** *"Turn to the Table of Contents. On the page 50 line, write the title 'What Is an Apostrophe? (continued)'."*

L34 *"Centered on the title line, between the two red margin lines, write the title 'What Is an Apostrophe? (continued)'."*

L34P L34 students need to begin a new practice page. **L56** students and above need to turn to page 51 before continuing the following steps.

Using Apostrophes to Form Other Plurals

L34 **Step 1 —** *"Skipping one baseline under the title line, comfortably close to the margin line, write the following: 'Rule 5: The plural forms of a letter, a number, a sign, or words mentioned as words all need an apostrophe "s"'.* You will need more than one line. Let's look at the following examples:

'There were three A's on her report card.'
'The skater received four 10's for her performance.'
'Six's were needed in the report.'
'We counted over 100 and's in the story.'

"What do we learn from these examples?"

STUDENTS: "It is just as the rule says. When a letter, a number, a sign, or words mentioned as words are used in their plural forms, they each need an apostrophe 's'."

L34 **Step 7 —** *"Starting on the next available baseline, comfortably close to the margin line, write the following examples, leaving one space between each one: 'three A's', 'four 10's', 'six 's', '100 and's'."*

Discovering More Rules for the Use of the Apostrophe

L78 **Step 1** — *"Skipping one baseline under our last examples, comfortably close to the left margin line, please write the following:* **'Rule 6: Possessive proper nouns already ending in "s" may either add an apostrophe alone or an apostrophe "s"; an apostrophe "s" is preferred except with a few proper names such as "Jesus" and "Moses"'.** *You will need more than one line."*

L78 **Step 2** — *"On the next two available baselines below the rule, starting each sentence comfortably close to the left margin line, write the following sentences on consecutive baselines:*

> **'Tess's class was very late in the evening.'**
> **'Jesus' disciples listened to his teaching.'**

"What do we learn from writing these sentences?"

STUDENTS: "The names of people ending in the letter 's' are made possessive by either adding an apostrophe alone or by adding an apostrophe and then another letter 's'."

L78 **Step 3** — *"Skipping one baseline below our last sentence, starting comfortably close to the left margin line, please write the following:* **'Rule 7: When speaking of two or more people, each of whom owns something separately, add the apostrophe or apostrophe "s" to the end of each name'."*

78 **Step 4** — *"On the next available baseline starting comfortably close to the left margin line, write the following sentence:*

> **'Jared's and Joel's bicycle tires need air.'**

"What does this rule teach us?"

STUDENTS: "We learn that separate ownership of the same kinds of things by two different people requires an apostrophe in each person's name."

L78 **Step 5** — *"Turn to page 52. Skipping one baseline below the title line, starting comfortably close to the left margin line, write the following:* **'Rule 8: When speaking of two or more people who own something together, add the apostrophe or apostrophe "s" to the end of only the last name mentioned'.**

L78 **Step 6** — *"On the next baseline, starting comfortably close to the left margin line, write the following sentence:*

> **'Jared and Joel's go-kart is in need of repair.'**

"What do we learn from this rule?"

| What Is an Apostrophe? (continued) | 51 |

Rule 5: The plural forms of a letter, a number, a sign, or words mentioned as words all need an apostrophe "s". three A's four 10's six #'s 100 and's

Rule 6: Possessive proper nouns already ending in "s" may either add an apostrophe alone or an apostrophe "s"; an apostrophe "s" is preferred except with a few proper names such as Jesus and Moses. Tess's class was very late in the evening. Jesus' disciples listened to his teaching.

Rule 7: When speaking of two or more people, each of whom owns something separately, add the apostrophe or apostrophe "s" to the end of each name. Jared's and Joel's bicycle tires need air.

Sample Page 51
Lesson 34

| 52 | What Is an Apostrophe? (continued) |

Rule 8: When speaking of two or more people who own something together, add the apostrophe or apostrophe "s" to the end of only the last name mentioned. Jared and Joel's go-kart is in need of repair.

Rule 9: When making compound words possessive, add the apostrophe or apostrophe "s" to the end of only the last word of the compound word. My sister-in-law's recipe for apple pie is my favorite.

Rule 10: We make indefinite pronouns possessive by adding an apostrophe and an "s" to the end of the word. Somebody's mitten was left in the car. Anyone's hat will work for the costume.

Sample Page 52
Lesson 34

We all know that successfully accomplishing a task requires great effort. Sometimes getting the job done is just plain hard work. If we persevere and are diligent, the rewards will come. Grammar Works is a training program. The lessons and the Notebook are push-ups and sit-ups. They may require the discipline of a marathon runner. We are equipping our students to be excellent communicators, and that is a worthy end.

---

52 | What Is an Apostrophe? (continued)

Rule 8: When speaking of two or more people who own something together, add the apostrophe or apostrophe "s" to the end of only the last name mentioned.
Jared and Joel's go-kart is in need of repair.

Rule 9: When making compound words possessive, add the apostrophe or apostrophe "s" to the end of only the last word of the compound word.
My sister-in-law's recipe for apple pie is my favorite.

Rule 10: We make indefinite pronouns possessive by adding an apostrophe and an "s" to the end of the word.
Somebody's mitten was left in the car.
Anyone's hat will work for the costume.

Sample Page 52
Lesson 34

What Is an Apostrophe? (continued) | 53

Rule 11: Possessive pronouns are already possessive and need no apostrophe.
Ours was fast.
Theirs was slow.

Rule 12: We make periods of time and amounts possessive by adding an apostrophe "s" to the end of the word.
Today's temperature was 80 degrees.
We used ten dollar's worth of gasoline.
It was an hour's time.

Sample Page 53
Lesson 34

STUDENTS: "There is only one go-kart. Both Jared and Joel own this go-kart. Because they own it together, we need to punctuate only the last name mentioned."

L78 **Step 7** — *"Skipping one baseline below our last example, starting comfortably close to the left margin line, write the following: '**Rule 9: When making compound words possessive, add the apostrophe or apostrophe "s" to the end of only the last word of the compound word'.**"*

L78 **Step 8** — *"On the next baseline starting comfortably close to the left margin line, write the following sentence:*

'*My sister-in-law's recipe for apple pie is my favorite.*'

"What do we learn from this rule?"

STUDENTS: "We learn that the last word in a compound word gets the apostrophe when the compound word owns something. In this case, the sister-in law owns the recipe."

Forming the Possessives of Pronouns

L78 **Step 9** — *"Skipping one baseline under the last example, starting comfortably close to the left margin line, write the following: '**Rule 10: We make indefinite pronouns possessive by adding an apostrophe and an "s" to the end of the word'.***

L78 **Step 10** — *"On the next baseline starting comfortably close to the left margin line, write the following sentences on consecutive baselines:*

'*Somebody's mitten was left in the car.*'
'*Anyone's hat will work for the costume.*'

"What do we learn from this rule?"

STUDENTS: "We learn that possessive indefinite pronouns are punctuated like regular singular nouns that own something. We just add an apostrophe and then the letter 's'."

L78 **Step 11** — *"Turn to page 53. Skipping one baseline under the title line, starting comfortably close to the left margin line, write the following: '**Rule 11: Possessive pronouns are already possessive and need no apostrophe'.***"*

L78 **Step 12** — *"On the next available baseline, starting comfortably close to the left margin line, write the following sentences on consecutive baselines:*

'*Ours was fast.*'
'*Theirs was slow.*'

"What do we learn with this rule?"

STUDENTS: "Possessive pronouns are already possessive and therefore do not need an apostrophe to show ownership."

Forming Other Possessives for Time and Amount Words

.78 **Step 13 —** *"Skipping one baseline under the last example, starting comfortably close to the left margin line, write the following:* **'Rule 12: We make periods of time and amounts possessive by adding an apostrophe "s" to the end of the word'.***"*

.78 **Step 14 —** *"On the next three consecutive baselines, starting each sentence comfortably close to the left margin line, write the following examples:*

> *'Today's temperature was 80 degrees.'*
> *'We used ten dollar's worth of gasoline.'*
> *'It was an hour's time.'*

"What do we learn from these examples?"

STUDENTS: "We learn that words in the possessive that refer to times or amounts, need to have an apostrophe and then a letter 's' added.

Let's Get Organized

.78 **Step 15 —** *"Turn to the Table of Contents. On the page 51, page 52, and page 53 lines, write the title* **'What Is an Apostrophe? (continued)'.** *Turn back to page 51. Centered on the title line on page 51, page 52, and page 53 of your* Notebook, *between the two red margin lines, write the **same title.**"*

Consistent Training Requires Perseverance

.78P We all know that successfully accomplishing a task requires great effort. Sometimes getting the job done is just plain hard work. If we persevere and are diligent, the rewards will come. *Grammar Works* is a training program. The lessons and the notebook are push-ups and sit-ups. They are sweat and labor and toil. They may require the discipline of a marathon runner. We are equipping our students to be excellent communicators, and that is a worthy end.

We are learning how to be accountable to the smallest of details.

What Is an Apostrophe? (continued) | 51

Rule 5: The plural forms of a letter, a number, a sign, or words mentioned as words all need an apostrophe "s".
three A's four 10's six #'s 100 and's

Rule 6: Possessive proper nouns already ending in "s" may either add an apostrophe alone or an apostrophe "s"; an apostrophe "s" is preferred except with a few proper names such as Jesus and Moses.
Tess's class was very late in the evening.
Jesus' disciples listened to his teaching.

Rule 7: When speaking of two or more people, each of whom owns something separately, add the apostrophe or apostrophe "s" to the end of each name.
Jared's and Joel's bicycle tires need air.

Sample Page 51
Lesson 34

---

52 | What Is an Apostrophe? (continued)

Rule 8: When speaking of two or more people who own something together, add the apostrophe or apostrophe "s" to the end of only the last name mentioned.
Jared and Joel's go-kart is in need of repair.

Rule 9: When making compound words possessive, add the apostrophe or apostrophe "s" to the end of only the last word of the compound word.
My sister-in-law's recipe for apple pie is my favorite.

Rule 10: We make indefinite pronouns possessive by adding an apostrophe and an "s" to the end of the word.
Somebody's mitten was left in the car.
Anyone's hat will work for the costume.

Sample Page 52
Lesson 34

What Is an Apostrophe? (continued) | 53

Rule 11: Possessive pronouns are already possessive and need no apostrophe.
Ours was fast.
Theirs was slow.

Rule 12: We make periods of time and amounts possessive by adding an apostrophe "s" to the end of the word.
Today's temperature was 80 degrees.
We used ten dollar's worth of gasoline.
It was an hour's time.

Sample Page 53
Lesson 34

Expectancies Learned or Reinforced in Lesson 34: Dialogue and Review

1. How do singular words show ownership? **L34** *(Singular words show ownership by adding an apostrophe and an "s" to the end of the word. "Man's hat", "dog's collar", "bus's window".)*

2. How do plural nouns that do not end in "s" show ownership? **L34** *(If the plural form of a word does not end in "s", the word shows ownership by adding an apostrophe and an "s" to the end of the word. "Men's athletics". "Mice's cheese".)*

3. How do the plural nouns that already end in "s" show ownership? **L34** *(If the plural form of a word already ends in "s", the word shows ownership by adding an apostrophe after the final "s". "Secretaries' desks", "Dogs' kennels", "buses' windows".)*

4. What do we call words that are created from two different words and are missing letters? **L34** *(We call these words "contractions". "Can't", "won't", "didn't", "haven't", "I'm", "we're".)*

5. What punctuation mark do we use to show missing letters or numbers when we combine two words into one? **L34** *(We use an apostrophe above where the letters or numbers are missing. "She'll" for "she will", "he's" for "he is" or "he was", "you've" for "you have", "'98" for "1998".)*

6. How do we punctuate the plural forms of letters, numbers, signs, or words mentioned as words? **L56** *(We punctuate the plural forms of letters, numbers, signs, or words mentioned as words with an apostrophe and then a letter "s". For example, "e's", "14's", "$'s", "the's".)*

7. How are proper nouns that already end in "s" made possessive? **L78** *(When proper nouns already end in "s", they may either add an apostrophe alone or an apostrophe and an "s" to the end of a name. The apostrophe "s" is the preferred form. The names "Jesus" and "Moses" need only the apostrophe. "Bess's apple pie".)*

8. When two or more people own something separately in the same sentence, how do we make these proper nouns possessive? **L78** *(When two or more people own something separately in a sentence, we add the apostrophe or apostrophe "s" to the end of each name. "John's and Sally's research papers".)*

9. When speaking of two or more people who own something together in the same sentence, how do we make these proper nouns show joint ownership of the same thing? **L78** *(When speaking of two or more people who own something together, we add the apostrophe or apostrophe "s" to the end of only the last name mentioned. "John and Sally's research paper", "Smith and Barney's Law Office".)*

10. How do we make compound words possessive in a sentence? **L78** *(When writing a possessive compound word, we add the apostrophe or the apostrophe "s" to the end of only the last word of the compound word. "Editor-in-chief's chair".)*

11. How do we make indefinite pronouns possessive? **L78** *(We make indefinite pronouns possessive by adding an apostrophe and an "s" to the end of the word. "Anybody's game".)*

12. How do we punctuate possessive pronouns? **L78** *(Possessive pronouns are already possessive and need no apostrophe. "Hers", "his", "theirs", "my", "mine", "ours", "your", "yours", "its".)*

13. How do we make words of time and amount possessive? **L78** *(Words of time and amount are made possessive by adding an apostrophe and an "s" to the end of the word. "Yesterday's weather", "dollar's worth", "hour's time".)*

Where Do I Go from Here?

- **L34**, **L56**, and **L78** go to **"Lesson 35"** on page 352.

What Materials Will I Need?

- **L34** will need penmanship paper, pencils, and red pencils.

- **L56** and **L78** will need *Grammar Notebooks,* pencils, and red pencils.

What Is an Apostrophe?

*Teacher Directions:
Students need to correct
the words that are using
apostrophes incorrectly
in the following
sentences. They should
rewrite these words in
the blank provided.
Worksheet 1 is for* **L34**
and above.

*Student Directions: Read
each sentence. Every
sentence has an error in
the use of the apostrophe
with singular and plural
nouns that show owner-
ship. Find the errors and
write the needed
correction at the end of
each sentence in the
blank provided.*

1. The childs' stuffed bear was lost.

    child's

2. The secretarie's notebooks were lost.

    secretaries'

3. The mens' seminar was at noon.

    men's

4. The mouses' house was warm.

    mouse's

5. The mices' food was dry.

    mice's

6. The calve's hay satisfied their hunger.

    calves'

7. Bobs' dog had a Frisbee.

    Bob's

8. Bob went to get his dogs's Frisbees.

    dogs'

9. The buse's mechanics were on strike.

    buses'

10. The foxes' tail was caught on the fence.

    fox's

1. The childs' stuffed bear was lost.

   _____

2. The secretarie's notebooks were lost.

   _____

3. The mens' seminar was at noon.

   _____

4. The mouses' house was warm.

   _____

5. The mices' food was dry.

   _____

6. The calve's hay satisfied their hunger.

   _____

7. Bobs' dog had a Frisbee.

   _____

8. Bob went to get his dogs's Frisbees.

   _____

9. The buse's mechanics were on strike.

   _____

10. The foxes' tail was caught on the fence.

    _____

Student Worksheet 1:

What Is an Apostrophe?

Student Directions:
Read each sentence.
Every sentence has an
error in the use of the
apostrophe with singu-
lar and plural nouns
that show ownership.
Find the errors and
write the needed
correction at the end of
each sentence in the
blank provided.

What Is an Apostrophe?

Teacher Directions: Students need to correct the words that are using apostrophes incorrectly in the following sentences. They should rewrite these words in the blank provided. Worksheet 2 is for **L78**.

Student Directions: Read each sentence. Every sentence has an error in the use of the apostrophe with singular and plural nouns that show ownership. Find the errors and write the needed correction at the end of each sentence in the blank provided.

1. Tesss' music gave her inspiration.
   Tess's

2. Jesus' and Moses' are important biblical people.
   Jesus   Moses

3. A dollars' value decreases on some days.
   dollar's

4. Rons' story was as true as Charlies' story.
   Ron's   Charlie's

5. Our's was the best effort.
   Ours

6. Johns' and Sally's car was red.
   John   Sally's

7. Marys' and her teacher's boots were in the hall.
   Mary's   teacher's

8. It was my father's-in-law fishing rod.
   father-in-law's

9. Anyones' advice will be welcome.
   Anyone's

10. An hours worth of time is needed to accomplish the task.
    hour's

1. Tesss' music gave her inspiration.

   _____

2. Jesus' and Moses' are important biblical people.

   _____

3. A dollars' value decreases on some days.

   _____

4. Rons' story was as true as Charlies' story.

   _____

5. Our's was the best effort.

   _____

6. Johns' and Sally's car was red.

   _____

7. Marys' and her teacher's boots were in the hall.

   _____

8. It was my father's-in-law fishing rod.

   _____

9. Anyones' advice will be welcome.

   _____

10. An hours worth of time is needed to accomplish the task.

    _____

What Is an Apostrophe?

Student Directions: Read each sentence. Every sentence has an error in the use of the apostrophe with singular and plural nouns that show ownership. Find the errors and write the needed correction at the end of each sentence in the blank provided.

54 | When Do I Use a Period?

Rule 1: A declarative sentence ends with a period.
The rain was coming down in buckets.

Rule 2: An imperative sentence may end with a period or an exclamation point.
Go to the teacher for more instructions.

Rule 3: Most abbreviations are followed by a period.

Gen. for General
Jan. for January
lbs. for pounds
oz. for ounce
A.D. for Anno Domini
P.M. for post meridiem
U.S. Grant for Ulysses Simpson Grant
MN for Minnesota

Sample Page 54
Lesson 35

When Do I Use a Period? (continued) | 55

Rule 4: A period needs to go inside the end quotation mark if the exact words of the speaker are declarative.
John said, "I am going to the store."

Rule 5: Abbreviations for the names of federal agencies or commonly recognized organizations are created by using the first letter of each key word. Each letter is capitalized and no periods are necessary.
FBI for Federal Bureau of Investigation (no periods—federal agency)
PTA for Parent–Teacher Association (no periods—common organization)
FDA for Food and Drug Administration (no periods—federal agency)
NATO for North Atlantic Treaty Organization (no periods—common organization)

Sample Page 55
Lesson 35

Lesson 35

When Do I Use a Period?

Punctuation Marks in a Sentence Are Like Road Signs on a Highway

L34 "If we can't read and understand road signs as we drive down the highway, we could make some very dangerous mistakes. A stop sign is red, has eight sides, and spells the word 'STOP'. It means something. A yield sign is yellow or red and white, has three sides, and spells the word 'YIELD'. It means something too. There are signs that tell us the kind of a curve that is coming down the road. There are signs that tell us we should slow down to 20 mph. All these signs, when comprehended, give us information that is important for safety on the highway.

"Punctuation marks in sentences are the same way. We have stop signs. We have yield signs. We have signs that tell us when someone is speaking and when someone is excited. They all mean something. We must use these signs so that our reader doesn't miss a curve and get lost out in the woods someplace. Reading the road signs of grammar is just as important as reading the road signs on the highway. In the next lessons, we are going to study the many road signs along our Grammar Highway."

L34P **L34** students need to be given loose-leaf penmanship paper to do the steps in this lesson. **L56** and above need to turn to page 54 in their *Grammar Notebook*. Use the Sample Page in the margin as a guide.

L34 **Step 1 —** "We already know that we end a declarative sentence and an imperative sentence with a period. A period is like a stop sign. Sometimes we may need to end an imperative sentence with an exclamation point because the imperative sentence has a lot of emotion. Most of the time, however, these sentences end with a period.

"We need to write down our first rule about the use of a period. *Skipping one baseline under our title line and starting comfortably close to the left margin line, please write the following:* **'Rule 1: A declarative sentence ends with a period'.** This will take more than one line."

L34 **Step 2 —** *"On the next available baseline, directly below Rule 1, starting comfortably close to the left margin line, write this sentence:* **'The rain was coming down in buckets'.** It requires a period because it is a declarative sentence."

L56P Have **L56** and **L78** students analyze, discuss, and mark this sentence in the following manner:

$$\overset{\text{S + HV +}}{\text{The rain was}} \overset{\text{AV}}{\text{coming}} \overset{\text{adv.}}{(\text{down})} \overset{\text{OP}}{[\text{in buckets}]}.$$

L34 **Step 3** — "Let's write the next rule concerning periods. *Skipping one baseline below your example for Rule 1, write this next rule: 'Rule 2: An imperative sentence may end with a period or an exclamation point'*. This may take more than one line."

L34 **Step 4** — *"On the next available baseline, directly below Rule 2, starting comfortably close to the left margin line, write this sentence: 'Go to the teacher for more instructions'*. It requires a period because it is an imperative sentence."

L56P Have **L56** and **L78** students analyze, discuss, and mark this sentence in the following manner:

$$\overset{\text{AV}}{\text{Go}} \overset{\text{OP}}{[\text{to the teacher}]} \overset{\text{adj.}}{[\text{for }(\text{more})} \overset{\text{OP}}{\text{instructions}]}.$$

TEACHER: "Do you remember what the subject is of every imperative sentence?"

STUDENTS: "It is the personal pronoun 'you'. In a previous lesson, we called it 'you understood'."

L34 **Step 5** — "Let's go to our next rule. *Skipping one baseline below the sample sentence for Rule 2, write the following: 'Rule 3: Most abbreviations are followed by a period'. Skipping one baseline below Rule 3, starting each abbreviation comfortably close to the left margin line, write the following abbreviations and their meanings on consecutive baselines: 'Gen. for General', 'Jan. for January', 'lbs. for pounds', 'oz. for ounce', 'A.D. for Anno Domini', 'P.M. for post meridiem', 'U.S. Grant for Ulysses Simpson Grant', 'MN for Minnesota'.* Two-letter abbreviations with no periods are now acceptable for states when written with zip codes and for countries."

L34 "'**Anno Domini**' is a Latin term that means in the year of the Lord used to indicate a date since the birth of Jesus. We say '**1998 A.D.**' '**Post meridiem**' is a Latin term that means after midday. That is why all times between noon and midnight have a '**P.M.**' following them. The abbreviation '**lb.**' for pound comes from the Latin word '**libra**' that means pound. If we have more than one pound, we add an 's' making the abbreviation '**lbs.**'"

Reviewing the Term "Acronym"

L34 **Step 6** — "We need to review the word 'acronym' at this point. By definition we have learned that an acronym is 'a word formed from the initial letters or groups of letters of words in a set phrase . . .' (Random House Dictionary © 1971) Our language is

54	When Do I Use a Period?

Rule 1: A declarative sentence ends with a period.
The rain was coming down in buckets.

Rule 2: An imperative sentence may end with a period or an exclamation point.
Go to the teacher for more instructions.

Rule 3: Most abbreviations are followed by a period.

Gen. for General
Jan. for January
lbs. for pounds
oz. for ounce
A.D. for Anno Domini
P.M. for post meridiem
U.S. Grant for Ulysses Simpson Grant
MN for Minnesota

Sample Page 54
Lesson 35

filled with these words. We have just written some examples of these. Do you know what AMA stands for? We take the words American Medical Association and grab the first letter of each word. Because it is a common organization, we do not need periods following each letter. This is how acronyms are made."

L56 "Many acronyms are used when working with computers, programming languages, and the Internet. In computer talk RAM means Random Access Memory. CPU means Central Processing Unit. PCI means Peripheral Component Interconnect. ISP means Internet Service Provider. ASCII means American Standard Code for Information Interchange. PCMCIA means Personal Computer Memory Card Interface Association. You get the picture. We will encounter some other acronyms a bit later."

Let's Get Organized

L56 **Step 7 —** *"Turn to the Table of Contents. On the page 54 line, write the title* **'When Do I Use a Period?'** *Turn back to page 54."*

L34 *"Centered on the title line, between the two red margin lines, write the title* **'When Do I Use a Period?'"**

Dictating More Rules for the Use of the Period

L34 **L34** students will need to turn their page over to continue this lesson. **L56** and above need to turn their attention to page 55 in the *Grammar Notebook.*

L34 **Step 1 —** *"Skipping one baseline below the title line, please write the following:* **'Rule 4: A period needs to go inside the end quotation mark if the exact words of the speaker are declarative'.** *Starting on the next available baseline directly below Rule 5, comfortably close to the left margin line, write the following the sentence:* **'John said, "I am going to the store."'**

"Look at where the period is used in this declarative sentence spoken by John. We have learned that a period is used at the end of a declarative sentence inside the end quotation marks."

L56 **Step 2 —** *"Skipping one baseline under our direct quote, please write the following:* **'Rule 5: Abbreviations for the names of federal agencies or commonly recognized organizations are created by using the first letter of each key word. Each letter is capitalized and no periods are necessary'."**

Step 3 — *"Starting on the next available baseline directly below Rule 5, comfortably close to the left margin line, write the following acronym for a federal agency:* **'FBI for Federal Bureau of Investigation'.** *On the next baseline below FBI, write* **'(no periods—federal agency)'."**

---

54 | When Do I Use a Period?

Rule 1: A declarative sentence ends with a period.
The rain was coming down in buckets.

Rule 2: An imperative sentence may end with a period or an exclamation point.
Go to the teacher for more instructions.

Rule 3: Most abbreviations are followed by a period.

Gen. for General
Jan. for January
lbs. for pounds
oz. for ounce
A.D. for Anno Domini
P.M. for post meridiem
U.S. Grant for Ulysses Simpson Grant
MN for Minnesota

Sample Page 54
Lesson 35

When Do I Use a Period? (continued) | 55

Rule 4: A period needs to go inside the end quotation mark if the exact words of the speaker are declarative.
John said, "I am going to the store."

Rule 5: Abbreviations for the names of federal agencies or commonly recognized organizations are created by using the first letter of each key word. Each letter is capitalized and no periods are necessary.
FBI for Federal Bureau of Investigation
(no periods—federal agency)
PTA for Parent–Teacher Association
(no periods—common organization)
FDA for Food and Drug Administration
(no periods—federal agency)
NATO for North Atlantic Treaty Organization
(no periods—common organization)

Sample Page 55
Lesson 35

.56 "We will enclose '(no periods—federal agency)' in what we call 'parentheses'. They look like this."

.56P Demonstrate what parentheses look like.

.56 "We use these marks sometimes when an expression has no necessary grammatical connection with the sentence or phrase with which it is working, but the information may still be important. For example, 'My car was prepared for the trip (as it always is), and I told them to be ready to go'."

"On the next baseline, write the following acronym for a common organization: 'PTA for Parent–Teacher Association'. On the next baseline below PTA, write '(no periods—common organization)'.

"On the next baseline, write the following acronym for a federal agency: 'FDA for Food and Drug Administration'. On the next baseline below FDA, write '(no periods—federal agency)'.

"On the next baseline, write the following acronym for a common organization: 'NATO for North Atlantic Treaty Organization'. On the next baseline below NATO, write '(no periods—common organization)'."

Reviewing End Punctuation Marks inside Quotation Marks

.78 Step 4 — "If the exact words of the speaker are declarative in nature, what will the end punctuation mark be inside the end quotation mark?"

STUDENTS: "It will usually be a period. If it is a statement with lots of emotion, we may use an exclamation point."

TEACHER: "If the exact words of the speaker are interrogative in nature, what punctuation mark will go inside the end quotation mark?"

STUDENTS: "We will need to use a question mark."

TEACHER: "If the exact words of the speaker are exclamatory, what punctuation mark would go inside the end quotation mark?"

STUDENTS: "We will need to use an exclamation point."

TEACHER: "If the exact words of the speaker are imperative in nature, what punctuation mark will go inside the end quotation mark?"

STUDENTS: "We will most often use a period, but if the statement has emotion, we can use an exclamation point."

TEACHER: "How do we determine the right punctuation mark at the end of a sentence before end quotation marks?"

STUDENTS: "We must determine the purpose of the sentence."

Let's Get Organized

L56   **Step 5 —** *"Turn to the Table of Contents. On the page 55 line, write the title 'When Do I Use a Period? (continued)'. Turn back to page 55."*

L34   *"Centered on the title line, between the two red margin lines, write the title 'When Do I Use a Period? (continued)'."*

Expectancies Learned or Reinforced in Lesson 35: Dialogue and Review

1. How do we end a declarative sentence? **L34** *(We end a declarative sentence with a period.)*

2. How do we end an imperative sentence? **L34** *(We end an imperative sentence with a period or an exclamation point.)*

3. What do we place after an abbreviation? **L34** *(We place a period after an abbreviation.)*

4. What do we place after the letters of an abbreviation of a common organization or a federal agency? **L56** *(No periods are necessary with common organizations or federal agencies.)*

5. If a direct quote is a declarative sentence, what punctuation mark do we use before the end quotation mark? **L34** *(A period is used inside an end quotation mark if the exact words of the speaker are a declarative sentence.)*

6. If a direct quote is an interrogative sentence, what punctuation mark do we use before the end quotation mark? **L34** *(A question mark is used inside an end quotation mark if the exact words of the speaker are an interrogative sentence.)*

7. If a direct quote is an exclamatory sentence, what punctuation mark do we use before the end quotation mark? **L34** *(An exclamation point is used inside an end quotation mark if the exact words of the speaker are an exclamatory sentence.)*

8. If a direct quote is an imperative sentence, what punctuation mark do we use before the end quotation mark? **L34** *(A period or an exclamation point is used inside an end quotation mark if the exact words of the speaker are an imperative sentence.)*

9. What is an acronym? **L34** *(An acronym is a word created by using the first letters from words that make up a set phrase. Y.M.C.A. stands for Young Men's Christian Association.)*

Where Do I Go from Here?

- **L34**, **L56**, and **L78** go to **"Lesson 36"** on page 357.

What Materials Will I Need?

- **L34** will need penmanship paper and pencils.

- **L56** and **L78** will need *Grammar Notebooks* and pencils.

Lesson 36
How Do I Use a Comma?

Starting with the Basics

12P There are many and varied uses of the comma. Not all the rules that govern the use of commas will be covered in this lesson. Many additional rules beyond this lesson are listed at the end of this lesson. Some of these rules will need to be covered in later lessons because some grammatical structures that require the use of a comma will have not yet been introduced.

When students understand such things as essential and non-essential clauses, for example, they will also understand further comma usage. For now we will stick to the basics.

L12 will watch the teacher demonstrate **Steps 1–4. L34** students will need a piece of loose-leaf penmanship paper. **L56** and above should turn to page 54 in their *Grammar Notebook*.

Singing the "Comma Happy Blues"

12P Prepare to demonstrate the exaggerated but thrilling **"Comma Happy Blues"**. Write a sentence for your students and throw commas in all over the place and then go to **Step 1.** We will learn that there are rules that govern the proper use of commas and that is what this lesson is all about.

56 **Step 1 —** "To use a comma or not to use a comma, that is the question. So many times students develop a condition called 'Comma Happy Blues'. They get so excited about seeing commas they just, put, them, in, any, place, they, want, because, it makes, them, so, happy. Of course there is a proper place and time for everything including when we use commas. Let's find out about how to use commas."

12 **Step 2 —** "A comma is a period with a tail. It is a way of telling us to take a small pause in our reading. It is like taking the time to take an extra breath if we are working hard. Commas help us organize our sentences so that we do not get confused. There are special times and special situations that require the use of a comma. We never want to put in too many. We don't want to put in too few. We want every sentence to have just the right number of commas and the exact meaning we intended."

12P First year students will watch and listen and use the sound of their own voice in directed discovery as the teacher demonstrates. Second year students, if they are ready, will try a

Rule 1: Commas separate items in a series. Jim needs pencils, paper, and glue for school.

Rule 2: Calendar dates and addresses of more than one part need commas. January 14, 1951, is my birthday. She lives at 305 Hazelwood Avenue, Henning, MN 56551.

Rule 3: A series of two or more prepositional phrases beginning a sentence requires a comma. In the middle of summer, we plan picnics.

Rule 4: Nouns of address need commas. John, please stop in after work.

Rule 5: Use a comma before a coordinating conjunction in a compound sentence. I go to town, and he goes to the farm.

Sample Page 56
Lesson 36

Rule 1: Commas separate items in a series.
Jim needs pencils, paper, and glue for school.

Rule 2: Calendar dates and addresses of more than one part need commas.
January 14, 1951, is my birthday.
She lives at 305 Hazelwood Avenue, Henning, MN 56551.

Rule 3: A series of two or more prepositional phrases beginning a sentence requires a comma.
In the middle of summer, we plan picnics.

Rule 4: Nouns of address need commas.
John, please stop in after work.

Rule 5: Use a comma before a coordinating conjunction in a compound sentence.
I go to town, and he goes to the farm.

Sample Page 56
Lesson 36

Examples of Commas Used in Series

The numbers 1, 2, 3, and 6 were removed from the hat.

We need nails, shingles, a sharp knife, and a tape measure to do the job.

Pencils, paper, and scissors are in the office.

Billy, Johnny, Amos, and George went camping.

A car needs to have gasoline, oil, and water to run well.

practice page on their own. **L34** students, of course, should not have a problem taking dictation and creating the following steps. **L56** and above should turn to page 56 in their *Grammar Notebook* and begin the creation of another notebook page.

Dictating the First Rule for Comma Use

L12   **Step 3** — *"Skipping one baseline below the title line, starting comfortably close to the left margin line, please write the following rule: 'Rule 1: Commas separate items in a series'."*

L12   *"On the next baseline just below Rule 1, starting comfortably close to the left margin line, write the following sentence: 'Jim needs pencils, paper, and glue for school'.* Do you see a list in this sentence? The list is a series of three nouns: pencils, paper, and glue. What does our rule say we need to do?"

> **STUDENTS:** "We need to put commas between the items in the list."

> **TEACHER:** "Where do we put the commas?"

> **STUDENTS:** "They go after the words 'pencils' and 'paper'."

> **TEACHER:** "You are right. They go between 'pencils' and 'paper' and between 'paper' and the words 'and glue'."

Practicing the Use of Items in a Series

L12   **Step 4** — "Let's look at five more examples of items in a series that will help us understand how to use commas."

L12P   Discuss the examples listed in this margin with your students. Write them on the board without the commas. Have them find the items that are in a series, and place commas where they are supposed to go.

Discovering Other Kinds of Items in a Series

L56P   On the pages that follow are examples of sentences illustrating the comma rules from this lesson. Write them on the board without commas. **L56** should also be able to analyze any of the sentences they might encounter in these lessons.

L56   **Step 5** — "Some items in a series use different grammatical structures to make lists. No matter what grammatical structure is being used, we need to place commas between items in a list if there are three or more items listed."

"Sometimes the list might be a series of action verbs with their direct objects as in this example:

'Mary ate the watermelon, washed the dishes, and cleaned the stove.'

"Where do we place commas here?"

STUDENTS: "We place commas after the direct objects 'watermelon' and 'dishes'."

TEACHER: "Good. Sometimes the items in a series might be sentences, as in the following sentence:

'Brian played golf at Bunker Hill, Kevin played golf at Hazeltine, and Doug played golf at the New Ulm Country Club.'

"Where do we place commas here?"

STUDENTS: "We place commas after 'Bunker Hill' and 'Hazeltine'."

TEACHER: "Right again. We can use a series of prepositional phrases too. Look at the following example:

'Abraham Lincoln once said that we are a government "of the people, by the people, and for the people".'

"One more time. Where do the commas go?"

STUDENTS: "They follow the first two 'people's'."

TEACHER: "Well done. In all of these, we see a list of three or more items. Items in a series might be nouns, verbs, phrases, numbers, names, or sentences. If they are items in a series, we separate them with commas. That is what Rule 1 for comma use is all about."

34 Step 6 — *"Skipping one baseline below the sentence 'Jim needs pencils, paper, and glue for school', starting comfortably close to the left margin line, write the following:* **'Rule 2: Calendar dates and addresses of more than one part need commas'.** Look at these examples."

34P Write the following examples on the board and explain the use of commas in these sentences.

"January 14, 1951, is my birthday."

34 Step 7 — "The name of the month and the exact date in that month are considered as the first part of a complete date. In this case January 14 is the first part. If we add the exact year, that is considered the second part of a complete date. In our example, 1951 is the second part. Rule 2 tells us that calendar dates of more than one part need commas. We need to place a comma after the number 14 and after 1951. They need to be separated from the rest of the sentence by commas.

---

56   How Do I Use a Comma?

Rule 1: Commas separate items in a series.
Jim needs pencils, paper, and glue for school.

Rule 2: Calendar dates and addresses
of more than one part need commas.
January 14, 1951, is my birthday.
She lives at 305 Hazelwood Avenue,
Henning, MN 56551.

Rule 3: A series of two or more prepositional phrases beginning a sentence
requires a comma.
In the middle of summer, we plan picnics.

Rule 4: Nouns of address need commas.
John, please stop in after work.

Rule 5: Use a comma before a coordinating conjunction in a compound sentence.
I go to town, and he goes to the farm.

Sample Page 56
Lesson 36

*"Starting on the baseline directly below Rule 2, comfortably close to the left margin line, write **a sentence** that tells when you were born. Give the **exact month, day, and year** and don't forget to place your **commas** correctly.* If we analyze this sentence, we will count all the parts of the date together as the subject."

L34 **Step 8** — "Here is another example:

'Wadena, Minnesota, is a great town'.

"In an address, the name of the town or the city is considered as one part. In this example, the city of Wadena is the first part of an address. If we add the name of the state where this town is located, we are using the second part of an address. In this example, the state of Minnesota is the second part of the address.

"Rule 2 tells us that addresses of more than one part need commas. We need to place a comma after Wadena. We need to place a comma after Minnesota. They are both separated from each other and the rest of the sentence with commas. Look at this example:

'She lives at 305 Hazelwood Avenue,
Henning, MN 56551.'

"This time the parts of the address are a little different, but the rule is the same. The exact street address is considered as one part. We need to put a comma after 305 Hazelwood Avenue. The city of Henning is another part and needs a comma after it. Minnesota together with the zip code is the third part. They all need to be separated from each other and the rest of the sentence with commas.

*"On the baseline directly below the sentence that tells the day you were born, comfortably close to the left margin line, write **a sentence** that tells where you live including your **street address, your city, your state, and your zip code.** If we analyze this sentence, the address and all of its parts together would be the OP of the preposition 'at'."*

L34 **Step 9** — "Look at this example. Why don't we place a comma after any of these parts of calendar dates or addresses?

'January 14 in Henning at 305 Hazelwood Avenue is the date of the birthday party in Minnesota.'"

STUDENTS: "The rule says that we need to use commas in calendar dates of more than one part and addresses of more than one part. All dates or addresses in this sentence are isolated parts. Isolated parts do not require being set off by commas."

TEACHER: "Thank you for listening."

L56 **Step 10 —** "We need to introduce another rule for the use of a comma. *Skipping one baseline below our example for Rule 2, starting comfortably close to the left margin line, write the following:* **'Rule 3: A series of two or more prepositional phrases beginning a sentence requires a comma'**. What do you see in the following examples:

> 'In the beginning of the program, the parents were thanked for their help.'

> 'On a Friday in the middle of summer, we'll go fishing.'

> 'Under the bed in the room at the top of the stairs, the dog slept soundly.'"

STUDENTS: "Every sentence in this list begins with more than one prepositional phrase. Sometimes there are three and even four prepositional phrases starting the sentence. After these introductory phrases, there is a comma."

"That is what our rule says. *Starting on the baseline directly below Rule 3, comfortably close to the left margin line, write the following sentence as an example of a series of two or more prepositional phrases beginning a sentence:* **'In the middle of summer, we plan picnics'**. *Don't forget to put in the* **comma**. *Don't forget to* **analyze** *your sentence."*

L56 **Step 11 —** *"Skipping one baseline below the last sentence, starting comfortably close to the left margin line, write the following:* **'Rule 4: Nouns of address need commas. Any time we want to directly talk to a person in our writing, we call the mentioning of that person's name a "noun of address"'**. Look at these examples:

> 'John, please stop in after work.'

> 'Could you find the time to see me, Mr. Hanson?'

> 'Well, partner, I think that horse will do just fine.'

> 'Tarnation, Hickory, you did it again!'

TEACHER: "Who are the people being addressed or talked to in these examples?"

STUDENTS: "In the first sentence John is being addressed. In the second it is Mr. Hanson. In the third it is someone given the name 'partner'. In the last example someone is talking to Hickory."

TEACHER: "Please notice that a noun of address is not always a personal name, as in the use of the word 'partner'. Also notice that the name of the person is not always at the beginning of a sentence. It can be at the end or in the middle. We separate the person being

---

56   How Do I Use a Comma?

Rule 1: Commas separate items in a series.
Jim needs pencils, paper, and glue for school.

Rule 2: Calendar dates and addresses of more than one part need commas.
January 14, 1951, is my birthday.
She lives at 305 Hazelwood Avenue, Henning, MN 56551.

Rule 3: A series of two or more prepositional phrases beginning a sentence requires a comma.
In the middle of summer, we plan picnics.

Rule 4: Nouns of address need commas.
John, please stop in after work.

Rule 5: Use a comma before a coordinating conjunction in a compound sentence.
I go to town, and he goes to the farm.

Sample Page 56
Lesson 36

Sample Page 56
Lesson 36

addressed from the rest of the sentence with the use of commas. The name of a person being addressed in the middle of a sentence needs commas before and after the name.

"Starting on the baseline directly below Rule 4, comfortably close to the margin, write the following: **'John, please stop in after work'.** *Remember where the* **comma** *needs to go. In analysis, 'John' is an* **'NA'***, which stands for a 'Noun of Address'."*

L56 **Step 12 —** "Another comma rule that would be good for us to know involves the joining of two sentences together to form what is called a compound sentence. *Skipping one baseline below our last example sentence, starting comfortably close to the left margin line, write the following:* **'Rule 5: Use a comma before a coordinating conjunction in a compound sentence'.** Do you remember the coordinating conjunctions?"

STUDENTS: "Yes. I believe they are 'and', 'but', 'or', 'for', 'nor', 'yet', and 'so'."

L56 "Right. Whenever we join two sentences together with a conjunction, we add a comma before the conjunction. We call two sentences joined together a compound sentence. Look at these examples:

'I am going to the library, and he is going to the store.'

'The baseball season was just beginning, but the fans were not excited.'

'The President visited Moscow, yet he was unable to persuade their leaders to reconsider their plans.'

TEACHER: "What do you see?"

STUDENTS: "If I analyze these sentences, I see there are two separate sentences in each example."

TEACHER: "How are those sentences joined together?"

STUDENTS: "They are joined together by using a comma first and then a coordinating conjunction."

L56 *"On the baseline directly below Rule 5, write the following example of a compound sentence:* **'I go to town, and he goes to the farm'.** What goes before the conjunction?"

STUDENTS: "We need to remember to place a comma before the conjunction if two sentences are being joined."

Take Time for a Writer's Workshop

L56P On another day, take time to review these comma rules or any of the lessons that might need reviewing. Ask your students to write examples of each rule. Have your students write a sentence that has a noun of address. Have them write a sentence that has three prepositional phrases at the beginning of the sentence. Writer's Workshop times are important. Direct application of what is being taught embeds these rules so students can use them at an automatic level in their writing.

Let's Get Organized

56   **Step 13 —** *"Turn to the Table of Contents. On the page 56 line, write the title* **'How Do I Use A Comma?'** *Turn back to page 56. Centered on the title line, between the two red margin lines, write the* **same title.***"*

Expectancies Learned or Reinforced in Lesson 36: Dialogue and Review

1. How do we punctuate a list of more than two items in a series whether that series is a list of nouns or verbs or whatever it might be? **L12** *(We separate the items from each other using commas. "John, Sally, Pete, and Jane went to the museum.")*

2. How do we punctuate calendar dates and mailing addresses of more than one part? **L34** *(Calendar dates or mailing addresses of more than one part are separated by commas. "I was born in Sleepy Eye, MN, on January 14, 1951.")*

3. How do we punctuate two or more prepositional phrases beginning a sentence? **L56** *(We need to place a comma following after the last prepositional phrase. "On the first day of the week, we work in the garden.")*

4. How do we punctuate a noun of address? **L56** *(Nouns of address need to be set apart by commas. "Mr. Smith, please stop by for a visit.")*

5. What is one way to join two sentences together using a comma? **L56** *(Two sentences may be joined together by using a coordinating conjunction with a comma preceding that conjunction. "He always trains for the marathon in the summer, but he takes it easy in the winter.")*

6. How many rules are there that govern the use of the comma? **L56** *(There are many rules. We can discover additional rules for comma use as we build our grammatical understanding.)*

Where Do I Go from Here?

- **L12** goes to **L12** "Scope and Sequence" Step 9.

- **L34, L56,** and **L78** go to "Lesson 37" on page 365.

What Materials Will I Need?

- **L34** will need penmanship paper and pencils.

- **L56** and **L78** will need *Grammar Notebooks* and pencils.

Discovering Additional Comma Rules

Use a Comma after the Following:

- Introductory words like yes, no, and well.
    "Well, how do you like it?"

- Introductory participial phrases and adverbial clauses.
    "When he finally came, I was gone."

- An interjection that expresses mild emotion.
    "My, that was a loud crash."

- The salutation and closing in a friendly letter.
    "Dear Mr. Johnson," "Sincerely yours,"

- A person's name that is followed by Sr., Jr., Ph.D., or M.D.
    "Bob's son is Bob, Jr."

- A prepositional phrase of four or more words starting a sentence.
    "In the very beginning, we worked hard."

Use a Comma to Separate the Following:

- A direct quote from the remainder of the sentence.
    "'I did it,' he stated proudly."

- Adjectives of equal value influencing the same noun.
    "He swam the cold, dark river."

- Words and phrases that have been transposed.
    "Call Mom for a ride if necessary." (Normal)
    "If necessary, call Mom for a ride." (Transposed)

Use Two Commas to Set Apart the Following:

- Appositives.
    "John Smith, the mayor, was reelected."

- Parenthetical expressions.
    "Your coat, I believe, is over there."

- Non-essential clauses.
    "The man who was reading looked sad." (Essential)
    "Jim, who was reading, looked sad." (Non-essential)

Additional Situations Where Commas Are Needed

- In numbers over 999.
    "1,000" "250,000,000"

- To indicate where words are omitted from parallel sentences.
    "Sally baked bread; Mary, some cookies."

Lesson 37

What Are Quotation Marks?

Using Paper Clips around a Direct Quote

L34 "Sometimes when we have loose papers and we don't want them to fly away, we take a paper clip and slip that paper clip over the pages. I suppose we could use a clothespin too. Regardless of what we might use, the pages are squeezed together.

"Often when we write, we need to record the exact words of a story character who is speaking. We cannot let these words fly away from us. We have to keep those words in a group so the reader knows that these are the exact words spoken by that character. In fact, every time someone speaks, we need to slip a good strong paper clip around those words on the front side and on the backside. Look at these sentences."

L34P Place the following sentences on the board without punctuation markings:

"'The sun is shining,' Furtive Fox said."

"'Go to the store for me,' Mom said."

"'How shall I get to the market?' Pensive Pig said."

"'What a great play at first base!' the coach said."

Discovering the Nature of a Direct Quote

L34P **L34** will need a piece of loose-leaf penmanship paper. **L56** and above need to turn their attention to page 57 in their *Grammar Notebook*.

L34 **Step 1** — "We have to put some paper clips in these sentences. We must find the exact words being spoken. In the first sentence, can you tell which words Furtive Fox is actually saying?"

STUDENTS: "Furtive Fox is telling us that the sun is shining."

TEACHER: "We need to paper clip those words together. Unlike the apostrophe, these paper clips are not just one comma flying above and between letters. The paper clips that we use look like two flying commas. They hover together like two hummingbirds at the beginning and at the end of the exact words that are spoken.

"We have a special name for these paper clips. They are called **'quotation marks'**. And they are very

---

What Are Quotation Marks? | 57

Rule 1: Quotation marks enclose the exact words of the speaker.

Rule 2: The part of the sentence that tells who is speaking is called the tag.

Rule 3: If a quote is a declarative sentence, and it comes before the tag, we place a comma before the last quotation mark.
"The sun is shining," Furtive Fox said.

Rule 4: The first word of a quote is capitalized.

Rule 5: If the quote is a declarative sentence, and it comes after the tag, we place a comma after the tag, and we place the end punctuation mark before the last quotation mark.
Furtive Fox said, "The sun is shining."

Sample Page 57
Lesson 37

---

58 | **What Are Quotation Marks? (continued)**

Rule 6: An imperative quote is punctuated like a declarative quote.
"Go to the store for me," Mom said.

Rule 7: If a quote is a question, use a question mark inside the quote.
"How shall I get to the market?" Pensive Pig said.

Rule 8: If the quote is an exclamation, use an exclamation point inside the quote.
"What a great play at first base!" the coach said.

Rule 9: Heavy written works or titles of paintings or specific names for planes, trains, ships, or spacecraft are underlined.

Sample Page 58
Lesson 37

What Are Quotation Marks? (continued) | 59

London Times (newspaper)
The Outsiders (book)
Flubber (movie)

Rule 10: Light written works like short stories, poems, songs, essays, chapter titles, or article titles use quotation marks.

"Stocks Break Records" (news article)
"The Red Wheelbarrow" (poem)
"Sentence Making" (chapter title)

Rule 11: Dialogue requires a new paragraph with every switch of speaker.

    "Have you handed in your composition using dialogue between two characters?" Mrs. Smith asked Jesse.
    "I cannot find it, Mrs. Smith!" Jesse exclaimed.

Sample Page 59
Lesson 37

---

60 | **What Are Quotation Marks? (continued)**

Rule 12: An indirect quote removes the quotation marks, adds the word "that", and changes the pronouns and verb forms if necessary.

"I want to go to the concert," said the band director.
The band director said that he wanted to go to the concert.

Rule 13: A divided quote uses a comma after the tag if the quote is carried over and a period after the tag if the quote is two separate sentences.
"The wind is very strong," said John, "but we must continue our work."
"The wind is too strong," said Jim. "We have to turn back."

Sample Page 60
Lesson 37

What Are Quotation Marks? 57

Rule 1: Quotation marks enclose the exact words of the speaker.

Rule 2: The part of the sentence that tells who is speaking is called the tag.

Rule 3: If a quote is a declarative sentence, and it comes before the tag, we place a comma before the last quotation mark.
"The sun is shining," Furtive Fox said.

Rule 4: The first word of a quote is capitalized.

Rule 5: If the quote is a declarative sentence, and it comes after the tag, we place a comma after the tag, and we place the end punctuation mark before the last quotation mark.
Furtive Fox said, "The sun is shining."

Sample Page 57
Lesson 37

Note to the Teacher:

You will notice throughout this entire curriculum and especially this lesson that we have had to indicate to you, the teacher, where to begin dictating to your students using, of course, quotation marks. Therefore, the dictation sections are indicated with double quotation marks. Any need for quotation marks within that dictation section (quotes, words used as words, sentences used as sentences, etc.) have then required alternating levels of single and double quotation marks.

(continued in margin on page 367)

important. Where do you think our paper clips need to go in this first sentence?"

STUDENTS: "We need to place those paper clips before the word 'The' and after the word 'shining'."

TEACHER: "Watch me as I do that."

L34P Demonstrate by placing quotation marks before and after the exact words spoken. Be sure to use the Sample Pages in the margins as your guide.

"Can you see why they look like two flying commas? We are paper clipping all the words together that Furtive Fox said. *Skipping one baseline below the title line, starting comfortably close to the left margin line, write the following:* **'Rule 1: Quotation marks enclose the exact words of the speaker'."**

L34 **Step 2** — "Now look at this Furtive Fox sentence a little more closely. How do we know who is speaking these exact words?"

STUDENTS: "The sentence tells us who is speaking by using the word 'said' together with the speaker's name."

TEACHER: "Right. At Christmas time many families give gifts to those they love. How do they know whose gift is under the tree?"

STUDENTS: "There is usually a tag on the package."

"Every sentence that uses quotation marks to tell what words are being spoken also uses a tag. The tag tells us to whom the words belong just like the tag on a gift at Christmas tells us whose gift it is. *Skipping one baseline below our last rule, starting comfortably close to the left margin, write the following:* **'Rule 2: The part of the sentence that tells who is speaking is called "the tag"'."**

L34 **Step 3** — "We need to do a little more investigating. What kind of a sentence is 'The sun is shining?' Is it a declarative sentence? Is it an interrogative sentence? Is it an imperative sentence? Or is it an exclamatory sentence?"

STUDENTS: "'The sun is shining' does not ask a question, it is not an order or request, and it is not an excited statement. That only leaves one from which to choose. It must be a declarative sentence because it is simply giving information."

"That is correct. Here is another rule of our language. *Skipping one baseline below Rule 2, starting comfortably close to the left margin line, write the following:* **'Rule 3: If a quote is a declarative sentence and it comes before the tag, we place a comma before the last quotation mark'."**

.34P As you work through these steps that follow, demonstrate the placing of proper punctuation marks as you speak.

.34 Step 4 — "Look where I have placed the comma. What is our rule really saying?"

STUDENTS: "If the quote is a declarative sentence, and if it is listed first and the tag is last, we place a comma right after the exact words spoken and right before the last quotation mark."

.34 Step 5 — *On the next available baseline below Rule 3, starting comfortably close to the left margin line, write the following sentence:* **"The sun is shining," Furtive Fox said'.** *Be sure to put the* **quotation marks** *and the* **comma** *in the right place.* I will do it on the board. Because the tag is at the end of the sentence, we end the sentence by placing a period after the word 'said'."

L34 Step 6 — "Let's switch the tag to the front of the sentence."

L34P Write a new "Furtive Fox" sample sentence on the board with the tag before the direct quote, including **proper** punctuation markings in place: "Furtive Fox said, 'The sun is shining.'"

L34 "Notice that the word 'The' is capitalized in the quote even though it is not the first word in our sentence. Do you know why? It is because it is the first word in our quote. Here is another rule governing quotes. *Skipping one baseline below the first sample sentence, starting comfortably close to the left margin line, write the following:* **'Rule 4: The first word of a quote is capitalized'.**"

L34 Step 7 — "Let's look at the example on the board. Where are the quotation marks?"

STUDENTS: "The quotation marks are placed around the words 'The sun is shining'."

TEACHER: "What punctuation mark is after the tag?"

STUDENTS: "If the tag is first, it looks like we need to place a comma after the tag."

TEACHER: "That is correct. We also know that every sentence must have an end punctuation mark. Where is our end punctuation mark placed?"

STUDENTS: "A period is placed inside or before the last quotation mark."

TEACHER: "So there is a comma after 'said' and the end punctuation mark is inside the quotation. That is what happens when the tag is in front of the quote."

Note to the Teacher (continued):

This was done, not to confuse you, but only to exemplify the proper use of quotation marks at these varying levels. There may also appear to be a discrepancy between stated rules for end punctuation and quotation marks and our application of same. This apparent discrepancy arose as a consequence of the use of double quotation marks to set apart the dictation sections for the teacher. If you have any questions regarding the proper use of quotation marks or end punctuation in relation to quotation marks for your students' Notebook pages, please refer to the Sample Pages in the back of this book. The quotation marks are represented there in the exact manner that your students should reproduce them.

Rule 1: Quotation marks enclose the exact words of the speaker.

Rule 2: The part of the sentence that tells who is speaking is called the tag.

Rule 3: If a quote is a declarative sentence, and it comes before the tag, we place a comma before the last quotation mark.
"The sun is shining," Furtive Fox said.

Rule 4: The first word of a quote is capitalized.

Rule 5: If the quote is a declarative sentence, and it comes after the tag, we place a comma after the tag, and we place the end punctuation mark before the last quotation mark.
Furtive Fox said, "The sun is shining."

Sample Page 57
Lesson 37

Rule 6: An imperative quote is punctuated like a declarative quote.
"Go to the store for me," Mom said.

Rule 7: If a quote is a question, use a question mark inside the quote.
"How shall I get to the market?" Pensive Pig said.

Rule 8: If the quote is an exclamation, use an exclamation point inside the quote.
"What a great play at first base!" the coach said.

Rule 9: Heavy written works or titles of paintings or specific names for planes, trains, ships, or spacecraft are underlined.

Sample Page 58
Lesson 37

"Skipping one baseline below Rule 4, starting comfortably close to the left margin line, write the following: 'Rule 5: If the quote is a declarative sentence and it comes after the tag, we place a comma after the tag, and we place the end punctuation before the last quotation mark'. On the next available baseline, comfortably close to the left margin line, write the following sentence: 'The Furtive Fox said, "The sun is shining"'."

Let's Get Organized

L56 **Step 8** — *"Turn to the Table of Contents. On the page 57 line, write the title* **'What Are Quotation Marks?'** *Turn back to page 57."*

L34 *"Centered on the title line, between the two red margin lines, write the title* **'What Are Quotation Marks?'"**

Placing Quotation Marks around an Imperative Sentence

L56P L56 and above need to turn their attention to page 58 in their *Notebook.*

L56 **Step 1** — "Look at the second sample sentence: '"Go to the store for me," Mom said'. What kind of a sentence is this quote?"

STUDENT: "It is an imperative sentence. Mom is telling me to go to the store."

TEACHER: "How is it punctuated?"

STUDENTS: "It is punctuated exactly like our first example where the quote was a declarative sentence."

TEACHER: "And that is our next rule.

"Skipping one baseline below the title line, starting comfortably close to the left margin line, write the following: 'Rule 6: An imperative quote is punctuated like a declarative quote'. On the next available baseline, comfortably close to the left margin line, write the sample sentence, '"Go to the store for me," Mom said'."

Placing Quotation Marks around Questions

L56 **Step 2** — "Look at our next sample sentence: '"How shall I get to the market?" Pensive Pig said'. How do we punctuate this example?"

STUDENTS:	"We place quotation marks around the exact words spoken by Pensive Pig."
TEACHER:	"What kind of a sentence is this direct quote?"
STUDENTS:	"It is an interrogative sentence. It asks a question."
TEACHER:	"What do we place after a question?"
STUDENTS:	"We need to place a question mark after a question."
TEACHER:	"Good. What do you think follows the last word 'said'?"
STUDENTS:	"Every sentence needs an end punctuation mark. If the tag is at the end of a sentence, we place a period after the tag."
TEACHER:	"I think you understand.

.56 *"Skipping one baseline below our last sentence, starting comfortably close to the left margin line, write the following: 'Rule 7: If a quote is a question, use a question mark inside the quote'. Starting on the next available baseline, write the following sentence: '"How shall I get to the market?" the Pensive Pig said'."*

Placing Quotation Marks around Exclamations

.56 **Step 3 —** "Look at our next sample sentence: '"What a great play at first base!" the coach said'. How do we punctuate this sentence?"

STUDENTS:	"Following the rules, we place quotation marks around the exact words spoken by the coach."
TEACHER:	"What kind of a sentence is this direct quote?"
STUDENTS:	"It is an exclamatory sentence. The coach is very excited."
TEACHER:	"What do we place after an exclamatory sentence?"
STUDENTS:	"We need to place an exclamation point."
TEACHER:	"Right.

56 *"Skipping one baseline below our last sentence, starting comfortably close to the left margin line, write the following: 'Rule 8: If the quote is an exclamation, use an exclamation point inside the quote'. Starting on the next available baseline, write the following sentence: '"What a great play at first base!" the coach said'. Remember to place a **period** after the tag."*

Do We Use Quotation Marks or Do We Underline a Title?

L78P We are going to introduce the use of quotation marks and underlining with titles. Students get confused about how to handle titles of books and songs and poems and the like. Do we use quotation marks or do we underline a title? Listen in on this conversation.

L78 **Step 4 —** "Jason, you look like a pretty strong fellow. Could you help me demonstrate a very important rule?"

> **JASON:** "If you are looking for a strong fellow, you have found your man."

> **TEACHER:** "I am going to go over and get an encyclopedia. Do you think you could hold that encyclopedia using both hands?"

L78P Hand him an encyclopedia volume. Give him several more volumes each time you ask if he can hold a few more. Keep piling them on until it is obvious that is takes something strong to hold them up.

> **JASON:** "No problem."

> **TEACHER:** "I want you to understand that your hands under that book need to be strong. Encyclopedias can be very heavy. Of course, newspapers and magazines can be very heavy too. I am going to get a few more books to represent magazines and newspapers. Can you hold a few more?"

> **JASON:** "No problem. My hands are strong!"

> **TEACHER:** "There are other written works that are also heavy. Dictionaries are heavy. Let me get a few more books to represent dictionaries. You can handle a few more books, can't you?"

> **JASON:** "Yes . . . yes . . . I think I can."

> **TEACHER:** "Do I see beads of perspiration forming on your head? No, I am sure not. There are still other written works that are heavy. Movie and play titles and document titles and opera titles and even ship, plane, train, and painting titles are heavy. We have to have a few more books to represent these."

> **JASON:** "Help!"

L78P The students start to get the picture. A drama develops. Can Jason hold all the encyclopedias or not? By the time I have transported all of the encyclopedias, and they are well past his nose, and he has broken out into a sweat, it is time to teach. First we set the encyclopedias down, however.

Discovering the Nature of Titles that Are Heavy and Light

78   **TEACHER:**   "You saw Jason trying to hold those heavy encyclopedias. He was using all the strength he had. If we could tie those encyclopedias together, could we use a paper clip and hang them from the ceiling?"

      STUDENTS: "That would be a foolish thing to do, especially if they were hanging over my head. They would come tumbling down."

      TEACHER: "The same is true of all book titles, all newspaper titles, all magazine titles, all long essay titles, all movie titles, all play titles, all long poem titles, all opera titles, all titles of paintings, and even the names of planes and ships and trains and spacecraft. These are very heavy and in order to hold them up in our writing, we need to underline them so they don't fall down."

      STUDENTS: "So the underlining would be like Jason's arms and hands."

      TEACHER: "That's right. Let's look at another angle. Sometimes we have written works that are not heavy at all. We could hang them from the ceiling with paper clips and they would not fall down. We have called these paper clips, 'quotation marks'.

"For example, the title of a short story is 'light'. We use quotation marks around it. The title of an article in a newspaper is light. The title of a short poem in a poetry book is light. A song title is light. Chapter titles from a book are light. Light written works use quotation marks. They can be hung with paper clips from the ceiling and they will not fall down. Heavy written works need more support. We place a line under them.

78   *"Skipping one line under our last sentence, comfortably close to the margin line write the following:* **'Rule 9: Heavy written works or titles of paintings or specific names for planes, trains, ships, or spacecraft are underlined'.***"*

Let's Get Organized

56   **Step 5 —** *"Turn to the Table of Contents. On the page 58 line, write the title* **'What Are Quotation Marks? (continued)'.** *Turn back to page 58. Centered on the title line, between the two red margin lines, write the* **same title.***"*

---

58 | What Are Quotation Marks? (continued)

Rule 6: An imperative quote is punctuated like a declarative quote. "Go to the store for me," Mom said.

Rule 7: If a quote is a question, use a question mark inside the quote. "How shall I get to the market?" Pensive Pig said.

Rule 8: If the quote is an exclamation, use an exclamation point inside the quote. "What a great play at first base!" the coach said.

Rule 9: Heavy written works or titles of paintings or specific names for planes, trains, ships, or spacecraft are underlined.

Sample Page 58
Lesson 37

Heavy written works are underlined or italicized.

Light written works use quotation marks.

In printed material, the publisher will use italics for a title instead of underlining.

What Are Quotation Marks? (continued) 59

London Times (newspaper)
The Outsiders (book)
Flubber (movie)

Rule 10: Light written works like short stories, poems, songs, essays, chapter titles, or article titles use quotation marks.

"Stocks Break Records" (news article)
"The Red Wheelbarrow" (poem)
"Sentence Making" (chapter title)

Rule 11: Dialogue requires a new paragraph with every switch of speaker.

"Have you handed in your composition using dialogue between two characters?" Mrs. Smith asked Jesse.
"I cannot find it, Mrs. Smith!" Jesse exclaimed.

Sample Page 59
Lesson 37

Using Quotation Marks for Titles That Are Light

L78 **Step 1** — *"Turn to page 59 in your* Grammar Notebook. *Skipping one baseline below the title line, starting comfortably close to the margin line, write the following on consecutive baselines:*

> '*London Times (newspaper)*'
> '*The Outsiders (book)*'
> '*Flubber (movie)*'.*"*

L78 **Step 2** — *"Skipping one baseline below our last example, write the following:* **'Rule 10: Light written works like short stories, poems, songs, essays, chapter titles, or article titles use quotation marks'."**

L78 **Step 3** — *"Skipping one baseline below Rule 10, write on consecutive baselines the following examples of written works that are light:*

> *'"Stocks Break Records" (news article)'*
> *'"The Red Wheelbarrow" (poem)'*
> *'"Sentence Making" (chapter title)'."*

L78 **Step 4** — "Let's look at some more examples. I will give you a title and I will tell you what it is. You tell me whether to underline it or use quotation marks.

1. E.T. (movie)

2. The Chicago Tribune (newspaper)

3. Time (magazine)

4. Titanic (ship)

5. "The Ransom of Red Chief" (short story)

6. Robinson Crusoe (book)

7. The Music Man (musical play)

8. "It's a Happy Day" (song)

9. Declaration of Independence (document)

10. World Book Encyclopedia (book)

11. "Students Turn Opportunity into Business" (News article)

12. Mona Lisa (painting)

13. Amahl and the Night Visitors (opera)

14. Spirit of St. Louis (plane)

15. "Stopping by the Woods on a Snowy Evening" (short poem)

16. "Punctuation" (chapter title)

17. <u>Gettysburg</u> (movie)

18. "The Red Wheelbarrow" (short poem)

19. <u>Apollo 9</u> (space ship)

20. "Greek Mythology" (chapter title)

21. <u>Pointing the Way to Literacy</u> (essay)

22. <u>Beowulf</u> (epic Poem)

Using *Italics* Instead of <u>Underlining</u>

78 **Step 5 —** "In printed material such as textbooks, newspapers, or magazines, instead of underlining, the publisher will print titles with slanted lettering. We call that type of print *'italics'*. When we write a paper that mentions titles of heavy written works using manuscript or cursive lettering, we cannot use italics. The only way we can tell our reader that we are writing a heavy written work is to underline the title."

Discovering Differences between Fiction and Nonfiction Writing

56 "There is a need to discuss the difference between fiction and nonfiction writing. A fictional story is a story that has been created in the author's imagination. It is unlikely that the characters are real though they may be based on people that the author has known. Although the story is pretend, it may be inspired by real-life experiences of the author or people the author has known. *The Wizard of Oz* or *Swiss Family Robinson* would be examples of fictional stories.

"A nonfiction book is true to life. It is a piece of writing about actual events. It may be about people who lived long ago or who are still living. A biography or life story about someone written by another person would be an example of nonfiction. A story about the life of George Washington is nonfiction. As we read great books, we can identify whether they are fiction or nonfiction books.

"As we read these kinds of books, we will discover that the authors use dialogue with quotation marks to help tell the story. Characters have conversations with each other. That is one of the ways the story is told."

Discovering the Nature of Dialogue

78 **Step 6 —** "Learning the use of quotation marks is very important in writing. If we want to add spice to our writing, we need to add conversation. Characters need to be talking to each other.

The exact words spoken by these characters are enclosed in quotation marks.

"In the case of a fictional story, the story is told by using conversation between two or more created characters. We learn more about the characters by what they say and how they respond to what is being said to them. It is really not any different in real life. We learn about others and they learn about us by what we say."

L78P Write the following sentences on the board. Be sure to draw clear and well-defined margin lines before you write. When writing this conversation, indent the dialogue every time there is a change of speakers. Each separate direct quote is a unique separate paragraph with a new tag. If a paragraph takes more than one line, we start the second line comfortably close to the margin line.

> "Have you handed in your composition using dialogue between two characters?" Mrs. Smith asked Jesse.
> "I cannot find it, Mrs. Smith!" Jesse exclaimed.
> "Are you sure that it isn't in your folder?" Mrs. Smith asked again.
> "I can't find anything in my folder," Jesse whined.
> "Maybe we need lessons on organization rather than on how to write a composition with dialogue," Mrs. Smith stated.

TEACHER: "What do we learn about the use of direct quotes in a conversation between two people?"

STUDENTS: "There is always a tag and every time there is a change of speaker, a new paragraph is started. If a paragraph needs more than one line, the second line is started comfortably close to the margin line."

TEACHER: "Excellent. Here is another rule that governs the use of dialogue.

"Skipping one baseline below our last example, starting comfortably close to the left margin line, write the following: 'Rule 11: Dialogue requires a new paragraph with every switch of speaker'."

L78 **Step 7** — *"Skipping one baseline below Rule 11, indenting five spaces from the margin line, write the following:*

> *'"Have you handed in your composition using dialogue between two characters?" Mrs. Smith asked Jesse.'*
> *'"I cannot find it, Mrs. Smith!" Jesse exclaimed.'"*

TEACHER: "Let's review. If we want to write a story and include a conversation between two of our chosen characters, what must we include?"

Sample Page 59
Lesson 37

STUDENTS:	"We must include dialogue. We must use quotation marks."
TEACHER:	"Yes. It is a very important part of writing stories. What do we need to do every time we switch from one speaker to another?"
STUDENTS:	"We must begin a new paragraph every time the conversation switches from one speaker to another."
TEACHER:	"What does that mean?"
STUDENTS:	"We start writing after we have moved in five spaces."
TEACHER:	"Good. Every time we switch between Jesse and Mrs. Smith, we have made a new paragraph. Making a new paragraph means we have indented five spaces from the margin line before we start our words."

Creating Conversation on Your Own

.78P Take time to help students create some conversation on a separate sheet of penmanship paper. Keep it simple. Tell students to choose two people or two animals and have them talk to each other. They need to make a new paragraph every time they change speakers. They need to enclose the exact words of the speaker in quotation marks. They need to include tags. They need to start a second line comfortably close to the margin line if the paragraph is longer than one line. They shouldn't be in a hurry. You may want to tell them that making dialogue is like recording a phone conversation.

Let's Get Organized

78 **Step 8** — *"Turn to the Table of Contents. On the page 59 line, write the title '**What Are Quotation Marks? (continued)**'. Turn back to page 59. Centered on the title line, between the two red margin lines, write the **same title.**"*

Discovering the Nature of Indirect Quotes

.78 **Step 1** — *"Turn to page 60 in your* Grammar Notebook. It is possible to take a sentence with a direct quote, remove the quotation marks, change some words, and create a sentence that tells us the same information as if we still had the quotation marks.

"Look at this example: 'Furtive Fox said that the sun was shining'. By using the word 'that' with the quotation marks removed, we can write a sentence that says almost the same thing as a direct quote with one difference.

What Are Quotation Marks? (continued) 59

London Times (newspaper)
The Outsiders (book)
Flubber (movie)

Rule 10: Light written works like short stories, poems, songs, essays, chapter titles, or article titles use quotation marks.

"Stocks Break Records" (news article)
"The Red Wheelbarrow" (poem)
"Sentence Making" (chapter title)

Rule 11: Dialogue requires a new paragraph with every switch of speaker.

"Have you handed in your composition using dialogue between two characters?" Mrs. Smith asked Jesse.
"I cannot find it, Mrs. Smith!" Jesse exclaimed.

Sample Page 59
Lesson 37

"An indirect quotation is not necessarily the exact words of another speaker. An indirect quote is the writer's own words about what the speaker said and not the speaker's actual words. Indirect quotes are less personal and sometimes more suitable for a particular writing task.

"Look at this next example: '"I want to go to the concert," said the band director'."

"We remove the quotes, add the word 'that', and change the pronoun 'I' to 'he'. If we change the verb form 'want' to 'wanted', what do we get?"

STUDENTS: "The band director said that he wanted to go to the concert."

TEACHER: "We call this kind of a quote an **'indirect quote'**.

L78 *"Skipping one baseline below the title line, starting comfortably close to the left margin line, write the following: **'Rule 12: An indirect quote removes the quotation marks, adds the word "that", and changes the pronouns and verb forms if necessary'.***"

"Skipping one baseline below Rule 12, comfortably close to the margin line, write the following on consecutive baselines:

'"I want to go to the concert," said the band director.'
'The band director said that he wanted to go
to the concert.'"

Discovering the Nature of Divided Quotes

L78 **Step 2** — "Sometimes a direct quote is divided in the middle by the tag. If that happens, we need to determine whether the quotes on either side of the tag are two separate sentences or if they are both part of the same sentence. Look at the following two examples:

'"The wind is very strong," said John, "but we must continue our work."'

'"The wind is too strong," said Jim. "We have to turn back."''"

L78P Make these examples available to your students.

TEACHER: "In the first example, the quote in front of the tag is only part of the sentence. The sentence is not finished and the rest of the sentence comes after the tag, so we put a comma after the name John. In the second example above, the tag is sandwiched between two separate sentences. We put a period after the name Jim because that is the last word in the first sentence. Another complete sentence follows.

"Skipping one baseline below our last example, starting comfortably close to the left margin line, write the following: 'Rule 13: A divided quote uses a comma after the tag if the quote is carried over and a period after the tag if the quote is two separate sentences'.

"On the next available baseline, comfortably close to the margin line, write the following on consecutive baselines:

> *'"The wind is very strong," said John, "but we must continue our work."'*

> *'"The wind is too strong," said Jim. "We have to turn back."'"*

et's Get Organized

.78   Step 3 — *"Turn to the Table of Contents. On the page 60 line, write the title 'What Are Quotation Marks? (continued)'. Turn back to page 60. Centered on the title line, between the two red margin lines, write the **same title**."*

Expectancies Learned or Reinforced in Lesson 37: Dialogue and Review

1. What do quotation marks probably indicate in a sentence? **L34** *(They indicate the exact words of the speaker.)*

2. What is a tag? **L34** *(A tag is the person saying the direct quote.)*

3. Where do the comma and period go if the direct quote is a declarative sentence and if the tag follows the quote? **L34** *(A comma precedes the last quotation mark and a period follows the tag if the direct quote is a declarative sentence.)*

4. What do we do with the first word of a direct quote? **L34** *(The first word of a direct quote needs to be capitalized.)*

5. Where do the comma and the end punctuation mark go if the tag is on the front of the direct quote? **L34** *(With the tag in the front, we separate the tag from the direct quote with a comma before the first quotation mark and place the end punctuation mark inside the last quotation mark.)*

6. How is an imperative quote punctuated? **L56** *(An imperative quote is punctuated like a declarative quote.)*

7. Where does the question mark and period go if the quote is a question and the tag follows the direct quote? **L56** *(The ques-*

60   What Are Quotation Marks? (continued)

Rule 12: An indirect quote removes the quotation marks, adds the word "that", and changes the pronouns and verb forms if necessary.

"I want to go to the concert," said the band director.
The band director said that he wanted to go to the concert.

Rule 13: A divided quote uses a comma after the tag if the quote is carried over and a period after the tag if the quote is two separate sentences.
"The wind is very strong," said John, "but we must continue our work."
"The wind is too strong," said Jim. "We have to turn back."

Sample Page 60
Lesson 37

tion mark precedes the last quotation mark and a period follows the tag.)

8. Where do the exclamation point and period go if the quote is an exclamation and the tag follows the direct quote? **L56** *(The exclamation point precedes the last quotation mark and a period follows the tag.)*

9. What is fictional writing? **L56** *(Fictional writing is a created story about characters from the author's imagination.)*

10. What is nonfiction? **L56** *(Nonfiction is writing that is a true to life account about actual events or people.)*

11. What is dialogue in a story? **L56** *(Dialogue is a conversation in writing between two or more characters.)*

12. What must we do with dialogue every time we switch speakers? **L78** *(Dialogue requires a new paragraph with every switch of speaker.)*

13. What do we do with "heavy" written works or titles of paintings or specific names for planes, trains, ships, or spacecraft? **L78** *(We underline them in handwritten reports. We use italics if we are using a word processor.)*

14. What do we do with "light" written works like short stories, poems, songs, chapter titles, or article titles? **L78** *(We enclose "light" titles in quotation marks.)*

15. How do we make an indirect quote? **L78** *(An indirect quote removes the quotation marks, adds the word "that", and changes pronouns or verb forms if necessary.)*

16. Why use an indirect quote? **L78** *(The writer may need to say what someone said, but using a direct quote may not fit well with the intended purpose of the writing.)*

17. How do we punctuate the tag of a divided quote? **L78** *(A divided quote uses a comma after the tag if the quote is carried over and a period after the tag if the second part of the direct quote is a separate sentence.)*

Where Do I Go from Here?

- **L34** goes to **L34** "Scope and Sequence" Step 27.

- **L56** has finished the **L56** "Scope and Sequence."

- **L78** goes to "Lesson 38" on page 379.

What Materials Will I Need?

- **L78** will need *Grammar Notebooks*, pencils, and copies of Worksheets for **"Lesson 38"** starting on page 384.

esson 38
What Are Semicolons and Colons?

A semicolon (;) is used to join two complete thoughts closely related in meaning.
We want to turn back; the wind and waves are strong.
Iowa grows acres of corn; it is a prosperous state.

Conjunctive adverbs join two sentences together using a semicolon and a comma.

also	however	nevertheless
besides	indeed	otherwise
consequently	instead	still
finally	later	then
furthermore	moreover	therefore
		thus

The trees were beautiful; therefore, we enjoyed the drive.
She drove; however, her car needed repair.

Sample Page 61
Lesson 38

| 62 | Semicolons and Colons (continued) |

A colon (:) is used before a list of items, after a salutation in a business letter, between the hour and minutes when telling time, between a chapter and verse in a Bible passage, or before a long quotation.
1:23 P.M.   Dear Sirs: Romans 3:23
Please buy the following: bread and cereal.
King David's first Psalm recorded in the Bible starts with these words: "Blessed..."

A colon never follows directly after a verb.
The people were John, Mary, and Cody.

Use a colon after an "...as follows:" or "...the following:" or following a noun.
The awards presented were as follows: the Peabody Award; the Best Writer Award; and the Barney Scholarship.
He knew four new words: reconcile, counsel, jeopardy, and sequence.

Sample Page 62
Lesson 38

L78 "In these last lessons of *Grammar Works,* we have looked at the use of apostrophes, commas, periods, and quotation marks. Knowing how to use all of these punctuation marks is very important if our writing is to effectively communicate our ideas. We must also learn how to use two other punctuation marks: the semicolon and the colon. That is what this lesson is all about."

Defining and Discovering the Nature of a Semicolon

L78 **Step 1 —** *"Turn to page 61 in your* Grammar Notebook. The semicolon and the colon have different jobs to do. We will look at the semicolon first. *Skipping one baseline below the title line, write the legal definition for a semicolon: 'A semicolon (;) is used to join two complete thoughts closely related in meaning'.*

L78 "The semicolon is sometimes used to connect two simple sentences instead of using a coordinating conjunction and a comma. Look at these examples."

78P Write the following sample sentences on the board. Be sure to use the Sample Pages a guide:

"Dr. Peterson was late; he had too many calls to make."

"The man was looking for his wallet; he had lost it at the mall."

"The food was good; the hamburgers were especially tasty."

L78 "In each example there are two separate sentences. The first sentence in each one is closely related to the second sentence. What are the two sentences in the first example?"

STUDENTS: "'Dr. Peterson was late' is one. The second is 'He had too many calls to make.'"

TEACHER: "How are they joined?"

STUDENTS: "Because they are so closely related in meaning, they are joined together with a semicolon."

L78 **Step 2 —** *"On the next available baseline under the definition of a semicolon, starting comfortably close to the left margin*

A semicolon (;) is used to join two complete thoughts closely related in meaning.
We want to turn back; the wind and waves are strong.
Iowa grows acres of corn; it is a prosperous state.

Conjunctive adverbs join two sentences together using a semicolon and a comma.
also   however   nevertheless
besides   indeed   otherwise
consequently instead   still
finally   later   then
furthermore moreover   therefore
                        thus

The trees were beautiful; therefore, we enjoyed the drive.
She drove; however, her car needed repair.

Sample Page 61
Lesson 38

A colon (:) is used before a list of items, after a salutation in a business letter, between the hour and minutes when telling time, between a chapter and verse in a Bible passage, or before a long quotation.
1:23 P.M.   Dear Sirs: Romans 3:23
Please buy the following: bread and cereal.
King David's first Psalm recorded in the Bible starts with these words: "Blessed..."

A colon never follows directly after a verb.
The people were John, Mary, and Cody.

Use a colon after an "...as follows:" or "...the following:" or following a noun.
The awards presented were as follows: the Peabody Award; the Best Writer Award; and the Barney Scholarship.
He knew four new words: reconcile, counsel, jeopardy, and sequence.

Sample Page 62
Lesson 38

---

line, write the following sentences that also use a semicolon. Place them on consecutive baselines:

> **'We want to turn back; the wind and waves are strong.'**
> **'Iowa grows acres of corn; it is a prosperous state.'"**

L78 **Step 3** — "Sometimes when joining two sentences, we need to use an explanatory expression or a special word called a **'conjunctive adverb'**. *Skipping one baseline below our last example, write the following: 'Conjunctive adverbs join two sentences together using a semicolon and a comma'. Starting on the next available baseline, comfortably close to the left margin line, write this list of common conjunctive adverbs: 'also', 'besides', 'consequently', 'finally', 'furthermore', 'however', 'indeed', 'instead', 'later', 'moreover', 'nevertheless', 'otherwise', 'still', 'then', 'therefore', and 'thus'.*"

Step 4 — "These words are used together with a semicolon to connect two sentences. This is also what a coordinating conjunction does ('and', 'but', 'or', 'for', 'nor', 'yet', 'so'). A comma is always placed between the adverb and the next sentence. *Skipping one baseline below our list of conjunctive adverbs, write the following two sentences on consecutive baselines:*

> **'The trees were beautiful; therefore, we enjoyed the drive.'**

> **'She drove; however, her car needed repair.'**

"What two sentences are being joined by the conjunctive adverbs 'therefore' and 'however'?"

STUDENTS: "The conjunctive adverb 'therefore' joins 'The trees were beautiful' with 'We enjoyed the drive.' The conjunctive adverb 'however' joins 'She drove' with 'Her car needed repair'.""

Defining the Nature of a Colon

L78 **Step 1** — *"Turn to page 62. Skipping one baseline below the title line, write the following definition of a colon: 'A colon (:) is used before a list, after a salutation in a business letter, between the hour and minutes when telling time, between a chapter and verse in a Bible passage, or before a long quotation'."*

Using a Colon with Time, Salutations, a List, and Bible Passages

L78P Write the following examples of colon usage on the board:

> "It is now 1:23 P.M."

> "Dear Sirs:"

"Please buy the following items: bandages, mosquito repellent, suntan lotion, and a swimming suit."

"Proverbs 3:5, 6"

"Romans 3:23"

Dictating Examples of Colon Usage

L78 **Step 2** — "We can see from these examples that the colon is used in a number of different ways. What are those ways according to the definition of a colon?"

STUDENTS: "A colon is used to separate the hour from minutes when writing a time. It is used after a salutation of a business letter. It is used to introduce a list. It is used to separate a chapter from a verse in a Bible passage."

TEACHER: "Well done.

On the next available baseline, starting comfortably close to the left margin line, write the following examples of colon usage leaving three spaces between each example: '1:23 P.M.' 'Dear Sirs:' 'Romans 3:23'. On the next available baseline, write the following sentence: 'Please buy the following: bread and cereal'."

Using a Colon before a Long Quotation

L78 **Step 3** — "We need to also use a colon to introduce a long quotation. 'King David's first Psalm recorded in the Bible starts with these words: "Blessed is the man who walks not in the counsel of the ungodly, nor stands in the way of sinners, nor sits in the seat of the scornful. But his delight is in the law of the Lord, and in that law does he meditate day and night . . ."'

On the next available baseline below the last sample sentence, starting comfortably close to the left margin line, write the following: 'King David's first Psalm recorded in the Bible starts with these words: "Blessed . . ."'"

Discovering an Ellipsis . . .

L78 **Step 4** — "Please note that we placed three periods after the word 'Blessed . . .' We have a special name for that. These three dots are called an **'ellipsis'**. They are used when we want to show that we are omitting words. An ellipsis can appear before or after a word. If it appears before a word, the omissions are before that word. If the ellipsis appears after the word, the omissions are after the word. An ellipsis is used because the words omitted are not important to the purpose of the writing.

62   Semicolons and Colons (continued)

A colon (:) is used before a list of items, after a salutation in a business letter, between the hour and minutes when telling time, between a chapter and verse in a Bible passage, or before a long quotation.
1:23 P.M.   Dear Sirs: Romans 3:23
Please buy the following: bread and cereal.
King David's first Psalm recorded in the Bible starts with these words: "Blessed..."

A colon never follows directly after a verb.
The people were John, Mary, and Cody.

Use a colon after an "...as follows:" or "...the following:" or following a noun.
The awards presented were as follows: the Peabody Award; the Best Writer Award, and the Barney Scholarship.
He knew four new words: reconcile, counsel, jeopardy, and sequence.

Sample Page 62
Lesson 38

A colon (:) is used before a list of items,
after a salutation in a business letter,
between the hour and minutes when telling
time, between a chapter and verse in a
Bible passage, or before a long quotation.
1:23 P.M.   Dear Sirs: Romans 3:23
Please buy the following: bread and cereal.
King David's first Psalm recorded in the
Bible starts with these words: "Blessed..."

A colon never follows directly after a verb.
The people were John, Mary, and Cody.

Use a colon after an "...as follows:" or
"...the following:" or following a noun.
The awards presented were as follows:
the Peabody Award, the Best Writer
Award, and the Barney Scholarship.
He knew four new words: reconcile,
counsel, jeopardy, and sequence.

Sample Page 62
Lesson 38

"Besides the ellipsis, of course, we see another use of the colon. How is the colon used with a long quote?"

STUDENTS: "We must place a colon directly before the long quote."

Other Uses of the Colon

L78   Step 5 — "There are a couple more things about colons that we need to learn. *Skipping one baseline below our long quote, starting comfortably close to the left margin line, write the following: 'A colon never follows directly after a verb'.*"

L78   Step 6 — "*Starting on the next available baseline, comfortably close to the left margin line, write the following sentence: 'The people were John, Mary, and Cody'.* Do we need a colon in this sentence?"

STUDENTS: "There is no colon needed. We cannot place a colon after the word 'were'. It is a verb."

L78   Step 7 — "*Skipping one baseline below the last sample sentence, starting comfortably close to the left margin line, write the following: 'Use a colon after an "... as follows:" or "... the following:" or following a noun'.*"

"*On the next available baseline, starting each sentence comfortably close to the left margin line, write the following examples on consecutive baselines:*

'*The awards presented were as follows: the Peabody Award, the Best Writer Award, and the Barney Scholarship.*'

'*He knew four new words: reconcile, counsel, jeopardy, and sequence.*'

"What do we learn from these sentences?"

STUDENTS: "We learn that a colon may follow a noun that precedes a list of items. A colon may also follow phrases like 'as follows:' or 'the following:' after which a list is also written."

Let's Get Organized

L78   Step 8 — "*Turn to the Table of Contents. On the page 61 line, write the following: 'What Are Semicolons and Colons?' On the page 62 line write the title 'Semicolons and Colons (continued)'. Turn back to page 61.*

"*Centered on the title line on page 61, between the two red margin lines, write the following title: 'What Are Semicolons and Colons?' Centered on the title line on page 62, between the two red margin lines, write the title 'Semicolons and Colons (continued)'.*"

Expectancies Learned or Reinforced in Lesson 38: Dialogue and Review

1. What is a semicolon used for? **L78** (*A semicolon is used to join two complete thoughts closely related in meaning.*)

2. What is a colon used for? **L78** (*A colon is used before a list of items, after a salutation in a business letter, between the hour and the minutes when telling time, between a chapter and a verse in a Bible passage, and before a long quotation.*)

3. What will a colon never follow? **L78** (*A colon will never follow a verb.*)

4. Besides the other uses for a colon already mentioned, where else may a colon be used? **L78** (*A colon may be used after ". . . as follows:" or ". . . the following:" or directly following a noun.*)

5. What is an ellipsis? **L78** (*An ellipsis is a series of three dots indicating the omission of words because these words are not important to the purpose of the writing.*)

6. How do we punctuate conjunctive adverbs? **L78** (*Conjunctive adverbs connecting two sentences have a semicolon preceding the conjunctive adverb, and a comma following them in a sentence.*)

Where Do I Go from Here?

- **L78** goes to **"Lesson 39"** on page 388.

What Materials Will I Need?

- **L78** will need *Grammar Notebooks* and pencils. **L78** will also need a book with a title page containing the information specified on page 389, a dictionary, an encyclopedia, a thesaurus, and (if you can obtain a copy) *The Readers' Guide to Periodical Literature.* You may want to have copies of the reference books introduced on pages 384 and 385.

Proper Punctuation

Teacher Directions: Explain to your students the directions for making needed corrections in the sentences for this exercise. Make sure your students are able to explain why they are making the changes.

Student Directions: Each of the following sentences may need periods, commas, apostrophes, quotation marks, semicolons, colons, capital letters, or other punctuation.

Fix each sentence by placing the proper punctuation where it belongs and place three lines under the lowercase letters that should be capital letters. For example: "sam" becomes "sam".

Be ready to explain why you are correcting the sentence the way that you do.

1. gen. u. s. grant defeated the fort at vicksburg, ms, during the civil war.

2. sally said, "i'm studying john f. kennedy's life for history."

3. "at 3:00 p. m. mr. roisum read the announcements," said capt. stenberg.

4. it's the best medicine, and it's very inexpensive.

5. the fbi said that no law had been broken.

6. on jan. 1, 2000, we will enter a new century.

7. "joel, please go to new york, ny, with that order."

8. after the start of the program, six lbs. of onions were delivered to battle lake, mn.

9. "we're going to the meeting, but we'll be late," said mayor holmgren.

10. the cat, the poodle, and the angel fish were the girl's (or girls') pets.

1. gen u s grant defeated the fort at vicksburg ms during the civil war

2. sally said im studying john f kennedys life for history

3. at 300 p m mr roisum read the announcements said capt stenberg

4. its the best medicine and its very inexpensive

5. the fbi said that no law had been broken

6. on jan 1 2000 we will enter a new century

7. joel please go to new york ny with that order

8. after the start of the program six lbs of onions were delivered to battle lake mn

9. were going to the meeting but well be late said mayor holmgren

10. the cat the poodle and the angel fish were the girls pets

1998 Grammar Works/Holly Hall Publications, Inc.   Lesson 38: What Are Semicolons and Colons?

Proper Punctuation

Student Directions: Each of the following sentences may need periods, commas, apostrophes, quotation marks, semicolons, colons, capital letters, or other punctuation.

Fix each sentence by placing the proper punctuation where it belongs and place three lines under the lowercase letters that should be capital letters. For example: "sam" becomes "sam".

Be ready to explain why you are correcting the sentence the way that you do.

Proper Punctuation

Teacher Directions: Explain to your students the directions for making needed corrections in the sentences for this exercise. Make sure your students are able to explain why they are making the changes.

Student Directions: Each of the following sentences may need periods, commas, apostrophes, quotation marks, semicolons, colons, capital letters, or other punctuation.

Fix each sentence by placing the proper punctuation where it belongs and place three lines under the lowercase letters that should be capital letters. For example: "sam" becomes "sam".

Be ready to explain why you are correcting the sentence the way that you do.

1. "listen, fella, i just stopped to help," said the ups man. "do you need help?"

2. john and sally's teacher was proud of their poem called "the moon."

3. yes, anybody's contribution will be appreciated.

4. the year's activities included a field trip to denver, co.

5. the swiss family robinson is a wonderful book. (or !)

6. please include the following items: a sweater, a pair of hiker's boots, a compass, a stocking cap, and a sleeping bag.

7. jn. 3:16 is an often quoted verse in the bible.

8. one of the most well known statements in the declaration of independence starts with these words: "we hold these truths to be self-evident that all men are created equal . . ."

9. uncle sam said, "let's go get an ice cream cone."

1. listen fella i just stopped to help said the ups man do you need help

2. john and sallys teacher was proud of their poem called the moon

3. yes anybodys contribution will be appreciated

4. the years activities included a field trip to denver co

5. the swiss family robinson is a wonderful book

6. please include the following items a sweater a pair of hikers boots a compass a stocking cap and a sleeping bag

7. jn 3 16 is an often quoted verse in the bible

8. one of the most well known statements in the declaration of independence starts with these words we hold these truths to be self-evident that all men are created equal

9. uncle sam said lets go get an ice cream cone

What Do We Find in Books? | 63

What is a title?
The title is the name of the book.

What is a title page?
The title page gives the name of the book, the author, and the publisher.

What is a Table of Contents?
The Table of Contents in the front of a book tells us what is in the book.

What is a glossary?
A glossary is a list of new words with definitions to help us understand the book.

What is an index?
The index in the back of the book is an alphabetical list of all subjects covered in the book.

Sample Page 63
Lesson 39

64 | What Do We Find in a Dictionary?

Words listed in a dictionary are written in alphabetical order.

Words listed in a dictionary are called entry words.
Entry words give us the correct spelling for a word.

The two words on the top of a dictionary page are called guide words.
Guide words tell us if a word is on that page.

Dictionaries give the definitions of words.
...the pronunciation of words.
...the syllables in a word.
...the parts of speech of words.
...the etymology of words.
...a sample sentence using the entry word.

Sample Page 64
Lesson 39

Library Skills (continued) | 65

Some words have more than one definition.
Some words can be used as a different part of speech.
Words called "homographs" are spelled the same but mean something different.

Dictionaries have special features.
Biographical Names sections list people.
Geographical Names sections list places.
The Atlas section has maps.

Encyclopedias arrange all topics alphabetically.
...use guide words like a dictionary.
...have pictures, diagrams, and illustrations.
...have a research guide to find more information.
...provide a list of related topics.

Sample Page 65
Lesson 39

66 | Library Skills (continued)

The card catalog has three different kinds of cards.
The title card lists the title of the book first.
The subject card lists the subject first.
The author card lists the author first.

Fiction books are arranged alphabetically.
Nonfiction books are arranged using a numbering system.
Almanacs, atlases, newspapers, magazines, and biographical materials are in a library.

The Readers' Guide to Periodical Literature is an index of magazine articles.
Each entry contains the title, the author's name, the magazine, the volume number, the page numbers, the date, and listings of illustrations, maps, or photos.

Sample Page 66
Lesson 39

Lesson 39
Developing Library Skills

Understanding Some Basic Parts that Make Up a Book

L12 "Good books are wonderful things. They rank right up there with downhill skiing and ice cream and sunsets and apple pie and grandma's home cooking and your favorite car and Valley-fair Amusement Park and the Fourth of July and fireworks and picnics and an ice-cold glass of lemonade on a hot summer day. Books are delicious and we can't eat enough of them. We all love stories, and to find a storyteller who can take us away to *Treasure Island* or to *Alice in Wonderland* or introduce us to Tarzan or Sherlock Holmes or Laura Ingalls Wilder is one of the greatest of joys. We have to learn about books."

L12P You will need to find books to use for examples. Make sure they have all of the features you will need to demonstrate. At **L12** your goal is to merely introduce this information. Show your students an example of each feature after you have introduced that feature.

L34P At **L34** your goal is to familiarize your students with the information. Have them look for the features in the books themselves. (You could point them out in **L3** and have them find them in **L4**.)

L56P **L56** and above should turn to page 63 in their *Grammar Notebook*. Show them the examples after they have completed entering the information into their *Notebooks*.

L12 **Step 1** — "The title of any book is written on the cover of the book and on the title page. It usually gives us a clue to the subject about which the book is written. All the important words in a book title are capitalized. **The title is the name of the book.**"

L56 *"Skipping one baseline below the title line, starting comfortably close to the left margin line write this sentence: 'What is a title?' On the next available baseline write the following: 'The title is the name of the book'."*

L12 **Step 2** — "The title page gives the name of the book, the author, and the publisher. We call the person who wrote the book the author. We call the person or company who created the book the publisher. We can also find out other information on the title page. If we look on the backside of the title page, we can learn what year the book was published. That is the copyright date."

.56 *"Skipping one baseline below our last sentence, write this sentence: 'What is a title page?' On the next available baseline, write the following: 'The title page gives the name of the book, the author, and the publisher'."*

.78 "Books today also have what is called an 'ISBN'. It is a number that is located on the backside of the title page. ISBN is an acronym for International Standard Book Number. Founded in 1872, a company called R. R. Bowker is the official ISBN agency for the United States. It produces reference products that form the cornerstone of the library and book selling communities. It keeps an accurate and current list of book references so that the ISBN is all we need to know if we want to order a book from a bookstore. Find a book that has an ISBN."

.12 **Step 3** — "When paging through a book, we will soon come to the Table of Contents. The Table of Contents tells us what is in the book. It is a list of all of the main sections in the book. We sometimes call these main sections chapters or units. The Table of Contents also has page numbers telling where each chapter begins."

.56 *"Skipping one baseline below our last sentence, write this sentence: 'What is a Table of Contents?' On the next available baseline, write the following: 'The Table of Contents in the front of a book tells us what is in the book'."*

.12 **Step 4** — "Sometimes books have a glossary, but not always. A glossary is a list of new words with definitions to help us understand the book. A glossary is usually a list of some of the more difficult words found in the book. It gives the meanings of these hard words to help us understand the book. We might have to look hard to find a book with a glossary in it. It might have to be a science book or a history book or some other kind of textbook. Usually a storybook would not have a glossary."

.56 *"Skipping one baseline below our last sentence, write this sentence: 'What is a glossary?' On the next available baseline, write the following: 'A glossary is a list of new words with definitions to help us understand the book'."*

12 **Step 5** — "At the back of some books, you will find an index. The index is an alphabetical listing of every topic covered in the text. It is a reference tool to help you quickly find your way to specific names or subjects. The index tells us the exact page numbers where subjects that are listed can be found."

56 *"Skipping one baseline below our last sentence, write this sentence: 'What is an index?' On the next available baseline, write the following: 'The index in the back of the book is an alphabetical list of all subjects covered in the book'."*

What Do We Find in Books? 63

What is a title?
The title is the name of the book.

What is a title page?
The title page gives the name of the book, the author, and the publisher.

What is a Table of Contents?
The Table of Contents in the front of a book tells us what is in the book.

What is a glossary?
A glossary is a list of new words with definitions to help us understand the book.

What is an index?
The index in the back of the book is an alphabetical list of all subjects covered in the book.

Sample Page 63
Lesson 39

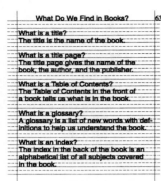

Sample Page 63
Lesson 39

Sample Page 64
Lesson 39

Let's Get Organized

L56   **Step 6** — *"Turn to the Table of Contents. On the page 63 line, write the title 'What Do We Find in Books?' Turn back to page 63."*

Understanding How a Dictionary Works

L12   Have a dictionary ready to use in this next part of the lesson.

L56   **L56** and above need to turn to page 64 in their *Grammar Notebook*.

L12   **Step 1** — "A dictionary is a book that contains very important information. When we know what can be found in a dictionary and how the information is arranged, the dictionary can be a very useful tool.

"The dictionary is full of words. These words are arranged in alphabetical order. Alphabetical order means that words are arranged according to the order of the letters in the alphabet. All of the words that start with the letter 'A' come first in alphabetical order. All of the words that start with the letter 'B' come next, and so on through the entire alphabet."

L34   "If two words start with the same letter of the alphabet, then we go to the second letters of these words to decide the order. If the first two letters are the same, we go to the third letter to decide the order, and so on."

L12   "It is important to learn to put words in alphabetical order because the words in a glossary, in an index, in encyclopedias, on the bindings of books on bookshelves in libraries, and even names of streets are often arranged alphabetically."

L56   *"Skipping one line under the title line, starting comfortably close to the margin line, write the following: **'Words in a dictionary are written in alphabetical order'.**"*

L12P   Make your own list of simple words using a dictionary. Choose some words starting with the same letter. Have your students work at arranging these words in alphabetical order.

L34P   Use words that start with the same letter, but the second letter is different. Make your lists more difficult as your students progress from one level to the next. To get you started, use the list provided with the next step. Place these words on the board and determine their alphabetical order.

L34   **Step 2** — "Look at this list of words. How would we arrange these alphabetically? Which word would come first? Which word would come second? 'Total', 'over', 'mace', 'no', 'school', 'make', 'look', 'like', 'book', 'may', 'come', 'are', 'out', 'ago', 'zoo', 'will'."

Step 3 — "The words that we look up in a dictionary are called **'entry words'**. The entry word tells us the correct spelling of the word for which we are looking. Entry words are usually in bold print and if we know the first few letters of the word, we can usually find the entry word we are looking for."

"Skipping one baseline below our last sentence write the following sentences on consecutive baselines: 'Words listed in a dictionary are called entry words'. 'Entry words give us the correct spelling for a word'."

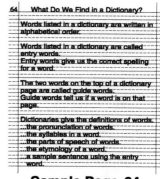

Sample Page 64
Lesson 39

Step 4 — "The two words at the very top of each dictionary page are called **'guide words'**. They are there to help us find the words on a page much more easily. The first guide word listed is the very first entry word listed on the page. The second guide word is the very last entry word written on the page. If we know how to alphabetize, then we can determine whether or not the word we are looking for is on this page. We can do that by deciding if the word we are looking for comes before the first guide word, after the second guide word, or between the two guide words on the page."

Turn to any page in your dictionary and point out the guide words and the entry words.

"Look at this example. Let's say the guide words on my page are 'fat' and 'favor'. Would the word 'apple' be on this page?"

STUDENTS: "The word 'apple' cannot be on this page because it does not fall between our guide words. 'Apple' starts with the letter 'A' and both 'fat' and 'favor' begin with the letter 'F'. The word that begins with the letter 'A' does not fit between the words that begin with the letter 'F'.

TEACHER: "How about the word 'father'? 'Father' starts with the letter 'F' just like the guide words do. Would the word 'father' be found on this page?"

STUDENTS: "The word 'father' would be found on this page. The first three letters of 'fat' and 'father' are the same. The additional fourth letter 'h' in 'father' tells us that it comes after the word 'fat'. Because we must use the third letters in 'favor' and 'father', the word 'father' would come before the word 'favor' because the letter 't' comes before the letter 'v'."

"Look more carefully at a dictionary page. Choose some words on that page and explain why these words fall between the guide words. Choose a few words that are not found on this page and explain why these words do not fit on the page you chose."

"Skipping one baseline below our last sentence, write the following sentences on consecutive baselines:

| 64 | What Do We Find in a Dictionary? |

Words listed in a dictionary are written in alphabetical order.

Words listed in a dictionary are called entry words.
Entry words give us the correct spelling for a word.

The two words on the top of a dictionary page are called guide words.
Guide words tell us if a word is on that page.

Dictionaries give the definitions of words.
...the pronunciation of words.
...the syllables in a word.
...the parts of speech of words.
...the etymology of a word.
...a sample sentence using the entry word.

Sample Page 64

Lesson 39

'The two words on the top of a dictionary page are called guide words.'

'Guide words tell us if a word is on that page.'"

A Dictionary Can Tell Us Much More about Entry Words

L34   **Step 5 —** "When we find the word we are looking for, the dictionary can tell us much about this word.

■ If we don't know what the word means, the dictionary will give us the **definition** or what the word means. Sometimes there is more than one definition.

■ If we need to know how to say the word, there is a **pronunciation guide** on the page. The pronunciation of the word itself is the very next thing following the entry word.

■ If the word has more than one syllable, the dictionary will place a black dot between letters at correct places breaking the word into **syllables.**

■ The dictionary will tell us what **part of speech** the word is, whether it is a noun, verb, adjective, adverb, preposition, conjunction, or interjection.

■ Sometimes the **etymology,** a big word for word origin or what language the word comes from, is included in the information about entry words. The entry word comes from a certain language. The etymology may tell us what the original word meant and from which language it comes. The etymology for the word dictionary or any word is set off in square brackets like these.

■ Finally, the dictionary often gives us a **sample sentence** or a sample phrase using the entry word correctly."

L56   *"Skipping one baseline below the last sentence, write the following on consecutive baselines:*

   'The dictionary gives the definitions of words.'

   '. . . the pronunciation of words.'

   '. . . the syllables in a word.'

   '. . . the parts of speech of words.'

   '. . . the etymology of a word.'

   '. . . a sample sentence using the entry word.'"

Let's Get Organized

.56   Step 6 — *"Turn to the Table of Contents. On the page 64 line, write the title **'What Do We Find in a Dictionary?'** Turn back to page 64. Centered on the title line, between the two red margin lines, write the **same title**."*

Practicing Dictionary Skills

.34P   Choose any dictionary page to look at with your students. Have your students answer the following questions.

1. What are the **guide words** on this page?

2. How many **syllables** do these words have? *(Choose five words with more than one syllable. Have your students figure out the number of syllables from the information on the dictionary page.)*

3. Where is the **pronunciation key?** *(You will need to explain that the symbols in this key are pronounced like the words that are printed beside them. The symbol letter "a" in a pronunciation for an entry word would say the same sound as the "a" in the word "at" or whatever word the key used. Point out the pronunciation key and explain how it works.)*

4. Can you find the **accent mark**? *(Explain that in the pronunciation of a word there is an element called an "accent mark". The accent mark is placed on the syllable that is spoken more loudly than the others.)*

5. What **part of speech** is the entry word? If it is a noun, what is its plural form?

6. What is the **definition** of the word? *(Have your students read the definition.)*

7. What are the **sample sentences or phrases** given for this word?

8. Point out any **illustrations or diagrams** for an entry word that help us better understand the meaning of a word.

9. Find a word that has an **etymology**. What is the etymology of the word?

10. Make up a list of ten words your students know. Have your students look them up in the dictionary and tell you what part of speech they are.

---

64 | What Do We Find in a Dictionary?

Words listed in a dictionary are written in alphabetical order.

Words listed in a dictionary are called entry words.
Entry words give us the correct spelling for a word.

The two words on the top of a dictionary page are called guide words.
Guide words tell us if a word is on that page.

Dictionaries give the definitions of words.
...the pronunciation of words.
...the syllables in a word.
...the parts of speech of words.
...the etymology of a word.
...a sample sentence using the entry word.

Sample Page 64
Lesson 39

Some words have more than one definition.

Some words can be used as a different part of speech.

Words called "homographs" are spelled the same but mean something different.

Dictionaries have special features.
Biographical Names sections list people.
Geographical Names sections list places.
The Atlas section has maps.

Encyclopedias arrange all topics alphabetically.
...use guide words like a dictionary.
...have pictures, diagrams, and illustrations.
...have a research guide to find more information.
...provide a list of related topics.

Sample Page 65
Lesson 39

Discovering the Nature of Words

L56 **Step 1 —** *"Turn to page 65 in your* Notebook. We need to look up the word 'pitch' in a dictionary. How many meanings does it have?"

STUDENTS: "I count at least 30 different definitions! Is that possible?"

TEACHER: "That is very possible. How many different parts of speech do you find?"

STUDENTS: "It can be used as a transitive verb. That means is has a caboose. It can be used as an intransitive verb. It can be use as a noun."

TEACHER: "Well done. These are dictionary skills that are important for you to know."

L56 *"Skipping one baseline under the title line, starting comfortably close to the margin line, write the following sentences on consecutive baselines:*

'Some words have more than one definition.'

'Some words can be used as a different part of speech.'

'Words called "homographs" are spelled the same but mean something different.'"

Special Features Found in a Dictionary

L56 **Step 2 —** "There are some special resource sections located in the back of most dictionaries. These sections provide us with specific topic-related information. We will list some of the more commonly found.

"Biographical Names: Here you will find lists of people who are famous or who were important in history. There you may find the pronunciation of the family name, the dates of birth and death, the nationality of the person, and a very short description explaining why the person is famous.

"Geographical Names: Here you will find the names of rivers and mountains, cities and states, countries and continents, oceans and bodies of water, and other places of historical or cultural significance. These entries may contain a pronunciation, some descriptive information and population. Sometimes the area of the geographical region is listed both in square miles and square kilometers. Length and height are also listed when appropriate.

"Atlas Section: You will find maps in this section of some dictionaries.

"Your dictionary may not have all of the sections listed above or it may have even more sections than we have mentioned here. *Skipping one baseline below our last sentence, starting comfortably close to the margin, write the following on consecutive baselines:*

'Dictionaries have special features.'

'Biographical Names sections list people.'

'Geographical Names sections list places.'

'The Atlas section has maps.'"

L56P Take your students on a tour of a dictionary. Try to find these unique features. You might find some other features also. There is much more information that is contained in a dictionary. This will be a good start.

Discovering the Nature of an Encyclopedia

L34   **Step 3** — "Encyclopedias are sets of books that contain articles about a great variety of topics. Every article is arranged in alphabetical order. Most letters of the alphabet have one whole volume devoted to topics starting with that letter."

L34P Find a set of encyclopedias. Select a topic to research. Point out the following:

1. Because everything is **arranged alphabetically,** we must choose the volume that includes the letters of the alphabet with which the name of our topic begins.

2. Like a dictionary, we need to use the **guide words** at the top of the pages to find an article about a chosen topic.

3. When we find our topic, we may see **pictures, diagrams, or illustrations** to help us understand the topic.

4. If we cannot find an article about a given topic, we should check the **research guide** to see if our topic is mentioned in articles about other topics.

5. After we have read the article, there may be a listing of different, **related topics** where we can go to find more information. We call looking for additional information in this manner cross-referencing.

L56   *"Skipping one baseline below our last sentence, starting comfortably close to the margin line, write the following on consecutive baselines:*

'Encyclopedias arrange all topics alphabetically.'

'. . . use guide words like a dictionary.'

Some words have more than one definition.
Some words can be used as a different part of speech.
Words called "homographs" are spelled the same but mean something different.

Dictionaries have special features.
Biographical Names sections list people.
Geographical Names sections list places.
The Atlas section has maps.

Encyclopedias arrange all topics alphabetically.
...use guide words like a dictionary.
...have pictures, diagrams, and illustrations.
...have a research guide to find more information.
...provide a list of related topics.

Sample Page 65
Lesson 39

'. . . have pictures, diagrams, and illustrations.'

'. . . have a research guide to find more information.'

'. . . provide a list of related topics.'"

Practicing with an Encyclopedia

L34P Have your students read information about your **home state.**

Have them read information about **Mt. Rushmore.**

Have them look up **George Washington.** Hold discussions about each of these. What do they learn?

Your Student Has a Snake in a Box? It Is Time to Seize the Moment!

L12P Encyclopedias are a wonderful place to go for "seize the moment" type teaching. When a student brings a unique snake to your attention and says, "Would you like to see the snake I have in this box?" it is time to either "seize the moment", run, or scream, whichever you prefer. Regardless of what you might do, now is when your student is extremely interested in snakes. He will find all sorts of information about snakes to be fascinating. What kinds of snakes are there? Where do snakes live? What do snakes eat besides people? What kind of snake did you catch? Why should snakes be left in the box rather than out of the box?

If you will take the time right now to show him where to look, how to look, and what kinds of information are available in the library, your inquisitive student will learn to eagerly do research on his own in a few years. It is worth the time and effort.

Let's Get Organized

L56 **Step 4** — *"Turn to the Table of Contents. On the page 65 line, write the title* **'Library Skills (continued)'.** *Turn back to page 65. Centered on the title line, between the two red margin lines, write the* **same title."**

Discovering the Card Catalog

L56 **Step 1** — *"Turn to page 66 in your* Notebook. With the increasing use of computers, the old card catalog format with its index cards is probably on its way to becoming obsolete. Card catalog skills, however, continue to be of value even when using new technologies.

"A library is a resource that has many books that may help us when we need to find information. It is important to know how to find a specific book that may be in a library. The card catalog is a tool to help us find books. Every book contained in the library is listed in the card catalog at least three times. There are three kinds of cards on which they are listed:

1. **"Title Card:** The name or title of the book is listed first on this card. The author and a short description of the contents of the book follow the title.

2. **"Subject Card:** The topic or the subject about which the book is written is found first on this card. The title of the book, the author, and a short description of the contents of the book follow the general subject heading.

3. **"Author Card:** The name of the author is the first thing found on this card. The title and a short description of the book follow the author's name."

L56 **Step 2 —** *"Skipping one baseline below the title line, starting comfortably close to the left margin line, write the following sentences on consecutive baselines:*

> *'The card catalog has three different kinds of cards.'*
>
> *'The title card lists the title of the book first.'*
>
> *'The subject card lists the subject first.'*
>
> *'The author card lists the author first.'"*

L56 **Step 3 —** "These cards may also contain what is called a 'Dewey Decimal System' number if they are nonfiction books. (Some libraries use the Library of Congress numbering system.) This number identifies in what section of the library the book may be found. These cards may also contain some information about the publisher of the book.

L56 "If we wanted to find out what books the library had about the subject 'dogs' with the old card catalog format, we could look for subject cards about the topic of 'dogs' under letter 'D'. If we knew the title of a specific book about dogs, such as *Only One Woof*, we would look for the title card under the letter 'O'. If we knew the name of an author who wrote books about dogs, we would search for the author card using the author's last name as a reference.

"Title cards, subject cards, and author cards under the old system are all arranged alphabetically. Therefore, if the author's name was George Smith, you would search for his name under 'S'."

---

66   Library Skills (continued)

The card catalog has three different kinds of cards.
The title card lists the title of the book first.
The subject card lists the subject first.
The author card lists the author first.

Fiction books are arranged alphabetically.
Nonfiction books are arranged using a numbering system.
Almanacs, atlases, newspapers, magazines, and biographical materials are in a library.

The Readers' Guide to Periodical Literature is an index of magazine articles. Each entry contains the title, the author's name, the magazine, the volume number, the page numbers, the date, and listings of illustrations, maps, or photos.

Sample Page 66
Lesson 39

Let's Go to the Library

L56P Go on a library field trip. Have your friendly librarian help you. Find the card catalog. Some libraries may still use card catalogs in large wooden cabinets with many small drawers; these drawers are all alphabetized. Some card catalogs are now computerized. If you are unfamiliar with how to find a book using the computer, ask the librarian for assistance. Choose some subjects of interest to your students like snakes perhaps. Show them how to find some books on these subjects.

Additional Information on How to Locate Books

L56   **Step 4** — "In addition to knowing what can be found in the card catalog, we must learn other important information about libraries. Let's look at some of the most useful information."

An Imaginary Trip to the Library

I. It is helpful to know how books are arranged in a library.

  A. Books of fiction are arranged alphabetically using the last name of the author.

  B. Many libraries arrange nonfiction books using the Dewey Decimal System.

   1. A man named Melvil Dewey created this system in 1876.

   2. There are ten subject areas numbered from 000 to 999.

     a) These ten groups are also divided into subdivisions.

     b) All nonfiction books fit into these ten subject areas.

   3. There is a Dewey Decimal Number on each card in the card catalog.

   4. The books on the shelves are arranged in an orderly fashion according to these numbers.

   5. To learn more about the Dewey Decimal System, we may need to ask a friendly librarian.

II. It is helpful to know what other resources are available in a library.

  A. There are reference books called almanacs.

   1. The *World Almanac* is a book that is filled with many current facts about the world.

2. The *Guinness Book of World Records* has lots of interesting pieces of information, including many spectacular feats and interesting accomplishments by a wide variety of people.

B. There are atlases, such as the *World Book Atlas*, that are filled with maps and geographical information.

C. There will be current newspapers from many different cities and towns available.

   1. We might find the *New York Times*.

   2. We might find the *Washington Post*.

   3. We might find our local town newspaper.

D. There are biographical reference books.

   1. We can go to a book called *Current Biography*, a monthly publication reporting on people in the news.

   2. We can go to a book called *Who's Who in America*, another book about important people.

E. There are many different periodicals that a library receives.

   1. Popular periodicals, called "magazines", are termed "periodicals" because they are printed and distributed on a periodic basis.

      a) Some magazines come out once a week.

      b) Some magazines come out once a month.

      c) Some magazines come out every other month.

      d) Some magazines come out quarterly.

   2. Professional periodicals are usually called "journals".

L56 *"Skipping one baseline below our last sentence, starting comfortably close to the margin line, write the following sentences on consecutive baselines:*

'Fiction books are arranged alphabetically.'

'Nonfiction books are arranged using a numbering system.'

'Almanacs, atlases, newspapers, magazines, and biographical materials are in a library.'"

66   Library Skills (continued)

The card catalog has three different kinds of cards.
The title card lists the title of the book first.
The subject card lists the subject first.
The author card lists the author first.

Fiction books are arranged alphabetically.
Nonfiction books are arranged using a numbering system.
Almanacs, atlases, newspapers, magazines, and biographical materials are in a library.

The Readers' Guide to Periodical Literature is an index of magazine articles. Each entry contains the title, the author's name, the magazine, the volume number, the page numbers, the date, and listings of illustrations, maps, or photos.

Sample Page 66
Lesson 39

Introducing the *Readers' Guide to Periodical Literature*

L78   **Step 5** — "Another resource that we need to know about is called the *Readers' Guide to Periodical Literature*. This reference tool can help us find magazine articles about many different subjects or about many different people. Hundreds of magazines are published every month. We can't subscribe to all of them. We can't keep track of all the articles that are being written. That is the job of the *Readers' Guide to Periodical Literature*."

L78P   Find the *Readers' Guide to Periodical Literature* in a local library. We need to take students on a little tour through some of the pages in this guide. Because this resource is such an important part of researching, many librarians have a class session ready and available to learn how to use this guide. Ask the librarian for help. If the librarian is unable to help you, point out the following with your students.

1. On the first inside pages you will see a listing of 200 magazines. The *Readers' Guide to Periodical Literature* indexes all the articles in each of these magazines.

2. These articles are listed by the author's last name and by subject headings and subheadings, alphabetically.

3. The author's name and the subject entries are written in **bold** type.

4. Each separate entry contains the following: the title of the article, the author's name, the name of the magazine, the volume number of the magazine, the pages where the article is located, the date of the magazine, and a listing of any illustrations, maps, or photos accompanying the article.

L78   **Step 6** — "Use the *Readers' Guide to Periodical Literature* to find a magazine article about a subject which interests you. Sometimes you may want to research a person who lived ten years ago. If you know the correct year, the *Readers' Guide to Periodical Literature* can help you. Libraries keep magazines for long periods of time. If your local library no longer has the article you need, they can get it for you from larger libraries.

"Once you have found an entry that interests you, write the name and the date of the magazine. Sometimes librarians provide special forms for this. It may also prove helpful to write the title of the article and the page numbers upon which that article appears. Take this information to the librarian and ask the librarian to find the magazine for you. Your article should be on the page indicated in the entry in the *Readers' Guide*."

ISLANDS—*cont.*

Puerto Rico

See also
Culebra Island (Puerto Rico)
ISLE AU HAUT (ME.: ISLAND)
Description and travel
See also
Hiking—Isle au Haut (Me.: Island)
ISLES, JOHN
Big Dipper variables. il *Sky and Telescope* v95 no6 p98-100 Je '98
ISO *See* Infrared Space Observatory
ISOMERASES
See also
Topoisomerases
ISOMERIZATION
See also
Photoisomerization
ISOMERS
See also
Enantiomers
ISOTOPES
See also
Helium—Isotopes
Osmium—Isotopes
Oxygen—Isotopes
Plutonium—Isotopes
Xenon—Isotopes
ISRAEL, ELLEN
about
Living with antiques: the New York apartment of Kentshire Galleries' Robert and Ellen Israel. M. Peppiatt. il pors *Architectural Digest* v55 no8 p118-23 Ag '98
ISRAEL, ROBERT
about
Living with antiques: the New York apartment of Kentshire Galleries' Robert and Ellen Israel. M. Peppiatt. il pors *Architectural Digest* v55 no8 p118-23 Ag '98
ISRAEL
See also
Economic assistance, American—Israel
Jews—Israel
Kibbutzim
Red Sea
Russians—Israel
Tennis—Israel
Anniversaries
The story of a success story: Israel's jubilee [cover story] E. Salpeter. il *The New Leader* v81 no6 p3-6 My 4-18 '98
Waiting for the teacher. A. Miller. il *Harper's* v297 no1778 p56-7 Jl '98
Antiquities
See also
Archeology—Israel
Bronze Age—Israel
Hazor (Ancient city)
Stele (Archeology)—Israel
Stone Age—Israel
Tel Dan site (Israel)
It's a very nice rock, but is it art? [lava fragment found in Israel could be man's first work of art] B. Pappas. il *Forbes* v162 no3 p39 Ag 10 '98
Armed Forces
Forces in Lebanon
See also
Lebanon—Israeli invasions, 1982-
Defenses
See also
Nuclear weapons—Israel
Foreign opinion
American
America's press: the Israeli bias. R. Fisk. *World Press Review* v45 no9 p48 S '98
How evangelicals became Israel's best friend [influence of dispensationalism; cover story] T. P. Weber. il *Christianity Today* v42 no11 p38-49 O 5 '98
Israel is special in U.S. eyes. *Society* v35 no5 p3-4 Jl/Ag '98
Foreign relations
Arab countries
See Jewish-Arab relations
Egypt—History
See also
Israel-Arab Wars, 1967-
Iraq
UNSCOMscam [M. Albright's involvement in U.S. squelching of UN weapons inspections of Iraqi sites and the implications for Israel] M. Peretz. *The New Republic* v219 no10 p12-14 S 7 '98
Lebanon
See also
Lebanon—Israeli invasions, 1982-
United States
American powerlessness? W. F. Buckley. *National Review* v50 no11 p67 Je 22 '98
How Israel calls the tune. M. Rodenbeck. *World Press Review* v45 no9 p11-12 S '98
Mideast burnout. P. W. Rodman. il *National Review* v50 no14 p22+ Ag 3 '98

United States—History
Israel and the United States [discussion of May 1998 article] N. Podhoretz. *Commentary* v106 no2 p5-8+ Ag '98
History
See also
Zionism
The man in the middle [efforts of R. J. Bunche] B. A. Weisberger. il por *American Heritage* v49 no3 p16+ My/Je '98
Remembering Golda on the centennial of her birth. L. C. Pogrebin. il pors *Ms.* v8 no6 p42-7 My/Je '98
The story of a success story: Israel's jubilee [cover story] E. Salpeter. il *The New Leader* v81 no6 p3-6 My 4-18 '98
Zion's justice [role of Supreme Court justices L. Brandeis and F. Frankfurter in the creation of Israel] S. G. Breyer. *The New Republic* v219 no14 p18-19 O 5 '98
Industries
See also
Check Point Software Technologies, Ltd.
Tourist trade—Israel
Politics and government
See also
Conservatism—Israel
Likud Party (Israel)
Political attitudes—Israel
The Bibi enigma. S. Nolen. il por *Maclean's* v111 no20 p24-5 My 18 '98
Religious institutions and affairs
See also
Millennialism—Israel
Territorial expansion
See also
Israel-Arab Wars, 1967- —Territorial questions
ISRAEL AND THE UNITED STATES
See also
Israel—Foreign opinion—American
ISRAEL-ARAB RELATIONS *See* Jewish-Arab relations
ISRAEL-ARAB WAR, 1948-1949
Diplomatic history
The man in the middle [efforts of R. J. Bunche] B. A. Weisberger. il por *American Heritage* v49 no3 p16+ My/Je '98
ISRAEL-ARAB WARS, 1967-
Occupied territories
See Israel-Arab Wars, 1967- —Territorial questions
Peace and mediation
See also
Israel-Arab Wars, 1967- —Territorial questions
Middle East peace conferences, 1991-
Reporters and reporting
America's press: the Israeli bias. R. Fisk. *World Press Review* v45 no9 p48 S '98
Robert Fisk [Middle East correspondent for the London Independent; interview] M. Rothschild. il por *The Progressive* v62 no7 p36-41 Jl '98
Territorial questions
See also
Gaza Strip
Middle East peace conferences, 1991-
Division and conflict in Israel: a Jewish-Christian exchange. Y. Landau and T. Getman. *The Christian Century* v115 no23 p786-8 Ag 26-S 2 '98
How evangelicals became Israel's best friend [influence of dispensationalism; cover story] T. P. Weber. il *Christianity Today* v42 no11 p38-49 O 5 '98
Israel needs a Palestinian state. S. Peres. il *World Press Review* v45 no7 p47 Jl '98
New nuances [U.S. stand on a Palestinian state] R. Satloff. *The New Republic* v219 no2 p15-16 Jl 13 '98
UNSCOMscam [M. Albright's involvement in U.S. squelching of UN weapons inspections of Iraqi sites and the implications for Israel] M. Peretz. *The New Republic* v219 no10 p12-14 S 7 '98
ISRAELI TENNIS PLAYERS *See* Tennis players
ISSUES IN SCIENCE AND TECHNOLOGY (PERIODICAL)
Something old, something new [Issues in science and technology online] K. Finneran. *Issues in Science and Technology* v14 no4 p33-4 Summ '98
ISSYK-KUL (KYRGYZSTAN: LAKE)
See also
Water pollution—Issyk-Kul (Kyrgyzstan: Lake)
ISTANBUL (TURKEY)
Description and travel
Little black book: Istanbul. il *Gourmet* v58 no3 p76 Mr '98
ISTOOK, ERNEST JIM, 1950-
about
Mischief in Congress, California. E. Doerr. il *The Humanist* v58 no3 p33-4 My/Je '98
IT *See* Interval training
ITALIAN COOKING *See* Cooking, Italian
ITALIAN GRAND PRIX *See* Automobile racing—Italy
ITALIAN PAINTING *See* Painting, Italian
ITALY
See also
Americans—Italy
Automobile racing—Italy
Aviation and state—Italy
Business ethics—Italy
Cividale del Friuli (Italy)

L78P Some libraries handle *Readers' Guides* for very specific fields of study such as medicine and business in addition to the *Readers' Guide* for periodicals. Ask your librarian about these.

L78 *"Skipping one baseline below your last sentence, starting comfortably close to the margin, write the following sentences on consecutive baselines:*

> **'The <u>Readers' Guide to Periodical Literature</u> is an index of magazine articles.'**

> **'Each entry contains the title, the author's name, the magazine, the volume number, the page numbers, the date, and listings of illustrations, maps, or photos.'"**

Let's Get Organized

L56   **Step 7 —** *"Turn to the Table of Contents. On the page 66 line, write the title **'Library Skills (continued)'**. Turn back to page 66. Centered on the title line, between the two red margin lines, write the **same title.**"*

Expectancies Learned or Reinforced in Lesson 39: Dialogue and Review

1. What is the name of a book called? **L34** *(The name of the book is called the title.)*

2. What is on the title page of a book? **L34** *(The title page gives the name of the book, the author and the publisher.)*

3. What is the Table of Contents? **L34** *(The Table of Contents in the front of the book tells us what is in the book and what page it is on.)*

4. What is a glossary? **L34** *(The glossary is a list of difficult words with definitions to help us understand the book.)*

5. What is the index? **L34** *(The index in the back of the book is an alphabetical list of all subjects covered in the book.)*

6. How are words written in a dictionary? **L34** *(Words in a dictionary are written in alphabetical order.)*

7. What are guide words? **L34** *(The two words on the top of a dictionary page are called "guide words". They tell us if the word we are looking for is on that page.)*

8. What can we learn about a word in the dictionary? **L34** *(The dictionary gives the definition, the pronunciation, the syllables, the parts of speech, the etymology, and a sample sentence using the word.)*

9. What are some special features of a dictionary? **L56**
(Dictionaries may have a Biographical Names section, a Geographical Names section, and an Atlas section.)

10. What do encyclopedias do? **L34** *(Encyclopedias arrange topics alphabetically, use guide words like a dictionary, have pictures, diagrams, and illustrations, have a research guide to look for more information, and provide a list of related topics.)*

11. What is a card catalog? **L56** *(The card catalog is a tool to help us find books. There are three different kinds of cards; the title card, the author card, and the subject card.)*

12. How are books of fiction arranged in a library? **L56** *(Books of fiction are arranged alphabetically according to the author's last name.)*

13. How are nonfiction books arranged in the library? **L56** *(Nonfiction books are arranged using a numbering system.)*

14. What are other references used in the library? **L56** *(Almanacs, atlases, newspapers, magazines, and biographical materials can also be found in a library.)*

15. What is the *Readers' Guide to Periodical Literature?* **L78** *(The* Readers' Guide to Periodical Literature *is an index of magazine articles.)*

16. What does each magazine entry in this index contain? **L78** *(Each magazine entry contains the title, the author's name, the magazine, the volume number, the page numbers, the date, and listings of illustrations, maps, or photos for that particular article.)*

Where Do I Go from Here?

- **L12** goes to **L12 "Scope and Sequence"** Step 7.

- **L34** goes to **L34 "Scope and Sequence"** Step 10.

- **L56** goes to **"Lesson 43"** on page 428.

- **L78** goes to **"Lesson 40"** on page 404.

What Materials Will I Need?

- **L56** and **L78** will need *Grammar Notebooks* and pencils. **L78** will also need blank envelopes.

What Is a Friendly Letter? | 67

July 29, 1997

Dear Mom,

How are you? I am fine. Camp is fun. Please send money.

I miss you. I wish you were here. See you soon.

Love,
Johnny

A friendly letter has five sections: a heading, a salutation, a body, a closing, and a signature.

The first word of every section, of every sentence, and all proper nouns are capitalized.

A comma is placed between the day of the month and the year, after the salutation, and after the closing.

Every new paragraph is indented five spaces.

Sample Page 67
Lesson 40

68 | Writing Thank You Notes and Invitations

May 3, 1995

Dear Korey,

Thank you for going to Trout Lake Camp with me. I really had a good time. I hope you did too. I enjoyed swimming during those hot days. I found out that I forgot my swimming suit on the clothesline outside our cabin. We called lost and found, but it was not there. Thank you for being my friend. I hope we can go to camp again next year.

Your friend,
Jared

The thank you note is just like the friendly letter.

The invitation is just like the friendly letter. The invitation includes who is doing the inviting, what the occasion is, when it is, and where it will be held.

Sample Page 68
Lesson 40

How Do I Address an Envelope? | 69

Student's Name
Address
City, State Zip Code
    Name of Person
    House Address
    City, State Zip Code

Student's Name
Address
City, State Zip Code
    Thanked Person
    Person's Street Address
    City, State Zip Code

Student's Name
Address
City, State Zip Code
    Invited Person
    Person's Street Address
    City, State Zip Code

Sample Page 69
Lesson 40

70 | How Do I Write a Business Letter?

Linden Park Resort
RR 2
Henning, MN 56551

July 4, 1997

Dr. Roger Beals
603 Douglas Ave.
Montevideo, MN 56265

Dear Dr. Beals:

I am on vacation, and I have misplaced my glasses. Please send me a new pair as soon as possible.

Sincerely yours,
Elmer E. Neumann

A business letter uses an inside address. Business letters use formal closings and a colon after the salutation.

Sample Page 70
Lesson 40

Lesson 40

Developing Letter Writing Skills

L34 "Letter writing is a very important skill to learn. A letter is a written form of communication. It is like talking to someone on paper or using e-mail instead of actually speaking to them in person. We often communicate or talk to someone in this manner when the other person is a distance away from us or anytime we are not able to speak to someone in person.

"E-mail is an immediate form of communication. It requires the use of a computer, internet access, and the proper e-mail address. Like letters on paper, e-mail letters can take several forms. A quick note to a close friend may be written in an extremely informal manner, but a more formal situation or business letter by e-mail should be written in the same form as a letter on paper. Letters on paper are also used in cases where there is a need for a permanent written record of what is being communicated. This lesson deals with learning the proper way to write a letter on paper.

"To write a letter, we will need paper, an envelope, some type of writing instrument, an address of the person to whom we are writing, and a stamp."

Discovering the Sections of a Letter

L34 **Step 1** — "There are several different types of letters. Some letters have more sections than others, but all letters have at least the following five sections:

1. **'Heading:** The simplest heading includes the month, the date, and the year written in numerals.

2. **'Salutation:** This is the greeting to the person to whom you are writing the letter. We usually use the word "Dear" together with the name of the person and then we follow that with a comma.

3. **'Body:** This is the main part of the letter where the information about which you are writing is contained. You might have one paragraph or many paragraphs.

4. **'Closing:** This is the "good-bye" of the letter. Sometimes we use the words "Sincerely yours" or just "Sincerely" with a

comma following. We can use almost anything appropriate including the closing, "Your friend".

5. **'Signature:** The signature is the name of the person who is writing the letter.'"

Discovering and Dictating the Friendly Letter

.34 **Step 2** — "There are two categories of letters: business letters and friendly letters. Business letter form is generally used for letters to and from officials and companies. The heading includes the address of the company. Friendly letters might take the form of a 'newsy' letter to friends, an invitation, or a thank you note. Let's begin our writing by learning the form of a friendly letter."

.34P **L34** students need to be given a piece of loose-leaf penmanship paper. **L56** and above need to turn to page 67 in the *Grammar Notebook*. If **L56** and above have done this lesson in previous years, they can begin writing their own friendly letter without going through the following steps. Help students fold their page into three equal columns and then make sure all the sections of the letter are included. This letter writing lesson will need to be spread out over several class periods.

.34 **Step 3** — "We are going to write a friendly letter. *Let's begin by folding our page into three equal, lengthwise columns.*"

.34 **Step 4** — "First we will write the heading which, in a friendly letter, is the date our letter is being written. *Skipping one baseline below the title line, starting in the third column, comfortably close to the folded margin line, write the **name of the month with a capital letter**. Skip a space and write the **day in numerals**. Follow the day with a **comma**. Skip one more space and then write **the year in numerals**. Say with me, 'The heading is the date the letter was written'.*"

.34 **Step 5** — "Next we will write the salutation which is the part of our letter where we greet the person to whom the letter is being written. *Starting on the next available baseline in the first column, comfortably close to the left margin line, write the greeting **'Dear Mom,'** beginning both words with a capital letter followed by a comma. Say with me, 'The salutation is the greeting'.*"

.34 **Step 6** — "*For the body of the letter, we will be starting on the baseline directly below the salutation. Indenting five spaces from the left margin line, starting each sentence with a capital letter and ending each with proper end punctuation, write the following sentences:* **'How are you?' 'I am fine.' 'Camp is fun.'**

©1998 Grammar Works/Holly Hall Publications, Inc.

Sample Page 67 (sidebar)

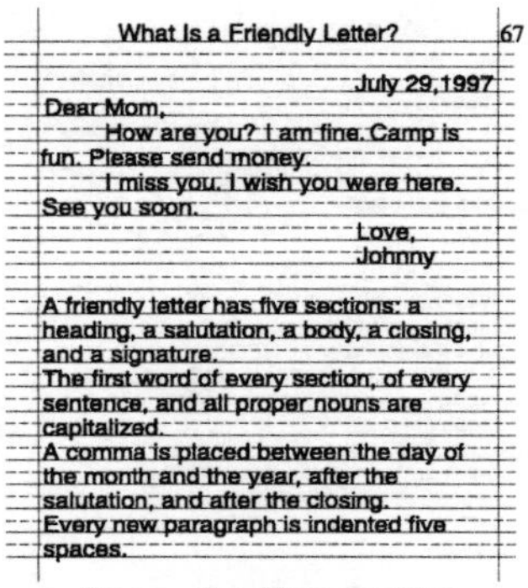

> What Is a Friendly Letter?   67
>
>   July 29, 1997
> Dear Mom,
>   How are you? I am fine. Camp is
> fun. Please send money.
>   I miss you. I wish you were here.
> See you soon.
>   Love,
>   Johnny
>
> A friendly letter has five sections: a
> heading, a salutation, a body, a closing,
> and a signature.
> The first word of every section, of every
> sentence, and all proper nouns are
> capitalized.
> A comma is placed between the day of
> the month and the year, after the
> salutation, and after the closing.
> Every new paragraph is indented five
> spaces.

Sample Page 67
Lesson 40

```
                            July 29,1997
Dear Mom,
        How are you? I am fine. Camp is
fun. Please send money.
        I miss you. I wish you were here.
See you soon.
                                Love,
                                Johnny

A friendly letter has five sections: a
heading, a salutation, a body, a closing,
and a signature.
The first word of every section, of every
sentence, and all proper nouns are
capitalized.
A comma is placed between the day of
the month and the year, after the
salutation, and after the closing.
Every new paragraph is indented five
spaces.
```

Sample Page 67

Lesson 40

'Please send money.' Starting on the baseline directly below your last sentence, indenting five spaces from the left margin line, write the following sentences: *'I miss you'. 'I wish you were here'. 'See you soon'.* Say with me, *'The body is the content of the letter'.*"

L34 **Step 7** — "Next we will write the closing. *Starting on the next available baseline in the third column, comfortably close to the folded margin line, write the word* **'Love,'** *with a capital letter and follow it with a* **comma.** *Say with me,* 'The closing is saying good-bye'.*"

L34 **Step 8** — "The last thing we write in our friendly letter will be the signature which is simply signing our name. *Starting in the third column, on the baseline directly under the word 'Love', comfortably close to the folded margin line, write* **your own name** *starting with a capital letter. Say with me,* 'The signature is the name of the person writing the letter'.*"

Discovering the Rules of Capitalization and Punctuation for Writing a Friendly Letter

L56 **Step 9** — "Let's look at our letter to see what capitalization and punctuation rules govern the writing of letters. Notice that we capitalized the first word of every section, every sentence, and, of course, any proper nouns. We placed commas between the numerals telling the day of the month and the year, after the salutation, and after the closing. We indented every new paragraph five spaces.

"*Skipping one baseline below your name, starting comfortably close to the left margin line, write the following sentences on consecutive baselines:*

> *'A friendly letter has five sections: a heading, a salutation, a body, a closing, and a signature.'*

> *'The first word of every section, of every sentence, and all proper nouns are capitalized.'*

> *'A comma is placed between the day of the month and the year, after the salutation, and after the closing.'*

> *'Every new paragraph is indented five spaces.'*"

Let's Get Organized

L56 **Step 10** — *"Turn to the Table of Contents. On the page 67 line, write the title* **'What Is a Friendly Letter?'** *Turn back to page 67. Centered on the title line, between the two red margin lines, write the* **same title.**"

Practicing a Friendly Letter

L34P As an assignment, have your students write a real letter to a friend. After we learn how to address an envelope later in this lesson, we will be able to send this letter.

Discovering the Nature of a Thank You Note

L34 **Step 1** — "The thank you note is written in exactly the same form as the friendly letter. The only difference is found in the body of the letter. Instead of writing 'newsy' information in the body as we did in the friendly letter, the body section of the thank you note is a message of thanks for gifts or for something someone has done for you."

L34P **L34** students need another piece of loose-leaf penmanship paper. **L56** students and above need to turn to page 68 in their *Grammar Notebook*. If **L56** and above have done this lesson in previous years, they can begin writing their own thank you note without going through the following steps. Have them fold their page into three equal columns and then make sure all the sections of the letter are included.

Dictating a Thank You Note

L34 *"Fold your paper once again into three equal, lengthwise columns. I am going to dictate a thank you note to you."*

L34 **Step 2** — "The heading for this thank you note is **'May 3, 1995'**. Where do we put it?"

> STUDENTS: *"We skip one baseline below the title line and write the date in the third column, comfortably close to the margin line."*

L34 **Step 3** — "The salutation **'Dear Korey,'** comes next. Where do we write this and how do we write it?"

> STUDENTS: *"On the next available baseline in the first column, comfortably close to the margin line, we write and capitalize the word **'Dear'** and the personal name **'Korey,'** and then place a **comma** after the word 'Korey'."*

> TEACHER: *"Please write **the salutation**."*

L34 **Step 4** — "The body begins with the sentence, 'Thank you for going to Trout Lake Camp with me.' Where do we begin the body of this letter?"

> STUDENTS: *"On the next available baseline, we indent five spaces and start a new paragraph."*

May 3, 1995

Dear Korey,

Thank you for going to Trout Lake Camp with me. I really had a good time. I hope you did too. I enjoyed swimming during those hot days. I found out that I forgot my swimming suit on the clothesline outside our cabin. We called lost and found, but it was not there. Thank you for being my friend. I hope we can go to camp again next year.

Your friend,
Jared

The thank you note is just like the friendly letter.
The invitation is just like the friendly letter. The invitation includes who is doing the inviting, what the occasion is, when it is, and where it will be held.

Sample Page 68
Lesson 40

May 3, 1995

Dear Korey,

Thank you for going to Trout Lake Camp with me. I really had a good time. I hope you did too. I enjoyed swimming during those hot days. I found out that I forgot my swimming suit on the clothesline outside our cabin. We called lost and found, but it was not there. Thank you for being my friend. I hope we can go to camp again next year.

Your friend,
Jared

The thank you note is just like the friendly letter.
The invitation is just like the friendly letter.
The invitation includes who is doing the inviting, what the occasion is, when it is, and where it will be held.

Sample Page 68
Lesson 40

TEACHER: *"Will you please write the sentence, 'Thank you for going to Trout Lake Camp with me'?"*

L34 Step 5 — "Please place these remaining sentences of the body of this thank you note directly after the first sentence. I will dictate them for you. Use as many lines as you need. *'I really had a good time. I hope you did too. I enjoyed swimming during those hot days. I found out that I forgot my swimming suit on the clothesline outside our cabin. We called lost and found, but it was not there. Thank you for being my friend. I hope we can go to camp again next year.'"*

L34 Step 6 — "The closing is 'Your friend'. We capitalize the first word but not the second word. Where do we put this closing?"

STUDENTS: *"On the next available baseline, in the third column, comfortably close to the folded margin line, we write 'Your friend,' with a capital letter on the first word and a comma following."*

TEACHER: "Right. *Will you please write the closing.*"

L34 Step 7 — "Every letter needs a signature. Where does the name 'Jared' go in this letter?"

STUDENTS: *"We place the name 'Jared' as the signature directly below the closing."*

TEACHER: *"Will you please write the name 'Jared' after the closing."*

L56 Step 8 — *"Skipping one baseline below the signature, starting comfortably close to the margin line, write the following: 'The thank you note is just like the friendly letter'."*

L34P Have your students write a real thank you note to someone who is in need of a thank you.

Discovering the Nature of an Invitation

L34 Step 9 — "An invitation is also written in the same form as the friendly letter. Once again, the only difference is what information we have written in the body of the letter. This time the body must contain very specific information. It must answer the following questions: 'Who is doing the inviting?' 'What is the event or occasion to which they are doing the inviting?' 'When is the event taking place?' 'Where will the event be held?'"

L56 *"Skipping one baseline below the sentence 'The thank you note is just like the friendly letter', write the following on consecutive baselines: 'The invitation is just like the friendly letter.' 'The invitation includes who is doing the inviting, what the occasion is, when it is, and where it will be held'."*

Let's Get Organized

.56 **Step 10 —** *"Turn to the Table of Contents. On page 68 line, write the title **'Writing Thank You Notes and Invitations'**. Turn back to page 68.*

.34 *"Centered on the title line, between the two red margin lines, write the title **'Writing Thank You Notes and Invitations'**.*"

Practicing the Writing of an Invitation

.34P Plan an occasion to which your students can invite someone they know. It could be as simple as inviting Grandma for cookies and milk, or it could be a birthday party or an open house to show what your students have been working on in school. Have students write an invitation to this event and then host the event.

Introducing the Term Acronym

.34 **Step 1 —** "We need to introduce the word **'acronym'** at this point. By definition an acronym is 'a word formed from the initial letters or groups of letters of words in a set phrase . . .'

"Sometimes we will receive an invitation on which you will see the letters RSVP. This is an acronym. An acronym is formed from the beginning letters of a number of different words used to represent entire words or phrases. The following are some examples:

> 'Parent Teacher Association becomes PTA'

> 'United States of America becomes USA'

> 'National Broadcasting Company becomes NBC'

"The French phrase, *'répondez, s'il vous plaît'*, meaning 'please respond', becomes RSVP. This is the polite and generally accepted way of asking you to kindly respond to the invitation so that the person who invited you knows ahead of time whether or not you plan to come. It is polite and proper for you to either call or write a short note to say 'Thank you for the invitation; we would love to come' or 'Thank you for the invitation; I'm very sorry that we will not be able to attend'."

Discovering the World of Acronyms

.34 **Step 2 —** "Acronyms are a very handy and acceptable method of making our language more efficient. Using too many of them in one place can become very confusing."

.34P You may want to duplicate the following acronym "sign" for your students on paper or on the board. It is purposely goofy.

---

68 | Writing Thank You Notes and Invitations

May 3, 1995

Dear Korey,

Thank you for going to Trout Lake Camp with me. I really had a good time. I hope you did too. I enjoyed swimming during those hot days. I found out that I forgot my swimming suit on the clothesline outside our cabin. We called lost and found, but it was not there. Thank you for being my friend. I hope we can go to camp again next year.

Your friend,
Jared

The thank you note is just like the friendly letter.
The invitation is just like the friendly letter. The invitation includes who is doing the inviting, what the occasion is, when it is, and where it will be held.

Sample Page 68
Lesson 40

"What if a sign in a community near you had the following acronyms?"

U	ASCS
S	SCS
D	WOTSWCD
A	

"You can see how confusing things can get if we are not familiar with these particular acronyms. Computer acronyms are the same way. Familiarity with these acronyms, of course, makes the difference. There are times when it would be better for the sake of an uninformed audience to use entire words even if it means using more space. We will discuss more about acronyms later. The acronyms on this sign mean the following:

'USDA is United States Department of Agriculture'

'ASCS is Agricultural Stabilization and Conservation Service'

'SCS is Soil Conservation Service'

'WOTSWCD is West Ottertail Soil and Water Conservation District'"

Discovering How to Address an Envelope

L34P L34 need to be given a piece of loose-leaf penmanship paper. **L56** and above need to turn to page 69 in their *Notebook*.

L34 Step 1 — "Now that we know how to write a letter, we must get the letter to the person to whom it is written. We need to learn how to address an envelope.

"We are going to divide our page into three equal sections. Counting the title line as number one, count down eight baselines. Darken the next available dotted line with a pencil all the way across the page. Continue to count down from line number eight to line number fifteen. Darken the next available dotted line with your pencil. We have created three sections about the same size as an envelope. We will use these three sections for writing addresses before we write on real envelopes. Let's practice by using the names and addresses of the people to whom we wrote our friendly letter, thank-you note, and invitation."

L34 Step 2 — *"Counting down six baselines from the title line, centering the name between the two red margin lines, and starting with a capital letter, write* **'Name of Person'**. This is where we would put your mother's name if you were going to write a letter to your mom."

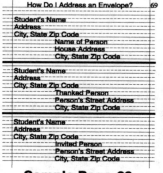

Sample Page 69
Lesson 40

34 **Step 3** — *"Starting on the baseline directly below the name, directly under the first letter of the name, capitalizing any proper nouns, write* **'House Address'.** This is where we would put the street address or rural route and box number of the person to whom we are sending the letter."

34 **Step 4** — *"Starting on the baseline directly under the first letter number of the street address, capitalizing any proper nouns, write the word* **'City,'** *followed by a* **comma.** *On the same line after the comma, write* **'State'** *followed by the word* **'Zip'.** There is no comma between the state and the zip code. This is where we would put the name of the city, the state, and the zip code of the person to whom we are writing the letter.

"All state abbreviations used with a zip code are two letter abbreviations that are capitalized without any punctuation mark following them:

> Minnesota = MN
> California = CA
> New York = NY, and so on.

"The zip code is a set of numbers that appears after the abbreviation of the state in an address. It is a number our postal system has assigned to a certain region's post office to help postal workers sort letters and get them to the proper place."

Writing the Return Address

34 **Step 5** — *"Skipping one baseline below the title line, comfortably close to the left edge of the envelope, write* **your own name.**

Step 6 — *"Starting on the baseline directly below your name, comfortably close to the left edge of the envelope, write* **your own street address or rural route and box number."**

Step 7 — *"Starting on the baseline directly below your street address, comfortably close to the left edge of the envelope, write the name of* **your city followed by a comma.** *On the same line after the comma, write the name of* **your state using two capital letters** *and then write* **your zip code."**

L34 **Step 8** — "Let's look at what we have written. The address that is centered on our envelope is the person's address to whom we intend to send the letter. The address in the upper left-hand corner is the **return address.** The return address is the address of the person who is sending the letter. We include a return address so the post office knows where to return the letter in case, for some reason, it cannot be delivered to the person to whom it is addressed."

Sample Page 69
Lesson 40

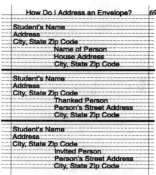

Sample Page 69
Lesson 40

L34P Have students practice writing the mailing addresses and return addresses for the thank you note and the invitation they have written on the upper two sections of their practice page.

Repeat the same steps for the **"Thanked Person"** envelope and the **"Invited Person"** envelope that were used to create the first model envelope. Use the Sample Pages as your guide.

When the time is right, the next step is to hand out real envelopes. Have students address the envelopes in the same manner. Tell them to imagine that there are dotted lines. Take the letters they have written in these exercises and prepare them for mailing.

Let's Get Organized

L56   **Step 9** — *"Turn to the Table of Contents. On the page 69 line, write the title 'How Do I Address an Envelope?' Turn back to page 69.*

L34   *"Centered on the title line, between the two red margin lines, write the title 'How Do I Address an Envelope?'"*

Discovering the Nature of a Business Letter

L34P **L34** will again use a piece of practice penmanship paper. **L56** and above will turn to page 70 in their *Grammar Notebook.*

L34   **Step 1** — "The business letter form is similar to that of the friendly letter. Each letter, however, has a different purpose. The friendly letter usually goes to someone we know. A business letter is written to someone with whom we have a business relationship.

"Business letters can be written in a block style where all sections of the letter start on the left margin. They can also place the heading, the closing and the signature to the right side of the paper. We will use the block style in this lesson.

"A business letter often requests information from a company or organization, orders a book or a product, or gives information that you have requested.

"A business letter has six parts. It contains the same five sections of the friendly letter but also has a new section called an **'inside address'**. The inside address is the address of the business that will be receiving the letter."

Sample Page 70
Lesson 40

L34   **Step 2** — "Skipping on the first available baseline below the title line, comfortably close to the left margin line, write **'Linden Park Resort'**. This is where you would start placing your complete mailing address in a business letter so the person responding to your letter can write you back. Remember to capitalize key words and proper nouns.

"On the baseline directly below 'Linden Park Resort', write **'R.R. 2'.** The letters 'R.R.' are an acronym for 'Rural Route'.

"On the baseline directly below the mailing address, write **'Henning, MN 56551'.**

"Skipping one baseline below the city, state, and zip code, comfortably close to the left margin line, write the date **'July 4, 1997'.** Including the date is important in a business letter so we know if the business concern has been handled promptly."

L34 **Step 3** — "Skipping one baseline, comfortably close to the left margin line, write the following mailing address, or 'inside address', on consecutive baselines:

> **'Dr. Roger Beals**
> **603 Douglas Ave.**
> **Montevideo, MN 56265'"**

L34 **Step 4** — *"Skipping one baseline below the city, state, and zip code, comfortably close to the left margin line, write the salutation,* **'Dear Dr. Beals:'** *followed by a* **colon** which looks like this. Every business letter uses a colon after the salutation."

L34P Demonstrate what a colon looks like. We will look at colons again in a later lesson.

L34 **Step 5** — "Now we can write the body of the letter. *On the next available baseline under the salutation, write the following sentences. Use as many lines as you need to. Remember to indent the first line five spaces.* It is a new paragarph.

> **'I am on vacation, and I have misplaced my glasses. Please send me a new pair as soon as possible.'"**

L34 **Step 6** — *"When you have finished writing the body, skipping one baseline under the last sentence of your letter, comfortably close to the left margin line, write the closing* **'Sincerely yours,'** *being sure to place a* **comma** *after it. On the next available baseline, below the closing, write the signature* **'Elmer E. Neumann'.** In a business letter we use a more formal closing than we might use in a friendly letter."

L56 **Step 7** — *"Skipping one baseline below the signature, comfortably close to the margin line, write the following sentences on consecutive baselines:*

> **'A business letter uses an inside address.'**

> **'Business letters use formal closings and a colon after the salutation.'**

Lesson 40: Developing Letter Writing Skills **413**

70 | How Do I Write a Business Letter?
Linden Park Resort
RR 2
Henning, MN 56551

July 4, 1997

Dr. Roger Beals
603 Douglas Ave.
Montevideo, MN 56265

Dear Dr. Beals:
   I am on vacation, and I have misplaced my glasses. Please send me a new pair as soon as possible.

Sincerely yours,
Elmer E. Neumann

A business letter uses an inside address. Business letters use formal closings and a colon after the salutation.

Sample Page 70
Lesson 40

70 How Do I Write a Business Letter?
Linden Park Resort
RR 2
Henning, MN 56551

July 4, 1997

Dr. Roger Beals
603 Douglas Ave.
Montevideo, MN 56265

Dear Dr. Beals:
    I am on vacation, and I have misplaced
my glasses. Please send me a new pair
as soon as possible.

Sincerely yours,
Elmer E. Neumann

A business letter uses an inside address.
Business letters use formal closings and
a colon after the salutation.

Sample Page 70
Lesson 40

Let's Get Organized

L56 **Step 9** — *"Turn to the Table of Contents. On the page 70 line, write the title 'How Do I Write a Business Letter?' Turn back to page 70."*

L34 *"Centered on the title line, between the two red margin lines, write the title: 'How Do I Write a Business Letter?'"*

Expectancies Learned or Reinforced in Lesson 40: Dialogue and Review

1. What are the five sections of a friendly letter? **L34** *(A friendly letter has a heading, a salutation, a body, a closing, and a signature.)*

2. What is the heading of a friendly letter? **L34** *(The heading is the date the letter was written.)*

3. What is the salutation of a friendly letter? **L34** *(The salutation is the greeting. It usually uses the word "Dear" with the name of the person who is getting the letter.)*

4. What is the body of a friendly letter? **L34** *(The body is the content of the letter.)*

5. What is the closing of a friendly letter? **L34** *(The closing of a friendly letter is saying good-bye.)*

6. What is the signature of a friendly letter? **L34** *(The signature of a friendly letter is the name of the person writing the letter.)*

7. What words need to be capitalized in a friendly letter? **L34** *(The first word of every section, of every sentence, and all proper nouns need to be capitalized.)*

8. Where do we put commas in a friendly letter? **L34** *(A comma is placed between the day of the month and the year, after the salutation, and after the closing in a friendly letter.)*

9. What do we do with every new paragraph? **L34** *(Every new paragraph is indented five spaces.)*

10. What is a thank you note? **L34** *(A thank you note is just like a friendly letter in structure. It is sent to tell someone how much you appreciated something they did for you.)*

11. What is an invitation? **L34** *(An invitation is just like a friendly letter in structure. It is sent to invite someone to participate in a planned activity.)*

12. What is in an invitation? **L34** *(The invitation includes who is doing the inviting, what the occasion is, when it is, and where it will be held.)*

13. What is an acronym? **L34** *(By definition an acronym is "A word formed from the initial letters or groups of letters of words in a set phrase.")*

14. What is a business letter? **L34** *(A business letter is a letter between two parties that have a common business interest.)*

15. What are the differences between a business letter and a friendly letter, a thank you note, and an invitation? **L34** *(A business letter uses formal closings and a colon after the salutation. A business letter also uses an inside address. The other letters use informal closings, have a comma after the salutation, and lack an inside address.)*

Where Do I Go from Here?

- **L34** goes to **"Lesson 6"** on page 114.

- **L56** goes to **L56** **"Scope and Sequence"** Step 12.

- **L78** goes to **"Lesson 41"** on page 416.

What Materials Will I Need?

- **L34** will need penmanship paper and pencils.

- **L78** will need *Grammar Notebooks* and pencils.

Lesson 41
Writing a Book Report

L12 "Let's discover the wonderful world of books. Books are so special. After we have learned to read, books can take us on adventures. We can learn about people and places. We can learn how to do things. We can read mystery stories.

"Some books tell us stories that are created by an author from his imagination. We call those stories 'fiction'. Some books are facts about real people and real events. These are called 'non-fiction'. We are going to learn about fiction books in this lesson.

"After we read our first story book, it helps to know all we can about that book. Books we read are often so exciting that we want to tell others about them. When we tell others about a book we have read, we are giving a book report.

"You might tell someone what the title of the book is. You could tell them who wrote the book. That would be the author. You could tell about the characters in the book and what they did. You could tell the story of the book. That is called the plot."

L12P Pick a fictional book that you have already read to the students. Ask the following questions about that book and show students where to look for that information:

"What is the name or title of the book?"

"Who is the author or the person who wrote the book?"

"Who are the main characters in the book?"

"What is the plot or what is the story about?"

If we will be consistent about doing this in the very first year that the student is reading, book reports will become more automatic and the transition from an oral report to a written one will be easier. As our students progress, questions will become more and more specific.

Understanding the Basic Tools of Excellent Fiction

L34P We want our students to understand the basic tools of a good fictional story. In order to do that we must introduce these. We will need to choose the best time to introduce this information to our students based upon their progress and ability to comprehend it and put it to use. Our students need to understand the following terms:

1. **Plot** *(What happens in the story? We call that the plot.)*

2. **Characters** *(Who are the main characters? Who are the good guys? We will call them the "protagonists". Who are the bad guys? We will call them the "antagonists".)*

3. **Conflict** *(What problem must the protagonist overcome? What does the protagonist want? What is stopping the protagonist from getting this?)*

4. **Consequences** *(What will happen if the problem is not solved?)*

5. **Suspense** *(Will the characters be okay? Is the story exciting? What unanswered questions are created? What exciting event is going to happen next?)*

6. **Setting** *(Where and when does the story take place?)*

7. **Dialogue** *(Are there conversations between characters?)*

8. **Theme** *(What message is the author trying to communicate? What lesson do we learn about life?)*

9. **Point of view** *(Who has the author chosen to tell the story? Is it one of the characters in the story? Is there a narrator telling the story?)*

10. **Resolution** *(What finally ends up happening in the story? Does the protaganist overcome his problem?)*

Defining the Parts of a Good Story | 71

1. The plot is what happens in the story.
2. The characters are who is in the story.
3. The protagonist is the good guy.
4. The antagonist is the bad guy.
5. Conflict is the problem the characters must overcome.
6. Consequences are what might happen if the problem is not solved.
7. Suspense is the excitement created by what might happen next.
8. Setting is where and when the story takes place.
9. Dialogue is the conversation between characters.
10. Theme is the author's message.
11. Point of view is who is telling the story.
12. Resolution is the conflict settled.

Conflict + Consequences = Suspense
Paying attention to details matters!

Sample Page 71
Lesson 41

Dictating the Tools of Good Fiction Writing

L34P L34 students need a piece of loose-leaf penmanship paper. **L56** and above need to turn to page 71 in their *Grammar Notebook*. Use the sample pages in the margin as a guide.

L34 **Step 1** — *"Skipping one baseline below the title line, comfortably close to the left margin line, write the following on consecutive baselines:*

> *'1. The plot is what happens in the story.'*

> *'2. The characters are who is in the story.'*

> *'3. The protagonist is the good guy.'*

> *'4. The antagonist is the bad guy.'*

> *'5. Conflict is the problem the characters must overcome.'*

> *'6. Consequences are what might happen if the problem is not solved.'*

'7. Suspense is the excitement created by what might happen next.'

'8. Setting is where and when the story takes place.'

'9. Dialogue is the conversation between characters.'

'10. Theme is the author's message about life.'

'11. Point of view is who is telling the story.'

'12. Resolution is the conflict settled.'"

L56 **Step 2** — "There is a special formula that every good story must have. When we write a story, we have to use this formula. Every good storyteller uses this formula. Every program on TV uses this formula. Every good book uses this formula.

"Skipping one line below our last sentence, write the following formula for a good story:

'Conflict + Consequences = Suspense'"

Discovering the Formula in "The Three Little Pigs"

L56 **Step 3** — "Every good story has characters that find themselves in a heap of trouble. Take the story of "The Three Little Pigs." Each little pig wants something. All three of them want to be safe, but only one can see the importance of building a strong house.

"The wolf at their door is a big problem. That is the **conflict**. Huffing and puffing makes the problem even bigger. The pigs want safety. The wolf wants bacon. What are the possible **consequences**? The wolf could either go to a pizza parlor or keep huffing and puffing until the house blows down. He chooses to keep huffing and puffing.

"Two houses fall down and what we feared would happen does happen. The first two pigs become breakfast for the big bad wolf.

"We can create fear by creating questions. Being fearful about the answers is called **"suspense"**. What will happen if the wolf keeps huffing and puffing? Will the house fall down? Will the little pigs survive? This kind of suspense is at work in every story. Suspense forces us to stay tuned to the next exciting episode.

"What finally ends up happening in the story is called the **"resolution"**. In this case, the third pig is safe because his house was secure.

"And what does the reader learn after finishing this story? That is the **theme**. We learn that the wolf might come to our door. If we aren't prepared for him, we could become his breakfast bacon. We learn that every brick is important. Each brick needs to be placed carefully and separately. We learn that working wisely is better than working hard, but foolishly. We learn that paying attention to details matters."

.34 **Step 4 —** *"On the next available baseline below our formula, comfortably close to the left margin line, write the following: 'Paying attention to details matters!'"*

Let's Get Organized

.56 **Step 5 —** *"Turn to the Table of Contents. On the page 71 line, write the title 'Defining the Parts of a Good Story'. Turn back to page 71."*

.34 *"Centered on the title line, between the two red margin lines, write the title: 'Defining the Parts of a Good Story'."*

Dictating a Book Report Resource Page

.56P **L56** and above need to turn to page 72 in their *Grammar Notebook*. Use the Sample Pages in the margin as a guide.

.56 **Step 1 —** "We are going to make a Book Report Resource Page. *Skipping one baseline below the title line, number from '1–20' on consecutive baselines to the left of the red margin line.* I am going to dictate some questions students should ask themselves when giving a book report. This page will be a resource for us when we need to prepare a report."

.56 **Step 2 —** *"Starting comfortably close to the left margin line on the line numbered one, write the following questions on consecutive baselines:*

> **'What is the title of my book?'**
>
> **'Why is the title a good one?'**
>
> **'Who is the author?'**
>
> **'What do I know about the author?'**
>
> **'What other books has the author written?'**
>
> **'What happened in the story?'**
>
> **'Who was my favorite character?'**
>
> **'Why did I like this character?'**
>
> **'Who was the antagonist?'**

Sample Page 71
Lesson 41

Sample Page 72
Lesson 41

Sample Page 72

Lesson 41

'What did these characters want?'

'What kinds of problems were there?'

'What did I fear might happen?'

'What were the most exciting moments?'

'Where did the story happen?'

'When did the story happen?'

'Who is telling the story?'

'Does the author use dialogue?'

'What did the book teach me?'

'Why should others read this book?'

'Is this book fact or fiction?'"

Let's Get Organized

L56 **Step 3** — *"Turn to the Table of Contents. On the page 72 line, write the title* **'Book Reports: Questions We Need to Ask'.** *Turn back to page 72. Centered between the two margin lines, write the* **same title."**

Expectancies Learned or Reinforced in Lesson 41: Dialogue and Review

1. What is a plot? **L34** *(A plot is what happens in the story. One event is linked to the next until a complete story is told.)*

2. What are characters? **L34** *(The characters are the people that are participating in the story.)*

3. What is a protagonist? **L34** *(The protagonist is the character who is generally the good guy.)*

4. What is an antagonist? **L34** *(The antagonist is the character who is generally the bad guy. Sometimes the bad guy can be a bad storm or a sickness or even a decision that needs to be made.)*

5. What is conflict? **L34** *(Conflict is a problem the protagonist must overcome. Conflict is created when the protagonist may not get what he wants or needs.)*

6. What are consequences? **L34** *(The consequences are what might happen if the problem is not solved.)*

7. What is suspense? **L34** *(Suspense is the excitement created about what might happen next.)*

8. What is the setting? **L34** *(The setting is where and when the story takes place.)*

9. What is the dialogue? **L34** *(The conversation between characters is called dialogue.)*

10. What is theme? **L34** *(Theme is the message or lesson the author is trying to communicate.)*

11. What is point of view? **L34** *(Point of view is who the author has chosen to tell the story. This person could be a character in the story. If it is one of the characters in the story, the author will use the pronoun "I". If a narrator tells the story, the author will use the pronouns "he" or "she" or "they".)*

12. What is the resolution? **L34** *(The resolution is what happens when the characters' problems are worked out.)*

13. What is the formula for a good story? **L34** *(The formula for a good story is Conflict + Consequences = Suspense.)*

14. What is one of the themes that "The Three Little Pigs" teaches us? **L34** *(One of the themes might be that attention to details really does matter.)*

Where Do I Go from Here?

- **L12** goes to **L12** "Scope and Sequence" Step 5.

- **L34** goes to **L34** "Scope and Sequence" Step 11.

- **L56** goes to "Lesson 15" on page 186.

- **L78** goes to "Lesson 42" on page 422.

What Materials Will I Need?

- **L56** will need *Grammar Notebooks,* pencils, red pencils, and copies of Worksheets.

- **L78** will need *Grammar Notebooks* and pencils.

- **Optional:** Teaching will be enhanced at **L56** by using adverb question "flags" as described in **"Lesson 15"**.on page 186.

How Do I Write a Paragraph?   73

I am thankful for my family. I am
thankful for my dad and mom. My dad
cheers me up when I'm sad. My mom
hugs me and listens to me when I have a
problem. My brother and sister play board
games with me when I am sick. I am
thankful for food and clothing and a warm
house. I am thankful that I can help with
chores around the house like lawn
mowing and vacuuming. I am thankful that
my family laughs together, plays together,
prays together, and works together.

A topic sentence is the first sentence in a
paragraph. It introduces what the
paragraph is about.
A paragraph is a group of sentences that
say something about the topic.

Sample Page 73
Lesson 42

74   What Is a Proofreading Checklist?

1. Have I read my paragraph out loud?
2. Does it read well?
3. Do all the sentences relate to my topic?
4. Are there words I can cross out?
5. Are there words I can add?
6. Are my words spelled correctly?
7. Are there sentences I can cross out to
   improve my paragraph?
8. Do I need to add more sentences?
9. Have I started every sentence with a
   capital letter?
10. Does every sentence have correct end
    punctuation?
11. Is my handwriting beautiful?
12. Have I shared my paragraph with
    someone?

A thesaurus is a valuable tool to help us
choose stronger words.

Sample Page 74
Lesson 42

Lesson 42

Phono-
sound or
speech

Writing Paragraphs

Mastering the Smallest of Details

L34 "Before we can become good writers, we must master the smallest of details. It is no different than building a house. We must start with a rock solid foundation.

"Our foundation for language development starts with **lines** and **circle segments** in a special pattern following a precise legal definition that creates a letter. These written symbols are letters or combinations of letters that we call **'phonograms'**. Each phonogram has a unique sound.

"We link phonograms to make **words** using the **spelling rules** of our language. Each word has a unique meaning. Each word has a job that it must do.

"We combine words to make **sentences** using the rules of **grammar**. Each sentence has a complete thought.

"In this next lesson, we will join sentences to make **paragraphs** using the guidelines for **composition**. These sentences must work together to make a paragraph just like phonograms work together to make words. The first sentence of a paragraph usually introduces the topic. That sentence is called the **'topic sentence'**. Each sentence contributes a supporting thought or a new idea to the topic sentence. Each paragraph discusses the specific topic introduced by the topic sentence.

"When we have mastered the writing of a paragraph, many paragraphs can be combined to make complete written works. Essays, short stories, reports, research papers, newspaper and magazine articles, and chapters in books are all made up of paragraphs. When we have mastered the art of writing excellent paragraphs, we are limited only by our imagination and our motivation."

L34P An easy and non-threatening way to have students write paragraphs at this level is to have them write one sentence a day. Have them choose a topic and write one sentence about that topic on Monday. Have them write a different sentence about that same topic each day on Tuesday, Wednesday, and Thursday. On Friday, have them read over the four sentences they have written and help them write a sentence that incorporates or is representative of the things they have talked about in their first four sentences. On the same day, or over the course of the next week, depending upon your students' developmental level, have your students copy their sentences on a piece of penmanship paper in paragraph form. Begin with the topic sentence they wrote on Friday. Be sure to indent the first sentence five spaces.

Choosing a Topic That Creates a Paragraph

L34 **Step 1** — "Before we write a paragraph, we need to choose a topic to write about. There are so many topics to choose from. We could make a list a mile long of all the topics that are available. Here are some examples:

> 'I am thankful for my family.'

> 'Sunday is my favorite day of the week.'

> 'I like to visit the zoo.'

> 'Fishing is my favorite hobby.'

> 'My dog is my best friend.'

"We are going to choose the first topic on being thankful for my family and learn to write a paragraph about that topic. Soon you will be able to write your own paragraph on a topic of your choice."

Creating a Topic Sentence

L56 **Step 2** — "Whatever topic you choose, you will need to develop the topic sentence. It is like building anything. It is a step-by-step process. Once we have chosen a topic, the first step is to think. We cannot write unless we first think.

"To help us think, we need to create a list of questions. Questions always cause us to think. The following is a sample list of questions that can be used to write our paragraph. Maybe you can think of others.

> 'Who is in my family?'

> 'What does my dad do that makes me thankful?'

> 'What does my mom do that makes me thankful?'

> 'What does my brother or sister do that makes me thankful?'

> 'What things that my family gives me am I thankful for?'

> 'What do you do together as a family?'

I am thankful for my family. I am
thankful for my dad and mom. My dad
cheers me up when I'm sad. My mom
hugs me and listens to me when I have a
problem. My brother and sister play board
games with me when I am sick. I am
thankful for food and clothing and a warm
house. I am thankful that I can help with
chores around the house like lawn
mowing and vacuuming. I am thankful that
my family laughs together, plays together,
prays together, and works together.

A topic sentence is the first sentence in a
paragraph. It introduces what the
paragraph is about.
A paragraph is a group of sentences that
say something about the topic.

Sample Page 73
Lesson 42

"These questions are just examples. We must remember that the writing process is first and foremost a thinking process. This is an important point. Before we can write, we must think. Questions help us to think. When we have our questions, then we can write.

"Every question that is asked is really a declarative sentence waiting to be written. Each new declarative sentence is designed to support the topic sentence.

"Questions help us to think. Turning the answers into declarative sentences helps us to write.

"We think and ask questions first; we answer questions and create declarative sentences second; we organize those declarative sentences later."

Dictating a Sample Paragraph

L56   **Step 3 —** *"Turn to page 73 in your* Grammar Notebook. *Skipping one baseline below the title line, indenting my paragraph five spaces, write the following sentences. Use as many consecutive lines as you need.*

> *'I am thankful for my family. I am thankful for my dad and mom. My dad cheers me up when I'm sad. My mom hugs me and listens to me when I have a problem. My brother and sister play board games with me when I am sick. I am thankful for food and clothing and a warm house. I am thankful that I can help with chores around the house like lawn mowing and vacuuming. I am thankful that my family laughs together, plays together, prays together, and works together.'"*

Defining a Topic Sentence and a Paragraph

L56   **Step 4 —** *"Counting up six baselines from the bottom of your page, starting comfortably close to the left margin line, write the following definition: 'A topic sentence is the first sentence in a paragraph. It introduces what the paragraph is about'."*

Step 5 — *"Starting on the next available baseline directly below the definition of a topic sentence, comfortably close to the left margin line, write the following definition: 'A paragraph is a group of sentences that says something about the topic'."*

Let's Get Organized

L56   **Step 6 —** *"Turn to the Table of Contents. On the page 73 line, write the title 'How Do I Write a Paragraph?' Turn back to* *page 73. Centered on the title line, between the two red margin lines, write the **same title**.”*

Dictating a Proofreading Checklist

L56 **Step 1 —** “When we write, we must always be careful to write accurately and say what we really mean to say. Proofreading means we seriously ask ourselves some very important questions. If we need to change something to improve our paragraph, that is proofreading.

“Turn to page 74 in your Notebook. *Skipping one baseline below the title line, place the numbers '1–12' to the left of the red margin line. Starting comfortably close to the left margin line, write the following on consecutive baselines:*

'Have I read my paragraph out loud?'

'Does it read well?'

'Do all the sentences relate to my topic?'

'Are there words I can cross out?'

'Are there words I can add?'

'Are my words spelled correctly?'

'Are there sentences I can cross out to improve my paragraph?'

'Do I need to add more sentences?'

'Have I started every sentence with a capital letter?'

'Does every sentence have correct end punctuation?'

'Is my handwriting beautiful?'

'Have I shared my paragraph with someone?'”

Proofreading Is So Important

L56 “Proofreading and revision are so important to the process of writing. We have to really care about our writing in order to make it a quality piece.

“When we read our writing out loud, we can find so many things that can be improved. Sometimes a sentence we thought fit very well really doesn't work at all. Sometimes we can see the need for a new sentence that would help our reader to understand better.

74	What Is a Proofreading Checklist?
1	Have I read my paragraph out loud?
2	Does it read well?
3	Do all the sentences relate to my topic?
4	Are there words I can cross out?
5	Are there words I can add?
6	Are my words spelled correctly?
7	Are there sentences I can cross out to improve my paragraph?
8	Do I need to add more sentences?
9	Have I started every sentence with a capital letter?
10	Does every sentence have correct end punctuation?
11	Is my handwriting beautiful?
12	Have I shared my paragraph with someone?

A thesaurus is a valuable tool to help us choose stronger words.

Sample Page 74
Lesson 42

"When we look at the words we have chosen, we need to decide whether they all work well or not. Maybe there is a better word we could use.

"Of course, we always need to spell correctly and use proper punctuation and capitalization.

"Sometimes other people can help us. If we have someone read our paragraph, they can tell us if we were successful and maybe give some suggestions for improvement. Of course, using beautiful handwriting will help our reader understand what we are trying to say."

Introducing a Thesaurus

L78 **Step 2** — "Proofreading and revising would not be complete without mentioning a **thesaurus**. A thesaurus is a treasury of words. It is a book where we can find synonyms and antonyms arranged in categories. This book is a valuable tool for making our written works interesting and colorful.

"When we are writing, we are often confined to a specific topic and in such cases there is always the danger of using the same words over and over again to express certain thoughts about that topic. This is when a thesaurus may prove a useful resource. Simply look up a word you wish to change and find a listing of other words that are possible substitutes. Word choice in our writing is so very important."

L78P Find a thesaurus and look up a simple word like "run" meaning to move with great speed. Show your students all the choices there are for this word. "What can a runner do? The runner can . . . sprint, scamper, dash, fly, race, tear, whisk, whiz, sweep, bolt, trot, bound, flit, spring, dart, boom, and even outstrip the wind." If nouns and verbs are the bones and sinews of speech, then it is important that we learn to pick just the right words to accomplish just the right effect.

L78 *"Skipping one baseline below the last sentence, write the following: 'A thesaurus is a valuable tool to help us choose stronger words'.* You will need more than one line."

Let's Get Organized

L56 **Step 3** — *"Turn to the Table of Contents. On the page 74 line, write the title 'What Is a Proofreading Checklist?' Turn back to page 74. Centered on the title line, between the two red margin lines, write the same title."*

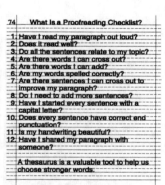

74	What Is a Proofreading Checklist?
1.	Have I read my paragraph out loud?
2.	Does it read well?
3.	Do all the sentences relate to my topic?
4.	Are there words I can cross out?
5.	Are there words I can add?
6.	Are my words spelled correctly?
7.	Are there sentences I can cross out to improve my paragraph?
8.	Do I need to add more sentences?
9.	Have I started every sentence with a capital letter?
10.	Does every sentence have correct end punctuation?
11.	Is my handwriting beautiful?
12.	Have I shared my paragraph with someone?

A thesaurus is a valuable tool to help us choose stronger words.

Sample Page 74
Lesson 42

Reviewing the Process of Writing a Paragraph

L56 **Step 4** — "Before we write, we need to choose a topic. We then need to ask questions about our topic. We need to ask lots of questions.

"This first thinking step is a vital step. We are looking for information about the topic. We are researching.

"Sometimes when we research, we go into the library of our own mind and use our own experiences. Other times we actually go to the library and use a book or a magazine article to help us with information. This preliminary thinking process is critical. We need to do our homework. We have to become an expert on the topic we have chosen.

"Once we have done our research and have asked all the right questions, we can start writing down our answers. We may not use all of them, but it is important for now to collect as much information as is possible. We start with an effective topic sentence and we build from there. Soon we will have a beautiful paragraph that says exactly what we want it to say."

Expectancies Learned and/or Reviewed in Lesson 42: Dialogue and Review

1. What is the first step in writing a paragraph? **L56** *(We need to pick a topic.)*

2. What do we do next? **L56** *(We need to begin researching that topic by asking questions about it.)*

3. When we have done the research, what do we do? **L56** *(We change all the questions we have discovered into declarative sentences that state facts and give information.)*

4. What is the next step? **L56** *(We write down our topic sentence and then organize the declarative sentences that tell about the topic sentence.)*

5. How important is it to proofread? **L56** *(Proofreading is very important. We need to be sure that our writing is the best it can be.)*

6. Why would I use a thesaurus? **L78** *(I would use a thesaurus to find just the right word to make my writing stronger.)*

Where Do I Go from Here?

- **L34** goes to **L34** "Scope and Sequence" Step 9.

- **L56** goes to "Lesson 40" on page 404.

- **L78** goes to "Lesson 43" on page 428.

What Materials Will I Need?

- **L56** and **L78** will need *Grammar Notebooks* and pencils. **L56** will need envelopes.

Sample Page 75
Lesson 43

Lesson 43

Creating an Outline

L56   "Developing tools that will help us understand what we are learning is very helpful. There are many tools that can help us with this. One of these tools is outlining."

L56   **Step 1 —** "Learning how to outline is a very important tool. *Turn to page 75 in your* Grammar Notebook. We are going to learn about outlining. An outline is a tool for organizing information we collect or plan to collect. We can use an outline to help us to write a report or to take notes on something we have read. Every outline is kept organized in the following manner."

L56P   Give your students a sample of an outline. There is a sample of an outline on the Sample Page in the margin. There is a sample outline in **"Lesson 39"** on Library Skills.

Dictate the following information to your students. Show them the manner in which an outline is organized. If your students do not know how to use Roman Numerals, it will be necessary to introduce this concept at this time.

L56   "We need to give our outline a title. We center the title on the title line. Key words in a title are always capitalized.

"An outline begins with a Roman Numeral followed by a period placed comfortably close to a left margin line. These Roman Numerals are the main points of our outline. We may have as many main points as we need to cover our topic, but we must have at least two. We may use a phrase or a sentence as a main point.

"On the next open baseline below the main point, we need to move about two spaces in from the left margin line. A capital letter with a period is used to list subpoints under our main points. We may have as many subpoints as we need, but we must have at least two. The first would be Capital A. The second would be Capital B and so on. The subpoints are always supporting and adding important information about the main point that they falls under.

"Again we need to move two spaces in. There may be details about a subpoint necessary for the report. An Arabic Numeral like "1, 2, 3, or 4" with a period following organizes these details under the subpoints. We may have as many details as we feel are necessary, but if we have a "1", we must have a "2". These details always support and give information about the subpoint that they fall under.

"It is possible to have details under the details. On this level use a lower case letter with a "close parenthesis" behind it. Again, we may have as many details under the details as we want, but we must have at least two. We will start using these details after we have indented two spaces under the Arabic Numerals."

Paraphrasing What We Are Learning

L56 "Any sentences we write in an outline or in a report need to be paraphrases of what we have learned. A paraphrase is simply writing sentences in our own words and not using the exact words of the text we are researching. Using an author's word-for-word material in what we write is fine if we give credit to the author. Not to give credit is wrong. That is called 'plagiarism'. Plagiarism is passing off someone else's written work as our own."

Creating an Outline on Our Own

L56 **Step 2 —** "When we are reading a textbook, we can take notes on what we are reading. Let's do some outlining together."

L56P Do one of the following three things on page 75 in the Notebook:

1. Have your students create an original outline if you feel they are ready. Find a typical chapter in a textbook. Let them work at making an outline. An outline is a great study tool. Outlining helps to embed information in our minds.

2. If the students need more practice before trying an outline on their own, dictate the outline about a summer vacation as it appears on the Sample Page in the margin.

3. If they still need more practice, dictate the outline called **"An Imaginary Trip to the Library"** beginning on page 398 of **"Lesson 39: Developing Library Skills."**

Remembering the Parts of an Outline

L56 **Step 3 —** "Remember that an outline may contain some or all of the following:

'A chapter title could be the **title** of our outline.'

'A number of key subheadings in this chapter could be our **main points.** We would use a **Roman Numeral** for these.'

How Do I Create an Outline? 75
I. Planning our trip.
    A. Out West or Coastal Georgia?
        1. Not Georgia—we always go there
        2. The West—where my Dad grew up
    B. Fly or drive?
        1. Flying is too expensive
        2. We will need to drive two cars
II. Where will we stay?
    A. In our tent
        1. Reserve campsites now!
        2. What if it rains?
        3. Two whole weeks in a tent?
    B. In a motel
        1. Motels are a lot nicer!
        2. Motels are a lot more expensive!
III. Where will we go?
    A. Not California—too far!
    B. Southwest
        1. Half as far
        2. Still some uncrowded areas

Sample Page 75
Lesson 43

Learning to outline is a skill that will help us to write clearly and comprehensively.

'Topic sentences in key paragraphs could easily be our **subpoints**. We would paraphrase these sentences and introduce them using **Capital Letters**.'

'The **details** could be found in the sentences in these paragraphs that are supporting the topic sentence. We would use an **Arabic Numeral** for those.'

'If any additional details like statistics would need to be located as **details under the details**, we would use a **lower case letter with a parenthesis.'"**

L56 **Step 4** — "By outlining key chapters, we are collecting information that may be helpful to us when we have to write a report. Instead of going back to the book, we can look at our notes on the outline and those notes can help us think about what we have already read. We are looking for facts when we research and take notes. We are collecting information.

"We are organizing our thoughts on a topic of interest. After we have collected our information from various sources, we are closer to writing a report on what we have learned.

"An outline form can also be used to write a story about an experience we have had. We aren't looking in a book this time. We are looking in our memory and reviewing our experiences. Could we come up with a title for one of these experiences? We would center it on our page. Were there some key ingredients to this experience? Those would be our main points. As you can see, an outline could prove to be a useful organizing tool."

L56P Continue to have your students practice their outlining skills until they understand outlining. Periodically pick a chapter in a subject area like science or social studies and have them outline it using the form as discussed in this lesson.

Let's Get Organized

L56 **Step 5** — *"Turn to the Table of Contents. On the page 75 line, write the title 'How Do I Create an Outline?' Turn back to page 75. Centered on the title line, between the two red margin lines, write the **same title.**"*

Expectancies Learned or Reinforced in Lesson 43: Dialogue and Review

1. Why do we outline? **L56** *(Outlining is an organized way of taking notes on what we read. It is also a way of organizing an experience or even a longer paper which may have many paragraphs.)*

How Do I Create an Outline? 75

I. Planning our trip.
  A. Out West or Coastal Georgia?
    1. Not Georgia—we always go there
    2. The West—where my Dad grew up
  B. Fly or drive?
    1. Flying is too expensive
    2. We will need to drive two cars
II. Where will we stay?
  A. In our tent
    1. Reserve campsites now!
    2. What if it rains?
    3. Two whole weeks in a tent?
  B. In a motel
    1. Motels are a lot nicer!
    2. Motels are a lot more expensive!
III. Where will we go?
  A. Not California—too far!
  B. Southwest
    1. Half as far
    2. Still some uncrowded areas

Sample Page 75
Lesson 43

2. How do we outline? **L56** *(We center the title and then use a series of symbols to keep order in our outline.)*

3. What symbols do we use? **L56** *(The main points use Roman Numerals. Sub-points under our main points use Capital Letters. Details about a subpoint use Arabic Numerals. Details under the details use a lower case letter with a parenthesis.)*

Where Do I Go from Here?

- **L56** and **L78** go to **"Lesson 44"** on page 432.

What Materials Will I Need?

- **L56** and **L78** will need *Grammar Notebooks* and pencils.

The State of Minnesota*

The state of Minnesota is nicknamed the Gopher State. As a farm state, its primary produce is dairy products. Minneapolis and St. Paul are the state's largest cities. About 4 million people live in this northern state where the temperatures can fall to 50 degrees below zero. The state has 10,000 lakes and the mighty Mississippi has its beginning in Lake Itasca in North Central Minnesota. Many years ago the Sioux and Chippewa Indians lived in the state. Minnesota became the 32nd state to enter the union on May 11, 1858.

*Information for this summary is taken from World Book, Volume 13, v. 1986, pages 496-510.

Sample Page 76
Lesson 44

Lesson 44
Writing a Summary

L56   "A summary is another note taking tool. It is condensing the main points of a book into one or two paragraphs. It is a brief statement made up of only a few sentences that quickly informs us of what was learned when a book or magazine article was read. Here is a good word picture describing the nature of a summary."

Discovering the Nature of A Summary

L56   **Step 1 —** "A gold prospector is looking for gold on a hillside. He is looking among many hundreds of rocks of various sizes and shapes. Sometimes he digs with his shovel. He is searching for gold nuggets. When we are reading, we are searching also. We are looking for gold nuggets too. When the prospector has found some of these precious nuggets, he puts them into a leather bag. They are special to him. A summary is a bag of gold nuggets."

L56   **Step 2 —** "To write a summary, it is necessary to focus on two points:

'What were the main points of my book or article?'

'What were the most important things I learned when I read this book or article?'

"Sometimes students write a summary of an article, chapter, or book on index cards. In this way, they can remember more easily what the book or article said after many days have passed. Note taking and summary writing are tools to help our memory.

"I am going to dictate a sample summary to you. If we were to look up information about the state of Minnesota, we could look in most encyclopedias. If we looked in the Volume 13, Letter 'M' 1986 *World Book*, we would find a lengthy discussion on Minnesota that starts on page 496 and ends on page 510. The fourteen pages of information are broken down into main points and subpoints with much detail.

"We only want a summary. We can't rewrite the whole article about Minnesota. We only want the gold nuggets."

Dictating a Summary

L56   **Step 3** — *"Turn to page 76 in your* Grammar Notebook. *Skipping one baseline below the title line, center the title* **'The State of Minnesota'** *between the two red margin lines. Skipping one baseline below this title, write the following paragraph. Remember to indent five spaces when you begin.*

'The State of Minnesota'

> **'The state of Minnesota is nicknamed the Gopher State. As a farm state, its primary produce is dairy products. Minneapolis and St. Paul are the state's largest cities. About 4 million people live in this northern state where the temperatures can fall to 50 degrees below zero. The state has 10,000 lakes and the mighty Mississippi has its beginning in Lake Itasca in North Central Minnesota. Many years ago the Sioux and Chippewa Indians lived in the state. Minnesota became the 32nd state to enter the union on May 11, 1858.'"**

L56P Have your students choose an encyclopedia entry. Have them find the "gold nuggets" and write a summary of what they read. They can then record this summary on page 76 in their *Grammar Notebook.*

Let's Get Organized

L56   **Step 4** — *"Turn to the Table of Contents. On the page 76 line, write the title* **'How Do I Write a Summary?'** *Turn back to page 76. Centered on the title line, between the two red margin lines, write the* **same title.***"*

Expectancies Learned or Reinforced in Lesson 44: Dialogue and Review

1. What is a summary? **L56** *(A summary is a brief paragraph that restates the main points of a much larger article.)*

Where Do I Go from Here?

- **L56** goes to **L56** "Scope and Sequence" Step 16.

- **L78** has completed the **L78** Scope and Sequence.

Comprehensive Checklist 4 for Lessons 34–44

1. How do singular words show ownership? **L34** *(Singular words show ownership by adding an apostrophe and an "s" to the end of the word. "Man's hat", "dog's collar", "bus's window".)*

2. How do plural nouns that do not end in "s" show ownership? **L34** *(If the plural form of a word does not end in "s", the word is shows ownership by adding an apostrophe and an "s" to the end of the word. "Men's athletics", "mice's cheese".)*

3. How do the plural nouns that already end in "s" show ownership? **L34** *(If the plural form of a word already ends in "s", the word shows ownership by adding an apostrophe after the final "s". "Secretaries' desks", "dogs' kennels", "buses' windows".)*

4. What do we call words that are created from two different words and are missing letters? **L34** *(We call these words "contractions". "Can't", "won't", "didn't", "haven't", "I'm", "we're".)*

5. What punctuation mark do we use to show missing letters or numbers when we combine two words into one? **L34** *(We use an apostrophe above where the letters or numbers are missing. "She'll" for "she will", "he's" for "he is" or "he was", "you've" for "you have", "'98" for "1998".)*

6. How do we punctuate the plural forms of letters, numbers, signs, or words mentioned as words? **L56** *(We punctuate the plural forms of letters, numbers, signs, or words mentioned as words with an apostrophe and then a letter "s". For example, "e's", "14's", "$'s", "the's".)*

7. How are proper nouns that already end in "s" made possessive? **L78** *(When proper nouns already end in "s", they may add an apostrophe alone or an apostrophe and an "s" to the end of a name. The apostrophe "s" is the preferred form. The names Jesus and Moses need only the apostrophe. "Bess's apple pie".)*

8. When two or more people own something separately in the same sentence, how do we make these proper nouns possessive? **L78** *(When two or more people own something separately in a sentence, we add the apostrophe or apostrophe "s" to the end of each name. "John's and Sally's research papers".)*

9. When speaking of two or more people who own something together in the same sentence, how do we make these proper nouns show joint ownership of the same thing? **L78** *(When speaking of two or more people who own something together, we add the apostrophe or apostrophe "s" to the end of only the last name mentioned. "John and Sally's research paper", "Smith and Barney's Law Office".)*

10. How do we make compound words possessive in a sentence? **L78** *(When writing a possessive compound word, we add the apostrophe or the apostrophe "s" to the end of only the last word of the compound word. "Editor-in-chief's chair")*

11. How do we make indefinite pronouns possessive? **L78** *(We make indefinite pronouns possessive by adding an apostrophe and an "s" to the end of the word. "Anybody's game".)*

12. How do we punctuate possessive pronouns? **L78** *(Possessive pronouns are already possessive and need no apostrophe. "Hers", "his", "theirs", "my", "mine", "ours", "your", "yours", "its".)*

13. How do we make words of time and amount possessive? **L78** *(Words of time and amount are made possessive by adding an apostrophe and an "s" to the end of the word. "Yesterday's weather", "dollar's worth", "hour's time".)*

14. How do we end a declarative sentence? **L34** *(We end a declarative sentence with a period.)*

15. How do we end an imperative sentence? **L34** *(We end an imperative sentence with a period or an exclamation point.)*

16. What do we place after an abbreviation? **L34** *(We place a period after an abbreviation.)*

17. What do we place after the letters of an abbreviation of a common organization or a federal agency? **L56** *(No periods are necessary with common organizations or federal agencies.)*

18. If a direct quote is a declarative sentence, what punctuation mark do we use before the end quotation mark? **L34** *(A period is used inside an end quotation mark if the exact words of the speaker are a declarative sentence.)*

19. If a direct quote is an interrogative sentence, what punctuation mark do we use before the end quotation mark? **L34** *(A question mark is used inside an end quotation mark if the exact words of the speaker are an interrogative sentence.)*

20. If a direct quote is an exclamatory sentence, what punctuation mark do we use before the end quotation mark? **L34** *(An exclamation point is used inside an end quotation mark if the exact words of the speaker are an exclamatory sentence.)*

21. If a direct quote is an imperative sentence, what punctuation mark do we use before the end quotation mark? **L34** *(A period or an exclamation point is used inside an end quotation mark if the exact words of the speaker are an imperative sentence.)*

22. What is an acronym? **L34** *(An acronym is a word created by using the first letters from words that make up a set phrase. "Y. M. C. A." stands for "Young Men's Christian Association".)*

23. How do we punctuate a list of more than two items in a series whether that series is a list of nouns or verbs or whatever it might be? **L12** *(We separate the items from each other using commas. "John, Sally, Pete, and Jane went to the museum".)*

24. How do we punctuate calendar dates and mailing addresses of more than one part? **L34** *(Calendar dates or mailing addresses of more than one part are separated by commas. "I was born in Sleepy Eye, MN, on January 14, 1951".)*

25. How do we punctuate two or more prepositional phrases beginning a sentence? **L56** *(We need to place a comma after the last prepositional phrase. "On the first day of the week, we work in the garden".)*

26. How do we punctuate a noun of address? **L56** *(Nouns of address need to be set apart by commas. "Mr. Smith, please stop by for a visit".)*

27. What is one way to join two sentences together using a comma? **L56** *(Two sentences may be joined together by using a coordinating conjunction with a comma preceding that conjunction. "He always trains for the marathon in the summer, but he takes it easy in the winter".)*

28. How many rules are there that govern the use of the comma? **L56** *(There are many rules. We can discover additional rules as we learn more about grammar.)*

29. What do quotation marks probably indicate in a sentence? **L34** *(They indicate the exact words of the speaker.)*

30. What is a tag? **L34** *(A tag indentifies the person saying the direct quote.)*

31. Where does the comma and period go if the direct quote is a declarative sentence and if the tag follows the quote? **L34** *(A comma precedes the last quotation mark and a period follows the tag if the direct quote is a declarative sentence.)*

32. What do we do with the first word of a direct quote? **L34**
(The first word of a direct quote needs to be capitalized.)

33. Where do the comma and the end punctuation mark go if the tag is on the front of the direct quote? **L34** *(With the tag in the front, we separate the tag from the direct quote with a comma before the first quotation mark and place the end punctuation mark inside the last quotation mark.)*

34. How is an imperative quote punctuated? **L56** *(An imperative quote is punctuated like a declarative quote.)*

35. Where do the question mark and period go if the quote is a question and the tag follows the direct quote? **L56** *(The question mark precedes the last quotation mark and a period follows the tag.)*

36. Where do the exclamation point and period go if the quote is an exclamation and the tag follows the direct quote? **L56** *(The exclamation point precedes the last quotation mark and a period follows the tag.)*

37. What is fictional writing? **L56** *(Fictional writing is a created story about characters from the author's imagination.)*

38. What is nonfiction? **L56** *(Nonfiction is writing that is a true-to-life account about actual events or people.)*

39. What is dialogue in a story? **L56** *(Dialogue is a conversation in writing between two or more characters.)*

40. What must we do with dialogue every time we switch speakers? **L78** *(Dialogue requires a new paragraph with every switch of speakers.)*

41. What do we do with "heavy" written works or titles of paintings or specific names for planes, trains, ships, or spacecraft? **L78** *(We underline them in handwritten reports. We use italics if we are using a word processor.)*

42. What do we do with "light" written works like short stories, poems, songs, chapter titles, or article titles? **L78** *(We enclose "light" titles in quotation marks.)*

43. How do we make an indirect quote? **L78** *(An indirect quote removes the quotation marks, adds the word "that" and changes pronouns or verb forms if necessary.)*

44. Why use an indirect quote? **L78** *(The writer may need to say what someone said, but using a direct quote may not fit well with the intended purpose of the writing.)*

45. How do we punctuate a divided quote? **L78** *(A divided quote uses a comma after the tag if the quote is carried over and a period after the tag if the quote is two separate sentences.)*

46. What is a semicolon used for? **L78** *(A semicolon is used to join two complete thoughts closely related in meaning.)*

47. What is a colon used for? **L78** *(A colon is used before a list of items, after a salutation in a business letter, between the hour and the minutes when telling time, between a chapter and a verse in a Bible passage, and before a long quotation.)*

48. What will a colon never follow? **L78** *(A colon will never follow a verb.)*

49. Besides the other uses for a colon already mentioned, where else may a colon be used? **L78** *(A colon may be used after "as follows:" or "the following:" or directly following a noun.)*

50. What is an ellipsis? **L78** *(An ellipsis is a series of three dots indicating the omission of words because these words are not important to the purpose of the writing.)*

51. How do we punctuate conjunctive adverbs? **L78** *(Conjunctive adverbs connecting two sentences have a semicolon preceding and a comma following them in a sentence.)*

52. What is the name of a book called? **L34** *(The name of the book is called the "title".)*

53. What is on the title page of a book? **L34** *(The title page gives the name of the book, the author, and the publisher.)*

54. What is the Table of Contents? **L34** *(The Table of Contents in the front of the book tells us what is in the book and where.)*

55. What is a glossary? **L34** *(The glossary is a list of difficult words with definitions to help us understand the book.)*

56. What is the index? **L34** *(The index in the back of the book is an alphabetical list of all subjects covered in the book.)*

57. How are words written in a dictionary? **L34** *(Words in a dictionary are written in alphabetical order.)*

58. What are guide words? **L34** *(The two words on the top of a dictionary page are called guide words. They tell us if the word we are looking for is on that page.)*

59. What can we learn about a word in the dictionary? **L34** *(The dictionary gives the definition, pronunciation, syllables, part of speech, etymology, and sample sentence using the word.)*

60. What are some special features of a dictionary? **L56** *(Dictionaries may have a Biographical Names section, a Geographical Names section, and an Atlas section.)*

61. What do encyclopedias do? **L34** *(Encyclopedias arrange topics alphabetically, use guide words like a dictionary, have pictures, diagrams, and illustrations, have a research guide to look for more information, and provide a list of related topics.)*

62. What is a card catalog? **L56** *(The card catalog is a tool to help us find books. There are three different kinds of cards: the title card, the author card, and the subject card.)*

63. How are books of fiction arranged in a library? **L56** *(Books of fiction are arranged alphabetically according to the author's last name.)*

64. How are nonfiction books arranged in the library? **L56** *(Nonfiction books are arranged using a numbering system.)*

65. What are other references used in the library? **L56** *(Almanacs, atlases, newspapers, magazines, and biographical materials can also be found in a library.)*

66. What is the *Readers' Guide to Periodical Literature*? **L78** *(The* Readers' Guide to Periodical Literature *is an index of magazine articles.)*

67. What does each magazine entry in this index contain? **L78** *(Each magazine entry contains the title, author's name, magazine, volume number, page numbers, date, and listings of illustrations, maps or photos for that particular article.)*

68. What are the five sections of a friendly letter? **L34** *(A friendly letter has a heading, salutation, body, closing, and signature.)*

69. What is the heading of a friendly letter? **L34** *(The heading is the date the letter was written.)*

70. What is the salutation of a friendly letter? **L34** *(The salutation is the greeting. It usually uses the word "Dear" with the name of the person who is getting the letter.)*

71. What is the body of a friendly letter? **L34** *(The body is the content of the letter.)*

72. What is the closing of a friendly letter? **L34** *(The closing of a friendly letter is saying good-bye.)*

73. What is the signature of a friendly letter? **L34** *(The signature of a friendly letter is the name of the person writing the letter.)*

74. What words need to be capitalized in a friendly letter? **L34** *(The first word of every section, of every sentence, and all proper nouns need to be capitalized.)*

75. Where do we put commas in a friendly letter? **L34** *(A comma is placed between the day of the month and the year, after the salutation, and after the closing in a friendly letter.)*

76. What do we do with every new paragraph? **L34** *(Every new paragraph is indented five spaces.)*

77. What is the thank you note? **L34** *(The thank you note is just like a friendly letter in structure. It is sent to tell someone how much you appreciated something they did for you.)*

78. What is an invitation? **L34** *(An invitation is just like a friendly letter in structure. It is sent to invite someone to participate in a planned activity.)*

79. What is in an invitation? **L34** *(The invitation includes who is doing the inviting, what the occasion is, when it is, and where it will be held.)*

80. What is an acronym? **L34** *(By definition an acronym is "a word formed from the initial letters or groups of letters of words in a set phrase".)*

81. What is a business letter? **L34** *(A business letter is a letter between two parties that have a common business interest.)*

82. What are the differences between a business letter and a friendly letter, a thank you note, and an invitation? **L34** *(Business letters use formal closings and a colon after the salutation. Business letters also use an inside address. The other letters use informal closings, have a comma after the salutation, and lack an inside address.)*

83. What is a plot? **L34** *(A plot is what happens in the story. One event is linked to the next until a complete story is told.)*

84. What are characters? **L34** *(The characters are the people that are participating in the story.)*

85. What is a protagonist? **L34** *(The protagonist is the character who is generally the good guy.)*

86. What is an antagonist? **L34** *(The antagonist is the character who is generally the bad guy. Sometimes the bad guy can be a storm or a sickness or even a decision that needs to be made.)*

87. What is conflict? **L34** *(Conflict is a problem the protagonist must overcome. Conflict is created when the protagonist may not get what he wants or needs.)*

88. What are consequences? **L34** *(The consequences are what might happen if the problem is not solved.)*

89. What is suspense? **L34** *(Suspense is the unanswered questions created by trying to resolve the problem. It is the excitement about what could happen next.)*

90. What is setting? **L34** *(The setting is where and when the story takes place.)*

91. What is dialogue? **L34** *(The conversation between characters is called dialogue.)*

92. What is theme? **L34** *(Theme is the message or lesson the author trying to communicate.)*

93. What is point of view? **L34** *(Point of view is who the author has chosen to tell the story. This person could be a character in the story, or it could be a narrator.)*

94. What is resolution? **L34** *(Resolution is the conflict settled.)*

95. What is the formula for a good story? **L34** *(The formula for a good story is Conflict + Consequences = Suspense.)*

96. What is one of the themes that "The Three Little Pigs" teaches us? **L34** *(One of the themes might be that attention to details really does matter.)*

97. What is the first step in writing a paragraph? **L56** *(We need to pick a topic.)*

98. What do we do next? **L56** *(We need to begin researching that topic by asking questions about it.)*

99. When we have done the research, what do we do? **L56** *(We change all the questions we have discovered into declarative sentences that state facts and give information.)*

100. What is the next step? **L56** *(We write down our topic sentence and then organize the declarative sentences that tell about the topic sentence.)*

101. How important is it to proofread? **L56** *(Proofreading is very important. We need to be sure that our writing is the best it can be.)*

102. Why would I use a thesaurus? **L78** *(I would use a thesaurus to find just the right word to make my writing stronger.)*

103. Why do we outline? **L56** *(Outlining is an organized way of taking notes on what we read. It is also a way of organizing an experience or even a longer paper which may have many paragraphs.)*

104. How do we outline? **L56** *(We center the title and than use a series of symbols to keep order in our outline.)*

105. What symbols do we use? **L56** *(The main points use Roman Numerals. Subpoints under our main points use Capital Letters. Details about a subpoint use Arabic Numerals. Details under the details use a lower case letter with a parenthesis.)*

106. What is a summary? **L56** *(A summary is a brief paragraph that restates the main points of a much larger article.)*

107. Why do I need to understand how our language works? *(If we do not understand how our language works, it controls us and we do not control it. It makes us a slave. We want it to be our servant. Well-practiced, well-polished communication skills are imperative if we expect doors of opportunity to open and stay open in the future.)*

108. What does this statement mean? "Precise grammar builds syntactical expectancies at an automatic level." *(Learning how our language works builds certain expectations about how sentences should be written and how language should be spoken. If we can use these understandings and they are automatic, language becomes a friend and a sharpened tool. Few obstacles will stand in our way of effective communication.)*

An Approach That Engages Our Students Produces Mastery

You have reached the end of *Grammar Works Part I*. It is our strong opinion that if students know and have practiced the principles contained in this text, they will display a mastery in their writing second to none.

They have been integrally involved in preparing their own *Grammar Notebook*. The student's *Grammar Notebook* will become a constant resource. Students should use it as a reference book for any questions they might have about their writing.

These principles have been laid into their brain one step at a time. They have been engaged at auditory, visual, vocal, kinesthetic, and written levels.

It has taken time. All things worth doing take this kind of an investment. You have followed the **"Scope and Sequence."** You have made modifications where necessary to accommodate the maturity level of the student. You have been patient as you have worked through each lesson. You have been creative. You have been innovative.

We hope that this text has helped to ensure that these principles are automatic and ready for use at the beck and call of your students.

Part 3:
Sample Pages

Sentences—Writing Words in Sequence

Rule 1: The first word of a sentence always begins with a capital letter.

She can see.

Rule 2: We must leave a space between words when we write.

Rule 3: Every sentence must end with proper end punctuation.

I can run.
The man can run.
The dog chews a bone.
The boy sits.
The child sings a song.

A sentence is a group of words making complete sense.

Sample Page A

Lesson 1

Telling

Declarative Sentences Practice Page

She can see.
I can run.
The man can run.
The dog chews a bone.
The boy sits.
The child sings a song.
The mother comes home.
We can play.
The girl finds a doll.
The mouse runs.

Sample Page B

Lesson 1

Interrogative Sentences Practice Page

Can she see?
Can I run?
Can the man run?
Does the dog chew a bone?
Does the boy sit?
Does the child sing a song?
Does the mother come home?
Can we play?
Does the girl find a doll?
Does the mouse run?

Sample Page C

Lesson 1

Command

Imperative Sentences Practice Page

Run to the school.
Play the game.
Go to sleep.
Say a kind word.
Take the train home.
Bring the Sunday paper.
Call your mother.
Come to the play.
Make up your mind.
Tell the truth.

Sample Page D

Lesson 1

Exclamatory Sentences Practice Page

Dad was right!
That was hard to do!
We found the gold coin!
Everybody was happy!
What a big ice cream cone that is!

Sample Page E

Lesson 1

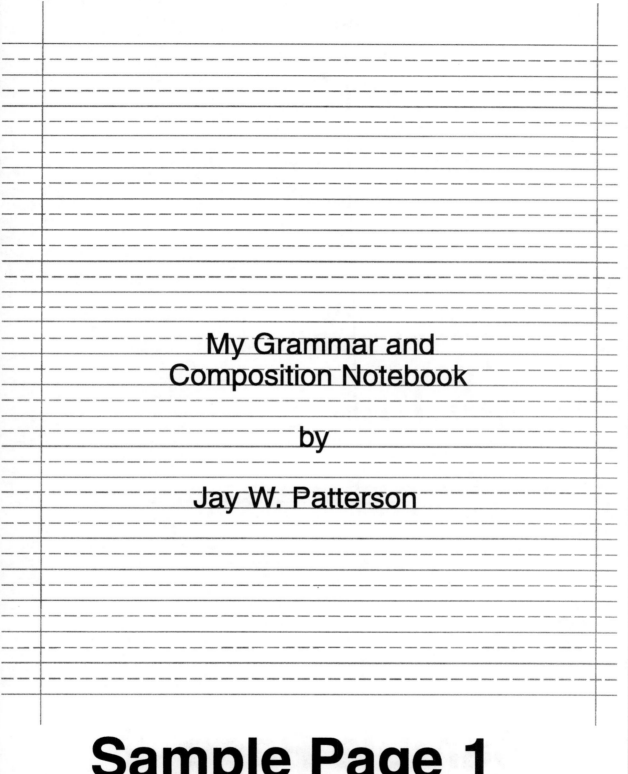

My Grammar and
Composition Notebook

by

Jay W. Patterson

Sample Page 1

Lesson 2

Sample Page 2
Lesson 3 (Blank)

Table of Contents

Sample Page 3

Lesson 2–18

Table of Contents (continued)

4

Sample Page 4

Lesson 19–32

Table of Contents (continued)

Sample Page 5

Lesson 32–39

6   Table of Contents (continued)

Sample Page 6

Lesson 39–44

Person	Place	Thing
man	school	bed
boy	street	top
mother	sea	time
child		chance

A noun is a naming word.
A noun names a person, place, or thing.
A singular noun speaks of one.
A plural noun speaks of more than one.

Sample Page 7

Lesson 4

Ideas	Qualities
democracy	trustworthiness
socialism	loyalty
capitalism	bravery
evolution	courage
creationism	integrity
liberalism	honesty
conservatism	patience
optimism	kindness
pessimism	thriftiness

An idea is a thought or concept formulated by the mind.
A quality is an inherent feature that makes a person, place, or thing what they are.

Sample Page 8

Lesson 4

What Are Common and Proper Nouns? | 9

Common Nouns	Proper Nouns
days	Sunday, Monday, and Tuesday
months	January, March, April, June, July, and August
holidays	Christmas, Easter, and Thanksgiving
titles	Miss, Mr., and Mrs.
	A Tale of Two Cities
	the President

A common noun is a general naming word that is not capitalized unless it is the first word in a sentence or part of a title. A proper noun is a special, particular naming word that is always capitalized.

Sample Page 9

Lesson 5

10 Common and Proper Nouns (continued)

continents	Europe, Asia, Africa, Anarctica, Australia, North America, and South America
names of	
people	John Smith
places	New York City Rocky Mountains
organizations	Boy Scouts of America
products	Coca-Cola
businesses	Sears
historical events	Civil War
nationalities	Norweigian
races	Caucasian
religions	Moslem and Christian
languages	Spanish and German
ships,planes,trains	Titanic
monuments	Lincoln Memorial
awards	Purple Heart
heavenly bodies	Mars and Neptune

Sample Page 10

Lesson 5

the child
a boy
an apple
the door
a dog
an egg
an hour
an honor

An article is a word that introduces a noun. There are three articles: "a", "an", and "the".
The article "an" is used with nouns that begin with a vowel sound.

Sample Page 11

Lesson 6

What Is an Action Verb?

do	eat	miss
go	stand	blow
see	bring	block
run	tell	sing
charge	ask	find
like	sit	take
hand	get	thank
live	call	dance
play	send	
make		
say		
come		

An action verb is a power word that gives strength and energy to a sentence.
An action verb expresses action or motion.

Sample Page 12

Lesson 7

What Is a Personal Pronoun? 13

	Singular	Plural
	I	we
	you	you
	he, she, it	they

Jared is going to the parade.
He is going to the parade.
The parade had ten marching bands.
It had ten marching bands.
Sally wanted to see the clowns.
She wanted to see the clowns.
Sam, Mark, and I went to the game.
We went to the game.

A personal pronoun is a part of English speech that takes the place of a noun.
A singular pronoun speaks of one.
A plural pronoun speaks of more than one.

Sample Page 13

Lesson 8

14   What Is an Indefinite Pronoun?

all	neither
another	nobody
any	none
anybody	no one
anyone	nothing
anything	one
each	other
either	others
everybody	some
everyone	somebody
everything	someone
many	something
most	somewhere
much	several

Indefinite pronouns are not specific about what or whom they are speaking of. Personal pronouns are quite specific about what or whom they are speaking of.

Sample Page 14

Lesson 9

Today I _____.
Yesterday I _____.
I have _____.

Singular	Plural

Present Tense

I go.	We go.
You go.	You go.
He, she, it goes.	They go.

Past Tense

I went.	We went.
You went.	You went.
He, she, it went.	They went.

Present Perfect Tense

I have gone.	We have gone.
You have gone.	You have gone.
He, she, it has gone.	They have gone.

Sample Page 15

Lesson 10

16   Conjugating (continued)

Singular	Plural
Past Perfect Tense	

Singular	Plural
I had gone.	We had gone.
You had gone.	You had gone.
He, she, it had gone.	They had gone.

Future Tense

Singular	Plural
I will go.	We will go.
You will go.	You will go.
He, she, it will go.	They will go.

Future Perfect Tense

Singular	Plural
I will have gone.	We will have gone.
You will have gone.	You will have gone.
He, she, it will have gone.	They will have gone.

Sample Page 16

Lesson 10

To Be	To Have
am	have
is	has
are	had
was	
were	Others
be, being, been	can
	could
	may, might
To Do	will, shall
do	would
does	must
did	should

HV + HV + HV + AV

I could have been singing in the choir.

A helping verb is a verb that helps the main verb. The helping verb or verbs and the main verb together make a verb phrase.

Sample Page 17

Lesson 11

18   What Is a Linking Verb?

am	tastes
is	looks
are	grows
was	smell
were	sound
becomes	stay
appears	remain
seems	and any form of the
feels	verb "to be"
	(be, being, been)

The child is a boy.
A boy becomes a man.
The apple tastes sour.

A linking verb is a joining word. A linking verb joins words that describe the subject or mean the same thing as the subject.

Sample Page 18

Lesson 12

The cat was chasing the mouse.
The mouse became afraid.
The farmer grows corn for the mice.
The mouse might have been caught.
The mouse ran into the farmhouse.
The mice have corn for breakfast.

If a word can be conjugated, it is a verb.
If a main verb is not on the linking verb list, it is an action verb.
A main verb may have helping verbs.
Linking verbs may be used as helping verbs.
Use the Is–Are Rule with verbs from "becomes" to "remain" to determine whether they are linking verbs or action verbs.
If a helping verb is the only verb and is not a linking verb, it is an action verb.

Sample Page 19

Lesson 13

The "What Kind?" flag
The "How Much?" flag
The "How Many?" flag
The "Which?", "Which One?", or
"Whose?" flag

"What Kind?" flag

The apple has red skin.

"What Kind?" flag   "How Many?" flag

An angry dog has no friends.

"Which?" flag   "What Kind" flag

The tallest building was Sears Tower.

"How Many?" flag   "Whose?" flag

Forty-two cats lived in our house.

"How Much?" flag   "What Kind?" flag   "What Kind?" flag

Much study is necessary for a hard test.

An adjective is a word that describes or influences a noun or pronoun.

Sample Page 20

Lesson 14

The "When?" flag
The "Where?" flag
The "Why?" flag
The "How?" flag
The "On What Condition?"or
"To What Extent?" flag

"When?" flag

Cats always purr.

"How?" flag   "When?" flag

Very smart dogs often bark.

"On What Condition?" flag   "When?" flag

Horses almost always run.

"Where?" flag

Will you sit here?

"Where?" flag

The mother sang softly.

An adverb is a word that describes or
influences a verb, an adjective, or
another adverb.

Sample Page 21

Lesson 15

after	below	by
before	beside, besides	except
during	between	for
since	down	like
to	from	of
till, until	in, into	with, within
about	inside, outside	without
above	near	in spite of
across	on, onto	because of
against	over	in addition to
among	through	instead of
around	toward	by means of
at	under	in back of
behind	up, upon	on account of

A preposition is a word used to relate its object to another word in the sentence.
A prepositional phrase begins with a preposition and ends with its object.
An object of a preposition (OP) is a noun or a pronoun.

Sample Page 22

Lesson 16

He rested after the race.
He found his wallet between the seats.
The girl walked without her shoes.

With strong workers, a group of Boy Scouts can clear much brush before sundown.

In addition to Boy Scouts, the police asked local citizens for help with the paper drive.

My son has experimented with rockets since 1990 because of an interest in jets.

They leaned against the wind and the rain and walked across the mountains and the prairie.

Sample Page 23

Lesson 16

and
but
or
for
nor
yet
so

The horse _and_ (conj.) the mule pulled the tractor
and (conj.) the wagon.
The junior choir _or_ (conj.) the senior choir will be
singing.
First we exercise, _but_ (conj.) then we run.
He cannot avoid the cold, _nor_ (conj.) can he stop
the wind.
Sally had to hurry, _for_ (conj.) she was late.

A coordinating conjunction is a word that
connects other words, phrases, or
clauses of equal importance.

Sample Page 24

Lesson 17

S + AV
S — AV

A cow eats.
A dog barks.
A bird sings.
A boy walks.
A baby cries.

A simple subject is a word about which something is being said.
A simple predicate is the main verb plus any helping verbs.
A simple sentence is a group of words that makes complete sense.

Sample Page 25

Lesson 18

The old, cranky dog was racing across the yard and under the fence.

A wise man walks through life with open eyes.

A shiny car was parked by the curb.

The baseball player dashed to second base.

The three boys quickly jumped over the ditch into the next field.

The complete subject is the simple subject plus all the words that influence it.
A complete predicate is the simple predicate plus all the words that influence it.

Sample Page 26

Lesson 19

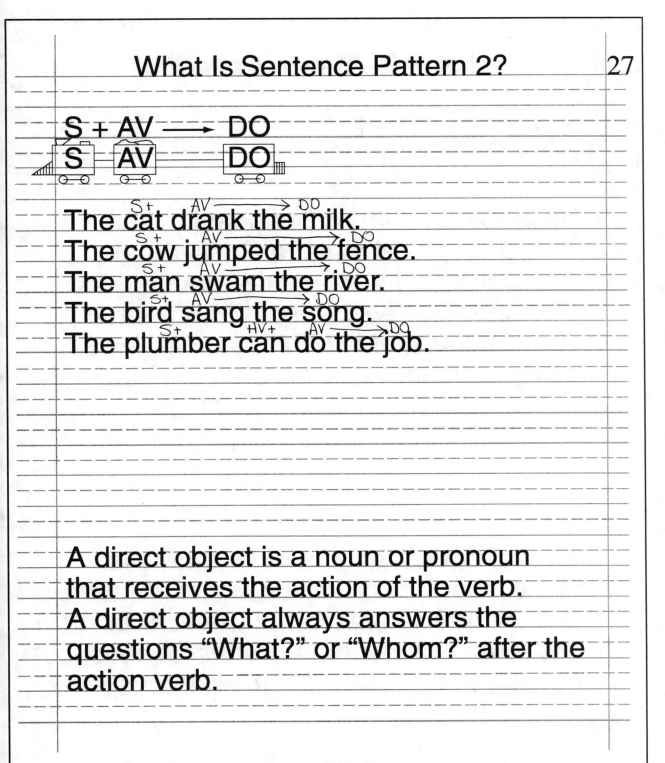

The cat drank the milk.
The cow jumped the fence.
The man swam the river.
The bird sang the song.
The plumber can do the job.

A direct object is a noun or pronoun that receives the action of the verb.

A direct object always answers the questions "What?" or "Whom?" after the action verb.

Sample Page 27

Lesson 20

What Is Sentence Pattern 3?

$$S + AV \longrightarrow IO + DO$$

| S | AV | IO | DO |

Mom fixed Bill a big breakfast.
The United States gave Russia grain.
The police officer gave the man a ticket.
The senator sent the governor a letter.
Grandfather told Johnny a story.
They gave the house a coat of paint.

An indirect object is a word that tells
"To Whom?" "For Whom?" "To What?" or
"For What?" the action of the verb is
done. An indirect object is the beneficiary
of what is happening in the sentence.

Sample Page 28

Lesson 21

©1998 Grammar Works/Holly Hall Publications, Inc

S + LV
S | LV

Present Tense

I am.	We are.
You are.	You are.
He, she, it is.	They are.

Past Tense

I was.	We were.
You were.	You were.
He, she, it was.	They were.

Present Perfect Tense

I have been.	We have been.
You have been.	You have been.
He, she, it has been.	They have been.

Sentence Pattern 4A has at least one subject and one linking verb.

Sample Page 29

Lesson 22

Sentence Pattern 4A (continued)

Past Perfect Tense

I had been.	We had been.
You had been.	You had been.
He, she, it had been.	They had been.

Future Tense

I will be.	We will be.
You will be.	You will be.
He, she, it will be.	They will be.

Future Perfect Tense

I will have been.	We will have been.
You will have been.	You will have been.
He, she, it will have been.	They will have been.

I am in the water.
He will be on time.
They were inside the house.
We had been below deck.
She has been in the pool.

Sample Page 30

Lesson 22

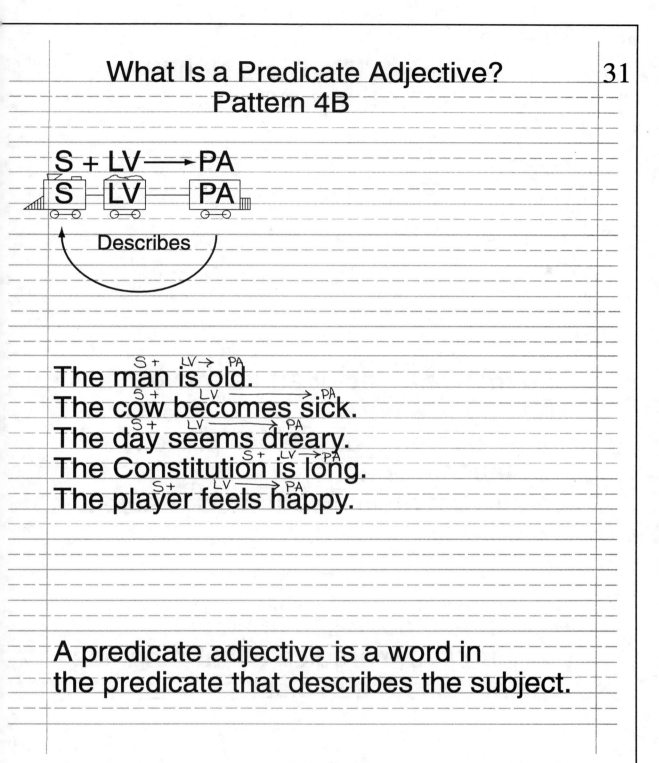

S + LV ⟶ PA

Describes

$\overset{S+}{\text{The}} \overset{LV}{\text{man is}} \overset{PA}{\text{old.}}$

The cow becomes sick.

The day seems dreary.

The Constitution is long.

The player feels happy.

A predicate adjective is a word in
the predicate that describes the subject.

Sample Page 31

Lesson 23

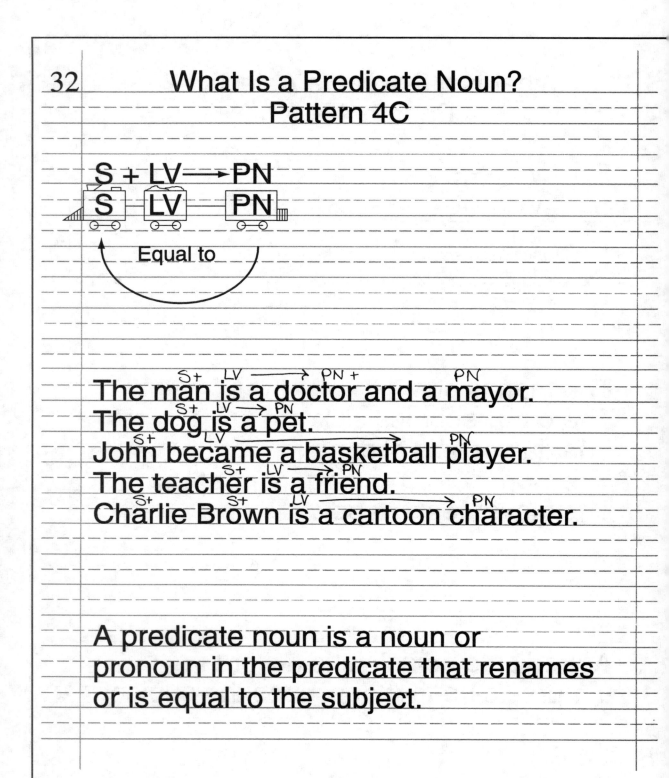

32   What Is a Predicate Noun?
Pattern 4C

S + LV ⟶ PN

Equal to

The man is a doctor and a mayor.
The dog is a pet.
John became a basketball player.
The teacher is a friend.
Charlie Brown is a cartoon character.

A predicate noun is a noun or
pronoun in the predicate that renames
or is equal to the subject.

Sample Page 32

Lesson 24

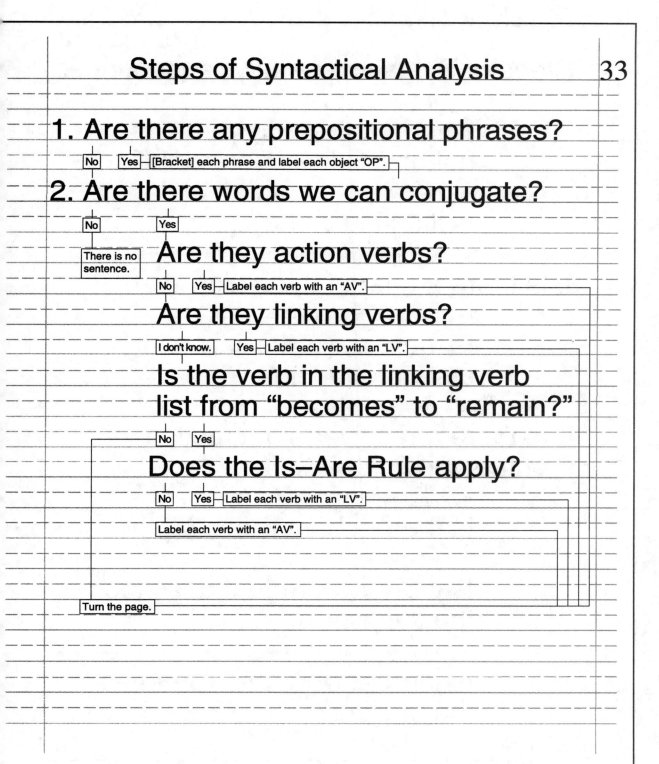

1. Are there any prepositional phrases?

No | Yes — [Bracket] each phrase and label each object "OP".

2. Are there words we can conjugate?

No | Yes

There is no sentence.

Are they action verbs?

No | Yes — Label each verb with an "AV".

Are they linking verbs?

I don't know. | Yes — Label each verb with an "LV".

Is the verb in the linking verb list from "becomes" to "remain?"

No | Yes

Does the Is–Are Rule apply?

No | Yes — Label each verb with an "LV".

Label each verb with an "AV".

Turn the page.

Sample Page 33

Lesson 25

©1998 Grammar Works/Holly Hall Publications, Inc.

Steps of Syntactical Analysis (continued)

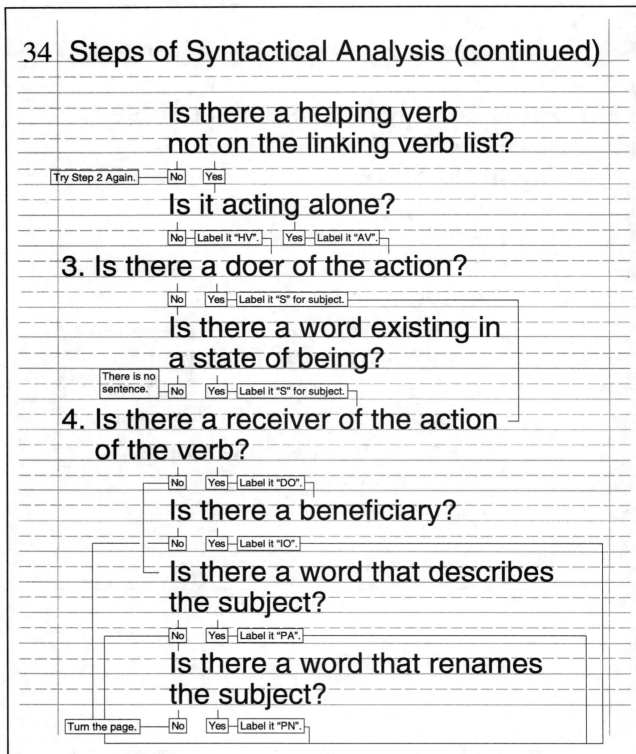

Is there a helping verb not on the linking verb list?

| Try Step 2 Again. | No | Yes |

Is it acting alone?

| No | Label it "HV". | Yes | Label it "AV". |

3. Is there a doer of the action?

| No | Yes | Label it "S" for subject. |

Is there a word existing in a state of being?

| There is no sentence. | No | Yes | Label it "S" for subject. |

4. Is there a receiver of the action of the verb?

| No | Yes | Label it "DO". |

Is there a beneficiary?

| No | Yes | Label it "IO". |

Is there a word that describes the subject?

| No | Yes | Label it "PA". |

Is there a word that renames the subject?

| Turn the page. | No | Yes | Label it "PN". |

Sample Page 34

Lesson 25

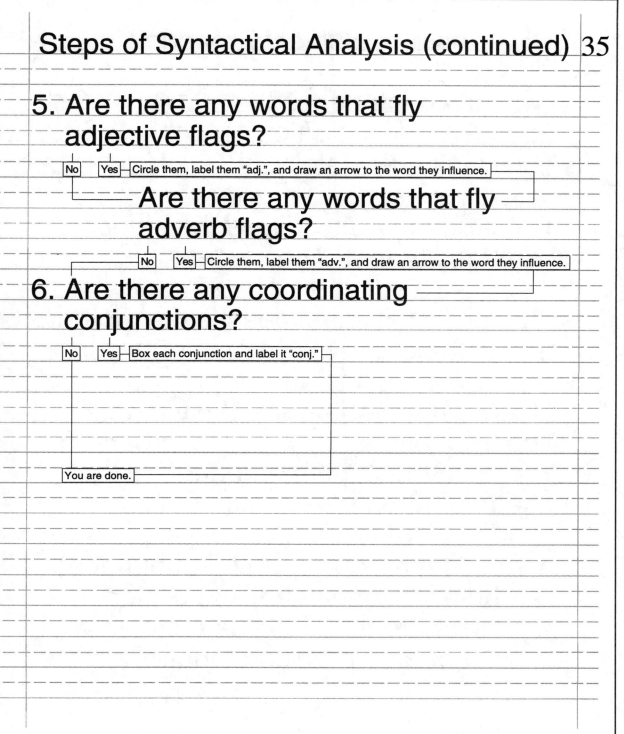

5. Are there any words that fly adjective flags?

No | Yes — Circle them, label them "adj.", and draw an arrow to the word they influence.

Are there any words that fly adverb flags?

No | Yes — Circle them, label them "adv.", and draw an arrow to the word they influence.

6. Are there any coordinating conjunctions?

No | Yes — Box each conjunction and label it "conj."

You are done.

Sample Page 35

Lesson 25

I run down the beach.
She gave Bill the cake.
They walked carefully.

The student is Jim. Jim is the student.
I am the student. The student is I.

The mother is Jean. Jean is the mother.
She is the mother. The mother is she.

The team members are Wolverines.
The Wolverines are team members.
They are the team members.
The team members are they.

A subject pronoun is any pronoun that
can be used in the subject position.
A subject pronoun may be used as a
subject or as a predicate noun.

Sample Page 36

Lesson 26

Subject Pronoun	Object Pronoun
Singular	**Singular**
I	me
you	you
he	him
she	her
it	it
Plural	**Plural**
we	us
you	you
they	them

An object pronoun is a form of a personal pronoun used in an object position.

An object pronoun may be used as a DO, IO, or OP.

Sample Page 37

Lesson 27

38 What Is an Object Pronoun? (continued)

Sheri and Joe traveled with John and Betty.

They traveled with them.

The cat and the dog ran over the fence.

They ran over it.

The coach and I tackled the quarterback.

We tackled him.

The mayor gave the police officer a new car yesterday.

He gave her a new car yesterday.

Sample Page 38

Lesson 27

George Johnson hated the alarm clock.
Monarch butterflies emerge from a
cocoon.
John, Sally, and Jim sold tickets for the
concert.
Harriet Tubman was called "Moses".
Spiders are found in the palaces
of kings.

A declarative sentence states a fact or
gives information and always ends with
a period.

Sample Page 39

Lesson 28

What Is an Interrogative Sentence?

What?	When?	Am?
Which?	Where?	Is?
Who?	Why?	Are?
To Whom?	How?	Was?
Whose?		Were?

Who was at the ball game with you?

Which teacher was responsible for the children?

What is the name of the man?

To whom do you refer?

Whose bicycle needs paint?

When will we go?

Why was the meeting canceled?

Am I going to the game?

An interrogative sentence asks a question and ends with a question mark.

Sample Page 40

Lesson 29

The mailman ate the candy.
Did the mailman eat the candy?

The President and the First Lady attended the Inaugural Ball.
Did the President and the First Lady attend the Inaugural Ball?

Books open doors to the past and make time without wings.
Do books open doors to the past and make time without wings?

Michael Jordan is a super player.
Is Michael Jordan a super player?

Preparation for a career requires study and hard work.
Does preparation for a career require study and hard work?

Sample Page 41

Lesson 29

What Is an Imperative Sentence?

(You) Clean the house.
(You) Go to the backyard.
(You) Jump in the lake.
(You) Wash the dishes.
(You) Run the mile in five minutes.
(You) Ask the mayor.

An imperative sentence gives a
command or makes a request.
An imperative sentence ends with a
period.

Sample Page 42

Lesson 30

How special you are!
That was an awesome play at first base!
What a wonderful person he was!
That is hot!
We won the game!
What marvelous eyes you have!
(You) Hit the brakes!
I love Minnesota hotdishes!
Uff Da! Bam! Zap! Pow! Bang! Hurrah!

Exclamatory sentences and interjections
display strong or sudden emotion.
They show excitement!
They always end with an exclamation
point!

Sample Page 43

Lesson 31

What Is a Possesive Pronoun?

I	my, mine
you	your, yours
he	his
she	her, hers
it	its
we	our, ours
you	your, yours
they	their, theirs

My car was running in your driveway.
His manner was kind in her presence.
Our plans were changed in spite of their objections.
Your honesty is wonderful!
Our calculator is inaccurate.

A possesive pronoun is a form of the subject pronoun that shows ownership of a noun.

Sample Page 44

Lesson 32

John's rake was missing.
It was Sally's car in the ditch.
The governor's race was very tight.

That red book is mine.
These blue coats are hers.
Those black tuxedos are Jim's.
This book is yours.

Mine is the red book.
Hers is the blue coat.
Jim's is the black tuxedo.

I cannot do that myself.
He walked uptown himself.
They helped with the project themselves.
We did it ourselves.

A possessive noun shows ownership of another noun and needs an apostrophe.

Sample Page 45

Lesson 32

How Do I Form Plural Nouns?

Rule 1: Regular nouns simply add "s".
dog dogs car cars

Rule 2: Nouns ending in the letters "s", "x", "z", "sh", or "ch" add "es".
buzz buzzes dish dishes
church churches bus buses

Rule 3: Letter names, numbers, signs like $'s, and words talked about as words are made plural by adding an apostrophe and an "s".

How many p's did you find in Mississippi?
There were four 10's used in the blueprint.
How many $'s were in the report?
Do count the number of the's on the first page.

Sample Page 46

Lesson 33

The "Y" Rules

Rule 4: Nouns ending in a consonant followed by a "y" change the "y" to "i" and add "es".
country countries sky skies

Rule 5: Nouns ending in a vowel followed by a "y" simply add "s".
turkey turkeys monkey monkeys

Rule 6: Most nouns that end in "f" or "fe" add "s". Some nouns that end in "f" or "fe" change the "f" or "fe" to "v" and add "es".
chief chiefs knife knives leaf leaves

Rule 7: Irregular nouns change the spelling of the singular to form the plural.
child children man men mouse mice

Rule 8: Some nouns stay the same in the singular and plural.
deer deer sheep sheep

Sample Page 47

Lesson 33

Forming Plural Nouns (continued)

The "O" Rules

Rule 9: Nouns ending in a consonant followed by the letter "o" simply add "es".
hero heroes tomato tomatoes

Rule 10: Nouns ending in a vowel followed by the letter "o" simply add "s".
radio radios rodeo rodeos

Rule 11: Musical terms ending in "o" simply add "s".
piano pianos solo solos

Rule 12: In compound nouns make the first word plural.
brother-in-law brothers-in-law
sister-in-law sisters-in-law
editor-in-chief editors-in-chief

Sample Page 48
Lesson 33

This is Tommy's bike.
The cat's food was in the pail.
Jim's car ran out of gas.
My teacher's smile was special.
The monkey's banana was in the tree.

Singular	Plural	Singular Possessive	Plural Possessive
child	children	child's	children's
turkey	turkeys	turkey's	turkeys'
calf	calves	calf's	calves'
dog	dogs	dog's	dogs'
secretary	secretaries	secretary's	secretaries'
man	men	man's	men's
bear	bears	bear's	bears'
cat	cats	cat's	cats'
mouse	mice	mouse's	mice's

Sample Page 49

Lesson 34

What Is an Apostrophe? (continued)

Rule 1: We make singular words show ownership by adding an apostrophe "s" to the end of the word.
My teacher's smile was special.

Rule 2: We make plural words not ending in "s" show ownership by adding an apostrophe "s" to the end of the word.
The children's toys were broken.

Rule 3: We make plural words that end in "s" show ownership by adding an apostrophe after the "s".
The boys' hats were found.

Rule 4: An apostrophe is used to show letters or numbers that are missing in a contraction.
did not didn't will not won't I am I'm
In the fall of '95, we traveled to Alaska.

Sample Page 50

Lesson 34

Rule 5: The plural forms of a letter, a number, a sign, or words mentioned as words all need an apostrophe "s".
three A's four 10's six #'s 100 and's

Rule 6: Possesive proper nouns already ending in "s" may either add an apostrophe alone or an apostrophe "s"; an apostrophe "s" is preferred except with a few proper names such as Jesus and Moses.
Tess's class was very late in the evening.
Jesus' disciples listened to his teaching.

Rule 7: When speaking of two or more people, each of whom owns something separately, add the apostrophe or apostrophe "s" to the end of each name.
Jared's and Joel's bicycle tires need air.

Sample Page 51
Lesson 34

Rule 8: When speaking of two or more people who own something together, add the apostrophe or apostrophe "s" to the end of only the last name mentioned.
Jared and Joel's go-kart is in need of repair.

Rule 9: When making compound words possessive, add the apostrophe or apostrophe "s" to the end of only the last word of the compound word.
My sister-in-law's recipe for apple pie is my favorite.

Rule 10: We make indefinite pronouns possessive by adding an apostrophe and an "s" to the end of the word.
Somebody's mitten was left in the car.
Anyone's hat will work for the costume.

Sample Page 52

Lesson 34

Rule 11: Possessive pronouns
are already possessive and need no
apostrophe.
Ours was fast.
Theirs was slow.

Rule 12: We make periods of time and
amounts possessive by adding an
apostrophe "s" to the end of the word.
Today's temperature was 80 degrees.
We used ten dollar's worth of gasoline.
It was an hour's time.

Sample Page 53

Lesson 34

Rule 1: A declarative sentence ends with a period.
The rain was coming down in buckets.

Rule 2: An imperative sentence may end with a period or an exclamation point.
Go to the teacher for more instructions.

Rule 3: Most abbreviations are followed by a period.

Gen. for General
Jan. for January
lbs. for pounds
oz. for ounce
A.D. for Anno Domini
P.M. for post meridiem
U.S. Grant for Ulysses Simpson Grant
MN for Minnesota

Sample Page 54

Lesson 35

Rule 4: A period needs to go inside the
end quotation mark if the exact words
of the speaker are declarative.
John said, "I am going to the store."

Rule 5: Abbreviations for the names of
federal agencies or commonly recognized
organizations are created by using the
first letter of each key word. Each letter is
capitalized and no periods are necessary.
FBI for Federal Bureau of Investigation
(no periods—federal agency)
PTA for Parent–Teacher Association
(no periods—common organization)
FDA for Food and Drug Administration
(no periods—federal agency)
NATO for North Atlantic Treaty Organization
(no periods—common organization)

Sample Page 55

Lesson 35

How Do I Use a Comma?

Rule 1: Commas separate items in a series.
Jim needs pencils, paper, and glue for school.

Rule 2: Calendar dates and addresses
of more than one part need commas.
January 14, 1951, is my birthday.
She lives at 305 Hazelwood Avenue,
Henning, MN 56551.

Rule 3: A series of two or more prepositional phrases beginning a sentence
requires a comma.
In the middle of summer, we plan picnics.

Rule 4: Nouns of address need commas.
John, please stop in after work.

Rule 5: Usa a comma before a coordinating conjunction in a compound sentence.
I go to town, and he goes to the farm.

Sample Page 56

Lesson 36

Rule 1: Quotation marks enclose the exact words of the speaker.

Rule 2: The part of the sentence that tells who is speaking is called the tag.

Rule 3: If a quote is a declarative sentence, and it comes before the tag, we place a comma before the last quotation mark.

"The sun is shining," Furtive Fox said.

Rule 4: The first word of a quote is capitalized.

Rule 5: if the quote is a declarative sentence, and it comes after the tag, we place a comma after the tag, and we place the end punctuation mark before the last quotation mark.

Furtive Fox said, "The sun is shining."

Sample Page 57

Lesson 37

Rule 6: An imperative quote is punctuated like a declarative quote.
"Go to the store for me," Mom said.

Rule 7: If a quote is a question, use a question mark inside the quote.
"How shall I get to the market?" Pensive Pig said.

Rule 8: If the quote is an exclamation, use an exclamation point inside the quote.
"What a great play at first base!" the coach said.

Rule 9: Heavy written works or titles of paintings or specific names for planes, trains, ships, or spacecraft are under-lined.

Sample Page 58

Lesson 37

<u>London Times</u> (newspaper)
<u>The Outsiders</u> (book)
<u>Flubber</u> (movie)

Rule 10: Light written works like short stories, poems, songs, essays, chapter titles, or article titles use quotation marks.

"Stocks Break Records" (news article)
"The Red Wheelbarrow" (poem)
"Sentence Making" (chapter title)

Rule 11: Dialogue requires a new paragraph with every switch of speaker.

"Have you handed in your composition using dialogue between two characters?" Mrs. Smith asked Jesse.

"I cannot find it, Mrs. Smith!" Jesse exclaimed.

Sample Page 59

Lesson 37

Rule 12: An indirect quote removes the quotation marks, adds the word "that", and changes the pronouns and verb forms if necessary.

"I want to go to the concert," said the band director.
The band director said that he wanted to go to the concert.

Rule 13: A divided quote uses a comma after the tag if the quote is carried over and a period after the tag if the quote is two separate sentences.
"The wind is very strong," said John, "but we must continue our work."
"The wind is too strong," said Jim. "We have to turn back."

Sample Page 60

Lesson 37

A semicolon (;) is used to join two complete thoughts closely related in meaning.
We want to turn back; the wind and waves are strong.
Iowa grows acres of corn; it is a prosperous state.

Conjunctive adverbs join two sentences together using a semicolon and a comma.

also	however	nevertheless
besides	indeed	otherwise
consequently	instead	still
finally	later	then
furthermore	moreover	therefore
		thus

The trees were beautiful; therefore, we enjoyed the drive.
She drove; however, her car needed repair.

Sample Page 61

Lesson 38

A colon (:) is used before a list of items, after a salutation in a business letter, between the hour and minutes when telling time, between a chapter and verse in a Bible passage, or before a long quotation.

1:23 P.M.   Dear Sirs: Romans 3:23

Please buy the following: bread and cereal.

King David's first Psalm recorded in the Bible starts with these words: "Blessed…"

A colon never follows directly after a verb.

The people were John, Mary, and Cody.

Use a colon after an "…as follows:" or "…the following:" or following a noun.

The awards presented were as follows: the Peabody Award, the Best Writer Award, and the Barney Scholarship.

He knew four new words: reconcile, counsel, jeopardy, and sequence.

Sample Page 62

Lesson 38

What is a title?
The title is the name of the book.

What is a title page?
The title page gives the name of the
book, the author, and the publisher.

What is a Table of Contents?
The Table of Contents in the front of
a book tells us what is in the book.

What is a glossary?
A glossary is a list of new words with definitions to help us understand the book.

What is an index?
The index in the back of the book is an
alphabetical list of all subjects covered
in the book.

Sample Page 63

Lesson 39

64   What Do We Find in a Dictionary?

Words listed in a dictionary are written in alphabetical order.

Words listed in a dictionary are called entry words.
Entry words give us the correct spelling for a word.

The two words on the top of a dictionary page are called guide words.
Guide words tell us if a word is on that page.

Dictionaries give the definitions of words.
...the pronunciation of words.
...the syllables in a word.
...the parts of speech of words.
...the etymology of a word.
...a sample sentence using the entry word.

Sample Page 64

Lesson 39

Some words have more than one definition.
Some words can be used as a different part of speech.
Words called "homographs" are spelled the same but mean something different.

Dictionaries have special features.
Biographical Names sections list people.
Geographical Names sections list places.
The Atlas section has maps.

Encyclopedias arrange all topics alphabetically.
...use guide words like a dictionary.
...have pictures, diagrams, and illustrations.
...have a research guide to find more information.
...provide a list of related topics.

Sample Page 65

Lesson 39

The card catalog has three different kinds of cards.
The title card lists the title of the book first.
The subject card lists the subject first.
The author card lists the author first.

Fiction books are arranged alphabetically.
Nonfiction books are arranged using a numbering system.
Almanacs, atlases, newspapers, magazines, and biographical materials are in a library.

The Readers' Guide to Periodical Literature is an index of magazine articles. Each entry contains the title, the author's name, the magazine, the volume number, the page numbers, the date, and listings of illustrations, maps, or photos.

Sample Page 66

Lesson 39

July 29, 1997

Dear Mom,

How are you? I am fine. Camp is fun. Please send money.

I miss you. I wish you were here. See you soon.

Love,
Johnny

A friendly letter has five sections: a heading, a salutation, a body, a closing, and a signature.

The first word of every section, of every sentence, and all proper nouns are capitalized.

A comma is placed between the day of the month and the year, after the salutation, and after the closing.

Every new paragraph is indented five spaces.

Sample Page 67

Lesson 40

May 3,1995

Dear Korey,

Thank you for going to Trout Lake Camp with me. I really had a good time. I hope you did too. I enjoyed swimming during those hot days. I found out that I forgot my swimming suit on the clothesline outside our cabin. We called lost and found, but it was not there. Thank you for being my friend. I hope we can go to camp again next year.

Your friend,
Jared

The thank you note is just like the friendly letter.
The invitation is just like the friendly letter.
The invitation includes who is doing the inviting, what the occasion is, when it is, and where it will be held.

Sample Page 68

Lesson 40

How Do I Address an Envelope?

Student's Name
Address
City, State Zip Code
Name of Person
House Address
City, State Zip Code

Student's Name
Address
City, State Zip Code
Thanked Person
Person's Street Address
City, State Zip Code

Student's Name
Address
City, State Zip Code
Invited Person
Person's Street Address
City, State Zip Code

Sample Page 69

Lesson 40

70   How Do I Write a Business Letter?

Linden Park Resort
RR 2
Henning, MN 56551

July 4, 1997

Dr. Roger Beals
603 Douglas Ave.
Montevideo, MN 56265

Dear Dr. Beals:
   I am on vacation, and I have misplaced my glasses. Please send me a new pair as soon as possible.

Sincerely yours,
Elmer E. Neumann

A business letter uses an inside address. Business letters use formal closings and a colon after the salutation.

Sample Page 70

Lesson 40

1. The plot is what happens in the story.
2. The characters are who is in the story.
3. The protagonist is the good guy.
4. The antagonist is the bad guy.
5. Conflict is the problem the characters must overcome.
6. Consequences are what might happen if the problem is not solved.
7. Suspense is the excitement created by what might happen next.
8. Setting is where and when the story takes place.
9. Dialogue is the conversation between characters.
10. Theme is the author's message.
11. Point of view is who is telling the story.
12. Resolution is the conflict settled.

Conflict + Consequences = Suspense
Paying attention to details matters!

Sample Page 71

Lesson 41

72 Book Reports: Questions We Need to Ask

1. What is the title of my book?
2. Why is the title a good one?
3. Who is the author?
4. What do I know about the author?
5. What other books has the author written?
6. What happened in the story?
7. Who was my favorite character?
8. Why did I like this character?
9. Who was the antagonist?
10. What did these characters want?
11. What kinds of problems were there?
12. What did I fear might happen?
13. What were the most exciting moments?
14. Where did the story happen?
15. When did the story happen?
16. Who is telling the story?
17. Does the author use dialogue?
18. What did the book teach me?
19. Why should others read this book?
20. Is this book fact or fiction?

Sample Page 72

Lesson 41

I am thankful for my family. I am thankful for my dad and mom. My dad cheers me up when I'm sad. My mom hugs me and listens to me when I have a problem. My brother and sister play board games with me when I am sick. I am thankful for food and clothing and a warm house. I am thankful that I can help with chores around the house like lawn mowing and vacuuming. I am thankful that my family laughs together, plays together, prays together, and works together.

A topic sentence is the first sentence in a paragraph. It introduces what the paragraph is about.
A paragraph is a group of sentences that say something about the topic.

Sample Page 73

Lesson 42

74   What Is a Proofreading Checklist?

1. Have I read my paragraph out loud?
2. Does it read well?
3. Do all the sentences relate to my topic?
4. Are there words I can cross out?
5. Are there words I can add?
6. Are my words spelled correctly?
7. Are there sentences I can cross out to improve my paragraph?
8. Do I need to add more sentences?
9. Have I started every sentence with a capital letter?
10. Does every sentence have correct end punctuation?
11. Is my handwriting beautiful?
12. Have I shared my paragraph with someone?

A thesaurus is a valuable tool to help us choose stronger words.

Sample Page 74

Lesson 42

©1998 Grammar Works/Holly Hall Publications, In

I. Planning our trip.
  A. Out West or Coastal Georgia?
    1. Not Georgia—we always go there
    2. The West—where my Dad grew up
  B. Fly or drive?
    1. Flying is too expensive
    2. We will need to drive two cars
II. Where will we stay?
  A. In our tent
    1. Reserve campsites now!
    2. What if it rains?
    3. Two whole weeks in a tent?
  B. In a motel
    1. Motels are a lot nicer!
    2. Motels are a lot more expensive!
III. Where will we go?
  A. Not California—too far!
  B. Southwest
    1. Half as far
    2. Still some uncrowded areas

Sample Page 75

Lesson 43

76   How Do I Write A Summary?

The State of Minnesota*

The state of Minnesota is nicknamed the Gopher State. As a farm state, its primary produce is dairy products. Minneapolis and St. Paul are the state's largest cities. About 4 million people live in this northern state where the temperatures can fall to 50 degrees below zero. The state has 10,000 lakes and the mighty Mississippi has its beginning in Lake Itasca in North Central Minnesota. Many years ago the Sioux and Chippewa Indians lived in the state. Minnesota became the 32nd state to enter the union on May 11, 1858.

*Information for this summary is taken from World Book, Volume 13, c. 1986, pages 496-510.

Sample Page 76

Lesson 44